Possible and Probable Languages

Possible and Probable Languages

A Generative Perspective on Linguistic Typology

FREDERICK J. NEWMEYER

Great Clarendon Street, Oxford OX2 6DP

Oxford University Press is a department of the University of Oxford.
It furthers the University's objective of excellence in research, scholarship,
and education by publishing worldwide in

Oxford New York

Auckland Cape Town Dar es Salaam Hong Kong Karachi
Kuala Lumpur Madrid Melbourne Mexico City Nairobi
New Delhi Shanghai Taipei Toronto

With offices in

Argentina Austria Brazil Chile Czech Republic France Greece
Guatemala Hungary Italy Japan Poland Portugal Singapore
South Korea Switzerland Thailand Turkey Ukraine Vietnam

Published in the United States
by Oxford University Press Inc., New York

First published 2005

British Library Cataloguing in Publication Data

Data available

Library of Congress Cataloguing in Publication Data

Newmeyer, Frederick J.

Possible and and probable langauges: a generative perspective on linguistic
typology / Frederick J. Newmeyer.

p. cm.

Includes bibliographical reference and index.

ISBN 0-19-927433-9 (alk. paper) – ISBN 0-19-927434-7 (alk. paper)

1. Typology (Linguistics) 2. Generative grammar. 3. Grammar, Comprative and
general. 4. Functionalism (Linguistics) I. title.

P204.N49 2005

415'.01–dc22

2005018556

Typeset by SPI Publisher Services, Pondicherry, India
Printed in Great Britain
on acid-free paper by
Biddles Ltd., King's Lynn

ISBN 0-19-927433-9 978-0-19-927433-8
0-19-927434-7 (Pbk.) 978-0-19-927434-5 (Pbk.)

1 3 5 7 9 10 8 6 4 2

Contents

Preface

A prominent American linguist once offered the opinion that languages can 'differ from each other without limit and in unpredictable ways' (Joos 1957: 96). Perhaps the most significant change of opinion in the field of linguistics in the past half-century, and one that unites linguists of all theoretical stripes, is that Joos was mistaken. We all know that there are things that grammars always do or never do, and things that they often do or rarely do. The topics of debate within the field have advanced from the question of whether the properties of grammars can vary without limit to the question of why they do not do so. I hope to have something useful to contribute to answering this latter question. In particular, this book is devoted to exploring cross-linguistic morphosyntactic variation within the general framework of assumptions that characterize generative grammar. But as the reader will discover, my conclusions challenge fairly fundamentally some central positions that have characterized mainstream generative approaches to linguistic typology for over two decades.

Chapter 1 is devoted more to clarifying the issues, both methodological and substantive, than to presenting concrete proposals. In particular, it is devoted to the question of how we *know* what is necessary in language, what is probable, and what is merely possible. The question is trickier than one might think; the answer is dependent on a host of underlying assumptions, not all shared by both formal linguists and functional linguists. Chapter 2 lays out the standard generative view concerning typological differences among languages: certain key constructs of the theory admit to 'parametric variation.' In the earlier Government-Binding approach, the theory's core principles themselves were parameterized. More recently, in the Minimalist Program, it is assumed that parametric differences among languages are localized in the lexicon. Chapter 3 is devoted not only to critiquing the parametric approach to variation, but also to the very idea that anything internal to Universal Grammar predicts why some morphosyntactic features are more common cross-linguistically than others. In one sentence: Universal Grammar predicts the set of possible languages, not the set of probable languages. Performance principles are responsible for the latter. Chapter 4, however, attempts to demonstrate the futility of throwing the baby out with the bathwater by abandoning formal grammar altogether. The distinction between knowledge of language and use of language, central to both the Saussurean and the Chomskyan views of language, is well supported empirically. Chapter 5 addresses the question of the relationship between performance pressure on grammar and the typological distribution of formal elements. It argues that the linkage is indirect. In particular, it makes the case that the principles and rules of grammar are not linked synchronically to their presumed functional motivations. Instead, the influence of function upon form—and therefore on the typological distribution of formal elements—is played out in language use and acquisition and (therefore) language change. A short Afterword precedes the list of references.

My greatest debts are to James McCloskey and Anna Siewierska, who read and commented on the original proposal and—in great detail—critiqued the pre-final version. I owe an equal note of appreciation to Martin Haspelmath, who provided a dozen pages of comments on the (almost) final product. This 'product' would have been greatly inferior without their input. The only reason that I did not incorporate all of their suggestions is that it would have been physically impossible to do so, given their markedly different perspectives on linguistic theory. I feel that having such comprehensive critiques from linguists with conflicting views on the nature of grammar has made for a much better book. Thank you again, Jim, Anna, and Martin!

Other linguist colleagues read and commented on material that was originally published in article form and was later incorporated into these pages. The following fall into that category and also deserve a statement of my appreciation: Judith Aissen, Joan Bresnan, Brady Clark, Peter Culicover, William Croft, Bart Defrancq, Scott Drellishak, Matthew Dryer, John Frampton, Martin Haspelmath, John A. Hawkins, Richard Hudson, Eloise Jelinek, Brian Joseph, Robert Levine, Joan Maling, Christopher Manning, Edith Moravcsik, Gereon Müller, Richard Oehrle, Martina Penke, Pierret Pica, Charles Reiss, Johan Rooryck, Anette Rosenbach, Peter Sells, Herb Stahlke, Thomas Wasow, Gabriel Webster, and Helmut Weiß. Finally, I should mention that the following articles of mine have resurfaced in modified form as sections of this book: Newmeyer (1998a, 2000b, 2001a,c, 2002a,b, 2003a, 2004a,b,c,d). A thanks to the editors of these publications for seeing them through to their initial publication.

1

On the Possible and the Probable in Language

1.1 Introduction

My goal in this initial chapter is to set the stage for what follows, by addressing a foundational cluster of questions inherent to the practice of linguistic typology. What does it mean to say that some grammatical feature is possible or impossible, or probable or improbable? Section 1.2 tries to pinpoint how one might identify a 'possible human language' and §1.3 raises some background issues relevant to the determination of why some language types appear to be more probable than others. Section 1.4 focuses on the major differences between formalists and functionalists with respect to the explanation of typological generalizations, using an extended published debate between Peter Coopmans and Bernard Comrie as a point of reference. A brief conclusion follows.

1.2 Possible human languages

This section explores the problem of identifying the set of possible human languages and explaining why just that set exists to the exclusion of others. Section 1.2.1 points out that this problem is as much a concern of functionalists as of formalists and §1.2.2 discusses how we might come to decide that a language type is literally impossible. Section 1.2.3 outlines two attempts to solve this problem empirically, namely, by attempting to teach subjects putatively impossible languages. The final subsection (§1.2.4) is devoted to the problem of explaining why certain logically possible language types are non-existent.

1.2.1 *Formalists and functionalists on the notion 'possible human language'*

The central goal of generative grammar from its inception has been to characterize the notion 'possible human language.' In an early formulation of this goal, Chomsky wrote:

The theory thus constructed is a theory of linguistic universals. Specification of the form of grammars *excludes certain infinite sets of sentences from consideration as possible natural languages*. . . . Procedures for evaluating grammars and determining structural descriptions impose strict conditions on the kinds of units that can be attributed to a natural language and the manner of their arrangement and interconnection. This general theory can therefore be regarded as a definition of the notion 'natural language'. (Chomsky 1962: 536–7; emphasis added)

The vocabulary of theoretical primitives, conventions for formulating rules, and so on are therefore chosen, not on the basis of an appeal to 'simplicity' in the abstract, but rather with the view in mind of excluding from the very possibility of formulation any process outside of the definition of 'natural language.' For example, it would be just as formally 'simple' for a language to form questions by regularly inverting the order of all the words in the corresponding declarative, rather than by fronting some particular constituent of the declarative. The theory of Universal Grammar (henceforth 'UG'), however, prohibits the former option by its failure to provide a mechanism for carrying out such an inversion operation. That is, the following rule type, while perhaps simple and elegant in the abstract, is not allowed by UG:

(1) $W_1 - W_2 - W_3 - \ldots - W_n \rightarrow W_n - \ldots - W_3 - W_2 - W_1$

In other words, given some hypothetical grammar, the theory of UG is designed to specify whether any human language could be characterized by that grammar. By the mid 1960s, the term 'possible' as applied to human languages came regularly to be used in the sense of *biologically* possible, or, put a different way, consistent with our innately determined attributes that allow any possible grammar to be attainable by a child under natural conditions of acquisition. Again, quoting Chomsky:

A theory of linguistic structure... proposes, then, that the child approaches the data with the presumption that they are drawn from a language *of a certain antecedently well-defined type*, his problem being to determine *which of the (humanly) possible languages* is that of the community in which he is placed (Chomsky 1965: 27; emphasis added)

As much as the mechanisms of generative theory have changed over the ensuing four decades and as much as the overall theory has splintered into rival frameworks, there is little debate over the question of pinning down as precisely as possible what constitutes a possible human language. My guess is that advocates of any formal framework would agree with Mark Baker that 'not all imaginable... grammatical properties are permissible. It seems that there are deep underlying principles that determine what properties can and cannot occur... in natural languages' (Baker 2001a: 35).

Functional linguists, no less than formalists, concern themselves with what is possible in human language. In the words of a leading functionalist:

[L]inguistic theory of any approach, 'formalist' or 'functional-typological', has as its central question, what is a possible language? This question can in turn be paraphrased as: of the logically possible types of languages, how do we account for what types actually exist? (Croft 1990: 44)

And Shibatani and Bynon (1995: 19) write that 'in a truly functional approach... [t]he range of the observed variation and its internal structures defined by crosslinguistic generalizations delimit the range of possible (segments of) human languages.' In other words, functionalists (and their allies who practice cognitive linguistics) are united with generative grammarians in the ultimate goal of linguistic theory. That which separates the different orientations is to be found at the level of specifics, in particular whether UG provides an innate module containing purely grammatical constructs. Functionalists in general envisage grammar 'as a sub-component of a... system in which the human linguistic capacity is linked to epistemic, logical, perceptual, and social capacities' (Siewierska 1991: 1), rather than being the semi-autonomous formal entity of most generative approaches. For that reason, one rarely finds reference to the construct 'Universal Grammar' per se in functionalist writings. Nevertheless, most adherents of the functionalist school see it as a major goal of linguistic theory to distinguish the possible from the probable.

1.2.2 *The problem of knowing what is possible*

But how do we *know* which features of grammar are possible and which are impossible? Unfortunately, there is no theory-independent way to talk about possibility and impossibility in language. By way of illustration, consider a recent paper by Mark Baker (Baker 2002). On the basis of an investigation of a small number of languages, Baker claims that no language is possible in which neither the subject nor the main verb move overtly to the highest functional head. Baker might very well be correct. But the problem is that such a claim of impossibility is so theory-laden that there is no way to evaluate it independently of the complex web of hypotheses that characterize early twenty-first century principles-and-parameters syntax—hypotheses that themselves are constantly undergoing revision. So let us turn then to the lower-level generalization that this proposal is intended to explain, namely that there is no (and can be no) language with the order of elements AUX-S-V-O. Here too non-trivial theoretical assumptions are at work. Clearly, we need to have some notion of *basic* order, since even in English we find AUX-S-V-O sequences (*Will you help me?*). Yet the notion of 'basic order' is one of the most notoriously difficult to pin down in grammatical theory (Brody 1984; Siewierska 1988; Newmeyer 1998b: ch. 6, §3.4.2). Continuing up the scale of generality does little to increase our confidence about claims of (im)possibility. There is a long-standing debate, for example, about which elements (if any) belong in a distinct category AUX (Pullum 1981a; Steele 1981) and theories differ markedly on their characterizations of subjects and objects and the role that these notions play in syntactic theory (Li 1976; McCloskey 1997; Davies and Dubinsky 2001). Hence, one is left with the (possibly) unpleasant feeling that any unhedged claim about either a universal or an impossible feature of language is necessarily suspect.

Confounding the problem still further are the risks of concluding the impossibility of a grammatical feature from its mere absence in a sample of languages. Baker's sample discussed above was very small. Presumably if we find a particular feature instantiated in one language, then that feature is possible, but how many absences does it take to conclude impossibility? There is simply no motivation for declaring that a grammatical feature is 'impossible' if it happens to be missing from some arbitrary number (or percentage) of languages (Newmeyer 1998b: ch. 6, §3). And yet, every linguist knows well that it is not the case that 'anything goes' in language. Some absences are at root uninteresting, since the non-existent phenomenon is logically impossible. Croft (2003: 50) gives the example of a language with indefinite first-person pronouns. Since indefinite pronouns are used when the referent is unknown to the hearer and 'first person refers to the speaker by definition and hence is known as such to the hearer,' the absence of such a language follows logically. But things are rarely that simple. There are grammatical features that have been observed in every language in the world (where one has taken the trouble to look for them) and there are grammatical features that have not been observed in any language, where logical necessity or logical impossibility are not at issue. Consider by way of example the following twenty-five claims of universality in morphosyntax. To the best of my knowledge, each is based on the best interpretation of the data that we now have at our disposal:[1]

(2) Some seemingly universal (or universally non-occurring) features of language:

a. Grammars cannot 'count past two.' That is, no morphosyntactic process refers to 'third position,' 'fourth position,' etc.
b. In no language can a syntactic process be sensitive to the segmental phonology of the lexical items undergoing the process (e.g. passivization confined to verbs that end in a consonant cluster).
c. In no language is a negative, or a question, or a command, or some other speech act formed by changing the first sound of the verb.
d. All languages make a grammatical distinction between sentences and noun phrases (Carstairs-McCarthy 1999).
e. No language has segmental–phonological conditions on word order (e.g. objects beginning with obstruents precede the verb, but otherwise follow it) (Martha McGinnis, p. c.).
f. There is no language in the world where words are made up of individual sound segments, each of which corresponds in systematic fashion to some aspect of the meaning of the word. That is, no language has a word like *blonk*, meaning 'elephant,' where initial 'b' denotes a living creature, a

[1] Some of these are a response to my Linguist List posting of 17 May 2004 asking for 'examples of phenomena that are not found in any language of the world (as far as we know), where there is no obvious functional explanation for that fact.'

following 'l' an animal, a following 'o' a mammal, a following 'n' a herbivore, and a following 'k' possessing a trunk.

g. In no language can an affirmative be turned into a negative by changing the intonation contour (Horn 1989).
h. Reduplication is never used to mark case (although it is commonly used for other inflectional categories such as aspect, tense, plurality, etc.) (Eric Raimy, p. c.; Grohmann and Nevins 2004).
i. No language allows more than four arguments per verb (Pesetsky 1995).
j. No language has a lexical item meaning 'not all', nor one for logical complements ('all but three,' etc.) (Horn 1972, 1989).
k. If conjoined phrases contain an element in the first person, then first-person agreement forms will always be used (Corbett 1991: 262).
l. In every language in which there is a person and number inflection, there is also a tense, aspect, and mood inflection (Bybee 1985: 267).
m. No language has nominal objects obligatorily in post-verbal position and sentential objects obligatorily in pre-verbal position (Luis Vincente, p. c.).
n. No language coordinates two NPs with a preposed conjunction (Stassen 2000).
o. In all languages in which the lexical possessor NP is case-marked, the pronominal possessor NP is case-marked as well (Moravcsik 1995; TUA #20).[2]
p. In all languages in which there is a marking alternation for objects in terms of definiteness and animacy, if indefinite or less animate objects are morphologically marked, then definite or more animate objects will also be morphologically marked (Lazard 1984; TUA #46).
q. In every language with an object agreement marker, that marker shares formal and semantic properties with an object personal pronoun (Moravcsik 1974; TUA #90).
r. In every language with any kind of overt marking (dependent marking, head marking, word order, etc.) in action nominalizations, that marking is also used in other constructions (Koptjevskaja-Tamm 1993; TUA #127).
s. In no language will the morphological bulk of affixes for direct cases, measured in number of syllables, exceed that of affixes for oblique cases (Haiman 1985; TUA #137).
t. In every language in which the property concept of shape is expressed through adjectives, then those of color and size are also expressed through adjectives (Dixon 1977; TUA #141).
u. In all languages in which adjectives are inflected, nouns are inflected as well (Moravcsik 1993; TUA #148).

[2] 'TUA' is short for 'The Universals Archive,' a marvelous online database coordinated by Frans Plank containing 2034 typological generalizations, along with pertinent discussion and references to the literature. The URL is <http://ling.unikonstanz.de:591/Universals/introduction.html>.

v. No language has more inflectional classes of adjectives than of nouns (Carstairs 1984; TUA #149).
w. In every language in which an adposition occurs as both an object marker and an allative marker, then it also occurs as a dative marker (Blansitt 1988; TUA #157).
x. In all languages in which the marker for NP conjunction has the same form as the comitative marker, the basic order is SVO (Stassen 1992; TUA #181).
y. In all languages in which there is incorporation of the nominal subject into the verb, there is also incorporation of the direct object (Kozinsky 1981; TUA #188).

The questions that must be raised are the following: (*a*) which of the features outlined in (2a-y) are *necessarily* universally occurring or universally prohibited as a consequence of our biological preprogramming (for grammar per se or for broader faculties not specific to language)? and (*b*) which are *incidentally* universally occurring or universally prohibited by virtue of the fact that if grammars were organized differently, communication (or other aspects of language use) would thereby be rendered less efficient in some way? The difficulty in answering those questions is the topic of the following section. First, however, we will examine the results of two attempts to teach subjects (subparts of) languages which all UG-based approaches consider impossible.

1.2.3 *Teaching 'impossible' grammars*

The first attempt to teach a subject putatively impossible grammatical processes was Smith and Tsimpli (1995)'s work with the savant Christopher. Christopher is unusual among savants in that, while he is cognitively impaired in a number of ways, he has an extraordinary talent for acquiring foreign languages—he has at least partial mastery of sixteen of them. Smith and Tsimpli set out to try to teach Christopher two languages to which he had not been exposed. The first was Berber, a language normally considered extremely difficult for native speakers of English. As expected, Berber posed no problems for Christopher. The second was a made-up language that they called 'Epun.' In many respects Epun has the properties of 'normal' languages and it was these properties to which Christopher was exposed at the start of the experiment. After he had mastered the basic regularities of the language, Smith and Tsimpli began to introduce 'impossible' constructions into Epun. These included the following:

(3) a. Structure-independent operations, such as suffixing an emphatic particle to the third orthographic word.
b. Structure-dependent, yet UG-anomalous, operations, such as negating an SVO sentence by fronting the verb and forming a past tense by fronting the object.
c. Morphological operations not attested in any language, in particular anomalous agreement patterns.

As it turned out, Christopher had extreme difficulties with (3a-b). What is particularly telling is the difference in behavior between Christopher and the normal control subjects, who were exposed to the same language. Both had trouble with structure-independent operations—not surprisingly, given their complexity by a variety of measures. But the control subjects did better than Christopher with respect to the structure-dependent anomalous operations. Evidently, the former were 'able to solve the problems by having recourse to central strategies of general intelligence' (Smith and Tsimpli 1995: 154), just the area in which Christopher was most deficient. Christopher, seemingly relying only on UG, was baffled by these operations. Interestingly, Christopher did much better than the controls in mastering the anomalous agreement patterns, suggesting to Smith and Tsimpli that 'the learning of the morphology and the lexicon is different in kind from the learning of syntax' (p. 155). In any event, Christopher's behavior seems to indicate that our biological preprogramming for language (i.e. UG) does indeed shape our acquisition of language and helps to delineate what is biologically possible in grammar.[3]

The second noteworthy attempt to teach subjects putatively impossible grammatical structures is described in Musso et al. (2003). In the first of two functional Magnetic Resonance Imaging (fMRI) studies, twelve native German speakers learned three grammatical rules of Italian and three UG-impossible rules using the Italian lexicon. The first of these latter rules was the placement of the negative word *no* always after the first word of the phrase; the second was the formation of interrogatives by the inversion of the linear sequence of words in the sentence; the third demanded that indefinite articles agree with the last noun of the phrase. In the second fMRI study, eleven native German speakers participated in a similar experiment, but this time with Japanese. The first two rules of 'unreal Japanese' paralleled those of 'unreal Italian.' Since Japanese has no articles, the third artificial rule was different. It involved creating a past tense by adding the suffix *-ta*, not to the verbal element, as in real Japanese, but on the second word counting from the right, in all sentences.

In fact, the subjects learned all of the rules, real and unreal, though they performed better on tasks involving the real ones. What is particularly interesting, however, are the differences in the functional imaging results with respect to the two classes of rules. The authors tested the change in blood-oxygen-level-dependent (BOLD) signal with respect to the type of rule learned. Their results showed a significant correlation between the increase in BOLD signal in the left inferior frontal gyrus and the online performance for the real, but not for the unreal language-learning tasks. In their view:

This stands as neurophysiological evidence that the acquisition of new linguistic competence in adults involves a brain system that is different from that involved in learning

[3] For a negative assessment of Smith and Tsimpli's conclusions, see Bates (1997); and for a reply to Bates, see Smith and Tsimpli (1997).

grammar rules that violate UG. More specifically, our results show that Broca's area has a key role in the acquisition of 'real' rules of language, independent of the linguistic family to which the language belongs.... [We] posit that this brain region is specialized for the acquisition and processing of hierarchical (rather than linear) structures, which represent the common character of every known grammar. (Musso et al. 2003: 777–8)

An important lesson to draw from the results of both Smith and Tsimpli and Musso et al. is that the notions 'possible' and 'impossible' need to be understood with respect to psychologically and neurologically normal processes. In both cases, the control subjects were able to master putatively 'impossible' grammatical rules (though, significantly, Christopher was not able to do so). What justifies their characterization as 'impossible,' then, is not their literal unattainability, but rather their neuropsychological deviance, in terms of how they are acquired and how they are mentally represented. This nuance, while seemingly justified, makes it all the more difficult to be sure that a non-occurring rule is, in fact, an impossible one.

1.2.4 *The problem of explaining what is possible*

In a previous section, I raised the following questions: (*a*) which of the features outlined in (2a-y) are *necessarily* universally occurring or universally prohibited as a consequence of our biological preprogramming (for grammar per se or for broader faculties not specific to language)? and (*b*) which are *incidentally* universally occurring or universally prohibited by virtue of the fact that if grammars were organized differently, communication (or other aspects of language use) would thereby be rendered less efficient in some way? These questions cannot be answered without answering an epistemologically prior one: why is there so little agreement on the precise nature of the human language faculty? There are a number of reasons, to which I now turn.

Perhaps the most serious problem is that the correct theory (whatever it might be) is greatly underdetermined by the principal sources of data used by linguists, either introspections about well-formedness and meanings in one's native language or the results of one-on-one fieldwork with consultants in a language not one's own. One need only glance at the vast majority of writings, from whatever framework, to see that other types of evidence generally play a very minor role.[4] Such is particularly the case in any work that attempts to draw cross-linguistic generalizations, which, of course, are prerequisites to zeroing in on what a

[4] Functionalists are rhetorically more committed to using non-introspective data than formalists, but it is not clear that the usage of such data by the former much exceeds that by the latter. To provide a telling example in support of my contention, in his editor's introduction to a collection of papers in cognitive and functional linguistics, Tomasello (1998: xiii) deplores the data that are used in generative grammar, which 'are almost always disembodied sentences that analysts have made up *ad hoc*... rather than utterances produced by real people in real discourse situations.' But significantly, only two contributors (Wallace Chafe and Paul Hopper) present segments of natural discourse, neither filling even a page of text. All of the other contributions employ the 'disembodied sentences' supposedly spurned by the cognitive–functional approach.

possible human language might be. The result is that virtually any framework is capable of formulating some interesting (and possibly true) generalization about grammatical patterning not easily formulable in any other framework, thereby heartening supporters of each framework to the idea that they are on the right track.

There are certainly any number of research papers that appeal to naturalistic and experimental data to bolster a particular theoretical position. The problem is that such data are, if anything, even more difficult to interpret than introspective data. Virtually every study that draws a theoretical conclusion based on a subject's reaction time in an experimental setting, on language loss in aphasia, on child (or adult) acquisition data, on spontaneous discourse, or whatever, has generated a rebuttal arguing that the facts lead in precisely the opposite direction. Introspective data are not as messy as they are often claimed to be (as has been demonstrated in Cowart 1997), nor other types as clean. Learning how to draw the correct conclusions from a combination of the two is perhaps the major task facing theoretical linguists in the twenty-first century.

The task of explaining the possibility or impossibility of some feature of language within a UG-based (i. e. generative) approach is more complex than in a functionalist one, since it necessarily involves hypothesizing which features of language fall under the purview of UG proper and which do not. This question is independent of that of 'innateness,' though the independence is not always appreciated. A UG property is by definition innate, but innateness is also the necessary property of a myriad of other faculties that might contribute to the explanation of what is possible or impossible. For example, a sentence with multiple self-embeddings like *The rat the cat the dog chased ate died*[5] has never been and never will be used in a natural discourse and one might be tempted to appeal to a UG constraint limiting the number of such embeddings. But that is hardly necessary, given the parsing difficulties that such sentences would pose. Yet, parsing principles themselves are presumably innate; we do not 'learn' how to parse sentences, given any reasonable definition of what it means to 'learn' something. Indeed the highly plausible innateness of parsing principles provides one of the best arguments for an innate UG. Since the former are (innately) fine-tuned to grammatical structure, it follows that at least certain aspects of grammatical structure must be innate as well.[6]

Generative grammarians, of course, have traditionally argued for (or, more often, assumed) the existence of domain-specific innate constructs, that is, those which are formulated in specifically 'linguistic' terms.[7] The existence of innate

[5] Intended reading: 'The rat died that was eaten by the cat that the dog chased.'

[6] I reserve until Chapter 4 discussion of stochastic approaches to grammar, e.g. Bod (1998), that provide alternative data-oriented approaches to parsing.

[7] Functionalists, in general, have rejected the idea of innate grammatical knowledge, while formalists, in general, have defended this idea. However, the Baldwin Effect (Hinton and Nowlan 1987) allows for the evolution of neural mechanisms that encode (functionally) beneficial attributes/behavior in a

language-specific principles has been motivated most often by arguments based on the 'poverty of the stimulus' available to the language learner. The idea is that there are not enough cues in the child's input to determine the grammar that has to be acquired, so important aspects of grammar must be innate.[8] But generativists have more and more come to appeal to the contribution of extralinguistic (but no less innate) faculties in explaining facts about language. Indeed, at least some prominent generativists have posited a much-diminished role for specifically linguistic constructs. Foremost among them is Chomsky. In Hauser, Chomsky, and Fitch (2002) it is suggested that the recursive property of language might be the sole attribute of UG proper (renamed 'Faculty of language—narrow sense' [FLN]), with the (not specifically linguistic) sensory-motor system and conceptual–intentional system ('Faculty of language—broad sense' [FLB]) taking over a lot of work previously attributed to UG. For example, they write:

> Many of the details of language that are the traditional focus of linguistic study (e.g., Subjacency, Wh-movement, the existence of garden-path sentences) may represent by-products of this solution [an optimal linking of the sensory-motor system and conceptual–intentional system by FLN], generated automatically by neural/computational constraints and the structure of FLB—components that lie outside of FLN. (Hauser, Chomsky, and Fitch 2002: 1574)

If Hauser, Chomsky, and Fitch are correct, then a remarkable convergence between the generative and functional-cognitive approaches is within the realm of possibility. On the other hand, many generativists, most notably Anderson and Lightfoot (2002), continue to argue for a rich set of domain-specific innate properties.[9]

Hence in many respects, the relationship between universality, possibility, and innateness is far from being a simple one. Consider another example. One's first thought might be that an impossible language is one in which some feature attributed to UG is absent. Such is not necessarily the case, however, since in all accounts, UG principles are stated in an implicational form, 'applying' only if certain conditions are met. To take a fairly simple case, the universality of extraction constraints on overt long-distance movement is not falsified by the fact that some languages lack overt long-distance movement. A hypothetically impossible language is one with such movement and without such constraints,

population that has a fair amount of plasticity at birth in brain wiring. Hence, there exists a mechanism by which UG principles might have become biologized without increasing the survival and reproductive possibilities for any particular individual who, by chance, happened to have acquired one or more of them. The Baldwin Effect has been pointed to as a means by which functionally motivated grammatical constraints might have become innate (see Newmeyer 1991; Kirby and Hurford 1997; Kirby 1998; Bresnan and Aissen 2002). For more remarks on the Baldwin Effect, see Ch. 5, §5.7.4.1.

[8] For a recent critique of one class of arguments based on the poverty of the stimulus, see Pullum and Scholz (2002) and, for rebuttals, see Fodor and Crowther (2002); Lasnik and Uriagereka (2002); Legate and Yang (2002); and Crain and Pietroski (2002).

[9] Chomsky's position (as put forward in Chomsky 2002) and that of Anderson and Lightfoot are compared and evaluated in Newmeyer (2003b), more positively for the latter than for the former.

not one in which evidence for such constraints is missing. A more complex case was put on the table by David Gil (1997, 2000, 2001). Gil has argued that classical generative theory, which posits a rich set of syntactic categories, is biased toward English and other languages in which numerous categories can be easily motivated. In Riau Indonesian and other languages of South-East Asia, the evidence points to a very small number, leading him to conclude that 'the imposition of familiar Eurocentric categories onto Riau Indonesian provides for a facile mode of grammatical description; however, it is essentially misguided' (Gil 1997: 188) and that 'much of the elaborate structures exhibited by most languages are incidental to universal grammar' (Gil 2001: 367). But in fact, it has never been claimed that every category provided by UG must be manifested in every language. The general assumption is that an adequate UG-based theory of categories hypothesizes implicational relations among categories (the presence of category X in a language implies the presence of category Y), but says nothing about the minimum (or maximum) possible number of categories. As far as I can tell, such hypotheses are not violated by the languages that Gil discusses.

Just as a feature of language can be innate without being part of UG, some feature of language might be universal without there being a UG-based explanation for its universality. To take a fairly trivial example, every language provides ways of talking about one's mother and father, the sun and the moon, the heart and the liver, and so on. Appeal to shared human experience suffices to explain that fact; there is no need to assume that the lexicalization of these concepts is encoded in our genes (which is not to say with complete confidence that it might not be). Along the same lines, it seems unlikely that UG needs to exclude sentences a million words long or those in which an adjective modifies a noun four clauses away with no agreement marking signaling the modification. There are obvious functional reasons—i.e. reasons based on usability—that would account for why ponderously long sentences are not used and why semantically opaque combinations of heads and modifiers are not grammaticalized.

But to complicate matters still further, the observation that some property of language has a plausible extragrammatical explanation is not in and of itself evidence for excluding that property from UG. Consider two examples. The first involves the structure dependence of grammatical rules, which has long been taken to be one of the distinguishing characteristics of UG (see Chomsky 1975). Numerous writers, beginning with Sampson (1978), have pointed out that virtually all complex behavior can be characterized by means of hierarchical structure, and have on that basis concluded that there is no reason to posit structure dependence as a feature of UG. But that conclusion does not follow. The structure dependence of grammatical rules might well have its evolutionary antecedence in some general human (or, more likely, biological) preference for structural solutions to complex problems. But structure dependence in grammar is a highly specific adaptation of this general preference, appealing to purely grammatical constructs (in particular, phrase structure). The evolutionary grounding of grammatical structure dependence in some generalized preference for structural solutions no more refutes the idea that the former is innate than the evolutionary grounding of eyes in simple light-sensitive cells refutes the innateness of eyes.[10]

Second, consider extraction phenomena. There are undoubtedly extractions of grammatical elements that are not found in any language, indeed are not *possible* in any language. For example, I doubt that in any language an element in the position of the word *father's* (in boldface) can be fronted in a question (4a-b):

(4) a. I asked whether the man who denied the claim that Bill's **father's** house was made of wood had the intention of visiting us.
b. *Whose did I ask whether the man who denied the claim that Bill's ___ house was made of wood had the intention of visiting us?

Intuitively, at least, linking the filler and the gap in (4b) poses problems for the parser that render unnecessary a UG-internal explanation. It is hard to imagine a parsing routine that would allow the hearer to hold the possessive interrogative in storage to the point where it would assign the position between *Bill's* and *house* as its locus of interpretation. A similar conclusion could be drawn from other, less dramatic, examples. One might then go on to conclude, along with Deane (1992), Kluender (1992), and others, that the UG constraint of Subjacency is superfluous and that its work can be taken over by extra-UG mechanisms. The problem with such a conclusion, as noted in Fodor (1984) and discussed in Newmeyer (1998b: ch. 3), is that the relationship between sentences excluded by putative UG principles and those posing interpretive challenges to the language user is far from being one-to-one. We find sentences that are constraint violations that pose no parsing difficulty (5a-b) and pairs of sentences of roughly equal ease to the parser, where one is grammatical and the other is a violation (6a-b and 7a-b):

(5) a. *Who did you prefer for ___ to win the game?
b. *What did the baby play with ___ and the rattle?

(6) a. *John tried for Mary to get along well with ___.
b. John is too snobbish for Mary to get along well with ___.

(7) a. *The second question, that he couldn't answer ___ satisfactorily was obvious.
b. The second question, it was obvious that he couldn't answer ___ satisfactorily.

Subjacency might very well have an ultimate functional motivation—a motivation that is reflected synchronically by the fact that many, if not most, violations

[10] Eisenbeiss (2002), Fanselow (1992), and Wunderlich (2004) discuss other phenomena that seem to fall under the same heading as structure dependence, namely being hypothesized properties of UG that are (intuitively) derivable from something broader. These include locality conditions, the i-within-i condition (Chomsky 1981), and economy of representation/derivation and preservation of asymmetric relations (Chomsky 1995).

of this principle are indeed difficult to parse. But whatever its origins, it appears that it is necessary to state it as a construct of grammar (whether innate or not), not one of an extragrammatical system such as parsing. Any formulation of Subjacency that can handle cases such as (5a–b), (6a), and (7a) would presumably generalize to handle (4b) as well. In other words, the impossibility of that latter sentence might well follow from a theory of UG in its narrow (generative) sense.

Paul Kiparsky in still-unpublished work (Kiparsky 2004) has proposed a set of criteria to distinguish UG-based universals from those with purely historical (and therefore ultimately functional) explanations. The former are distinguished from the latter by being exceptionless,[11] process-independent, being able to interact with other grammatical constraints, and constituting pathways for analogical change. Kiparsky proffers what is typically called the 'Animacy Hierarchy' (Hale 1973; Silverstein 1976) as an example of a UG principle, noting that it is at work in phenomena as disparate as split-ergativity, number agreement, and the positioning of adjectival possessors.[12] He points to 'Pica's generalization' (Faltz 1977/1985; Pica 1987) as an example of a generalization whose explanation lies outside of UG. Faltz and Pica noted that complex reflexives (like English *-self* forms) typically differ from simple monosyllabic reflexives in allowing object antecedents, needing to be bound locally, and lacking a possessive form. Kiparsky explains how the (non-exceptionless) constellation of properties associated with complex reflexives tends to arise historically and provides a number of arguments that, in any event, the generalization does not lend itself to formulation in UG terms. It remains to be seen if Kiparsky's criteria generalize to distinguish in the desired way a wide variety of diverse phenomena.

Finally, there are some (apparently) exceptionless universals that have no immediately obvious UG-based *or* non-UG-based accounts. A particularly interesting one is discussed in Cysouw (2003), where it is noted that no language known has a 'true' first-person plural form. That is, a language might have a form referring to the speaker and the hearer or to the speaker and one or more third persons, but not to multiple speakers. Such a gap is perhaps unexpected, since there are numerous examples of what Mühlhäusler and Harré (1990: 201–2) call 'mass speaking': 'football chanting, ritual mass speaking, as in a church service, the mass speaking of children at play, and finally the reactions of a concert audience [and] what occurs at political rallies.' It is interesting that *some* language has not grammaticalized this person reference.[13]

[11] Cf. Chomsky (1988: 62): 'The principles of universal grammar are exceptionless, because they constitute the language faculty itself.'

[12] Citing Wierzbicka (1981), Kiparsky asserts that, contrary to what is often assumed, the hierarchy does not admit to a functional explanation.

[13] Anna Siewierska (p.c.) has suggested that 'true' first-person plurals need no encoding because the relevant parties (the speakers) are all in one place and can see each other, and Martin Haspelmath (p.c.) has remarked that innovations always begin with individual speakers, not with groups of speakers.

In this book I take a cautious approach to attributing some particular feature of grammar to UG (though not as cautious as most functional or cognitive linguists will feel comfortable with). First, I will assume that UG determines grammatical architecture in its broad lines: the interaction of the components devoted to syntax, morphology, semantics, and phonology, as well as the form that grammatical rules (constraints, principles, etc.) may take. In my view, the similarities among the 6000 or so of the world's languages are too striking and various alternative possibilities for the organization of grammars are so *a priori* plausible that I cannot convince myself that what we find in human language represents an 'optimal' (functionally engineered) solution. For example, why is it 'better' for syntax to be blind to segmental phonology? Having made that point, I must stress that this book takes no position on *the precise nature* of this grammatical architecture. While I will advance ideas as to what one might find in UG and what one might not find, it is not my purpose in this book to propose a comprehensive theory of UG.

Second, I will assume that certain more specific universals of grammar are determined by UG in the absence of a convincing alternative 'externally based' account. For example, Horn's observation that no language allows an affirmative to be turned into a negative by changing the intonation contour (2g) has, in my view, precisely that property. Something in UG—and I am for the present content to be agnostic on precisely what—prevents the existence of just such languages. On the other hand, I suspect that the majority of the putative universals in (2) are not consequences of UG at all. It seems implausible, for example, (and here I am relying on nothing but my own professional intuitions) that the generalization that adjective inflection implies noun inflection (2u) is encoded in our genes. My guess is that most of (2a-y) will turn out not even to be universal after more languages are investigated in depth. As Bickel (2001: 2) has pointed out, 'cross-linguistic surveying cannot in principle contribute to the definition of what is possible and what not in human languages,' since the next language observed might well reveal some feature previously thought to be impossible. By way of illustration:

> Recent examples include the discovery of syntactic ergativity in the absence of morphological ergativity (Donohue and Brown 1999), of syntactic ergativity in complementation (Bickel and Nichols 2001), or of pronoun borrowing (Thomason and Everett 2001). An earlier example was object-before-subject constituent order (Pullum 1981b). (Bickel 2001: 2)

Dryer (1997b) concurs, pointing out that before the publication of Seiler (1985) it was believed that no language had a phonologically null plural and a non-null singular, and before the publication of Dimmendaal (1983), a language with gender on nouns but not on pronouns was thought to be impossible. Dryer goes on to argue that exceptionless universals are so rare that linguists' time would be better spent formulating statistical universals than searching for absolute ones.

Finally, I will ascribe to UG those constructs for which a convincing argument from the poverty of the stimulus indicates that they could have never been learned inductively. Subjacency has precisely this property, as argued in Hoekstra and Kooij (1988) and summarized in Newmeyer (1998b: ch. 2, §5.3.1). I will *not* assume, however, that innateness is the default hypothesis for any grammatical principle that has in the past been ascribed to UG or has a universal 'feel' to it. I regard any claim of grammatical innateness as an empirical hypothesis that requires a vigorous defense.

1.3 Probable and improbable human languages

Grammatical features that seem to characterize a great majority of languages, but not all, are easy to find. Perhaps the best known are those found (and derived from) the seminal work in linguistic typology, Greenberg (1963). While this paper proposed several dozen typological universals, those that immediately attracted the greatest deal of attention and inaugurated the most extensive research program are the ones that correlate the basic order of subject, object, and verb with other grammatical features. Even though Greenberg worked with a convenience sample of only thirty languages, some of the correlations that he noted seemed too striking to be accidental. Consider, for example, the correlation between word order and adposition order. Greenberg's sample contained six languages with VSO order, all of which were prepositional; thirteen SVO languages, which were overwhelmingly prepositional; and eleven SOV languages, all postpositional (see Table 1.1). Such correlations, it was widely agreed, could not be due to chance.

The most exhaustive survey of typological correlations between basic word order and some other grammatical feature is Dryer (1992). Based on a study of 625 languages, Dryer found the statistically significant correlations of VO and OV order that are represented in Table 1.2.[14]

In every case that I am aware of, neither the VO correlates nor the OV correlates are exceptionless. In other words, a VO language in which the article precedes N', an OV language in which the manner adverb precedes the verb, etc.,

TABLE 1.1. *Correlations between word order and adposition order (Greenberg 1963)*

	VSO	SVO	SOV
Prep	6	10	0
Postp	0	3	11

[14] Dryer conflated VSO and SVO languages into one category, on the basis of his belief that their typological correlates are largely the same (see Dryer 1991 for a defense of this idea and Chapter 4, §4.6.2, of the present book for critical discussion).

TABLE 1.2. *Correlation pairs reported in Dryer (1992) (the 'Greenbergian correlations')*

VO correlate	OV correlate
adposition—NP	NP—adposition
copula verb—predicate	predicate—copula verb
'want'—VP	VP— 'want'
tense/aspect auxiliary verb—VP	VP—tense/aspect auxiliary verb
negative auxiliary—VP	VP—negative auxiliary
complementizer—S	S—complementizer
question particle—S	S—question particle
adverbial subordinator—S	S—adverbial subordinator
article—N′	N′—article
plural word—N′	N′—plural word
noun—genitive	genitive—noun
noun—relative clause	relative clause—noun
adjective—standard of comparison	standard of comparison—adjective
verb—PP	PP—verb
verb—manner adverb	manner adverb—verb

are merely 'probable languages.' Languages with the reverse correlations are both possible and attested.

Thousands of other robust, but not exception-free, generalizations have been discussed in the typological literature. What follows is a listing of twenty-five randomly chosen grammatical features (or correlations of features) that fall into that category. For the sake of consistency, each is stated in terms of 'improbability':

(8) Some 'improbable languages':
  a. A language with morphemes for both number and case on the same side as the noun, where the case morpheme is closer to the head noun than the number morpheme (Greenberg 1963; TUA #7).
  b. A language with basic SOV order that is not agglutinative (Lehmann 1973; TUA #11).
  c. A language in which the verb agrees with the direct object, but not with the subject, or one in which the verb agrees with the indirect object, but not the direct object (Croft 1988; Moravcsik 1988; TUA #45).
  d. A language in which verbs agree in number, but not in person (Plank 1994; TUA #1058).
  e. A language in which case has a zero realization (or a zero allomorph) which is not absolutive or nominative (Dixon 1994; TUA #1108).
  f. A language in which the adjective precedes the noun, but a number word follows the noun (Hawkins 1983; TUA #75).
  g. A language in which the noun precedes the demonstrative, but the relative clause precedes the noun (Hawkins 1983; TUA #88).

h. A language with a gender distinction for second-person singular pronouns, but not for third-person singular pronouns (Greenberg, Osgood, and Jenkins 1963; TUA #93).
i. A language whose basic order is consistently OV, but in which interrogative markers precede the verb (Lehmann 1973; TUA #108).
j. A language whose basic order is SVO, but where the negative marker does not occur between the subject and the verb (Dryer 1988b; TUA #109).
k. A language in which nouns precede demonstratives, but where adjectives precede nouns (Dryer 1988a; TUA #114).
l. A language with NP-internal agreement, where adjectives inflect for the dual, but demonstratives do not do so (Plank 1989; TUA #142).
m. A language which has overt *wh*-fronting and special marking in yes–no questions (Cheng 1991/1997; TUA #1117).
n. A language with case affixes on nouns that are not suffixed (Hawkins and Gilligan 1988; TUA #170).
o. A language whose basic order is SOV, but which has complex syllable structure (Lehmann 1973; TUA #196).
p. A language with adverb as a distinct word class, but without adjective as a distinct word class (Hengeveld 1992; TUA #248).
q. A language with a number opposition for nouns, but not for pronouns (Vardul' 1969; TUA #255).
r. A language which has VOS basic order and verbal inflection (Bybee 1985; TUA #278).
s. A language with specialized topic markers that is not SOV (Gundel 1988; TUA #377).
t. A language with personal pronouns accompanied by an indefiniteness marker (Moravcsik 1969; TUA #1120).
u. A language with personal possessive prefixes where the genitive follows the noun (Ultan 1978; TUA #455).
v. A language in which the direct object is morphologically marked in a particular sentence, but the indirect object is not (Sedlak 1975; TUA #484).
w. A language that has passives with agent phrases, but lacks passives without agent phrases (Keenan 1985; TUA #1121).
x. A language in which a dual and a plural are distinguished in the 1st person exclusive form of a pronoun, but not also distinguished in the inclusive (Moravcsik 1978; #580).
y. A language with agglutinative morphology that has grammatical gender (Renault 1987; #589).

The question, then, is whether it is the task of UG to capture robust, but not exceptionless, generalizations. Such a question rarely arose in early transformational grammar, given that the typical publication focused on the analysis of one language only (which was not necessarily English, however, despite what is often charged). There was in fact a brief discussion in *Aspects of the Theory of Syntax* of the theoretical treatment of grammatical processes that are not fully excluded from UG, but rather are in some sense 'unnatural,' that is, unlikely to occur in the grammars of very many languages. Chomsky advocated the idea that the notational conventions of the theory be designed so as to facilitate the capturing of natural processes, but to complicate the statement of unnatural ones. Consider his discussion of the English auxiliary (Chomsky 1965: 42–5). Aux may contain as its maximal expansion a tense morpheme, a Modal, a Perfect morpheme, and a Progressive morpheme. Among the ways that such a situation might logically manifest itself are illustrated in (9) and (10). In (9) the linear ordering between elements is always the same, in that, for example, Modal may precede Progressive, but never follow it. In (10), on the other hand, the relationship among the elements is 'cyclic,' in the sense that a second Tense–Modal–Perfect–Progressive ordering can follow the first:

(9) a. Tense
 b. Tense Modal
 c. Tense Perfect
 d. Tense Progressive
 e. Tense Modal Perfect
 f. Tense Modal Progressive
 g. Tense Perfect Progressive
 h. Tense Modal Perfect Progressive

(10) a. Tense Modal Perfect Progressive
 b. Modal Perfect Progressive Tense
 c. Perfect Progressive Tense Modal
 d. Progressive Tense Modal Perfect
 e. Tense Perfect
 f. Modal Progressive

(9) and (10) contain an equivalent number of symbols and, from that point of view, are equally complex. However the linear regularity of (9), not only represents the true situation for English, but is a commonplace one in the languages of the world. The cyclic regularity of (10) is 'not characteristic of natural language' (Chomsky 1965: 43). Hence the theoretical motivation for the parentheses notation, which allows the twenty symbols of (9) to be collapsed to the four (to the right of the arrow) of (11):

(11) Aux → Tense (Modal) (Perfect) (Progressive)

No corresponding notational convention allows for the collapsing of (10). But note that UG does not absolutely exclude the situation exemplified in (10). That is, no constraint prohibits the following set of rules from being part of the grammar of English, or their analogs from being part of the grammar of some other language:

(12)

$$\text{Aux} \rightarrow \left\{ \begin{array}{l} \text{Tense Modal Perfect Progressive} \\ \text{Modal Perfect Progressive Tense} \\ \text{Perfect Progressive Tense Modal} \\ \text{Progressive Tense Modal Perfect} \\ \text{Tense Perfect} \\ \text{Modal Progressive} \end{array} \right\}$$

However, such a grammar must 'pay' for its typological unnaturalness by requiring a complicated set of rules, not susceptible to being collapsed by any abbreviatory convention provided by UG.

Chomsky's discussion set the tone for most subsequent generative-based typological work. The dominant idea has been that it is the job of UG, not merely to distinguish the class of possible languages from the class of impossible languages, but also to distinguish the class of probable languages from the class of improbable languages. It is the second of these two propositions that much of this book will be devoted to rebutting.

1.4 Two methodological approaches to capturing typological generalizations

Before turning to more substantive issues, it might prove useful to highlight and evaluate the methodological differences between formalists and functionalists in the manner in which typological generalizations (particularly non-absolute ones) might be captured. Let's take some fairly easily observed generalization that is manifested in about 90 per cent of languages of the world and not manifested in about 10 per cent. Functionalists have been most likely to take the generalization at face value and to put forward some user-based explanation of why more languages would be likely to work in some particular way than in some other way. Formalists, on the other hand, have tended to focus on developing some principle of UG from which the majority tendency among the world's languages is predicted to follow. In general, this UG principle is arrived at by an intensive analysis of one or two languages instantiating the typological generalization, rather than by comparative work. As far as the minority of languages that seem *not* to instantiate the UG principle are concerned, typically either some grammar-complicating rule or principle is attributed to them or they are ignored entirely.

By focusing on an extended exchange in the 1980s between Bernard Comrie (the functionalist) and Peter Coopmans (the formalist) I will attempt to demonstrate some of the limitations of formalist methodology in accounting for typological generalizations, which, as a consequence, have given functionalists a leg-up in the field of typology, independently of the intrinsic ability of a UG-based theory to handle typological generalizations.[15]

The opening salvo was fired in Comrie (1981), the first edition of his *Language Universals and Linguistic Typology.* After laying out the functional–typological approach, Comrie charges that argumentation for universal principles in the generative approach 'is almost entirely aprioristic, with virtually no appeal to actual data supporting the position being argued for' (4). By 'actual data,' Comrie means a rich variety of cross-linguistic data, since he does acknowledge that generativists 'study a single language in depth' (4). He goes on to argue that generativist methodology 'has led to the positing of putative language universals which then crumble as soon as presented with data from other languages' (7). Comrie's most developed argument to illustrate the point involves the X-bar schema, which claims that for a given language, for all phrase types, specifiers uniformly precede their heads or follow their heads, as do all complements. He notes that this universal, which 'was originally proposed on the basis of English data' (7), does indeed seem to work for that language, as illustrated in (13):

(13) a. *the* book
b. *must* go

However, a look at Malay, where the determiner follows the noun but the auxiliary precedes the verb, shows that at best we are dealing with a tendency, not an absolute universal:

(14) a. surat *itu* 'letter that'
b. *akan* membaca 'will read'

But even worse, even the weaker claim that the X-bar schema represents a tendency:

> ... turns out to be invalid as an attempt to characterize variation across languages. The number of languages in which determiners follow nouns and auxiliaries follow verbs is small, while there are many languages—including most languages of the widespread canonical SOV type (see chapter 4)—that have determiners preceding the noun but auxiliaries following the verb ... (Comrie 1981: 7–8)

Such elementary errors on the part of generative grammarians, Comrie suggests, result from 'the theoretical and practical deficiencies of trying to work on language universals on the basis of a single language' (9).[16]

Few more negative reviews have appeared in the literature than that of the Comrie book by Peter Coopmans (Coopmans 1983). Coopmans accuses Comrie of a 'general misapprehension about the universals posited in generative

[15] A thoroughgoing critique of the mainstream generativist approach to typology is reserved for Chapter 3.

[16] In current principles-and-parameters work, nouns are generally considered to be heads of phrases that are complements to phrases headed by determiners and verbs heads of phrases that are complements to phrases with auxiliary heads. So Comrie's critique might continue to be relevant.

grammar' (457), which, far from being surface generalizations induced from simple inspection of a great number of languages, hold only at a high level of abstraction. So, as far as Comrie's critique of X-bar theory is concerned, this theory:

> ... constrains the phrase structure rules of a particular grammar and should not be construed as a generalization of existing word order correlations on a par with the various universals in surface word order typology. An empirical refutation of a particular X-bar theory will show that some grammar requires PS rules which are incompatible with that theory; the refutation will be as convincing as the (partial) grammar offered ... Comrie does not argue for any particular PS rules, least of all for any rules which contravene some particular theory of PS rules. (Coopmans 1983: 457)

But neither, in fact, does Coopmans. In other words, while Coopmans reiterated in admirably clear fashion how the notion 'universal' is to be understood in a UG-based theory, he brought the reader no closer to an understanding of how the *surface* differences between English and Malay might be explained, nor to an explanation of the fact that *superficially at least* X-bar theory appears to be contradicted in part by cross-linguistic generalizations about the ordering of specifiers and heads. After all, the only data that we have at our disposal are 'superficial.' Explanations might well involve a highly abstract chain of inference, but they are still at root accounts of the data.

Coopmans went on to provide some examples of how abstract UG principles might be applied to the explanation of phenomena of interest to typologists. One involves the discussion of the phenomenon of preposition stranding in Lightfoot (1981) and the attempt to explain why it is allowed in English (15a, 16a), but disallowed in French (15b, 16b):

(15) a. John was talked to ___
b. *Jean était parlé à ___

(16) a. Who did you talk to ___?
b. *Qui avez-vous parlé à ___?

Coopmans endorsed Lightfoot's account, which is based on differences in the abstract case systems of the two languages. Given the hypothesis that English prepositions assign objective case to the position they govern after the application of movement and that French prepositions assign oblique case at D-structure before movement, along with further assumptions about UG requirements on the level of Logical Form, the typological difference between English and French is said to follow.

The greater part of Coopmans's review was devoted to trying to undermine certain functional explanations for typological generalizations put forward in Comrie's book. For example, Comrie presented, endorsed, and provided a functional explanation for the 'Accessibility Hierarchy' governing the ability of NP positions to be relativized in simple main clauses (Comrie 1981: 148–55):

(17) *THE ACCESSIBILITY HIERARCHY (AH) GOVERNING RELATIVIZATION* (Comrie and Keenan 1979; Keenan and Comrie 1977, 1979)

SU > DO > IO > OBL > GEN > OCOMP

'>' means 'is more accessible than.' 'SU,' 'DO,' 'IO,' 'OBL,' 'GEN,' and 'OCOMP' stand for 'subject,' 'direct object,' 'indirect object,' 'major oblique case NP,' 'genitive,' and 'object of comparison,' respectively. The relevant constraints for accessibility are stated as follows (Comrie and Keenan 1979: 652–3):

(18) SUBJECT RELATIVE UNIVERSAL

All languages can relativize subjects.

(19) ACCESSIBILITY HIERARCHY CONSTRAINT
a. If a language can relativize any position on the AH with a primary strategy, then it can relativize all higher positions with that strategy.
b. For each position on the AH, there are possible languages which can relativize that position with a primary strategy, but cannot relativize any lower position with that strategy.

A strategy is considered primary if it is the one used to form relative clauses on *subjects* for that language. The sets of positions in (20) are those that AH predicts to be relativizable (and are illustrated with an actual language manifesting them taken from Keenan and Comrie's sample), but not those sets of positions in (21):

(20) a. SU, DO, IO, OBL, GEN, OCOMP (Urhobo)
b. SU, DO, IO, OBL, GEN (French)
c. SU, DO, IO, OBL (Korean)
d. SU, DO, IO (Roviana)
e. SU, DO (Tongan)
f. SU (Tagalog)

(21) *SU, DO, GEN; *SU, OBL, OCOMP; *SU, DO, GEN; and 55 others

Coopmans attempted to show that the generalization embodied in the hierarchy is incorrect (in other words to show that Comrie had 'explained' a non-existent generalization), by pointing out that in certain cases direct objects are easier to extract than subjects. *That*-trace phenomena provide clear examples in illustration of the point:

(22) a. Who do you think Bill saw ___?
b. Who do you think ___ saw Bill?

(23) a. Who do you think that Bill saw ___?
b. *Who do you think that ___ saw Bill?

(24) a. the man who you think Bill saw ___
b. the man who you think ___ saw Bill

(25) a. the man who you think that Bill saw ___
b. *the man who you think that ___ saw Bill

The Empty Category Principle (ECP), a principle of UG (Chomsky 1981), determines relativization possibilities in (22–25), illustrating (to Coopmans's satisfaction) the unreasonableness of attempting a functional explanation. Coopmans went on to argue that the relevant generalization does not even apply to grammatical relations. Rather, it is purely structural. As noted in Cinque (1981), subjects in Italian can be relativized with *che*, so that would count as a 'primary strategy' for Keenan and Comrie:

(26) La proposta che è stata fatta è assurda
'The proposal that has been made is absurd'

But what determines relativization possibilities with this primary strategy is whether the position is marked with a preposition or not. So one can form relative clauses in Italian with *che* from predicative (that is, post-copular) NPs (27) and even from some temporal adverbials (28), because in such cases there is no preposition marking the point of extraction:

(27) a. Era *un gentiluomo*
'He was a gentleman'
b. Il gentiluomo [$_{S'}$ che era] gli impedì di reagire in malo modo
'The gentleman that he was prevented him from reacting nastily'

(28) a. La proposta Banfi era stata bocciata *il giorno prima.*
'The proposal made by Banfi had been rejected the day before'
b. Il giorno [$_{S'}$ che la proposta Banfi fu bocciata] non c'era nessuno.
'The day that the proposal made by Banfi was rejected nobody was there'

There can be no cut-off point for grammatical relations, according to Coopmans, because grammatical relations are not even the relevant descriptive parameter for the generalization. So we can see how Coopmans had mounted a two-pronged attack on the typological–functional wing. First he rejected the typological generalization itself, by arguing for the primacy of structural principles over relational ones. That in turn cast doubt on functional explanation in general, given that it was so easy for Comrie to provide one for a (putatively) false generalization.

The next shot was fired by Comrie, who was granted the luxury of a reply to Coopmans's review (Comrie 1984). As far as preposition stranding was concerned, Coopmans (and the analysis by Lightfoot that he adopted) played right into Comrie's hands. Comrie had no difficulty in showing that the desired correlation between case-assignment possibilities and the possibility of stranding barely extends past English and French. Some case-rich languages *are* stranding (e.g. Old English), while most case-poor languages (indeed, most languages in general) are not stranding (Haitian Creole was Comrie's example). In other words, Coopmans could not have picked a worse example to illustrate the ability of generative grammar to capture a typological generalization. On the surface, at least, the explanatory abilities of the principle that he pointed to was counter-exemplified by the great majority of languages in the world and he proposed no supplementary principles to account for these problematic cases.

Comrie then turned to *that*-trace phenomena, which Coopmans pointed to as challenging the basis of the AH. Coopmans had appealed to the ECP to explain the impossibility of sentence (29):

(29) *the girl that you think that ___ will come

But as is well known, in Italian the literal translation of (29) is fine:

(30) la ragazza che credi che ___ verrà

Why is this sentence not an ECP violation as well? As Comrie noted, Rizzi (1982) had an answer. Subject postposing and the possibility of null subjects are linked. So if extraction takes place from postposed position, there would be no ECP violation. In other words, sentence (30) would derive in part from:

(31) ___ verrà la ragazza

But Comrie went on to point out the lack of generality of Rizzi's solution. Portuguese, like Italian, allows *that*-trace sentences (see (32)), yet it does not permit subject postposing:

(32) a menina que você acredita que ___ vai chegar

Comrie noted that Zubizarreta (1982) had attempted to solve this problem by arguing that *que* in Portuguese is a relative pronoun, not a complementizer, so there would be no '*that*-trace' (ECP) violation. Comrie continued:

> What is lacking [in the approach defended by Coopmans] is an investigation of the range of variation found across languages with respect to this phenomenon, so that we might have at least some hope of knowing whether or not the theoretical analyses proposed have some chance of accounting for the range of phenomena they are supposed to cover.... If French can avoid the constraint by replacing a complementizer by a pronoun (*que* → *qui*), and Portuguese can do this even where complementizer and pronoun are homophonous, then why does this possibility not exist in English, replacing *that* by *who* (or even leaving it as *that* if the relative clause introducer *that* in English is analyzed as a pronoun) to give **the girl that I think who will come*? (Comrie 1984: 160–1)

Again, Comrie was quite successful, I think, in demonstrating that Coopmans' UG-based approach had little to contribute to the understanding of typological variation in language. In each case, any seeming exception to a UG-based explanation of a typological feature was patched up by a special assumption for the language in question. What is particularly ironic here, in my view, is that generative grammarians are always the first to say that isolated facts are not sufficient to demolish a principle. Yet Coopmans had no problem with rejecting the AH—an extremely robust, though not exception-free, typological generalization—on the basis of a couple of facts from a couple of languages. And he never felt obligated either to provide an explanation of why the AH *does* seem to hold fairly reliably, or to explain the range of variation that one finds in cases where it does not seem to hold.

The fourth article in the series, Coopmans (1984), continued the attack on Comrie, but focused in particular on the typological work of John Hawkins (Hawkins 1979, 1980, 1982). The three papers by Hawkins recast many of the Greenbergian correlations as chains of implications, as for example:

(33) a. SOV → (AN → GN)
 b. VSO → (NA → NG)
 c. Prep → (NA → NG)
 d. Postp → (AN → GN)

Some of Coopmans's article was devoted to pointing out and correcting redundancies in the formulation of Hawkins's implicational universals. But the bulk of the paper had goals that can only be described as 'schizophrenic.' On the one hand, Coopmans questioned 'whether H[awkins's] approach [which focused on surface typological generalizations] represents a productive research strategy at a stage of investigation when plausible principles of some explanatory depth already exist' (Coopmans 1984: 58). But on the other hand, he devoted several pages to explaining how UG principles can explain such generalizations. I do not feel that it is being overly uncharitable to Coopmans to analogize him to some (probably non-existent) theoretical physicist who scorns the work of experimentalists as being superficial and obsessively data-oriented, but then claims as a significant result the providing of a theoretical framework from which the experimental results follow.

Let us look at a couple of the Greenbergian correlations that Coopmans said that UG theory is capable of explaining. One was Greenberg's Universal #12, for which a UG-based explanation was put forward in Emonds (1980). On the basis of a sample of sixteen languages, six of them VSO, Greenberg proposed the following universal:

(34) Universal #12: 'If a language has dominant order VSO in declarative sentences, it always puts interrogative words or phrases first in interrogative word questions.' (Greenberg 1963: 83)

Emonds analyzed VSO languages as having an underlying SVO order with movement of V out of VP to COMP:

(35) The derivation of VSO languages (Emonds 1980)

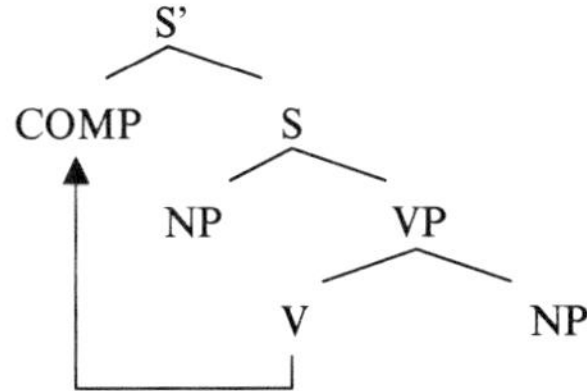

Emonds further assumed that 'the existence of [sentence-initial] COMP in the language entails a *wh*-fronting transformation' (Emonds 1980: 44) and that all movements to pre-subject position are attractions to a sentence-initial COMP node (den Besten 1983). Given this conjunction of assumptions, Coopmans said that Emonds had succeeded in explaining Universal #12. In a nutshell, since VSO formation is analyzed as attraction to a left-positioned COMP, the presence of that COMP attracts the *wh*-phrase as well.

The problem is that the surface generalization that Emonds set out to explain—Greenberg's Universal #12—is not exceptionless. According to Dryer (1991), a significant proportion of verb-initial languages (16 per cent) have *wh-in-situ*.[17] In other words, Emonds was in the awkward position of having 'explained' a non-existent universal. Now of course, Emonds and Coopmans might well have appealed to some independently motivated principle applying in the residual 16 per cent that would mask the effects of the *wh*-fronting process that UG required them to manifest (though I cannot imagine what it might be) or they might have wished to argue that these languages are not really VSO (though I cannot imagine why they would not be). The fact that they did not do so is indicative of the lack of seriousness with which typological generalizations have typically been approached by generative grammarians. Even more problematically, it appears to be the case that a crucial assumption in Emonds's chain of reasoning is incorrect, namely that initial COMP entailing *wh*-fronting. While every VO language known has an initial COMP (Hawkins 1990), Dryer notes that 42 per cent of SVO languages are *wh-in-situ*.

Coopmans attempted to explain another apparent universal. He noted that in Greenberg's thirty languages sample, there were no instances of VSO languages with the order REL-N (Greenberg 1963: 106, n. 20). Coopmans reasoned as follows: We have already seen that VSO languages have both sentence-initial COMP and a *wh*-fronting operation. If we assume that UG demands that the head of an NP in a relative clause be immediately adjacent to the *wh*-element in COMP (in order to establish the proper binding relation), then it follows that the order of elements in VSO languages must be N-REL:

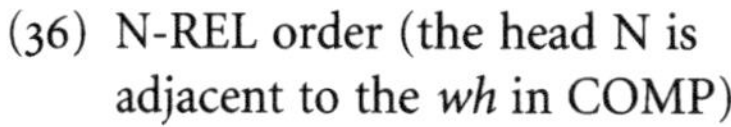
(36) N-REL order (the head N is adjacent to the *wh* in COMP)

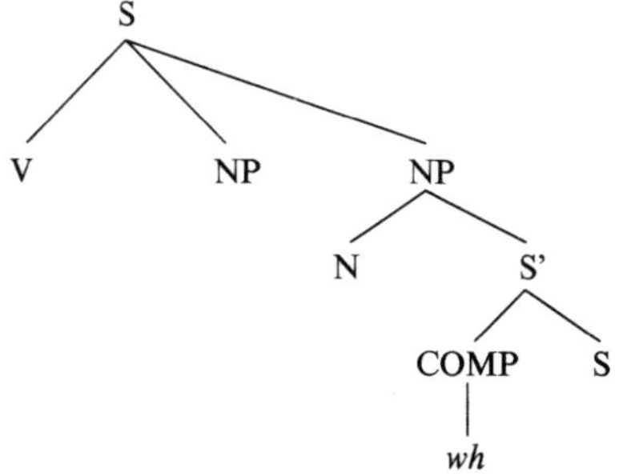

[17] Dryer's figures are adjusted to eliminate genetic and areal bias. His presentation did not distinguish VSO from VOS languages. Given that the former greatly outnumber the latter, that fact should have no bearing on the present discussion.

If the order were Rel-N, there would be no adjacency:

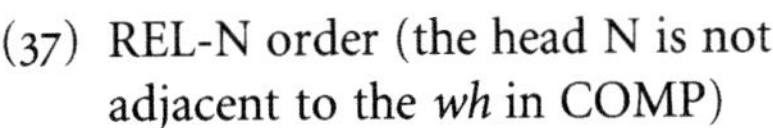

(37) REL-N order (the head N is not adjacent to the *wh* in COMP)

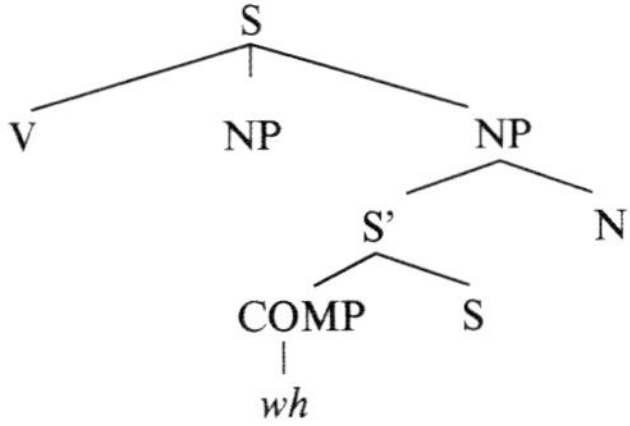

Here again, many questions can be raised. First, the argument goes through only for VSO languages in which relative clauses involve movement of a *wh*-element into COMP. Second, SVO languages manifest N-REL order almost to the same extent that VSO languages do. In Matthew Dryer's 324 language database, only one language (Chinese) correlates VO order with REL-N ordering. Yet, Coopmans's explanation for why VSO languages should be N-REL does not generalize to SVO languages. And finally, any VSO language with deep REL-N ordering could easily achieve the surface N-REL ordering necessary for binding simply by extraposing the relative clause (such extraposition is widespread in the world's languages). Coopmans provided no account for why this option might not be chosen.

To summarize, the standard generative approach to typological generalizations, epitomized by Coopmans's papers from the 1980s, leaves a lot to be desired. Surface generalizations of the Greenbergian sort are at first scorned as trivial and uninteresting, but then provided with an account within the general envelope of UG that takes little responsibility for explaining those cases in which they do not hold. Not much has changed in the ensuing two decades. As we will see in the following few chapters, even though generativists have come more and more to advocate UG-internal explanations of typological generalizations, they have done little to overcome the methodological limitations that have plagued this genre of explanation from the beginning.

1.5 Conclusion

Most theoretical linguists, from whatever camp, consider that it is a central goal of theoretical work on grammar to distinguish possible grammatical processes from impossible ones and—for the former—to explain why some possible processes seem more common than others. As we have seen, the theoretical and methodological obstacles to achieving this goal are legion. The following chapters are devoted to reorienting generative grammarians in a direction that is better able to capture the distinction between the possible and the probable in language than has generally been manifest in UG-based research.

2

Parameterized Principles

2.1 Introduction

This chapter is devoted to presenting the principal means within generative theory by which typological generalizations have been captured, namely, by the parameterization of principles of Universal Grammar. It begins (§2.2) with a look at early work in generative-based typological analysis, before parameters were introduced. Section 2.3 presents the Government-Binding approach to parameters and §2.4 their treatment within the Minimalist Program. Sections 2.5 and 2.6 discuss parameter- and typology-related issues with respect to language acquisition and language change respectively, and are followed by a brief conclusion (§2.7).

2.2 Early generative syntactic typology

Questions of language typology did not occupy center stage in the first couple of decades of work in generative syntax. The earliest work for the most part tended to be in-depth studies of some particular construction or set of constructions in one particular language, with the goal of motivating or providing additional support for some abstract grammatical principle. That is, there was little comparative work devoted to explicating the possible range of grammatical variation across languages. The reason for the relative absence of such studies is not hard to understand. The program of generative grammar prioritizes the uncovering of highly abstract generalizations about grammar. But their discovery necessitates an intensive look at individual languages. Therefore in the early stages of the theory, the most important task was seen to be to focus on the properties of English or French or Hidatsa or some other particular language, and to leave typological studies for a later date.

There was also a tendency, in retrospect an unfortunate one in my opinion, to dismiss surface variation among languages (the subject of typological studies in the Greenbergian tradition) as not meriting serious attention from grammatical theorists. For example, a passage in Chomsky's *Aspects of the Theory of Syntax* seems to de-emphasize the search for (and presumably explanation of) the sorts of typological generalizations that Greenberg had outlined in his famous paper of two years earlier:

> Modern work has indeed shown a great diversity in the surface structures of languages. However, since the study of deep structure has not been its concern, it has not attempted to show a corresponding diversity of underlying structures, and, in fact, the evidence that has been accumulated in modern study of language does not appear to suggest anything of this sort.... Insofar as attention is restricted to surface structures, the most that can be expected is the discovery of statistical tendencies, such as those presented by Greenberg (1963). (Chomsky 1965: 118)

As argued in Newmeyer (1998b: 351), a full reading of the section of *Aspects* in which this quote appears tends to temper somewhat its more extreme (though common) interpretation, namely that Chomsky felt that the explanation of typological generalizations was not a job for theoretical linguists. This passage was embedded in a long discussion of how at deep levels of analysis, languages are more similar to each other than they are at surface levels. That is, Chomsky was combating the tendency, manifest in both earlier structuralist models and the nascent functional–typological approach, to *restrict attention* to surface structure. Nevertheless, the passage did indeed invite the conclusion that typology lacked interest. That fact, combined with the fact that Chomsky himself never took on typological issues in the period, tended to discourage generative syntacticians from delving into the question of capturing cross-linguistic generalizations.

Even so, there were a number of pre-1980 typologically oriented studies in generative syntax, many of which referred explicitly to the seminal Greenberg paper. These studies had the following (overlapping) goals: to argue that syntax, as well as phonology, should avail itself of markedness conventions (§2.2.1); that languages can be shown to be more typologically consistent at a deep level of structure than at the surface (§2.2.2); and that principles of UG provide the key to solving typological problems (§2.2.3). Let us look at them in turn.

2.2.1 *Syntactic typology and markedness theory*

Consideration of the relative commonness of a grammatical process acted as a guide to theory construction in the early days of transformational generative grammar, particularly in phonology. In the initial chapters of *The Sound Pattern of English* (Chomsky and Halle 1968), the naturalness of a phonological rule was calculated essentially as the inverse of the number of distinctive feature specifications needed to formulate it. That is, UG was assumed to provide an evaluation metric such that the more commonly attested processes (say, those applying to natural classes of elements) were easier to state than the less commonly attested ones. The problem, addressed in chapter 9 of that book, was that feature counting alone did not suffice to distinguish cross-linguistically common processes from cross-linguistically rare ones. For example, all other things being equal, no more feature specifications are required for a language to unround all rounded back vowels than to unround all rounded front vowels. Yet, the former process is extremely rare cross-linguistically, while the latter relatively common. To deal with this problem Chomsky and Halle introduced a set of *marking conventions* into the theory, which tied naturalness to evaluation. The common unrounding process would be cost free in terms of the metric, while the rare one would be costly. These conventions were further developed in Kean (1975).

The mid 1960s saw the first application of markedness theory to syntactic analysis. The criteria for determining whether a process is marked or not appear to have been determined largely, if not wholly, on typological distribution: more common cross-linguistically was considered to be less marked grammatically. For example, Bach (1965) proposed to handle certain Greenbergian word-order correlations by means of marking conventions internal to the grammar. He speculated that the following correlations seemed consistent with Greenberg (1963):

(1) a. SVO & N Rel ordering
    b. SOV & Rel N ordering

In the framework of syntactic analysis current at the time, relative clauses were adjoined to their heads by means of embedding transformations. So it would follow that for SVO languages like English, the relative clause would be embedded after the head noun and for SOV languages like Japanese before the head noun. In Bach's view, such a treatment led to a missed generalization, in that the assumed predictability of the placement of the relative in each language type did not follow from anything broader. To remedy this situation, Bach proposed to handle the word-order correlations by means of marking conventions. He wrote that since OV languages like Japanese typically 'have preposed desentential nominal modifiers... we do not have to state the rule shifting "REL" to a position before the noun for Japanese separately but can state in our general theory that this rule is predictable from the basic order of Japanese sentences' (Bach 1965: 10–11). The grammars of the minority of languages that violate (1a-b) would require special complicating statements overriding the marking conventions.

The only other case of which I am aware of markedness being appealed to in syntax in pre-principles-and-parameters models to handle typological generalizations is found in Hale (1976).[1] Hale called attention to the typologically rare phenomenon of defining the notion 'subject' in terms of the language's case system (found in Warlpiri and other 'non-configurational' languages) instead of configurationally. He suggested that marking conventions single out this phenomenon as highly marked, presumably by requiring more language-particular descriptive machinery than is necessary to characterize configurationally assigned grammatical relations.

It is interesting to speculate why markedness theory was so little appealed to by generative syntacticians in this period. Part of the explanation is certainly

[1] It was not uncommon in the 1970s, however, to find some rare or unusually complex grammatical process described as a 'marked' one (for example, see Chomsky 1977b). The typological implications of such a characterization were rarely investigated, however.

that few generativists were engaged in comparing language types in enough depth to draw the relevant markedness generalizations. But more profoundly, I think that the hesitancy to appeal to markedness derived from the feeling that the concept lacked explanatory power altogether—'marked' simply being another word for 'uncommon' and 'unmarked' for 'common.' In the 1960s and 1970s, as today, most generativists felt that a true explanation had to appeal to the intricate interaction of rules and/or principles of complex deductive structure.

2.2.2 *Deep structure and typological consistency*

For the most part, generative solutions to typological problems before 1980 appealed to a central concept in syntactic theory at the time—the difference between deep structure and surface structure. Bach (1970) was the first to argue for the underlying order in a particular language being different from surface order as a step toward explaining a set of seeming exceptions to the Greenbergian correlations. That language was Amharic, a Semitic language spoken in Ethiopia. Unlike most Semitic languages, Amharic is predominately SOV on the surface. Nevertheless, the language has a number of what Bach regarded as 'non-SOV-like' properties: it is prepositional; it has both prefixes and suffixes; honorifics precede names; relative clauses can either precede or follow the head noun; there are alternatives to verb-final order; it has verb–object agreement, which is unusual for an SOV language; and it exhibits 'gapping' behavior (Ross 1970) more like a VO language than an OV language. In other words, Amharic would seem to have at least as many 'VO correlations' as 'OV correlations.'

Bach argued that underlyingly Amharic is VSO, based on an intricate argument involving possessives. In that language, *yə-* is prefixed in possessive constructions:

(2) a. yə-ne bet 'my house' (yə + ine + bet)
b. yə-səwiyyəw 'the man's house'

In keeping with the standard view of the time, Bach assumed that such possessives were derived from relative clauses. Indeed, relatives in Amharic also use *yə-* as a verbal prefix. The idea of identifying the two instances of *yə-* was given further support by their similar morphosyntactic behavior, in that both are deleted after prepositions. Bach's next assumption was that relative clauses derive from a structure like:

(3) yə $[_{s}\text{VXNP}_{i}\text{Y}]$ NP_{i}

Consider, now, his derivation of *yəne bet* 'my house,' given a verb-initial deep structure:

(4) a. yə [all- ine bet] bet
be me house house
b. yə [all- ine] bet deletion of identical NP

c. yə [ine] bet copula deletion
d. yə + ine bet *yə-* attachment

If copula deletion does not apply, *yə-* attachment affixes *yə-* to the verb immediately to its right, thereby deriving *the house that I had.* Now, Bach argued, if we had assumed that Amharic were SOV instead of VSO, two rules of *yə-* attachment would be needed, one for possessives, and one attaching it to verbs at the *end* of the clause, thereby missing the generalization that *yə-* is attached to the following lexical element, no matter what it might be.

As argued at some length in Hudson (1972), Bach's analysis was not problem-free, even given the assumptions of late 1960s generative syntax. For one thing, it required an extra rule shifting the verb, the necessity of which was purely a consequence of positing an underlying order for Amharic different from the surface order. By complicating the syntactic derivation at the expense of simpler underlying representations, Bach was setting the stage for the next few decades' work in generative typology. Indeed, following Bach, it became generally assumed that the Greenbergian (and other typological) correlations hold at the deepest syntactic level, with inconsistency and irregularity being a product of the distorting effect of language-particular movements. Problematically in the case of Bach on Amharic, however, in order to get the analysis to work he had to assume that the underlying order of the relative clause and its head noun is Rel–N, even though the great majority of verb-initial languages manifest the opposite order.

As a final point of interest, semiticists are united in considering VSO to be the original word order of Amharic, with its verb finality a consequence of centuries of contact with the neighboring Cushitic languages. In this respect, then, Bach's analysis reinforced the sorts of analyses that were then current in phonology (e.g. Chomsky and Halle 1968), where the underlying structure typically represented a historically antecedent stage of the language.

A similarly structured argument is found in Tai (1973), which argued purely on the basis of grammar-internal simplicity that Chinese is SOV. Tai went on to point out that a benefit of his analysis was the explanation of why Chinese manifests SOV correlations. As he noted, if deep structure order is more revealing of typology than surface structure order, it would come as no surprise that the deep order motivated on theoretical grounds would be a better predictor of type than the surface order.

2.2.3 *UG principles and the solution of typological problems*

Generative interest in typology took a new turn with the publication of John R. Ross's classic paper on gapping (Ross 1970), which was perhaps the first to argue explicitly that principles of UG can solve typological problems. Ross, in calling attention to Greenberg's 'important paper' (p. 249), noted a correlation between a language's ordering of verb and object and the directionality of the rule of

Gapping, which in a conjoined sentence deletes the verb in one conjunct under identity with the verb in the other. VO languages like English gap to the right, while OV languages like Japanese gap to the left:

(5) I ate fish, Bill ate rice, and Harry ate roast beef ⇒
I ate fish, Bill ___ rice, and Harry ___ roast beef

(6) Watakusi-wa sakana-o tabe, Biru-wa gohan-o tabeta ⇒
I fish eat Bill rice ate
'I ate fish, and Bill ate rice'

Watakusi-wa sakana-o, Biru-wa gohan-o tabeta
I fish Bill rice ate
'I ate fish, and Bill rice'

In other words, we find gapping possibilities (7a) and (7b). (7c), however, does not seem to exist:

(7) Possible Gapping orders
a. SVO + SO (English)
b. SO + SOV (Japanese)
c. *SO + SVO (unattested)

Ross suggested that a UG condition specifies that the order in which Gapping operates depends on the order of elements at the time that the rule applies. If the identical elements are on left branches, Gapping applies forward; if they are on right branches, it applies backward. This hypothesis seemed to be supported by Russian, which has fairly free word order:

(8) ja pil vodu, i Anna pila vodku
↓
Ø (SVO + SO)
I drank water and Anna (drank) vodka

(9) ja vodu pil, i Anna vodku pila
↓
Ø (SO + SOV)

Ross was assuming a 'Scrambling' rule for Russian, so Scrambling must have preceded Gapping in one of these derivations (depending on what the underlying order of Russian is). Now, to make things more complicated, Russian also has SO + SVO:

(10) ja vodu, i Anna pila vodku
S O S V O

Given his other assumptions, along with the assumption that Gapping is an 'anywhere rule,' Ross noted that the ordering in (10) leads to the conclusion that Russian must be underlyingly SVO. In other words, Ross had, to his satisfaction, proposed a UG constraint on deletion and used that constraint to settle the problematic question of the basic order of Russian.

Too many problems were immediately uncovered with Ross's analysis to lead to its general adoption by the community of generative syntacticians (see, for example, Jackendoff 1970; Maling 1972). However, a more successful demonstration of how generative theory can be used to settle problems of interest to typologists was put forward in Emonds (1976). Emonds took on the question of basic word order in German, which is problematic because main clauses and subordinate clauses differ with respect to the placement of the tensed verbal element. In main clauses the finite verb is generally in second position (hence the characterization of German as a 'V2 language'), while in embedded clauses the verb is final in the verb phrase:

(11) a. Gestern **ist** er nach Hause gekommen
'Yesterday he came home'
b. Welches Buch **können** the Studenten nehmen?
'Which book can the students take?'

(12) a. Ihm tat es leid, dass er gestern nach Hause gekommen **war**
'He was sorry that he came home yesterday'
b. Er weiss nicht, welche Bücher die Studenten genommen **haben**
'He doesn't know which books the students took'

Emonds constructed an ingenious argument that, given the Structure Preserving Constraint (SPC), the principle of UG which his book was devoted to motivating, the only possible underlying order for German is SOV:

(13) Structure Preserving Constraint (Emonds 1976): Rules that distort basic phrase structure configurations apply only in topmost ('root') clauses

If the SPC is correct, German and Dutch *have to be* SOV. Consider what are perhaps the two most plausible deep structure orders for German, V2 (14a) and SOV (14b):

(14) a. b.

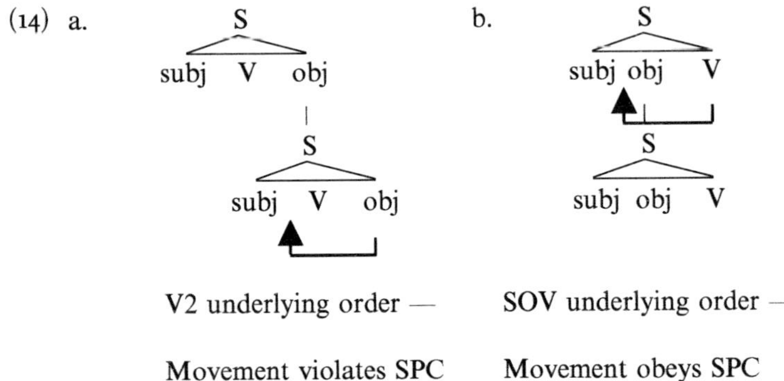

If German were underlyingly V2, as in (14a), a rule would be required in subordinate clauses to move the object to the left of the verb. But such a rule would violate the SPC, as it would distort a basic phrase-structure configuration in a non-root clause. On the other hand, if German is underlyingly SOV, as in (14b), then a rule applying in the main clause moves the verb to the left of the object. But such a rule would be perfectly fine, since non-structure-preserving rules can apply in root clauses. Hence it follows that the basic order of German is SOV.[2]

Let us turn to another example of how UG was applied to the solution of typological questions in early generative syntax. It has long been known that verb-final languages are much less likely to exhibit *wh*-fronting than VO languages, but much more likely to have sentence-final question particles. Table 2.1 from Dryer 1991: 455–66 provides the data supporting such an idea.[3]

The root of the typological correlation between verb finality, lack of *wh*-fronting, and final question particles has been on the generative research agenda for over three decades. Baker (1970) proposed a universal rule of Question Movement, in which a *wh*-type element moves to the left to replace an abstract question morpheme 'Q.' Q is the question particle for languages that have one (in English it is realized as *if* or *whether*). SOV languages have Q on the right, so these languages keep their Q and, given that *wh*-fronting is obligatorily to the left, do not have this rule. Bresnan (1970) identified 'Q' with the category 'COMP' (i.e. 'Complementizer') and suggested that only languages with clause-initial COMP permit a COMP-substitution transformation, thereby accounting for the fact that long-distance movements are in general excluded in OV languages. Bach (1971), working with a slightly different set of assumptions from Bresnan, concluded that movement of question words will always be to the left and that such movement will never occur in SOV language. These conclusions followed from the assumptions that *wh*-fronting must be unbounded, that the element moved by this rule is attracted to a verb that governs questions (which might be an abstract performative verb), and that UG allows only leftward movement rules to be unbounded.

TABLE 2.1. *Proportion of languages with* wh-in-situ *and final question particles, by word-order type (Dryer 1991)*

	V-final	SVO	V-initial
Wh-in situ	71	42	16
Final Q particles	73	30	13

[2] And indeed, most generative grammarians who have taken on the question of basic order in German (and in Dutch, which manifests similar behavior) have concluded on the basis of other considerations that these languages are SOV (e. g. Bach 1962; Bierwisch 1963, 1966; Koster 1975; Bennis and Hoekstra 1984). However, applying some of the assumptions of Kayne 1994, Zwart 1993, 1997 and Koster 1994 argue that Dutch is SVO with a great deal of leftward movement of complements.

[3] The figures in the 'Final Q particles' row give the proportion of final question particles out of the total number of final and initial particles. Languages with no question particles at all, or those whose particles occur non-peripherally, are not counted.

Indeed, since the early 1970s, most treatments have assumed that a Q or *wh*-feature in C° is in some way responsible for triggering movement.[4]

Finally, let us turn to the early treatment of null subject phenomena. This issue has a special place in generative typology, as the division of languages between those that require subjects of tensed clauses and those that do not is probably the typological difference among languages that has received the most intensive study. The long history of the analysis of such phenomena begins with Perlmutter (1971), which noted that in French, one can question the object of a subordinate or relative clause introduced by *que*, but not the subject:

(15) a. Qui a-t-il dit que Martin avait envie de voir?
'Who did he say that Martin felt like seeing?'
b. *Qui a-t-il dit que s'est évanoui?
'Who did he say (that) fainted?'

(16) a. la personne à qui il a dit que Nicole a donné l'argent
'the who he said (that) Nicole gave the money to'
b. *la personne qu'il a dit que va venir ce soir
'the person that he said (that) is going to come tonight'

Perlmutter also pointed out that subjects, both thematic and non-thematic, can be null in Spanish, but not in French:

(17) a. *Avons travaillé toute la journée '(We) worked all day long'
b. Hemos trabajado todo el día '(We) worked all day long'

(18) a. Il pleut / *Pleut 'It is raining'
b. *Él llueve / Llueve 'It is raining'

He proposed the following surface structure constraint (or 'filter') for French to distinguish it from Spanish:

(19) Any sentence other than an Imperative in which there is an S that does not contain a subject in surface structure is ungrammatical.

Perlmutter noted that more languages appear to behave like Spanish than like French, pointing to similar phenomena in Italian, Serbo-Croatian, Arabic, Hebrew, Hausa, Warlpiri, and Basque.

Now, what about English? In many ways it appears to behave like French, in particular by prohibiting deleted subjects after the complementizer *that* and by requiring subjects in simple tensed clauses:

(20) a. *What did he say that happened?
b. *the events that he said that happened
c. *Raining

[4] A notable early exception is Grimshaw (1977), which, on the basis of an appeal to the autonomy of syntax, rejected the idea of a semantically based feature driving syntactic movement.

But English differs from French in that deleted embedded subjects are possible if the complementizer is deleted as well:

(21) a. What did he say happened?
 b. the events that he said happened

Perlmutter accounted for this typological difference between English and French by means of the assumption that English, like French, is subject to constraint (19), but that in English the deletion of *that* entails the pruning of the S node:

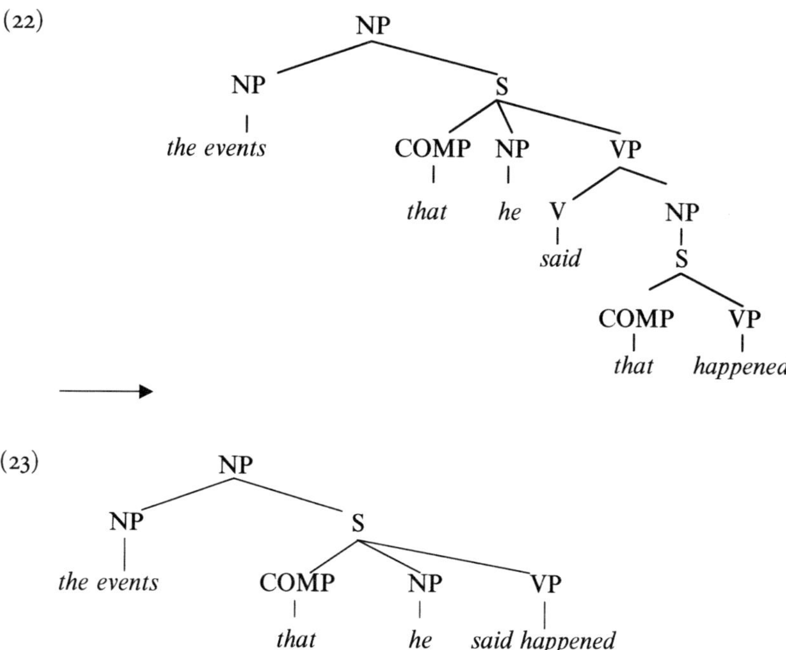

Chomsky and Lasnik (1977) took a somewhat different tack in accounting for the differences between languages like French and those like Spanish. They argued that Filter (19) is, in fact, universal. The locus of the major differences among languages with respect to the presence of subjects is whether free deletion of pronominal subjects is permitted. Spanish was posited to have such a deletion rule, resulting in the non-application of the filter. As a result of their particular analysis, languages like Spanish came to be known informally as 'pro-drop languages.'

It was soon realized that there are 'intermediate' languages like Dutch and Icelandic, in which null personal pronominal subjects are forbidden, yet which allow extraction of a subject clause headed by a complementizer (see Maling and Zaenen 1978). Sentences (24–25) provide an illustration from Dutch.

(24) *(ik) heb ze allemal gezien
I have them all seen
'I saw all of them'

(25) wie$_i$ vertelde je dat e$_i$ gekomen was
who said you that come was
'who did you say that had come?'

Taraldsen (1980) and Pesetsky (1982) adapted to formal analysis a long-standing (functional) principle to the solution to this problem, namely that there is a correlation between the allowing of null subjects and the richness of the language's inflectional system.[5] In their analysis, Dutch and Icelandic are said to be basically pro-drop languages (explaining the possibility of (25)), but the inflection of these languages is not rich enough to license null thematic subjects.

Finally, Kayne (1980) suggested the existence of another correlation with null subjects and unconstrained embedded subject extractions: the possibility of subject inversion. So, the sentences of (26) are grammatical in Italian, but not their word-for-word translations in English and French:

(26) a. Hanno telefonato molti amici.
b. Sono arrivati molti amici.

(27) a. *Have telephoned many friends.
b. *Have arrived many friends.

(28) a. *Ont téléphoné beaucoup d'amis.
b. *Sont arrivés beaucoup d'amis.

We will turn to the discussion of subsequent approaches to null subjects in §2.3.4.

2.3 The Government-Binding program for capturing parametric variation

The transition from the Extended Standard Theory of the 1970s to the Government-Binding (GB) theory of the 1980s brought with it a novel way of accounting for cross-linguistic generalizations. The leading idea was that the principles of UG are 'parameterized,' that is, they differ within fairly strict limits from one language to another (§2.3.1). The GB approach is introduced in §2.3.2 and exemplified in §2.3.3. Subsequent subsections discuss the clustering of grammatical properties based on a single parameter setting (§2.3.4), the typological implications of the core–periphery distinction (§2.3.5), markedness relations within core grammar (§2.3.6), Mark Baker's Parameter Hierarchy (§2.3.7), and the problem of constraining parameters and their possible settings (§2.3.8).

[5] For a recent typological study bearing on the question of subject omissibility and inflection, see Bickel (2003).

2.3.1 *Luigi Rizzi and the parameterization of Subjacency*

Generative syntax was propelled in a typological direction as a result of an ingenious idea put forward by Luigi Rizzi in the late 1970s. The story begins with an important proposal in Chomsky (1973). Chomsky set out to unify most of the constraints on extraction proposed in Ross (1967) under the principle of Subjacency.[6] On the basis of English data, Chomsky suggested that Subjacency prohibits a moved element from crossing two (or more) bounding nodes, where bounding nodes are S and NP. So consider Subjacency violation (29), whose tree representation is (30):

(29) *What did you wonder where Bill put?

(30)

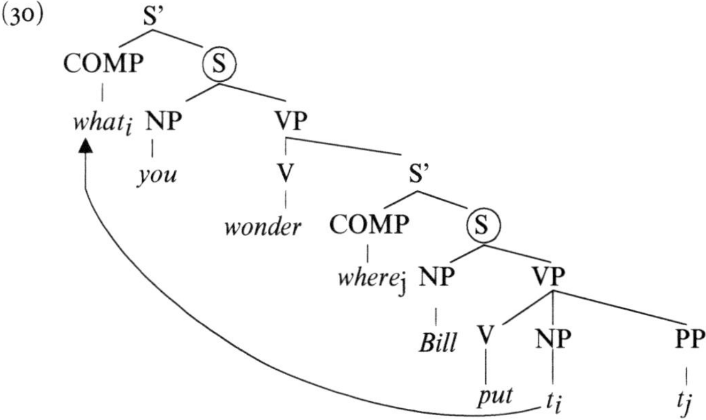

Movement of *what* to the highest COMP crosses the two circled bounding nodes, so the sentence is ungrammatical. Rizzi (1982), however, observed that Italian allows sentences of the form of (29), as we can see in (31a–b):

(31) a. Il solo incarico che non sapevi a chi avrebbero affidato è poi finito proprio a te.
'The only charge that you didn't know to whom they would entrust has been entrusted exactly to you.'

b. Tuo fratello, a cui mi domando che storie abbiano raccontato, era molto preoccupato.
'Your brother, to whom I wonder which stories they told, was very troubled.'

Rizzi's solution to this problem was to suggest that the notion of 'bounding node' is *parameterized*. Different languages have different bounding nodes. In Italian, S' is a bounding node, but S is not:

[6] For clarity of exposition, in the remainder of this section I update somewhat terminology and notation.

(32)

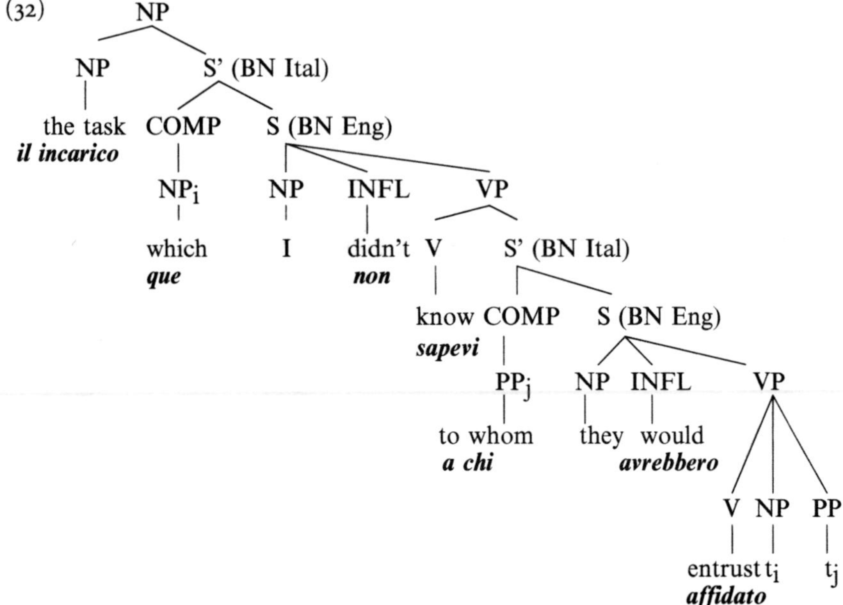

Therefore, the Italian sentence is grammatical and the English sentence is not. Later work suggested that other languages with overt *Wh*-Movement are stricter than English. For example, Russian has this rule:

(33) a. kogo ljubit Marija (Russian; Freidin and Quicoli 1989)
who-ACC loves Mary-NOM
'who does Mary love?'

b. ja znaju kogo Marija ljubit
I know who-ACC Mary-NOM loves
'I know who Mary loves'

But the *wh*-phrase may not be extracted from its clause:

(34) *kogo govorit Ivan čto Marija ljubit
who-ACC says Ivan that Mary-NOM loves
'Who does Ivan say that Mary loves?'

Hence it would seem to follow that in Russian both S and S' are bounding nodes.

2.3.2 *The Government-Binding program and typology*

Rizzi's idea that seemingly major differences between languages might be reduced to small differences in the setting of a particular parameter triggered an enormously productive research program, which was incorporated into the structure of the nascent Government-Binding theory. The research program of GB was to attempt to derive all (or at least most) linguistic complexity from a set of interacting principles and to attribute differences among languages to slightly different settings of the parameters associated with these principles. Hence, the term 'principles-and-parameters' (P&P) came almost immediately to be used alongside 'government-binding' to describe the approach.[7] As Chomsky characterized the approach in *Lectures in Government and Binding* (*LGB*; Chomsky 1981):

> What we expect to find, then, is a highly structured theory of UG based on a number of fundamental principles ... with parameters that have to be fixed by experience. If these parameters are embedded in a theory of UG that is sufficiently rich in structure, then the languages that are determined by fixing their values one way or another will appear to be quite diverse, since the consequences of one set of choices may be very different from the consequences of another set; yet at the same time, limited evidence, just sufficient to fix the parameters of UG, will determine a grammar that may be very intricate ... (Chomsky 1981: 3–4)

LGB proposed the following subsystems of UG, each characterized by a small number of principles:

(35) The subsystems characterizing the Government-Binding theory:
   a. Government theory, whose principles govern relations between heads and dependents.
   b. Binding theory, whose principles govern relations between anaphoric elements (including null elements) and their antecedents.
   c. Bounding theory, whose principles govern the relation between moved elements and their gaps.
   d. Case theory, whose principles define Case-marked positions, and the consequence of an element occupying (or not occupying) such a position.
   e. Control theory, whose principles govern the choice of antecedents for the null element PRO.
   f. Theta theory, whose principles govern the distribution of arguments.
   g. X-bar theory, whose principles govern phrase-structure configurations.

GB ushered in a dramatic change in the mainstream generative attitude to cross-linguistic variation and its theoretical treatment.[8] Since a central goal of syntactic theory was to identify the various subsystems of UG and to characterize the degree to which they might vary (now understood as 'be parameterized') from language to language, value was placed on the investigation of a wide variety of languages, particularly those with structures markedly different from some of the more familiar European ones. As far as capturing typological generalizations within P&P is concerned, Chomsky wrote:

[7] Confusingly, some linguists use the term 'principles-and-parameters' to encompass the current Minimalist Program and some do not. Strictly speaking, the Minimalist Program is not a version of P&P, given the diminished role for UG principles per se (see below, §2.4).

[8] Some of the material in the following paragraphs first appeared in Newmeyer (1998b: 353–5).

Within the P&P approach the problems of typology and language variation arise in somewhat different form than before. Language differences and typology should be reducible to choice of values of parameters. A major research problem is to determine just what these options are, and in what components of language they are to be found. (Chomsky 1995: 6)

In this regard, it is instructive to observe Chomsky's changing attitude to Greenbergian typological work. In 1981, Chomsky offered what was perhaps his first favorable reference to this line of research:[9]

Universals of the sort explored by Joseph Greenberg and others have obvious relevance to determining just which properties of the lexicon have to be specified in this manner in particular grammars—and to put it in other terms, just how much must be learned as grammar develops in the course of language acquisition. (Chomsky 1981: 95)

By 1982 he was writing that 'Greenberg universals ... are ultimately going to be fairly rich.... They have all the difficulties that people know, they are "surfacey," they are statistical, and so on and so forth, but nevertheless they are very suggestive' (Chomsky 1982a: 111). In 1986, they are considered 'important, ... yielding many generalizations that require explanation ...' (Chomsky 1986b: 21). And more recently still:

There has also been very productive study of generalizations that are more directly observable: generalizations about the word orders we actually see, for example. The work of Joseph Greenberg has been particularly instructive and influential in this regard. *These universals are probably descriptive generalizations that should be derived from principles of UG.* (Chomsky 1998: 33; emphasis added)

2.3.3 *Some examples of GB parameters*

Let us now consider a few examples of parameters proposed in the GB period which were applied to capturing typological differences among languages. Probably the best known (and certainly the easiest to discuss) is the Head Parameter, that is, the parameter that specifies head–complement order. It is generally the case that languages put their complements to each head consistently on the right of the head or on the left of the head. So in English, complements are canonically all on the right:

(36) a. $_{\text{VP}}$[throw - the ball]
b. $_{\text{NP}}$[refusal - (of) the offer]
c. $_{\text{PP}}$[in - the room]
d. $_{\text{AP}}$[fond - (of) linguistics]

[9] Looking at things from the other side of the fence, most typologists are and have always been theoretically grounded in functionalist approaches and thus tend to be fairly hostile to the basics of the generative program (see, for example, Comrie 1989: ch. 1). Still, Greenberg (1978: 1–2) could write that his 'typological, inductive, and empirical [approach to universals] does not... dogmatically exclude work more oriented to the generative approach' (see similar remarks by Ferguson 1978 in the same volume). And even Comrie has referred approvingly to 'one of the most interesting recent developments in linguistic typology... the entry of generative syntax into the field' (Comrie 1988: 458).

In GB research it was at first assumed that UG provides a simple D-structure parameter along the lines of (37) that would have as a consequence the capturing of a significant portion of the Greenbergian correlations (see Chapter 1, Table 1.2):

(37) HEAD PARAMETER—Complements are consistently to the left or to the right of the head.
  a. HEAD-LEFT (English, Swahili, ...)
  b. HEAD-RIGHT (Japanese, Lakhota, ...)

The late 1980s proposals that nominal phrases are headed by Determiner, sentences by Tense, and full clauses by Complementizer (Abney 1987; Chomsky 1986a; Fukui 1986) further strengthened the case for a Head Parameter, since they entailed profound structural parallels between these categories and categories with less controversial structures, like VP and PP.

The idea was that in the course of acquisition, English-acquiring children would come to set this parameter as in (37a), while Japanese-acquiring children would set it as in (37b). There has been, however, considerable controversy as to which system of principles is responsible for this particular parameter. For Stowell (1981), it was the job of X-bar theory to capture the generalization that heads (tend to) either precede or follow their complements. Stowell proposed a parameter of phrase structure with two possible values: heads-before-complements or heads-after-complements. Thus the correlation that VO languages tend to be prepositional, while OV languages tend to be postpositional, follows automatically. Later researchers within GB (e.g. Travis 1984, 1989; Koopman 1984) were more likely to point to Case and/or Theta theory as the locus of the typological generalization. That is, they proposed that languages (tend to) uniformly assign theta-roles and Case to the left or to the right.

Notice the descriptive simplicity of (37). Other parameters, say, those determining whether a language is null subject or not, configurational or not, and so on, have been thought to be equally simple. In this respect, it has been standard practice to compare parameters to rules, arguing that the latter tend to be cumbersome and complex, whereas the former admit to simple and elegant formulations.

Many of the best-known typological generalizations are implicational in nature: 'If a language has property X, then it is likely to have property Y.' A major challenge confronting GB was to demonstrate that it was not only able to capture implicational cross-linguistic generalizations, but that it was able to do so better than functionalist approaches, which typically recognize no level more abstract than surface structure and have no real equivalent to abstract parameter settings. Implicational relations among typological features have generally been derived from implicational relations among parameter settings (see especially Baker 2001a and §2.3.7 below). For example, as noted above, verb-final languages tend not to allow *wh*-fronting. Explanations of this generalization within GB and later formal models have taken the following form:

(38) HEAD-RIGHT ⊃ 'PARAMETER X' (where an indirect consequence of Parameter X is that *wh*-fronting is impossible)

For example, Fukui (1986) argued that a parametric feature of head-final languages is that they lack a Specifier for COMP. Since this category provides a landing site for moved *wh*-elements, it follows that in such languages *wh*-fronting is impossible. For Kim (1990), the analogs of *wh*-elements in movementless languages are actually quantifiers and therefore undergo Quantifier Raising at LF, rather than overt *wh*-fronting. And more recently, Cheng (1991/1997) has addressed a related correlation, namely, that between the presence of final question particles (a typological feature of head-final languages) and the impossibility of syntactic *wh*-fronting. Based on the economy principles provided by the Minimalist Program (MP), she proposes a theory of 'clausal typing,' whereby a language must choose one of these two methods of 'typing' questions.[10]

Parameters have not only been assumed to be descriptively simple, but it has been taken for granted that they are small in number as well. I have never seen any estimate of the number of binary-valued parameters needed to capture all of the possibilities of core grammar that exceeded a few dozen (about thirty or forty in the view of Lightfoot 1999: 259). Smallness of number serves more than just aesthetic purposes. Fodor (2001b: 734) observes that 'it is standardly assumed that there are fewer parameters than there are possible rules in a rule-based framework; otherwise, it would be less obvious that the amount of learning to be done is reduced in a parametric framework.'

Finally, there is the question of whether all parameters are applicable to all languages, that is, assuming binary values for each parameter, whether each has the setting + or − for each language. I think that the standard answer to this question has been 'yes,' an answer facilitated by the architecture of P&P syntax, which allows for a rich variety of covert operations. So a parameter that might seem at first glance irrelevant to a particular language (e.g. one governing *wh*-extraction in a language in which *wh*-phrases are *in situ*) would still be relevant to *covert wh*-extraction. Still, there have been proposals which, in effect, say that certain parameters are simply non-applicable to certain languages. Hale (1983) argues that in non-configurational languages like Warlpiri, UG constrains lexical structure, but not phrase structure. Hence parameters relevant to phrase structure have neither positive nor negative values in Warlpiri. And Milsark (1985) suggests that the Case Filter is inapplicable to certain languages, including Finnish.

2.3.4 *Predicting the clustering of typological properties*

As typological generalizations go, the Greenbergian correlations are fairly straightforward. But not surprisingly, a major goal of GB was to show that by means of highly abstract parameters, an unexpected (and previously unnoticed)

[10] See below (§2.4.2) for an explanation of the correlation between verb finality and absence of *wh*-fronting based on the antisymmetric program of Kayne (1994).

clustering of typological properties could be predicted. In other words, any demonstration that the putatively rich deductive structure of parameters could lead to new discoveries would tend to demonstrate that a parametric approach was on the right track. This idea was quickly put into practice with respect to the Null Subject Parameter. In the original formulations of this parameter within GB, those found in Chomsky 1981, it was predicted that null subject languages should manifest the (not obviously related) properties in (39) (null subject Spanish is contrasted with non-null subject English):

(39) a. Missing subjects (*Llueve* 'It is raining')
 b. Free inversion in simple sentences (*Leyó el libro María* 'Read the book Mary')
 c. Long *wh*-movement of subject across *wh*-islands (*el hombre que me pregunto a quién vio* 'the man who I wonder whom (he) saw')
 d. Empty resumptive pronouns in embedded clauses (*ésta es la muchacha [que me pregunto [quién cree [que ___ puede...]]]* 'this is the girl who I wonder who thinks that (she) may...')
 e. Apparent violations of the *that*-trace filter (*¿Quién dijiste que salió temprano?* 'Who did you say (*that) left early?')

The properties of (39a–e) have an intuitive relation among each other, in that all but (39c) have some connection to empty elements in subject position. Nevertheless, it does not logically follow that if a language allows (or disallows) one of them, it would necessarily allow (or disallow) all of them. So the idea that the presumed clustering followed from one single parameter setting was seen as a sign that the parametric approach was on the right track.[11]

An extremely influential paper, Pollock (1989) (which itself built on the analysis in Emonds 1978), was devoted to characterizing, in terms of parametric theory, a clustering of differences between English and French. In French, VP-adverbs, clausal negation, and floated quantifiers follow finite main verbs, while in English they precede them:

(40) a. Jean embrasse souvent Marie.
 b. *Jean souvent embrasse Marie.

(41) a. *John kisses often Mary.
 b. John often kisses Mary.

(42) a. Jean (ne) mange pas de chocolat.
 b. *Jean (ne) pas mange de chocolat.

(43) a. *John eats not chocolate.
 b. John does not eat chocolate.

[11] For expository reasons, I delay illustrating the concrete mechanism proposed within P&P syntax for handling null subjects to Ch. 3, §3.2.2.5.

(44) a. Les enfants mangent tous le chocolat.
b. *Les enfants tous mangent le chocolat.

(45) a. *The children eat all chocolate.
b. The children all eat chocolate.

Pollock suggested that the IP node be split into at least three separate projections—T(ense)P, Neg(ative)P, and Agr(eement)P. In his analysis, both English and French have the following structure for negative clauses:

(46)
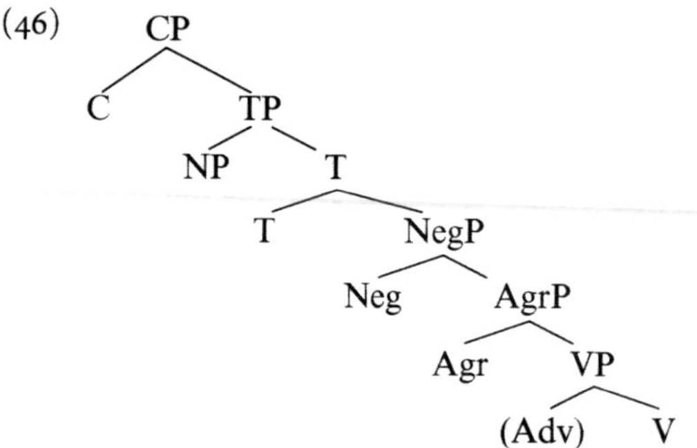

Given a structure like (46), accompanied by a number of additional assumptions, the following parameter distinguishes French and English as far as the phenomena represented in (40–45) are concerned:[12]

(47) Verb Movement Parameter:
a. Lexical verbs move to a higher inflectional position (French)
b. Lexical verbs do not move to a higher inflectional position (English)

Another example of a deep parameter that seemed to predict an unexpected clustering of properties was put forward in Hale (1982). Extending the proposal of Hale (1976) (mentioned in §2.1 above), Hale suggested that in non-configurational languages X-bar theory is parameterized differently than in configurational ones, a proposal that he revised again in Hale (1983), where he suggested that it is the Projection Principle that is parameterized. In both cases, he argued that a single parameter setting predicts a rich case system, free word order, lack of NP movement, lack of pleonastic NPs, use of discontinuous expressions, complex verb words, and free or frequent omission of arguments. Again, it is not obvious that we would find a clustering of this constellation of properties.

As a final example, Snyder (2001) has argued for a Compounding Parameter, stated as follows:

[12] Pollock's analysis has been extensively revised in the past fifteen years, though many of its key features have been retained. For a literature review, see Belletti (2001).

(48) Compounding Parameter:
 a. The grammar disallows formation of endocentric compounds during the syntactic derivation (unmarked value)
 b. The grammar allows formation of endocentric compounds during the syntactic derivation (marked value)

Given current assumptions in mainstream versions of P&P syntax (Larson 1988; Hale and Keyser 1993; Marantz 1993), the same underlying mechanisms that are responsible for the formation of endocentric compounds also license resultative constructions like (49):

(49) John painted the house red.

Snyder looked at seventeen languages from thirteen different families and found that in all cases but one (Basque) the possibility of resultatives correlates with the possibility of forming endocentric compounds, thereby lending support to his proposed parameter.

2.3.5 *The typological implications of the core versus periphery distinction*

Chomsky and Lasnik (1977) introduced a novel construct into generative theory, that of 'core grammar' (see also Chomsky 1977a: 6). They wrote:

> We will assume that UG is not an 'undifferentiated' system, but rather incorporates something analogous to a 'theory of markedness.' Specifically, there is a theory of core grammar with highly restricted options, limited expressive power, and a few parameters. (Chomsky and Lasnik 1977: 430)

Core processes were described as those that are 'optimal in terms of the evaluation metric,' essentially those whose characterization was captured by the constraints, universally applicable filters, and so on that were posited in late 1970s Extended Standard Theory. Non-core processes, on the other hand, 'we may think of as the syntactic analogue of irregular verbs.' The distinction between core grammar and non-core processes (the latter which were soon described as those pertaining to the 'periphery')[13] came to play a central role in *Lectures on Government and Binding*, which appeared four years later. The set of core grammars was now conceived of as the set of grammars resulting from the fixing of the parameters of UG in all possible ways. Outside core grammar lay 'a periphery of marked elements and constructions' (Chomsky 1981: 8), incorporating:

> ... borrowings, historical residues, inventions, and so on, which we can hardly expect to—and indeed would not want to—incorporate within a principled theory of UG. (Chomsky 1981: 8)

Chomsky wrote in *LGB* that 'we do not expect to find chaos in the marked periphery of language' (p. 70). And indeed, phenomena that he attributed to the

[13] The first published use of the term 'periphery' in this technical sense is found, I believe, in van Riemsdijk (1978).

periphery (or suggested might be found there) seem more systematic in their behavior than that of 'irregular verbs' and included elliptical expressions (p. 27), 'exceptional case marking' constructions such as *I believe her to be clever* (p. 66), and picture noun reflexives such as *John thinks that the picture of himself is not very flattering* (p. 216).

Now then, what is the relevance of the core–periphery distinction for language typology? One's first thought might be that there is a robust correlation between core processes and typologically common ones and between peripheral processes and typologically rare ones, and Chomsky implied that such might be the case:

> How do we delimit the domain of core grammar as distinct from marked periphery? ... [We] rely heavily on grammar-internal considerations and *comparative evidence*, that is, on the possibilities for constructing a reasonable theory of UG and considering its explanatory power in *a variety of language types*... (Chomsky 1981: 9; emphasis added)

Early studies that attribute some typologically rare construction to processes of the marked periphery include those of preposition-stranding (van Riemsdijk 1978; Hornstein and Weinberg 1981) and relative clauses that do not manifest $[_{NP}$ NP S] structure (Cinque 1982).

Chomsky has always expressed uneasiness about the core–periphery distinction. In interviews conducted in 1979 and 1980 he mentioned that he does 'not even think that it is clear whether we should make a sharp distinction between core and periphery' (Chomsky 1982a: 108) and a decade later the distinction was merely an 'expository device' (Chomsky 1991b: 449), possibly posing a dangerous distraction for the grammarian:[14]

> When the study of language is able to extricate itself from prejudice, dogma, and misunderstanding, we will, I believe, dismiss [the periphery of marked exceptions] as tenth-order effects resulting from uninteresting accident, focusing our attention on the deeper properties and principles that lead to real explanation and understanding of essential properties of the human mind. At that point we will no longer distinguish core and periphery. (Chomsky 1991a: 42)

I am not aware of any more recent references in Chomsky's writings to the core–periphery distinction. The question then arises as to how Chomsky and his co-thinkers would approach phenomena both typologically rare and/or (seemingly) falling outside the scope of the central machinery provided by the theory. The answer is far from clear. Such phenomena have played a limited role in current minimalist work.[15]

[14] Joseph (1992: 318) has felicitously remarked that Chomsky now regards the periphery as no more than a 'holding station' for seemingly recalcitrant phenomena.

[15] A distinction with properties somewhat similar to that between core and periphery is that between narrow syntax and P-syntax, to which we turn in §2.4.1.

2.3.6 *Markedness relations within core grammar and typological inconsistency*

Chomsky (1981) also pointed to markedness relations within core grammar, as well as those between the core and the periphery.[16] He gave no concrete illustrations, but it must have seemed evident at the time that not all combinations of parameter settings are as 'natural' (in some intuitive sense of the word) as others. Languages in which all heads do not uniformly precede or uniformly follow their complements of course do exist, as do languages with heads on the right and *wh*-fronting. Yet it seemed counterintuitive to assign to the marked periphery correlations of constructions that manifested some typological inconsistency. Rather, the usual assumption has been that such inconsistency is a reflex of marked relations within core grammar. That is, the idea was that typologically rare features should require a more complex formulation than typologically common ones, perhaps by requiring special marked parameter settings, by violating an implicational statement among parameter settings, or something else along these lines.

For example, Chinese is consistently head final except in the rule expanding X' to X^o (if the head is verbal it precedes the complement). Note that Chinese manifests the ordering V-NP, but NP-N:

(50) you sange ren mai-le shu (Huang 1982)
HAVE three man buy-ASP book
'Three men bought books'

(51) Zhangsan de sanben shu
Zhangsan three book
'Zhangsan's three books'

Huang (1994) captured this situation by a phrase-structure schema that complicates somewhat the Chinese instantiation of the X-bar schema:

(52) a. $XP \rightarrow YP\ X'$
b. $X' \rightarrow YP\ X'$
c. $X' \rightarrow$ c'. X^o YP iff $X = [+v]$
c''. YP X^o otherwise

Hence, deviation from typological consistency is reflected in a more complex grammar. Pointing to a different subsystem of principles, Travis (1989) suggested that Chinese has a marked parameter setting for word order. Normally, if a language is head final, it assigns Case and Theta-Role to the left, as in (53a). However Chinese has a special setting that violates this default ordering, namely (53b):

(53) a. Unmarked setting: HEAD-RIGHT ⊃ THETA-ASSIGNMENT TO LEFT & CASE-ASSIGNMENT TO LEFT
b. Marked setting (Chinese): HEAD-RIGHT & THETA-ASSIGNMENT TO RIGHT & CASE-ASSIGNMENT TO RIGHT

[16] And Chomsky (1986b: 147) also mentioned the possibility of markedness relations internal to the periphery.

Several appeals to grammar-complicating statements whose design is to predict deviations from some typological generalization are found in Kayne (1994) (for a sketch of Kayne's program, see below, §2.4.2). There exist 'typologically inconsistent' languages such as Vata which have final complementizers, but in which *wh*-elements move to the left. Kayne gives a rough sketch of how such languages have more complicated grammars than those with the expected correlation. Cinque (1996) also attempts to explain typological generalizations—and exceptions to them—in Kayne's framework. For example, Kayne predicts that no language will have N-Dem and Num-N. But some languages, including Berber, Welsh, Hebrew, and Zapotec, do manifest this constellation of features. According to Cinque, such languages 'pay the price' for their deviance by requiring an extra movement of demonstratives.

Finally, there have been a number of attempts to derive the relative rarity of VSO languages with respect to SVO languages by positing that more rules are involved in the derivation of the former than of the latter. For example, Emonds (1980) argued that Irish and other VSO languages are SVO throughout the greater part of the derivation. Such languages have a late rule that fronts the verb before the subject. As Emonds put it (1980: 44), such languages are 'more complicated, therefore rarer.' Emonds was writing just before the advent of GB; presumably the 'extra rule' account could be assimilated to the 'marked parameter setting' account.

Not all generative grammarians, however, assume that unmarked values of some parameter are necessarily reflected by more languages having properties that reflect that value than by those that reflect the marked value. In this vein Lightfoot (1991: 12) has remarked that

> [t]he fact that the Italian setting for the [null subject] parameter seems to be much more common across languages than the English setting does not entail that it is less marked, since markedness values do not reflect statistical frequency. In fact Berwick's (1985) Subset Principle predicts that the Italian setting should be marked. The Subset Principle requires children to 'pick the narrowest possible language consistent with evidence seen so far'. (Berwick 1985: 237)
>
> The Italian setting of the parameter entails a language that is broader than one with the English setting (because in Italian subjects may or may not be phonetically expressed), and therefore the English setting must be unmarked. (p. 290)

For Lightfoot, in other words, learnability considerations determine the marking of a parameter setting, not the relative number of grammars in the world manifesting that setting.

2.3.7 *Mark Baker's Parameter Hierarchy*

Given the importance of parameters in the P&P approach, one might assume that the pages of the generative-oriented journals would be filled with articles devoted to working out the relevant implicational relations among parameters with the ultimate goal of deriving the more robust generalizations that have been uncovered in the past few decades of typological investigation. Nothing could be farther from the truth, however. Many articles and books posit a particular parameter (and associated settings) to distinguish one language or dialect from another and most introductions to transformational syntax devote a few pages (but rarely more) to how cross-linguistic generalizations might be captured. But with one exception, researchers have not attempted a comprehensive treatment of parameters and their settings. That exception is Mark Baker's book *The Atoms of Language: The Mind's Hidden Rules of Grammar* (Baker 2001a).[17] Baker takes seriously the P&P program for typology and proposes an intricate 'Parameter Hierarchy' (PH) in which implicational relations between parameters and their settings are made explicit. Figure 2.1 presents his final version of that hierarchy.[18]

The PH is to be interpreted as follows. Each of the boldfaced expressions is a particular parameter, while their settings are in small capitals. If Parameter X has logical priority over Parameter Y, then X is written higher than Y and is connected to Y by a downward slanting line. If two parameters are not ranked with respect to each other, then they are written on the same line and separated by a dash. Such is the case only for the Head Directionality Parameter (HDP) and the Optional Polysynthesis Parameter (OPP). The logical independence of these two parameters leads to four possible 'choices,' each represented by a branching line: 'head first' for the HDP and 'no' optional polysynthesis for the OPP; 'head first' for the HDP and 'yes' optional polysynthesis for the OPP; 'head last' for the HDP and 'yes' optional polysynthesis for the OPP; and 'head last' for the HDP and 'no' optional polysynthesis for the OPP. If there are no further parametric choices to be made, given a particular setting of a particular parameter, then the branch ends in a terminal symbol *. Beneath the asterisk, languages are listed that have this combination of parameter settings. As a consequence, structurally similar languages should end up being close on the diagram, and dissimilar languages far apart.

In Baker's account, the clustering of typological features is a consequence of the formulation of the parameters themselves and the hierarchical relations among them. To take a simple case, VO languages tend to be prepositional because the notion 'head' enters into the definition of the Head Directionality Parameter and verbs and prepositions are heads of their respective phrases. More subtly, all polysynthetic languages are predicted to be non-configurational (in fact, Baker rejects the idea of a separate 'Configurationality Parameter' as in

[17] *The Atoms of Language*, however, presents an unusual challenge to the critical reader. It is not a 'research monograph' in the usual sense of the term, but rather, as the dust cover puts it, a 'book for a general audience.' Very little knowledge is presupposed about the intricacies of grammatical theory. Baker's book, then, is possibly unique in the annals of science publishing, in that it is a popularization of research results that were never argued for in the scholarly literature in their full technically elaborated form. Unfortunately I see no alternative but to regard and evaluate the book as if it presents research results, even though the claims that it makes are typically presented in an extremely informal manner, given the intended audience.

[18] Baker also points to three other parameters, one governing *wh*-fronting and two governing domains for anaphors, that he cannot place in the hierarchy.

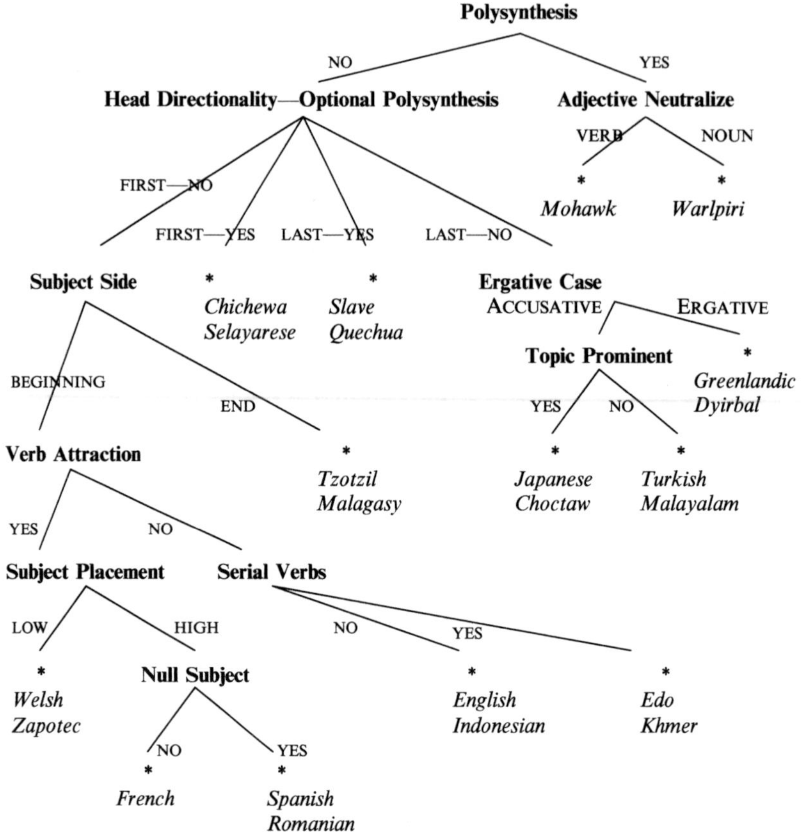

FIGURE 2.1. The Parameter Hierarchy (Baker 2001a: 183)

Hale 1983), since a positive value for the Polysynthesis Parameter treats full arguments as mere adjuncts, with corresponding freedom of occurrence. And head-initial languages are claimed never to be either ergative or topic prominent, since the branch leading to the Ergative Case Parameter originates from the setting 'last' for the Head Directionality Parameter and the Topic Prominent Parameter branches from the Ergative Case Parameter. In a similar manner, the non-existence is predicted of a polysynthetic language that has serial verbs, a subject-final language without a distinct category of 'adjective,' and a subject-final language with optional polysynthesis.

Baker's account of why certain typological features are more common than others is more indirect. Essentially, the more 'choices' a language learner needs to make, the rarer the language type is claimed to be. As far as VO versus OV is concerned:

Since the difference between English-style word order and Japanese-style word order is attributable to a single parameter [Head Directionality], there is only one decision to make by coin flip: heads, heads are initial; tails, heads are final. So we expect roughly equal numbers of English-type and Japanese-type languages. (Baker 2001a: 134)

Why are VSO languages so much rarer than SVO languages, then? Because two more parameters enter into the characterization of the former than of the latter:

Within the head-initial languages, however, it requires two further decisions [the value for the Subject Placement Parameter and the value for the Verb Attraction Parameter] to get a verb-initial, Welsh-type language: Subjects must be added early and tense auxiliaries must host verbs. If either of these decisions is made in the opposite way, then subject-verb-object order will still emerge. If the decisions were made by coin flips, we would predict that about 25 per cent of the head-initial languages would be of the Welsh type and 75 per cent of the English type. This too is approximately correct... (Baker 2001a: 134)

In other words, one-way implications fall out naturally from the PH. If a language has serial verbs, then it must have the setting 'no' for the Verb Attraction Parameter. But a 'no' setting for this parameter does not entail the presence of serial verbs. Rather it predicts a 50:50 chance of serial verbs.[19]

2.3.8 Constraints on possible parameters

Practically from the inception of parametric theory, attempts began to rein in parameters, that is, to find some way of constraining them and/or limiting their number. Practitioners of GB perceived immediately the danger inherent in the approach, namely that the amount of parametric variation postulated among languages and the number of possible settings for each parameter could grow so large that the term 'parameter' would end up being nothing but jargon for 'language-particular rule.' In this unfortunate scenario, as many different parameters and parameter settings would be needed as there are construction types in language. Thus doing GB would become nothing more than listing a set of 'parameters,' each one a description of a recalcitrant fact in some language. In fact, in a 1984 *GLOW Newsletter*, Hans Bennis and Jan Koster warned of this very possibility:

[19] To this extent, then, the PH answers the criticism of Haspelmath (2004: 561–2) that a P&P model is not very good at explaining one-way typological implications. Haspelmath cites the following (p. 562) as examples of such implicational relationships: (1) if a language has VO order, the relative clause follows the head noun, though the converse is not necessarily true (Dryer 1991); (2) if a language has case marking for inanimate direct-object NPs, it also has case marking for animate direct object NPs, but not necessarily the converse (Comrie 1989: ch. 6); (3) if a language has a plural form for inanimate nouns, it also has a plural form for animate nouns, but not necessarily the converse (Corbett 2000); (4) if a language uses a reflexive pronoun with typically self-directed actions, then it also uses a reflexive pronoun with typically other-directed actions, but not necessarily the converse (König and Siemund 2000); (5) if a *wh*-phrase can be extracted from a subordinate clause, then it can also be extracted from a verb phrase, but not necessarily the converse (Hawkins 1999). None of the generalizations is expressed by the PH, however.

Parametric syntax and phonology have quickly become very popular. Of necessity, this has led to some excesses: too often ill-understood differences among languages are simply attributed to some new *ad hoc* parameter. (Bennis and Koster 1984: 6)

In this section I will discuss some of the attempts to constrain parameters that have been proposed over the years.

Perhaps the first constraint on parameters and certainly the longest standing is the Lexical Parameterization Hypothesis (LPH):[20]

(54) Lexical Parameterization Hypothesis (Borer 1984; Manzini and Wexler 1987; Webelhuth 1992): Values of a parameter are associated not with particular grammars, but with particular lexical items.

At least some version of the LPH seemed justified by virtue of the fact that even within a particular language different lexical items at times behave differently with respect to particular UG principles. For example, many languages have up to a half-dozen different anaphors and pronominals, each of which might differ in terms of their binding possibilities and overall distribution. Consider some examples involving Principles A and B of the binding theory of Chomsky 1981, which are stated below:

(55) Principle A. An anaphor is bound in its governing category.
Principle B. A pronominal is free in its governing category.

(56) β binds α iff
β c-commands α, and β and α are coindexed.

(57) γ is a governing category for α iff
γ is the minimal category that contains α and a governor for α and has a subject.

It turned out that the notion 'governing category' would not only have to be defined differently from language to language, but also differently *within* each language, depending on the particular anaphor or pronominal. For example, among its set of anaphors, Korean has *cakicasin*, which must be locally bound and *caki*, which allows both local and higher-sentence antecedents, with a preference for the latter (Moon 1995):

(58) Bill$_i$-i [John$_j$-i cakicasin$_{*i/j}$-ul miwehanta]-ko malhayssta
Bill-NOM John-NOM self-ACC hate-COMP said
'Bill$_i$ said that John$_j$ hates self$_{*i/j}$'

[20] A number of versions of the LPH have been proposed. To cite one example, Clahsen, Eisenbeiss, and Penke (1996) have proposed the 'Lexical Learning Hypothesis' (LLH), in which language acquisition proceeds through the interplay between UG principles and the identification of functional elements such as inflectional affixes, determiners, complementizers, etc. The child's task is to discover—based on positive evidence—which grammatical concepts are lexicalized. Languages thus differ only with respect to which concepts they lexicalize. It remains to be investigated to what extent the LLH differs empirically from the LPH.

(59)

Bill$_i$-i	[John$_j$-i	caki$_{i/j}$-lul	miwehanta]-ko	malhayssta
Bill-NOM	John-NOM	self-ACC	hate-COMP	said

'Bill$_i$ said that John$_j$ hates self$_{i/j}$'

Icelandic has an anaphor, *sig*, whose binding domain is quite different from both English *x-self* and the two just discussed in Korean. Contrast the following two sentences containing the anaphor *sig* (Maling 1984; Manzini and Wexler 1987):

(60)

Jón$_j$	segir	að	Maria$_i$	elskar	sig$_{i/*j}$
John	says	that	Maria	loves	REFL

(61)

Jón$_j$	segir	að	Maria$_i$	elski	sig$_{*i/j}$
John	says	that	Maria	loves (SUBJUNCTIVE)	REFL

The requirement for *sig* is that its governing category be the minimal category containing *sig*, its governor, and a 'referential' tense (that is, an inherently defined tense, as opposed to a subjunctive). Icelandic also has a pronominal *hann*, whose governing category is different from that of *sig*, because the domain in which it must be free (not have an antecedent) is a domain containing any tense at all:

(62)

Jón$_j$	segir	að	Maria	elski	hann$_i$
John	says	that	Maria	loves (SUBJUNCTIVE)	him

(63)

*Jón$_j$	skipaði	mér	að	raka	hann$_i$
John	ordered	me	to	shave	him

Apparently, the governing category for *hann* is the minimal domain containing *hann*, its governor, and *any* tense. (62) is possible since the governing category for *hann* is the lower clause. *Hann* is free in that governing category. But (63) is impossible, since the lower clause, lacking tense, is not the governing category for *hann*. *Hann* is illicitly bound by *Jón*, the subject of the higher clause.

Even in English, a language with only a couple of anaphors, reflexive and reciprocal anaphors seem to have different properties. The reflexive anaphor *themselves* is categorically impossible as subject of an embedded tensed clause, while the reciprocal anaphor *each other* does occur in that position, at least in informal speech:

(64) John and Mary think that [*themselves/?each other are the best candidates].

Chomsky and others have also put forward a metatheoretical reason for advocating the LPH. If it is correct, the argument goes, then there is only one human language outside of the lexicon and hence language acquisition becomes simply a matter of learning lexical idiosyncrasies. As Chomsky put it:

> Apart from lexicon, [the set of possible human languages] is a finite set, surprisingly; in fact, a one-membered set if parameters are in fact reducible to lexical properties.... How else could Plato's problem [the fact that we know so much about language based on so little direct evidence—FJN] be resolved? (Chomsky 1991a: 26)

Fukui (1988) argues that the LPH is too strong. There are many properties of grammars and typological differences among grammars that do not seem to be lexically based. Take a language's basic word order. Whether a language is SVO or SOV has nothing obviously to do with the lexicon, no matter how broadly conceived.

As a second example of a non-lexically-based parametric difference among languages, Fukui suggests that languages might differ in their number of bar levels. According to Fukui and Speas (1986), Japanese constituents are X′, not X″. That is, Japanese lacks functional categories such as DET, INFL, and COMP (Fukui considers the 'complementizers' *to* 'that,' *ka* 'Q,' etc. to be members of the category 'P'). Along the same lines, Suchsland (1993) argues that the internal complexity of German phrases leads to the conclusion that that language has one more bar level in the VP than English:

(65) dass sie [$_{V'''}$ meinem Kollegen [$_{V''}$ leider [$_{V''}$ die Bücher [$_{V'}$ noch immer
that she my-DAT colleague unfortunately the books yet always

[$_{V'}$ nicht [$_{V'}$ zurückgegeben hat]]]]]]
not returned has
'that unfortunately she has not yet returned the books to my colleagues'

Another non-lexical parameter that seems to separate languages is the degree of adjacency required between heads and complements. Ewert and Hansen (1993) call attention to the following differences between English and German, where the latter language seems to be more lax than the former in terms of adjacency requirements:

(66) a. a father proud of his daughter
b. a husband loyal to his wife

(67) a. *a proud of his daughter father
b. *a loyal to his wife husband

(68) a. der auf seine Tochter stolze Vater
b. ein seiner Frau treuer Ehemann

Finally, not all lexical items are involved in parametric variation. We would not expect a language in which the word for 'eat,' for example, takes its complements to the right and the word for 'drink' takes its complements to the left. It seems to be mostly *functional categories* that are involved in parameters (for development of this view, see especially Ouhalla 1991a). Note that functional categories (those headed by elements such as complementizers, tense and aspectual morphemes, and determiners) often do manifest particular lexical properties in terms of restrictions of ordering and (perhaps) adjacency. In Nupe, for example, the complementizer *gànán* precedes the clause that it introduces; the complementizer *o*, which occurs in the focus construction, follows it (Zepter 2000):

(69) a. mi kpaye [gànán Musa lå èbi] (Nupe: Zepter 2000)
I think COMP Musa took knife
'I think that Musa took the knife'

b. ebi Musa lá o
knife Musa take COMP
'[it's] a knife that Musa took'

The above facts led Fukui (1988) to posit two revisions to the Lexical Parameterization Hypothesis. The first, the Ordering Restriction Hypothesis, specifies that non-lexical parameters are limited to ordering restrictions. The second, the Functional Parameterization Hypothesis, posits that only functional elements in the lexicon (that is, elements such as Complementizer, Agreement, Tense, etc.) are subject to parametric variation. This latter hypothesis represents an updating of the proposal in Borer (1984) that parameters are located in the 'inflectional system' and is illustrated by an example of a difference between Lebanese Arabic and Hebrew:

(70) hkit maʔ-o la Karim (Lebanese Arabic)
talked-I with-him to Karim
'I talked with Karim'

(71) *dibarti 'im-a (le/s.el) Anna (Hebrew)
talked-I with-her to/of Anna
'I talked with Anna'

Both examples involve clitic doubling of the object of the preposition. In Borer's theory, clitics absorb the case feature of the head they are attached to, so in both sentences the object of the P is deprived of Case, violating the Case Filter. However, Lebanese Arabic has an inflectional rule of preposition insertion as 'saving device,' which Hebrew lacks. Hence there is no Case Filter violation in Lebanese Arabic.

Finally, it has been generally assumed that parameters have binary settings: 'The values of each parameter form no continuum and in the ideal case just amount to two' (Longobardi 2003: 108). I am not aware of any empirical arguments for binarity, but I assume that restricting settings in such a way is motivated on learnability grounds. At least all formal studies of parameter acquisition and change have, to my knowledge, taken binarity for granted (see, for example, Clark and Roberts 1993; Gibson and Wexler 1994; Wu 1994; Niyogi and Berwick 1997).

2.4 Parameters and typology in the Minimalist Program

The transition from Government-Binding to the Minimalist Program in the early 1990s entailed a profound rethinking of how cross-linguistic generalizations might best be captured. Section 2.4.1 discusses the relevance of mechanisms internal to the MP to the issues that concern us here. The two subsections that follow are concerned with the typological relevance of Richard Kayne's antisymmetric program (§2.4.2) and the trend for capturing cross-linguistic variation in terms of 'microparameters' (§2.4.3). Section 2.4.4 is a brief summary.

2.4.1 *Minimalist mechanisms and typology*

The problem of capturing cross-linguistic variation within the MP is circumscribed by the fact that, at least superficially, it presents a very sparse ontology. The levels of D-structure and S-structure are no longer posited to exist and the computational system (or 'narrow syntax' as it has come to be called) consists solely of the basic operations Merge and Move, subject to economy conditions (the nature of which have changed fairly radically over the past decade and a half). The locus of language-particular differences is assumed to reside in functional categories and, in particular, their heads. To that extent, the MP carries over a version of the Functional Parameterization Hypothesis. By way of illustration, McCloskey (2002) argues that whether or not a language makes productive (fully grammaticalized) use of resumptive pronouns depends on the inventory of C-type elements that the language makes use of. And in Pesetsky and Torrego (2001), whether or not a language has Subject-Aux Inversion depends on the featural properties of C.

In the early MP (Chomsky 1995), functional heads could be either strong or weak with respect to their visibility at the PF interface. Strong features are visible at PF if they are not checked before the interface, while weak features are not visible. The result of this difference is that if the feature is strong, there is overt movement, either of a phrase to the SPEC position of a higher functional category or of a head to a higher head position. If the feature is weak, no visible movement is triggered.

Given the above set of assumptions, consider some examples of how the early MP proposed to capture some parametric differences among languages. The functional categories AGR and T were posited to contain both N-features and V-features, each of which could be either strong or weak:

> Since the strength of N- and V-features on AGR is at least conceptually independent of their strength on T, the four combinations of features on AGR can combine freely with the four combinations on T to yield sixteen possible language types... English has strong N-features on T but weak V-features. The strong N-features require a DP (subject) to move to Spec of AGRsP before Spell-Out; the weak V-features permit the V to stay in VP... French raises the verb to T before Spell-Out and it is pronounced to the left of the adverb [as in example (40a) above—FJN].... Chomsky also suggests that the N-features of AGR and T might be weak in verb-initial languages such as Irish. With weak N-features on all functional heads, the subject and object of verbs in these languages could remain in the VP until after Spell-Out. If the V-features of T and/or AGR were strong, the verb would be forced to raise from the VP prior to Spell-Out in these languages, yielding a VSO order of major constituents. (Marantz 1995: 372–3)

Note that surface word order in this account is a consequence of movement to a functional projection. Indeed, in the MP virtually all surface grammatical properties, even control (if one adopts the position of Hornstein 1999), result from movement.

In recent MP work (e.g. Chomsky 2001), the strong–weak feature distinction has been abandoned. Instead, movement is triggered by the need to eliminate uninterpretable features. Given that this idea has been instantiated in several versions, none of which seems to be in a predominant position, it is difficult to say with any confidence what the implications for parametric variation (and hence typology) might be. Chomsky does continue to refer to parameters, as, for example, the 'OV/VO parameter' (Chomsky 2001: 36). And that same article devotes several pages to a parameter that distinguishes languages with object shift from those languages that lack it. Object shift is the process found in Scandinavian and other languages that can move objects to the left across a clause-medial adverb (Holmberg 1986; Thráinsson 2001). (72b) is an example from Icelandic:

(72) a. Nemandinn las ekki bókina
student-the read not book-the
'The student did not read the book'

b. Nemandinn las bókina$_i$ ekki t$_i$
'The student did not read the book'

Chomsky proposes a (rather complex) parameter assigning a particular feature to a functional head in shifting languages, which has the effect of triggering the desired movement. Nevertheless, for whatever reasons, proposals for capturing parametric differences among languages seem to be less of a priority for Chomsky now than in previous years.

In one important respect, the MP completely reverses the conception of grammatical organization that was predominant in the earlier GB approach. In GB, movement was optional, its output being constrained by some relevant UG principle. So Move-α would freely apply to (73a) to derive (73b)

(73) a. e was seen Mary
b. Mary$_i$ was seen e$_i$

If this optional movement rule failed to apply, the resultant ungrammatical sentence, *was seen Mary*, would be ruled out by the Case Filter. But in the MP, all processes are obligatory, triggered by features of functional heads. The revised approach necessitated some rethinking as far as capturing typological generalizations is concerned. Recall that a standard assumption in early transformational grammar, generally maintained under GB, was that D-structure represents the level at which one finds typological consistency and that optional rules create, for each particular language, typologically inconsistent structures. But the MP has no level of D-structure, nor does it allow optionality in the syntax per se. How then to capture formally departures from canonical typological correlations? Fukui (1993), writing with early MP assumptions, proposed relaxing the wholesale ban

TABLE 2.2. *Alternate orderings for basic orders (Steele 1978)*

basic order	VOS	VSO	SOV	SVO
very common alternate	VSO SVO	VOS	OSV	—
common alternate	—	SVO	SVO	—

on optionality, suggesting that optional operations are possible if they produce a structure consistent with the parameter value of the language. Otherwise, any deviation from the parameter setting of the language could not be optional, but would have to be triggered by a particular feature of a functional head. Note that the 'very common' alternate orderings for VO and OV languages preserve head directionality (Table 2.2).

So, Japanese allows scrambling of the order of subject and verb, but not of the order of verb and object:

(74) a. John-ga sono-hon-o katta (koto)[21]
John-NOM that-book-ACC bought (the-fact-that)
'John bought that book'
b. sono-hon-o John-ga katta (koto)
c. *John-ga katta sono-hon-o (koto)

This fact is explained by Fukui's principle: sentence (74b) preserves OV order, while (74c) illicitly creates VO order.[22] Now consider *wh*-fronting and NP-movement in English:

(75) a. What$_i$ did John buy t$_i$?
b. John$_i$ was killed t$_i$

Note that these operations create derived non-canonical OV order. Fukui devotes considerable space to arguing that these two operations could not possibly be optional and hence are consistent with his principle.[23]

An interesting typological prediction follows from Fukui's approach. It predicts that of the six word-order types, only SOV and VOS languages will allow optional reordering of subject and object. We have already seen an example from

[21] Fukui added *koto* 'the fact that' in order to avoid the unnaturalness sometimes caused by the lack of a topic in independent clauses in Japanese.

[22] Japanese does, however, have sentences where 'right-dislocated' objects can occur postverbally (Tanaka 2001):

(i) John-ga yonda yo, LGB-o
John-NOM read LGB-ACC
'John read it, LGB'

Such sentences might well pose a problem for Fukui's principle, particularly if they are analyzed as instances of Scrambling, as advocated by Tanaka.

[23] Some languages, however, do apparently have optional *wh*-fronting, that is, cases where the fronting is reported to have no semantic or discourse consequences. For an MP analysis of the Athabaskan language Babine-Witsuwit'en, which seems to have this property, see Denham (2000).

Japanese for the former; Fukui cites Chung (1990) on Chamorro for an example of the latter.[24]

More recently, optionality has typically been handled within the MP by means of optional features on functional heads. So Miyagawa (2001) derives the fact that Japanese has Scrambling (as well as other typological differences between Japanese and English) by positing that such heads can optionally manifest the Extended Projection Principle (EPP) property.

There are a number of other ways that the advent of the MP led to a reanalysis of how certain typological facts about languages might be captured. Consider binding domains, discussed above, as an example. While tagging each anaphor with a specification of its binding domain is consistent with the LPH, the idea that binding domains themselves might vary from language to language runs counter to the idea that *all* differences among languages are lexical, that is, that grammatical principles are universal and invariant. In a number of papers, Peter Cole and his associates (Cole and Sung 1994; Cole and Wang 1996; Cole and Hermon 1998) have argued that, universally, reflexives have local antecedents at LF, a circumstance that involves LF movement of reflexives that do not overtly manifest this property. In the view of these authors, certain typological properties of (what are superficially) long-distance reflexives automatically follow: as observed in Pica (1987), they are monomorphemic, are subject-oriented, and have a certain blocking effect (see the brief discussion of 'Pica's Generalization' in Chapter 1, §1.2.4)

One could make a similar point about bounding and Subjacency. The Rizzian idea that languages differ in terms of their bounding nodes is incompatible with the LPH. A number of attempts have been made to locate cross-linguistic differences in bounding possibilities in differences in functional category inventories. For example, Richards (2001) suggests that languages differ as to whether CP or IP admit to multiple specifiers. This paper argues that a host of differences among languages follows from this distinction, including differences in scrambling, superiority, and crossover effects (for a related proposal, see Sabel 2002).

One need only look at the evolution of the treatment of serial verbs to see how the shift from GB to the MP has engendered a shift in the way that parameters are viewed. A serial verb construction (SVC) is a sequence of verbs which act together as a single predicate, without any overt marker of coordination, subordination, or syntactic dependency of any other sort. Consider an example from Sranan:

(76) Kofi naki Amba kiri
Kofi hit Amba kill
'Kofi struck Amba dead'

One of the many problems in their analysis is that SVCs manifest 'argument sharing.' A single argument is associated with two or more predicates, leading to what on the face of it is a violation of the Theta-Criterion. In a GB treatment,

[24] I have found few references in the literature to the Fukui paper. I suspect that its theoretical assumptions were overtaken by and rendered unformulable in subsequent developments in the MP.

Baker (1989) proposed a parameter that, in effect, allowed this UG principle to be weakened:

(77) Generalized Serialization Parameter (Baker 1989: 519)
VPs {can/cannot} count as the projection of more than one distinct head.
CAN: Yoruba, Sranan, Ijo, Ewe...
CANNOT: English, French, Swahili, Japanese...

More recently, Collins (1997) has reinterpreted the SVC in minimalist terms, locating the parameter in the functional category system:

(78) Serialization Parameter (Collins 1997: 493)
I (tense) {can/cannot} license multiple Vs
CAN: Yoruba, Sranan, Ijo, Ewe...
CANNOT: English, French, Swahili, Japanese...

Nevertheless, not all MP-based parameters are attributed to differences in functional categories. A long-studied typological difference among languages is whether *wh*-elements occur *in situ*, as in Japanese, or are displaced, as in English (§2.2.3 above and Table 2.1). In one popular view, the distinction between the two types of languages is purely phonological. For the former languages, the tail of a movement chain is pronounced; for the latter, the head (Bobaljik 1995; Groat and O'Neil 1996; Pesetsky 1998).

Another example of parametric variation not generally attributed to differences of properties of functional heads involves the MP reinterpretation of the Head Parameter. Most commonly, the process of linearization (and hence order between heads and complements) is assumed to take place at the point of transfer from the syntax (where linear order is hypothesized to be irrelevant) to the sequence of operations which readies the syntactic object for processing by the phonology, where linear order is of central importance (see Chomsky 1995; Takano 1996; Fukui and Takano 1998; Uriagereka 1999). On this conception, a linearization statement for English would look something like the following:

(79) For a syntactic object $\{\alpha,\beta\}$, if α is a head and β is a complement, then α precedes β.

Complicating any attempt to make precise the MP approach to typological variation is the distinction between processes that apply in the 'narrow syntax' and those syntactic processes, like linearization, that apply in the phonological component (formerly PF, now more frequently the 'P-syntax'). The idea behind P-syntax (which was present as a level in antecedent models as well) is that there exists a set of operations, different in kind from those characteristic of the central computational system, which takes the formal objects created by the syntax and incrementally transforms them into the kinds of representations which can be operated on by the morphophonology, the prosody, and the phonology. These operations have a historical kinship both with the 'stylistic' and 'post-cyclic' rules of classical transformational grammar, and with the readjustment rules of Chomsky and Halle (1968). Chomsky (1995) suggested that the adjunction of phrases as represented by processes such as extraposition, right-node raising, VP-adjunction, and scrambling might lie outside of the computational system in its narrow sense (the output of Merge, Move, etc.). Chomsky (2001) increases the set of operations that might be said to occur outside narrow syntax, including, most importantly, head movement (see also Boeckx 2001).[25] There is a lot that is unclear about the narrow syntax/P-syntax distinction. One has to agree with McCloskey (1999: 207) that 'at present we have no theory whatsoever of what the properties of such [PF] movements might be.' In any event, there is no obvious implication for capturing typological variation inherent in the narrow syntax/P-syntax distinction, nor, to be fair, has there been claimed to be one.

2.4.2 *Kayne's antisymmetric program and typology*

Kayne (1994) proposed a much-discussed approach to formal syntax sharing many properties of the MP, but distinct in certain ways from the general thrust of Chomsky's minimalist theorizing. Unlike mainstream minimalism, the Kaynean program was designed from the start with the explanation of typological generalizations in mind.

It has been known since the early 1970s that grammars are replete with left–right asymmetries: cross-linguistically, the best-motivated movement rules displace elements to the left, antecedents tend to be to the left of their coreferential anaphors and pronominals, fillers tend to be to the left of their gaps, and so on. Kayne proposed to capture these generalizations, and many others as well, by means of a novel conception of the relationship between hierarchical structure and linear order, namely the Linear Correspondence Axiom (LCA). Informally put, the idea of the LCA is that if one non-terminal node c-commands another (that is, is higher in the branching structure than another), then it must precede it as well. In other words, '[p]hrase structure in fact always completely determines linear order and consequently that if two phrases differ in linear order, they must also differ in hierarchical structure' (Kayne 1994: 3). Kayne argues that the fundamentals of X-bar theory follow from this hypothesis, rather than needing to be stipulated as axioms of a distinct subsystem of grammar. Note also that the generalization about movement being solely to the left follows directly. Any rightward movement would constitute a straightforward violation of the LCA, since it would result in the moved element both c-commanding and following the movement site.

A perhaps startling conclusion of the LCA is that all languages have to manifest (underlyingly) Specifier-Head-Complement ordering—in other words SVO order for sentential constituents. The idea that specifiers are initial is reasonably uncontroversial, since subjects and displaced *wh*-phrases are almost always initial and they have both been analyzed since the 1980s as occupying specifier position

[25] For a defense of the idea that head movements are purely syntactic, see Zwart (2001).

(and it is widely agreed that VSO languages derive from a prior SVO order). Needless to say, the idea that all languages are underlyingly VO is more controversial. However, such a conclusion seems forced by the LCA. To illustrate, consider two possibilities: SVO order (80) and SOV order (81):

(80)
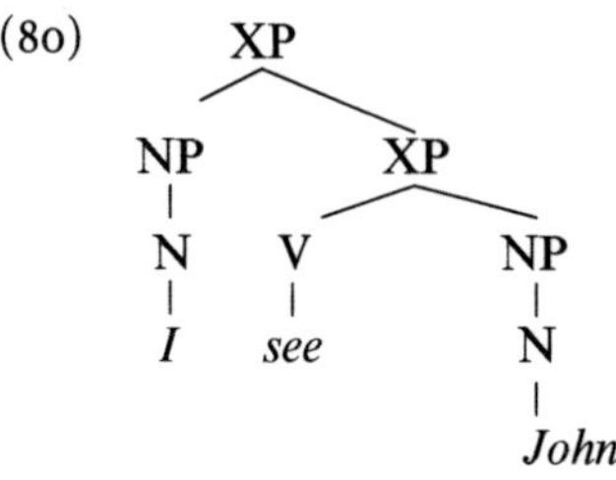

(81)*
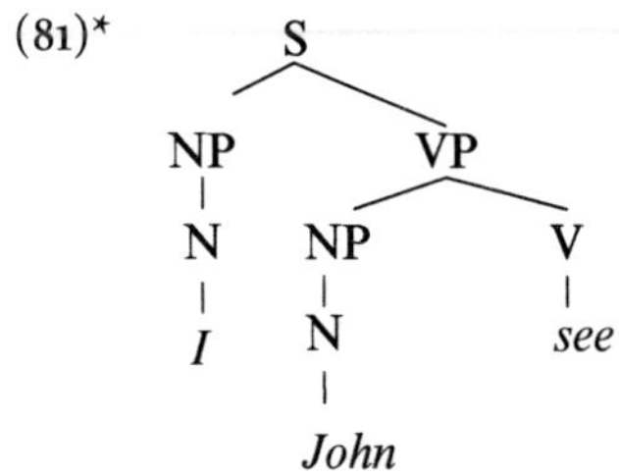

Structure (81) violates the LCA, because *see* c-commands *John* but does not precede it. In other words, SOV ordering has to be derived from leftward movement of the object over the verb.[26]

Let us now review some typological consequences of the LCA. Since Kayne assumes that the LCA underlies the entire set of syntactic representations, all complement–head ordering must result from movement. Even postpositions have to start out as prepositions:

(82)
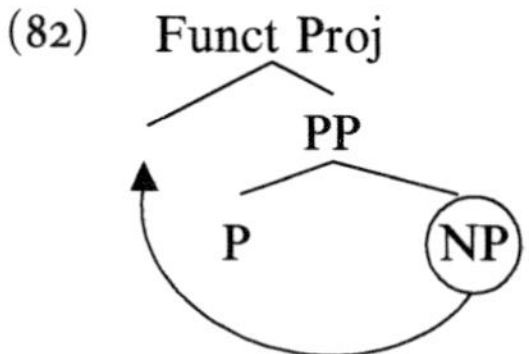

Kayne pointed to an interesting prediction that follows from this movement, namely that we would expect to find agreement between postpositions and their complements, but not between prepositions and their complements. That would be predicted under the LCA, he argues, since the (moved) object NP is in a specifier-head relation with the postposition and agreement between specifiers and heads is commonplace.

[26] But see Haider (2000a,b) for arguments that more typological predictions follow from the assumption that the universal underlying order of languages is OV, rather than VO.

Kayne also proposed an explanation of the fact that, in general, languages with clause-final complementizers do not allow *wh*-fronting. Final complementizers arise from movement of IP into SPEC, CP, just as other correlates of verb finality (including verb finality itself) arise from leftward movement:

(83)

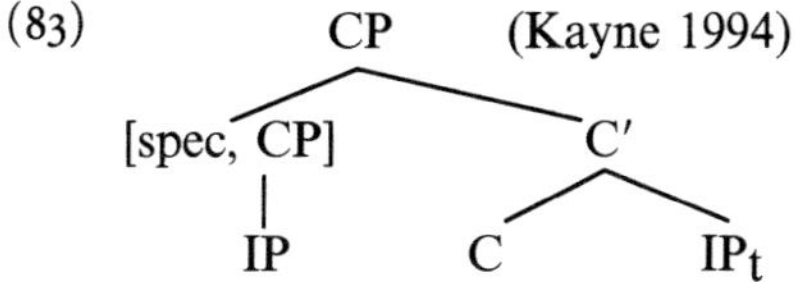

But once IP occupies SPEC,CP, there is no longer a landing site for *wh*-fronting. Hence the correlation in question is predicted.

The typological consequences of Kayne's program are further explored in Cinque (1996). For example, he takes on the following universal from Greenberg (1963):

(84) Universal 20: When any or all of the items (demonstrative, numeral, and descriptive adjective) precede the noun, they are always found in that order. If they follow, the order is either the same or its exact opposite. (Greenberg 1963: 87)

This universal is refined considerably in Hawkins (1983):

(85) For prepositional languages:
 a. NDem & NA (Swahili, Fulani, Bahasa Indonesian ...)
 b. DemN & NA (Maori, Baure, Douala, Tunen ...)
 c. DemN & AN (Greek, Maya, Norwegian ...)
 d. *NDem & AN

 e. NNum & NA (Swahili, Douala, Tunen ...)
 f. NumN & NA (Maori, Baure, Bahasa Indonesian ...)
 g NumN & AN (Greek, Maya, Norwegian ...)
 h. *NNum & AN

(86) For postpositional languages:
 a. NDem & NA (Selepet, Mojave, Diegueño ...)
 b. DemN & NA (Burmese, Kabardian, Warao ...)
 c. DemN & AN (Burushaski, Hindi, Japanese ...)
 d. *NDem & AN

 e. NNum & NA (Selepet, Mojave, Kabardian, Warao ...)
 f. NumN & NA (Burmese, Hixkaryana, Ubykh ...)
 g NumN & AN (Burushaski, Hindi, Japanese ...)
 h. *NNum & AN

In other words, postpositional languages follow the same ordering restrictions as prepositional languages. Why should this be? Cinque assumes that universal basic order is as follows:

(87)

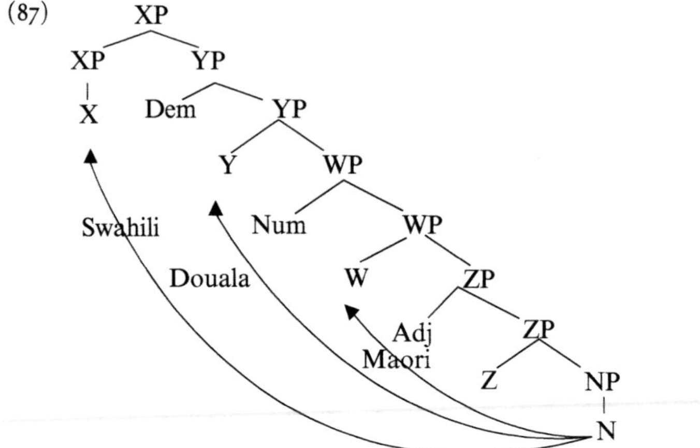

N either remains *in situ* or raises as indicated. If postpositional languages were 'symmetric' to prepositional ones, we would expect, he argues, mirror-image rightward movement. But if that were the case, then we would predict the non-existence of postpositional languages with both DemN & NA. In such languages, there would be no way for the N to occur between the Dem (on the extreme right) and the A (on the left). But in fact such languages exist.

So, given antisymmetry, there are essentially two possibilities for postpositional languages. Either nothing moves, resulting in Dem-Num-Adj-N order, as in Hindi, or there are successive leftward movements of the complements of the functional heads Z, W, and Y:

(88)

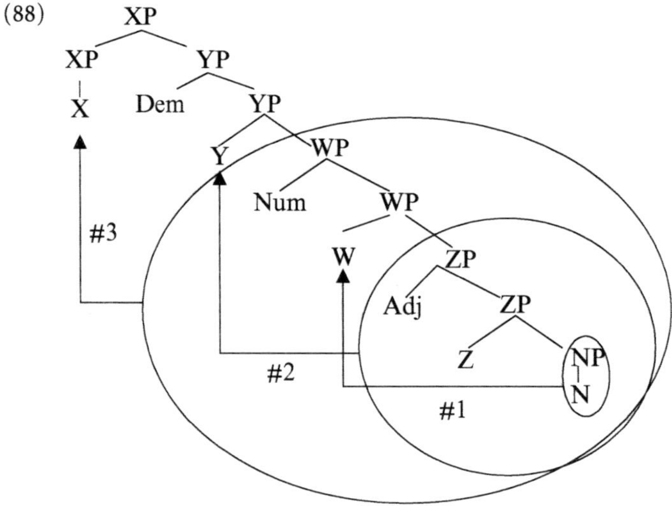

If all of these steps apply, the result is N Adj Num Dem, i.e. the mirror image of the underlying order. Cinque argues that independent support for these movements is provided by the fact that intermediate steps appear to exist: steps #1 and #2 only, resulting in Dem N Adj Num (Kabardian and Warao) and step #1 only, resulting in Dem Num N Adj (Burmese, Kokama, and Ubykh).[27]

2.4.3 *Microparameters*

The parameters proposed in GB and in the early MP for the most part were what Baker (1996) calls 'macroparameters' and what Pica (2001) calls 'metaparameters,' that is, dimensions of variation for which every language in the world is assumed to have a feature (+ or −) and which are associated with a clustering of diverse typological properties. The methodology going along with the idea of macroparameters has typically been to compare unrelated languages, or fairly distantly related ones, to ascertain how the values of the parameters in question might be differently set in those languages. The move to locating parametric differences among languages in differences in their functional projections has gone hand-in-hand with a different methodology for zeroing in on the formal differences among languages. Consider another thread in Richard Kayne's overall research program as an example. Much of his comparative work in the early 1980s focused on teasing out a parametric difference between two languages, more often than not French and English, and attempted to derive a range of differences between the two languages from differences in the setting of the particular parameter (see especially Kayne 1984). But 'in the early to mid-1980s, it became apparent to [him] that direct comparison of French and English raised difficult problems to a greater extent than a direct comparison of French and Italian' (Kayne 2000b: 4). The essence of the problem is that, close as they are in the grand scheme of things, English and French are simply too different in too many ways. Hence the difficulty in determining which syntactic properties of one language are linked by different settings of the same parameter to which syntactic properties of the other language.

But even French and Italian differ from each other in significant ways. The ideal situation then would be to compare speech varieties that differ from each other only in terms of (most ideally) one or, failing that, only a few variables. Kayne remarks:

> If it were possible to experiment on languages, a syntactician would construct an experiment of the following type: take a language, alter a single one of its observable syntactic properties, examine the result and see what, if any, other property has changed as a consequence. If some property has changed, conclude that it and the property that was altered are linked to one another by some abstract parameter. Although such experiments cannot be performed, I think that by examining pairs (and larger sets) of ever more closely

[27] Cinque's paper has many footnotes that raise, and attempt to solve, potential problems for his analysis. Space does not permit a discussion of them here.

related languages, one can begin to approximate the results of such an experiment. To the extent that one can find languages that are syntactically extremely similar to one another, yet clearly distinguishable and readily examinable, one can hope to reach a point such that the number of observable differences is so small that one can virtually see one property covarying with another. (Kayne 2000b: 5–6)

In other words, in Kayne's view, this *microparametric* variation is the best testing ground for the hypothesis that syntactic variation can be reduced to a finite set of parameters.

A focus on microparameters immediately poses the question once again of how many distinct parameters there are—after all, one can point to a seemingly unlimited number of differences between any two speech varieties. And this question in turn raises the question of how many distinct languages/dialects there are. As Kayne notes, one commonly estimates that there are 4000–5000 languages in the world. But the number is surely higher if all dialects 'of the same language' that differ in some way syntactically from each other are taken into account:

... in Northern Italy alone one can individuate at least 25 syntactically distinct languages/dialects solely by studying the syntax of subject clitics. More recently, I have had the privilege of participating in a Padua-based syntactic atlas/(micro)comparative syntax project with Paola Benincà, Cecilia Poletto, and Laura Vanelli, on the basis of which it is evident that one can easily individuate at least 100 syntactically distinct languages/dialects in Northern Italy. A very conservative estimate would be that present-day Italy has at least 500 syntactically distinct-languages/dialects. 500,000 would in consequence, I think, then be a very conservative extrapolation to the number of syntactically distinct languages/dialects in the world at present. (Kayne 2000b: 7)

Comparing the grammars of *individuals* could easily lead to the estimate that there are five billion or so distinct grammars differing by one or more parameter settings. This poses no problem for Kayne, since 'the number of independent binary-valued syntactic parameters needed to allow for 5 billion syntactically distinct grammars is only 33 (2 raised to the 33rd power is about 8.5 billion)... it seems plausible that the child is capable of setting at least that many syntactic parameters' (Kayne 2000b: 8).

My impression is that an increasing number of publications in which parameters are proposed to distinguish one speech variety from another take Kayne's words to heart and focus on microparametric differences between the varieties.

2.4.4 *Summary*

As we have seen, the theoretical constructs of the MP have been applied to the characterization and explanation of cross-linguistic variation. However, I feel that it is justified to write in summary that capturing typological generalizations is not at the heart of the MP agenda, as it was for the GB agenda. The MP does indeed provide *mechanisms* to capture such generalizations, namely parameterizing the identity, positioning, and featural make-up of the functional categories available in any particular language. But the very structure of GB, which had at its core a small number of principles each of which admitted a small number of parameter settings, invited a marriage between grammatical and typological theory. Such is not the case for the MP.

2.5 Parameters, typology, and language acquisition

Chomsky on numerous occasions has attributed the property of innate knowledge not merely to the principles of UG, but to the set of possible parameters as well. In this view, the sole significant task for the child is to 'fill in' the proper settings, perhaps being guided by an (also presumably) innate awareness of which grammatical properties are 'marked' and which are unmarked. The following passage is typical:

> [W]hat we 'know innately' are the principles of the various subsystems of S_0 [= the initial state of the language faculty—FJN] and the manner of their interaction, and the parameters associated with these principles. What we learn are the values of these parameters and the elements of the periphery... The language that we then know is a system of principles with parameters fixed, along with a periphery of marked exceptions. (Chomsky 1986b: 150–1)

If Chomsky is right, then the task of language acquisition is an utterly trivial one for the child. As Janet Fodor put it, learning a language would be no more difficult than playing the game of '20 questions'. (Fodor 2001b: 734)

Language acquisition has always been at the center of the generative program and parameter theory provides no exception to this generalization. But many linguists have found somewhat troubling the idea that markedness relations are a property of synchronic grammar. The reason is that there could easily be a degree of circularity in the claim that some feature of grammar (a violation of X-bar, a special parameter setting) is more 'marked' than another. The problem derives from the fact that markedness is typically concluded from cross-linguistic rarity, but then cross-linguistic rarity is explained in terms of markedness. With this problem in mind, David Lightfoot has suggested that claims of markedness require independent motivation:

> For specific proposals concerning marked values to entail testable claims, these claims will have to hold in an 'external' domain, a domain other than that of the distribution of morphemes or grammatical well-formedness. Claims to explanatory adequacy will have to be grounded in such domains. Natural candidates for such a domain wherein markedness proposals make empirically testable claims are language change and acquisition. (Lightfoot 1979: 77)

What is the empirically testable claim about language acquisition that follows from a markedness proposal? The null hypothesis is that '[t]he "unmarked case" can be understood as the child's initial hypothesis about language (in advance of any data)' (Williams 1981: 8; see also Lebeaux 1987 and Rizzi 1986). In terms of grammatical development, '[w]e would expect the order of appearance of structures in language acquisition to reflect the structure of markedness in some respects' (Chomsky 1981: 9). Chomsky went on to speculate that:

> Universals of the sort explored by Joseph Greenberg and others have obvious relevance to determining just which properties of the lexicon have to be specified in this manner in particular grammars—and to put it in other terms, just how much must be learned as grammar develops in the course of language acquisition. (Chomsky 1981: 95)

If the order of acquisition is a function of the markedness of the construct being acquired and claims of markedness are based in part on cross-linguistic frequency, then we would naturally expect that early-acquired constructs would be cross-linguistically frequent. And indeed, two prominent specialists in the field of language acquisition (who typically disagree with each other on many theoretical issues) have drawn just such a conclusion:

> [I]n determining which notions are encoded in a language's morphology, the child is faced with a formidable search problem… [B]y imposing a weighting on the child's hypotheses, one could account for the large disparities in the prevalence of various grammatical encodings in the world's languages, and in the speed of acquisition of various encodings by children. (Pinker 1984: 168–71)

> One intriguing possibility is that the relative accessibility for children of alternative schemes for partitioning meaning in a given conceptual domain is correlated with the frequency with which these schemes are instantiated in the languages of the world.… It is plausible that relative frequency is correlated with 'ease' or 'naturalness' for the human mind. (Bowerman 1985: 1306)

More recently, Mark Baker has attributed the property of innate knowledge to his Parameter Hierarchy (see above, §2.3.7). He remarks that 'it would make sense if children, too, instinctively work their way down the hierarchy, taking advantage of its logical structure to avoid agonizing over needless decisions' (Baker 2001: 192) and goes on to suggest that 'the parameter hierarchy provides a logical flowchart that children use in the process of language acquisition' (p. 195).

Hyams (1986), however, has rejected the view that the unmarked case can be identified with the child's first hypothesis in language acquisition. As she points out, 'we would not assume that a grammar which generates complex structures is necessarily more marked than a grammar which generates only simple sentences, solely because the former appears later in the developmental sequence than the latter' (p. 158). She opts instead for a 'relational or relative' definition of markedness, one which has explicitly more typological implications. In this approach, markedness relations are determined by universal formal criteria, as are the implicational relations among them. Thus the presence of null subjects in and of itself would not necessarily be marked or unmarked. However, UG would specify that if a language does allow them, then the unmarked option would be to allow subject inversion as well, thereby capturing the typological generalization that null subjects and inversion tend to go together. Hyams tentatively suggests that marked correlations between features present more of a learning challenge for the child than unmarked ones.

Most researchers now reject the idea that stages of language acquisition reflect in any direct way the structure of grammatical theory in terms of relations between parameters and their settings. We will turn to more recent views of the acquisition of parameter settings and their implications for our concerns in Chapter 3, §3.2.2.7.

2.6 Parameters, typology, and language change

Just as one might expect a correlation between unmarked parameter settings, cross-linguistic frequency, and early first-language acquisition, one might also expect a correlation between unmarked parameter settings, cross-linguistic frequency, and the likelihood of a particular language change. That is, one might expect that changes from marked parameter settings to unmarked ones would be more common than the reverse change. Roberts (1999) and Roberts and Roussou (2002) have made a proposal that would seem to have such a consequence, though they do not say so in so many words. They take the (early) MP position that the 'strong' value of a feature triggers overt movement and that the 'weak' value triggers covert movement. They further assume that the weak value is always the unmarked value, that the strong value is the marked value, and that the default value in language acquisition is the unmarked (hence weak) value. They apply this conjunction of assumptions to the explanation of the loss of verb movement (i.e. V-to-I) movement in the history of English and other well attested changes. As I read their account, it would seem to follow that one would expect a general historical tendency to abandon (overt) movement.[28]

Roberts (1998) has also suggested that parametric theory might be applied to historical reconstruction. Suppose that we wish to determine the setting (+ or −) of a particular parameter in a protolanguage. We can use 'the traditional methodology of reconstruction' to conclude that the proto-setting was '−' if the daughter languages present themselves as in (89):

(89)

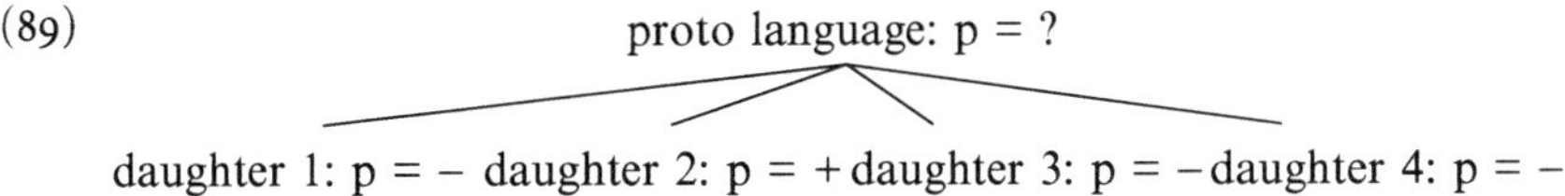

[28] See Ishikawa (1999) for a discussion of how a change from weak to strong might take place. A number of scholars (e.g. Wurzel 1994) have claimed that when a privative opposition is given up, it is the unmarked member that survives. Exemplifications of this idea tend to involve phonology and morphology, rather than syntax, and their relationship to (generative) parameter theory is not clear. For a collection of papers on markedness and change, again with an uncertain relationship to UG parameters, see Andersen (2001).

According to Roberts, one would conclude that the protolanguage has the '–' setting, given that it manifests itself in three of the four daughter languages.[29]

In a number of publications, David Lightfoot (1991, 1999) has made claims about parametric change that have implications for typology. Lightfoot distinguishes between two types of change. One involves changes of parameter settings and the other includes grammaticalization, morphological changes, such as the loss of gender markers (Jones 1988), the reduction in verbal desinences, and the loss of subjunctive mood. He points to six features that are characteristic of parametric change: each new grammatical property is manifested by a cluster of new phenomena; the new property sets off a 'chain reaction' of further changes; it spreads rapidly and manifests an S-curve; an earlier structural property becomes obsolescent; significant change in meaning occurs; and (as a prior condition) the change was triggered by shifts in unembedded data only. Among examples of parametric change in the history of English, Lightfoot includes the change from OV to VO order; the ability of the infinitival *to* marker to transmit case-marking and head-government properties of a governing verb; the loss of inherent D-structure oblique case; the reanalysis allowing the stranding of prepositions; the recategorization of the premodal verbs; and the loss of the ability of verbs to move to a governing INFL position.

2.7 Conclusion

We find typological studies framed in generative theory from almost the very inception of that approach to grammar. However, the commitment of generativists to account for cross-linguistic variation was greatly facilitated by the introduction of the Government-Binding theory in the early 1980s and its conception that principles of grammar are parameterized, different languages allowing different setting for particular parameters. The parametric program continues to this day, though it is perhaps less evident how to handle typological generalizations within the Minimalist Program than within GB.

[29] It is not clear that this idea is compatible with the one expressed in the preceding paragraph. We would not expect reconstruction by 'majority rule' to work if some changes are more likely than others.

3

Parameters, Performance, and the Explanation of Typological Generalizations

3.1 Introduction

My goal in this chapter is to launch a frontal assault not just on the parametric approach to grammar, but also on the very idea that it is the job of Universal Grammar per se to account for typological generalizations. I contrast two approaches to typological variation in grammar. In one approach, variation is captured largely by means of parameters, directly tied either to principles of UG or to functional projections provided by UG. In the other approach, variation is captured by means of extragrammatical principles. I argue that the second approach is better supported than the first. To be specific, I challenge the idea, current since Chomsky (1981), that the overall structure of linguistic theory is something along the lines of (1):

(1) Some central features of (currently predominant) linguistic theory:
   a. Principles of Universal Grammar (or, more recently, a set of functional projections provided by UG), which have
   b. Different parameter settings for different languages (thereby accounting for language-particular differences).
   c. By means of (1a) and (1b), typological variation is accounted for.
   d. A residue of marked (language-particular) morphosyntactic properties.

The alternative position which I defend here is presented in (2):

(2) Some central features of an alternative way of looking at linguistic theory:
   a. Unparameterized principles of Universal Grammar.
   b. Language-particular rules constrained by these UG principles.
   c. Extragrammatical principles that account for typological variation.

Under position (2), neither UG principles nor functional categories are associated with a range of parameter settings. Rather, language-particular differences are captured by differences in language-particular rules. Accompanying this view, the burden of accounting for typological generalizations is shifted from competence to performance.

Before proceeding further, it is crucial that I specify what I mean by 'language-particular rule.' I have two rather different types of device in mind. First, and less interestingly, the notion encompasses the formal mechanisms devised to handle phenomena whose explanation seems to lie outside the scope of the core principles of principles-and-parameters syntax (from whatever period). In a GB approach, then, language-particular rules would encompass processes assigned to the marked periphery like Exceptional Case Marking (see Chapter 2, §2.3.5), deletions like VP Ellipsis, 'stylistic' and phonology-sensitive processes like Heavy-NP-Shift, the residue of idiosyncratic filters, and so on. Given the still-inchoate state of much minimalist theorizing, it is more difficult to characterize what a language-particular rule would be in that general approach. Candidates include XP adjunctions such as Extraposition, Right-Node Raising, VP-Adjunction, and Scrambling and processes that might apply in the 'P-syntax,' such as those sensitive to linear order and those sensitive to phonological conditions.

The second sense of 'language-particular rule' is unique to the present work. Essentially, they are parameter-settings 'detached' from the parameters themselves (which are hypothesized not to exist). So, as was noted in Chapter 2, it is frequently assumed that UG provides a 'Head Parameter' like (3), with settings (also provided by UG) like (3a) and (3b) or else (in the MP) linearization statements, parameterized as in (4a-b):

(3) HEAD PARAMETER: Complements are to the left or to the right of the head.
   a. HEAD-LEFT (English, Swahili . . .)
   b. HEAD-RIGHT (Japanese, Lakhota . . .)

(4) a. For a syntactic object { α,β }, if α is a head and β is a complement, then α precedes β. (English, Swahili . . .)
   b. For a syntactic object { α,β }, if α is a head and β is a complement, then α follows β. (Japanese, Lakhota . . .)

In my alternative view, UG would still specify that phrases are headed (and hence in the process of acquisition children would still be driven to identify the position of the head). However, what they would acquire for each of the four languages mentioned would simply be a rule along the lines of (5a-d):

(5) a. English: Complements are to the right of the head.
   b. Swahili: Complements are to the right of the head.
   c. Japanese: Complements are to the left of the head.
   d. Lakhota: Complements are to the left of the head.

Now consider a broad UG principle like Subjacency. In the traditional GB view, Subjacency is stated something along the lines of (6), with parameter settings as in (6a-c) (see Chapter 2, §2.3.1):

(6) SUBJACENCY: No moved element may cross two or more bounding nodes, with the choice of bounding nodes parameterized as follows:
 a. English chooses S.
 b. Italian chooses S'.
 c. Russian chooses S and S'.

In my alternative way of looking at things, Subjacency could still exist as a UG principle, but would be stated much more broadly, as in (7):

(7) SUBJACENCY (REVISED): There are limits on the structural distance between the launching and landing site of a moved element.

Move-α, then, if we make a set of assumptions that otherwise characterize GB, would be formulated somewhat differently in English, Italian, and Russian. However, in no language would Move-α be totally 'free.' That is, given the UG principle of Subjacency, Move-α will always be bounded to some degree or other. Similarly, given the approach to bounding compatible with minimalist assumptions, namely that such effects are derived from the number and properties of the specifiers of CP and IP (see Chapter 2, §2.4.1), in my alternative conception the component of the grammar specifying phrase structure would simply have different rules expanding CP and IP.

To take another example, it has been assumed since the early 1980s that an important parameter separating languages is whether *Wh*-Movement takes place in the (narrow) syntax or in LF (after Spell-Out). In the view adopted here, grammars are simply formulated so that some contain a rule of overt movement and others a rule of covert movement. If the choice of overt or covert movement can be derived from some other feature of the language, then well and good, but, again, there is no UG-provided specification that languages have some global property, or some local property tied to a feature of a functional head, which divides them into overt movers and covert movers.

One's first reaction to these remarks might well be that I am advocating a 'less constrained' grammatical theory than advocates of principles-and-parameters syntax have generally assumed, given that in my alternative view, UG has a diminished role to play. To a certain extent, such is true. However, I have two points to make in defense. The first is that the degree to which a theory can be constrained is itself constrained by empirical reality. And empirical reality, as I see it, dictates that the hopeful vision of UG as providing a small number of principles each admitting of a small number of parameter settings is simply not workable. The variation that one finds among grammars is far too complex for such a vision to be realized. The second is that the degree of grammatical variation is in fact highly constrained, but much more by performance factors than by UG. Hopefully, the truth of both points will become apparent as the chapter unfolds.

Section 3.2 makes the case that the arguments that have been advanced in favor of a parametric approach are defective. Put simply, there is no evidence that parametric approaches are any more successful than rule-based approaches. In §3.3 I argue that typological generalizations are simply irrelevant for a theory of UG. Section 3.4 argues that the burden of accounting for cross-linguistic generalizations should be shifted away from competence and to performance and §3.5 is a brief conclusion.

3.2 Against a parametric approach to grammar

In §3.2.1 I review what I call the 'standard story' on the parametric approach to typological variation, drawing mainly on material from the previous chapter. Section 3.2.2 is a lengthy discussion outlining what I consider sound arguments for rejecting the idea that UG principles (or functional projections provided by UG) are parameterized.

3.2.1 *The 'standard story' on the superiority of the parametric approach*

It should prove useful to frame the discussion by outlining what have typically been the main selling points for a parameter-based theory over a rule-based theory. They are enumerated in (8):

(8) The standard story on parameters (and how they contrast with rules):

a. Parameters are descriptively simple, whereas rules are (generally) not (Chapter 2, §2.3.3).
b. Parameters have binary settings (an idea which is inapplicable to rules) (Chapter 2, §2.3.8).
c. Parameters are small in number; the number of rules is open-ended (Chapter 2, §2.3.3).
d. Parameters are hierarchically/implicationally organized, thereby accounting for both order of first language acquisition and typological generalizations (there is nothing comparable for rules) (Chapter 2, §2.3.7).
e. Parameters are abstract entities with a rich deductive structure, making possible the prediction of (unexpected) clusterings of morphosyntactic properties (Chapter 2, §2.3.4).
f. Parameters and the set of their possible settings are innate (and therefore universal). Rules are not (normally) assumed to be drawn from an innate set (Chapter 2, §2.5).
g. Parameter settings are easily learned, while rules are learned with much greater difficulty (Chapter 2, §2.5).
h. Parametric change is directional (marked setting to unmarked setting). Also (unlike morphological and grammaticalization-related changes), parametric change leads to clustering, sets off a chain reaction of other changes, spreads rapidly and manifests an S-curve, leads to the obsolescence of an earlier structural property, involves significant change in meaning, and is triggered by shifts in unembedded data only (Chapter 2, §2.6).

One can readily understand the appeal of the conjunction of hypotheses (8a-h). If they are correct, then the parametric view of language is far-ranging in explanatory power. However, the remainder of this chapter will argue that they are not correct. Taking these hypotheses in order, I will argue that the facts are at least as supportive of a rule-based account of variation (2a-c) as of a parametric account (1a-d).

3.2.2 *The deficiencies of parameter-setting models*

This section will take each argument in turn that has been presented in support of parameter-setting models and point out its deficiencies. I will attempt to demonstrate that in all cases, a rule-based account is either more adequate than a parameter-based one or that, when all the facts are taken into account, they are empirically indistinguishable.

3.2.2.1 Descriptive simplicity

Let us begin by looking at the question of parameters and rules simply from the point of view of formal description. I take it as uncontroversial that parameters are motivated only to the extent that they lead overall to more formal simplicity. If as many parameter settings are needed in a parameter-based model as rules would be needed in a rule-based one and the former turn out to be as complex as the latter, then clearly nothing is gained by opting for parameters.

In fact, I see no reason to think that there is any gain in descriptive simplicity with parameters. Consider first the differences between adjective–noun ordering in English and French. Cinque (1994) points to the following contrasts:

(9) a. un **gros** ballon **rouge**
b. a **big red** ball

(10) a. un tissu **anglais cher**
b. an **expensive English** fabric

(11) a. an **old** friend (= friend who is aged or friend for a long time)
b. une **vieille** amie (= friend for a long time)
c. une amie **vieille** (= friend who is aged)

In Cinque's account, the facts of (9–11) result from the following parametric differences between French grammar and English grammar:

(12) a. French has postnominal adjectives (as in 9a) because of a parametric difference with English that allows N-movement in the former language, but not in the latter.
b. *Cher* has scope over *anglais* in (10a) because French has a parametric difference with English that triggers movement of an N-ADJ constituent.
c. In (11), the two positions for *vieille* in French, but only one for *old* in English, result from a parametric difference regarding the feature attraction possibilities of functional categories in the two languages.

As Bouchard (2003) stresses, the problem with such an account is that the word 'parameter' is used as nothing more than a synonym for the word 'rule.' There is no increase in descriptive elegance, economy, or whatever in Cinque's account over an account which does no more than say that English and French have different rules of adjective placement.

In any number of cases a parametric approach seems simpler than a rule-based one only because no one has ever attempted to capture the full complexity of any one language by means of them. Consider English word order. English is not uniquely SVO. As we can see in (13), other orders of subject, verb, and object are possible:

(13) a. The last lecture Mary really hated. (OSV)
  b. Drink the whole bottle, John never would. (VOS)
  c. Away ran John. (VS)

In a rule-based model, presumably English would have an underlying SVO order and the sentences of (13) would be generated by means of optional movement rules. But the point is that simply characterizing English as manifesting the parameter 'head first' is not sufficient. Either a separate 'parameter' would have to be posited to allow for (13a-c), effectively using the word 'parameter' as a not very enlightening synonym for the word 'rule,' or their derivation would have to be consigned to the 'marked periphery.' Neither alternative results in any gain in overall simplicity.

In general, parametric accounts have been vague on which phenomena in the language under discussion need to be handled by some extra-parametric mechanism. An exception is the discussion of Hixkaryana in Baker (2001a), based on an earlier proposal in Kayne (1994). This language for the most part manifests OVS word order, an order which is extremely rare typologically:

(14) kanawa yano toto Hixkaryana (Derbyshire 1985)
  canoe took person
  'the man took the canoe'

One's first thought might be that what is needed is a parameter allowing for OVS order. But in fact Baker rejects the idea that a special word-order parameter is involved here. Rather, following Kayne, he argues that Hixkaryana is (parametrically) SOV and allows the fronting of VP by a movement rule (the language does in fact have SOV as variant order):

(15) S[OV] $\longrightarrow$ [OV]S

In other words, in this account word order is determined both by a parameter and by a language-specific rule. Such a treatment undercuts the attractiveness of a parametric approach. That is, it is no longer a matter of comparing a theory with parameters (and all their virtues) with a theory with rules (and their lack of virtues). Rather, it is a matter of comparing a theory with parameter settings *and* rules versus one with rules alone. On the basis of Occam's razor, one would be forced to renounce the idea of any *a priori* desirability of a parametric theory.

The dilemma here is that if the scope of parameters is expanded (to include the English and Hixkaryana cases), then 'parameter' has simply become a synonym for 'rule' (a danger inherent in parametric theory noted long ago by Safir 1987: 78). If parameters are kept simple and few in number, then grammatical theory needs to characterize the properties of rules, just as it would have to in a purely rule-based approach.[1]

3.2.2.2 Binarity

In general, where features have been posited in morphosyntax, they have been assumed to be binary, just as in phonology. But binarity in phonology has a conceptual basis, in that it is rooted in categorical perception (Richard Wright, personal communication). It goes without saying that such an account does not generalize to the morphological or syntactic properties of language.

In fact, there is little evident binarity in morphosyntax. The number of genders, numbers, and cases in a particular language might be two, but it might be more than that (one thinks of the heroic, but failed, attempt in Jakobson (1936/1971) to reduce the cases of Russian to sets of binary distinctions). Along the same lines, there is little reason to think of grammatical relations, thematic roles, and so on as lending themselves to characterization in terms of binary oppositions. Where binarity has been posited in syntax, it has not been very successful. It is generally assumed that the categories N, A, P, and V are decomposed into binary features, as in Table 3.1:[2]

But as Baker (2003: 2) has astutely observed, 'this theory is widely recognized to have almost no content in practice. The feature system is not well integrated into the framework as a whole, in that there are few or no principles that refer to these features or their values.' Indeed, there is little reason to believe that this or

TABLE 3.1. *Categories and features (Chomsky 1970)*

	+N	−N
+V	A	V
−V	N	P

[1] Interestingly, Chomsky has remarked with respect to the principles-and-parameters approach that '[t]here remains a derivative sense in which a language *L* is a "rule system" of a kind: namely, the rules of *L* are the principles of UG as parameterized for *L*' (Chomsky 1991b: 417).

[2] To be accurate, prepositions were not incorporated into the feature system until Jackendoff (1977), though Jackendoff's system of cross-classification differed from Chomsky's. Aside from the fact that adding prepositions completes the symmetry of the system, the strongest argument for their inclusion that I am aware of is found in Lefebvre and Muysken (1988). They argue that if [-V, -N] is taken to represent the unspecification of features (or their underspecification), one is on the way to explaining why N, A, and V are often grammaticalized as P over time.

any pair of binary feature specifications for the four major categories could be well motivated. To begin, *any* such breakdown necessarily makes the very weak claim that four of the six combinations involving two categories are 'natural'; in the system illustrated in Table 3.1, only the pairs A-P and V-N are unnatural. And yet, it is difficult to see what might be unnatural about either of them. In the course of the history of English, for example, we have seen adjectives become prepositions (e.g. the word *like*), and, as pointed out in Baker (2003), APs and PPs can be appended to a transitive clause to express the goal or result of the action, but NPs and VPs cannot:

(16) a. John pounded the metal flat. (AP)
b. John threw the ball into the barrel. (PP)
c. *John pounded the metal a sword. (NP)
d. *John polished the table shine. (VP)

Likewise, gerunds cross-linguistically manifest both N-related properties and V-related properties to varying degrees. Even more problematically, there are numerous attested generalizations involving three out of the four categories: P, A, and V are Case assigners in some languages, and, in English, N, A, and P, but not V, allow QP specifiers (for more examples along these lines, see Reuland 1986 and Muysken and van Riemsdijk 1986, and for detailed criticism of the feature system for categories, see Stuurman 1985; Déchaine 1993; and Wunderlich 1996):

(17) a. Whose [$_N$book] is that?
b. How [$_A$red] was the sunset?
c. How much [$_P$over] the limit are we?
d. *How fast [$_V$cycling] was Lance Armstrong?

As far as parameters are concerned, some have indeed been assumed to have binary settings, such as those that determine whether a language is configurational or not, whether it has (overt) *wh*-fronting or not, and so on. But many others are not (evidently) binary. So for example, the possible binding domains across languages have been argued to be in a subset relation with respect to each other, rather than contrasting in binary fashion:

(18) Domains for binding of anaphoric elements (Manzini and Wexler 1987)
γ is a governing category for α iff
γ is the minimal category that contains α and a governor for α and
a. can have a subject or, for α anaphoric, has a subject β, $\beta \neq \alpha$; or
b. has an Infl; or
c. has a Tense; or
d. has a 'referential' Tense; or
e. has a 'root' Tense;
if, for α anaphoric, the subject of γ is accessible to α.

Likewise, there is nothing (evidently) binary about the possible bounding nodes for Subjacency, about the number of specifiers a DP can take, or about any number of other syntactic properties that might distinguish one language from another.

In a sense, binarity was built into the early MP by means of the (binary) distinction between strong and weak features. Languages differ in terms of the binary feature specifications of functional heads; if the relevant feature of the head is strong, there is overt movement; if the feature is weak, then there is movement in LF. But the problem is that it has never been clear how to relate many parametric differences among languages to the distinction between strong and weak features (one thinks of binding and bounding domains again, for example). And thinking of parametric choices as binary choices is less evident in current instantiations of the MP, where notions like 'interpretable' and 'uninterpretable' have replaced 'strong' and 'weak.' Perhaps each functional head is associated with two features, one interpretable and one uninterpretable, but it is not obvious why that should be the case.

In short, parameters do not clearly have binary settings, and in that respect parameter settings do not differ from rules.

3.2.2.3 Smallness of number

How many parameters are there? The answer depends, of course on what is in the marked periphery. Certainly hundreds have been proposed since the notion was introduced around 1980. Lightfoot, as noted in the previous chapter, considers thirty or forty to be a reasonable number from the perspective of language acquisition, but goes on to make the disconcerting comment that 'a single issue of *Linguistic Inquiry* may contain 30–40 proposed parameters' (Lightfoot 1999: 259). Such has been the norm since the introduction of parametric theory. Consider the papers in the *Proceedings of the North Eastern Linguistic Society Conference* (volume 15, from 1985), several of which propose parameters of variation. Some of these in fact do seem fairly general, including one distinguishing nominative/accusative languages from ergative/absolutive languages. But others have the appearance of being uncomfortably language-particular, including one that states that Finnish is immune to the Case Filter; one which has *Wh*-Movement pass through INFL in Yoruba; and one that states that a preposition must be properly governed in Dutch in order to be a proper governor itself.

If we can (for purposes of argument) make the assumption that there is one binary parameter setting for each functional head, we need 'simply' count the number of functional heads to determine the number of parameters. And how many functional heads are there? If Cinque (1999) is right, there are at least thirty-two functional heads in the IP domain alone (possibly multiplied by the number of verb forms, i.e. finite/infinitive/past participle, etc.):

(19) Functional heads in the IP domain (Cinque 1999):

a. $\text{Mood}_{\text{Speech Act}}$	b. $\text{Mood}_{\text{Evaluative}}$	c. $\text{Mood}_{\text{Evidential}}$
d. $\text{Mood}_{\text{Epistemic}}$	e. T(Past)	f. T(Future)
g. $\text{Mood}_{\text{Irrealis}}$	h. $\text{Mod}_{\text{Necessity}}$	i. $\text{Mod}_{\text{Possibility}}$
j. $\text{Mod}_{\text{Volitional}}$	k. $\text{Mod}_{\text{Obligation}}$	l. $\text{Mod}_{\text{Ability/permission}}$
m. $\text{Asp}_{\text{Habitual}}$	n. $\text{Asp}_{\text{Repetitive(I)}}$	o. $\text{Asp}_{\text{Frequentative(I)}}$
p. $\text{Asp}_{\text{Celerative(I)}}$	q. T(Anterior)	r. $\text{Asp}_{\text{Terminative}}$
s. $\text{Asp}_{\text{Continuative}}$	t. $\text{Asp}_{\text{Perfect(?)}}$	u. $\text{Asp}_{\text{Retrospective}}$
v. $\text{Asp}_{\text{Proximative}}$	w. $\text{Asp}_{\text{Durative}}$	x. $\text{Asp}_{\text{Generic/progressive}}$
y. $\text{Asp}_{\text{Prospective}}$	z. $\text{Asp}_{\text{SgCompletive(I)}}$	aa. $\text{Asp}_{\text{PlCompletive}}$
bb. Voice	cc. $\text{Asp}_{\text{Celerative(II)}}$	dd. $\text{Asp}_{\text{SgCompletive(II)}}$
ee. $\text{Asp}_{\text{Repetitive(II)}}$	ff. $\text{Asp}_{\text{Frequentative(II)}}$	

On the basis of a look at fifteen languages, fourteen of them Indo-European (from only four subfamilies), Longobardi (2003) proposes thirty binary parameters for DP. Cinque (1994) divides Adjective Phrase into at least five separate maximal projections encoding Quality, Size, Shape, Color, and Nationality. Beghelli and Stowell (1997) break down Quantifier Phrase into projections headed by *Wh*, Neg, Distributive, Referential, and Share. CP has also been split into a dozen or more projections, including ForceP, FocusP, and an indefinite number of Topic Phrases (Rizzi 1997). Facts pertaining to clitic inversion and related phenomena in some northern dialects of Italian have led to the positing of Left Dislocation Phrase, Number Phrase, Hearer Phrase, and Speaker Phrase (Poletto 2000). Damonte (2004) proposes projections corresponding to the set of thematic roles, including Reciprocal, Benefactive, Instrumental, Causative, Comitative, and Reversive Phrases. We have seen Verb Phrase split into two projections, one headed by V and the other by 'v' (Chomsky 1995). Zanuttini (2001) posits four distinct Negative Phrase projections for Romance alone and McCloskey (1997) argues that at least three subject positions are needed. The positing of a new functional projection (and hence a new parameter) to capture any structural difference between two languages has led to what Ackerman and Webelhuth (1998: 125) have aptly called 'the diacriticization of parameters.'

Other proposals have led to a potentially exponential increase in the number of functional projections and their interrelationships, and hence in the number of parameters. For example, Giorgi and Pianesi (1997) have mooted the possibility of 'syncretic categories,' that is, those that conflate two or more otherwise independent ones, as, for example, TP/AgrP. Along similar lines, Bobaljik (1995), Thráinsson (1996), and Bobaljik and Thráinsson (1998) suggest that languages differ not only by the settings of their parameters, but by the very existence in a particular language of the functional categories in which they are situated (see also Fukui 1995). Such a proposal leads to at least a ternary value for each parameter: positive, negative, or not applicable. Complicating things still further, Ouhalla (1991a) argues that an important dimension of parametric variation among languages is the relative ordering of embedding of functional categories. So for example, in his analysis, in Berber and Chamorro, the AgrP projection is below the TnsP projection, while in English and Welsh, TnsP is below AgrP.

One might, of course, argue along with Cinque and contra Ouhalla that the ordering among functional categories is universal. In that view, languages would differ parametrically in their lexicalization possibilities, some functional categories being lexicalized in some languages, but not in others. However, transferring the parametric choice to the lexicon neither decreases the number of potential parameters nor gives them an edge over rules. First, the number of parameters is not reduced, since the burden of specifying whether a functional category is present in a particular language or not has merely been transferred to the lexicon. Second, the statement that some language makes the parametric choice that lexical item L licenses functional projection P is indistinguishable from the statement that there is a language-particular rule involving L that specifies P.

Recall from the previous chapter (§2.4.3) that in order to account for microparameters and the 'some number substantially greater than five billion' grammars that might exist in the world (Kayne 2000b: 8), Kayne calculates that only thirty-three binary-valued parameters would be needed. His math may be right, but from that fact it does not follow that only thirty-three parameters would be needed to capture all of the microvariation that one finds in the world's languages and dialects. In principle, the goal of a parametric approach is to capture the set of *possible* human languages, not the set (however large) of actually existing ones. One can only speculate that the number of such languages is in the trillions or quadrillions. In any event, Kayne's own work suggests that the number of parameters is vastly higher than thirty-three. Depending on precisely what counts as a parameter (Kayne is not always clear on that point), just to characterize the difference among the Romance dialects discussed in the first part of Kayne (2000b) with respect to clitic behavior, null subjects, verb movement, and participle agreement would require several dozen distinct parameters. It is hard to avoid the conclusion that characterizing just a few more differences among the dialects would lead to dozens of new parameters.

If the number of parameters needed to handle the different grammars of the world's languages, dialects, and (possibly) idiolects is in the thousands (or, worse, millions), then ascribing them to an innate UG to my mind loses all semblance of plausibility. True, we are not yet at the point of being able to 'prove' that the child is not innately equipped with 7846 (or 7,846,938) parameters, each of whose settings is fixed by some relevant triggering experience. I would put my money, however, on the fact that evolution has not endowed human beings in such an exuberant fashion.

Nobody is in a position say how many parameters are necessary in a parametric account, any more than one is in a position to say how many rules are necessary for any given language in a rule-based approach. But I see no reason to conclude that the number of the former is significantly less than the number of the latter.

3.2.2.4 Hierarchical/implicational organization

The most detailed proposal by far of the hierarchical relations among parameters is Baker (2001a), discussed in some detail in the previous chapter. For ease of reference, I reproduce his Parameter Hierarchy (PH) in Figure 3.1.

The great potential appeal of the PH is its architectural simplicity. All choices branch from a single parametric node, namely the Polysynthesis Parameter, which is the most basic parametric choice that language learners need to make. Furthermore, with one exception (the PH puts the Head Directionality and Optional Polysynthesis parameters at the same level), all branching (and hence all choices) are binary. One binary choice leads inexorably to another, with parameters on collateral branches playing, in principle, no role in any particular choice.

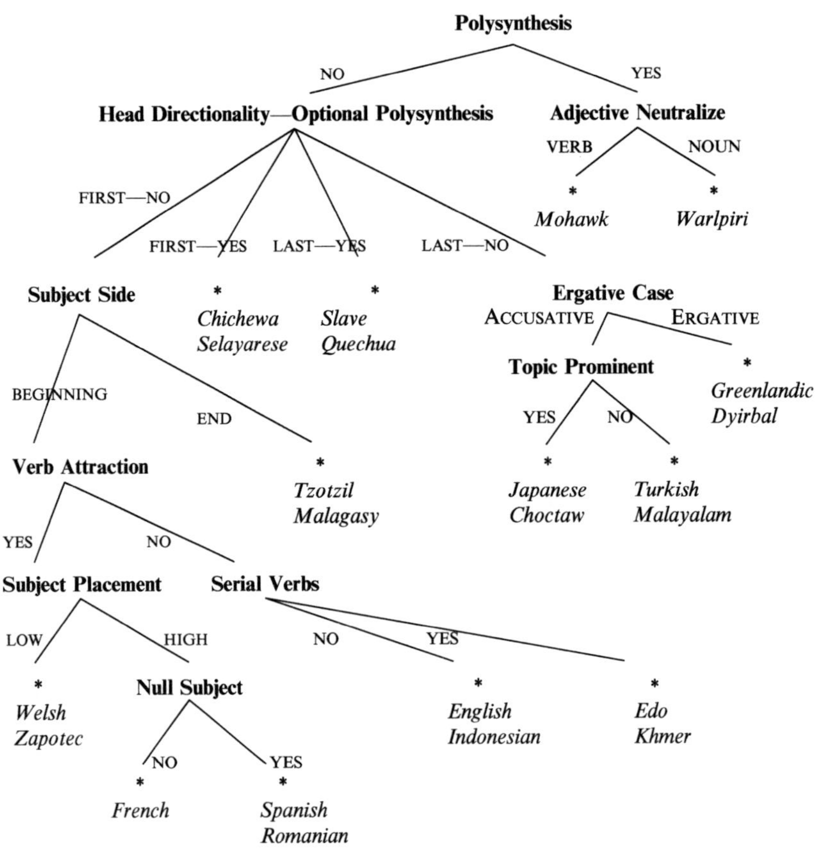

FIGURE 3.1. The Parameter Hierarchy (Baker 2001a: 183)

Unfortunately, the typological evidence argues against a model of parametric choice with properties remotely that simple. Take the Ergative Case Parameter as an example. In the PH, this parameter comes into play only for head-final languages without optional polysynthesis. But what Baker really wants to say, I think, is that only languages with these typological properties can be *ergative*. Somehow, speakers of head-initial languages have to know (or come to know) that their language is accusative. Nothing on the PH conveys the information that accusativity is, in essence, the 'default.' Along the same lines, nothing in the PH conveys information about whether ergative languages can have serial verbs, whether languages that neutralize adjectives can be verb–subject, or whether topic prominent languages can have null subjects. Recording this information in the PH would considerably complicate its architecture, since doing so would require that branches cross each other or some equivalent notational device.

There are serious problems as well with the idea that the rarity of a language type is positively correlated with the number of 'decisions' (i.e. parametric choices) that a language learner has to make. Baker's discussion of verb-initial languages implies that for each parameter there should be a roughly equal number of languages with positive and negative settings. That cannot possibly be right. There are many more non-polysynthetic languages than polysynthetic ones, despite the fact that whether a language is one or the other is a matter of a yes–no choice. The same point could be made for subject-initial head-first languages vis-à-vis subject-last ones and non-optional polysynthesis languages vis-à-vis optional polysynthetic ones. Most problematically of all, the Null Subject Parameter is the lowest parameter of all in the PH, implying that null subject languages should be rarer than verb-initial languages. However, according to Gilligan (1987), a solid majority of the world's languages are null subject.[3]

The PH is also rife with purely empirical problems. To 'start at the top,' Baker assigns a positive value of the Polysynthesis Parameter to both Mohawk and Warlpiri, despite extreme typological differences between them. Among other things, Mohawk makes heavy use of incorporation and has no overt case marking, while Warlpiri has rich case marking. The problem with distinguishing the two languages by means of a case-marking parameter is that Baker wants case marking to fall out from the Head Directionality Parameter, since most head-final languages have case marking. But as Table 3.2 shows, a sizeable percentage of head-first languages have case marking, while 36 per cent of head-last languages lack it. None of these languages would appear to have any place in the PH.[4]

[3] Baker (2001a: 169) suggests that '[w]hen the study of null subject phenomena is taken out of its original, Romance-centric context, we may discover that the Null Subject Parameter is essentially the same thing as the Optional Polysynthesis Parameter.' Unfortunately, his rationale for this speculation is not presented in sufficient detail to allow adequate evaluation.

[4] Baker (2001a: 177) remarks that the difference between Mohawk-type languages and Warlpiri-type languages is 'induced by the Adjective Neutralization Parameter,' but I do not understand how.

TABLE 3.2. *Percentage of languages of each type with explicit dependent (case) marking (Siewierska and Bakker 1996)*

V-initial	V-medial	V-final
42	30	64

Furthermore, the PH posits that a positive value for the Polysynthesis Parameter automatically suggests adjective neutralization, that is, adjectives belonging to the class of nouns or verbs, rather than forming a category of their own. But it is far from being the case that adjective neutralization is limited to polysynthetic languages. According to Dixon (1977), in Chinese, Thai, and in many Austronesian languages, adjectives belong to the class of verbs, while in Arabic, Tagalog, and in many Dravidian and Bantu languages, adjectives belong to the class of nouns. Again, there is no place for such languages in the PH.

Moving further down the hierarchy, one finds more curious features. The Ergative Case Parameter applies only to head-final languages and indeed the great majority of languages with ergative case are head-final. The problem is that agreement morphology can also be ergative (as Baker himself notes, p. 181). However, such languages tend to be either verb-initial (as in Chamorro and Sahaptin) or verb-final (as in Abkhaz and Canela-Kraho) (see Nichols 1992). Since the parameters that determine verb-finality and verb-initiality could not be farther apart on the PH, it is far from clear how the two subcases of ergative agreement marking could be treated in a unified fashion and how both could be unified parameter-wise with ergative case marking (should that be desirable). To cite a different example, the Serial Verb Parameter is placed to allow only SVO languages to manifest this phenomenon, even though Schiller (1990) gives examples of SOV and VOS languages with serial verbs. In fact, Crowley (2002: xi) has offered the opinion that 'OV [is the] order of most serializing languages.' And only a subset of SVO languages are permitted to have a positive value for the Null Subject Parameter, even though null subject languages can be SOV (Turkish) and VSO (Irish).

The PH represents an attempt to revive the 'holistic typologies' that dominated the field in the nineteenth and early twentieth centuries. The idea was to divide the languages of the world into a small number of basic 'types' (in the nineteenth century 'agglutinating,' 'isolating,' etc.), from which other typological properties were predicted to follow automatically. Most typologists have abandoned holistic approaches, simply because they do not work. Most seriously, typological properties tend to cross-classify with each other, rather than being organized hierarchically. It is clearly the case that not all problems with the PH are 'structural' in the sense that the very architecture of the hierarchy prevents an adequate statement of the relevant generalization. Indeed, Baker is to be commended for pushing the UG-parametric approach as far as he has—and certainly much farther than anyone else has done. One would naturally expect empirical problems in a pioneering work of this sort. But the bulk of problems are crucially structural. No hierarchy of the general form of the PH is capable of representing the parametric choices that the child is hypothesized to make. Needless to say, from that fact we have no right to conclude that *no* parametric approach of any sort can succeed. But the burden, I feel, is on those who have an alternative that equals Baker's PH in detail and coverage, while at the same time providing an empirically more adequate model.

3.2.2.5 Clustering

From one parameter setting is it possible to derive diverse, seemingly unrelated, properties that hold across many unrelated languages? This subsection is devoted to arguing that there is little reason to think so. I begin by pointing out that clustering within individual languages can be handled by a rule-based model as elegantly as by a parametric model. Moreover, the clustering predicted to follow from the Null Subject Parameter simply does not exist and there is little reason to believe that certain differences between English and French that have been based on a single difference in parameter setting generalize beyond those languages. Indeed, there is not that much robust clustering in general. I go on to discuss some consequences of the Lexical Parameterization Hypothesis and the typological predictions of Kayne's antisymmetric program. The final section is a summary.

'Clustering' in a single language To begin, many studies that point to parameters and clustering give evidence from only a *single* language, or a few very closely related languages or dialects. For example, Roberts (1993b) argues that a single parametric change in the history of French triggered loss of simple inversion in questioning, the loss of V2 order, and the change of French from null subjecthood to obligatory subject status. But he provides no evidence that the properties attributed to this parameter are linked cross-linguistically. Likewise, the centerpiece of Lightfoot (1991) is the claim that a wide-ranging clustering of properties resulted from six new parameter settings in the history of English. But again, the prediction that particular parameter settings have particular clustering effects is not tested with respect to other languages.

In fact, rule-based models, even those found in the earliest approaches to generative grammar, are also able to handle clustering effects within a single language. Consider the following phrase structure and transformational rules proposed in Chomsky (1957):[5]

(20) a. AUX → TNS (M) (*have* + *en*) (*be* + *ing*)
b. affixal element + verbal element → verbal element + affixal element

[5] I have changed some of the category labels for clarity of exposition.

From these simple rules, a host of seemingly unrelated properties follows: the fact that on the surface the perfect and progressive in English are overlapping and discontinuous, the impossibility of double modals, the site for the insertion of supportive *do*, some of the peculiarities of contraction, and more. Nothing can be concluded from (20) about the clustering of those properties in any other language, but, of course, no claims have ever been made to that effect.

The Null Subject Parameter The very few claims of parametric clustering across a wide variety of languages have not been borne out. Consider the best-studied parameter in the P&P approach—the Null Subject Parameter.[6] Perhaps the first concerted goal of early GB was to arrive at the crucial parametric difference between null subject languages like Spanish and Italian on the one hand and non-null subject languages like English and French on the other. Indeed, Chomsky proposed no fewer than three versions of the parameter in the first two years of GB. His first solution, proposed in Chomsky (1981), was to suggest that in null subject languages, the empty subject is a base-generated empty category. The Null Subject Parameter is that in such languages, AGR acts as a proper governor:

(21)

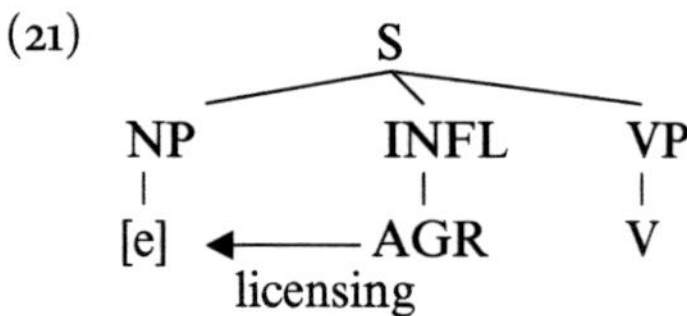

Later in the same book he revised his analysis, suggesting that the empty subject is PRO. What distinguishes null subject languages is the possibility of affix-movement taking place in the syntax, leaving the subject ungoverned (and thereby licensing the PRO):

(22)

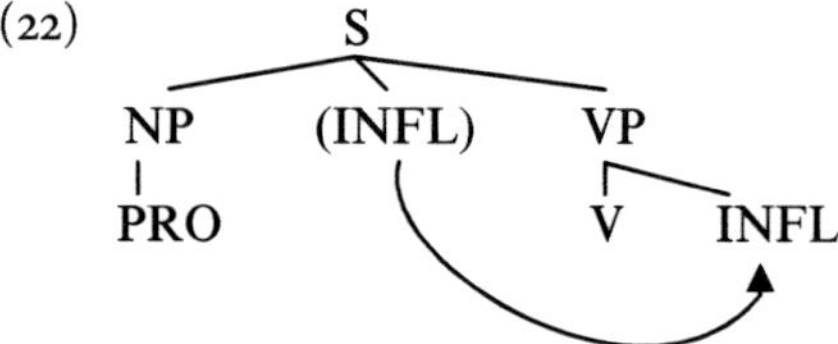

His third version of the parameter was proposed in Chomsky (1982b). Null subjects are now analyzed as being 'pro,' that is, an empty 'ordinary' pronoun. The presence of pro is licensed by a sufficiently rich inflection on AGR:

(23)

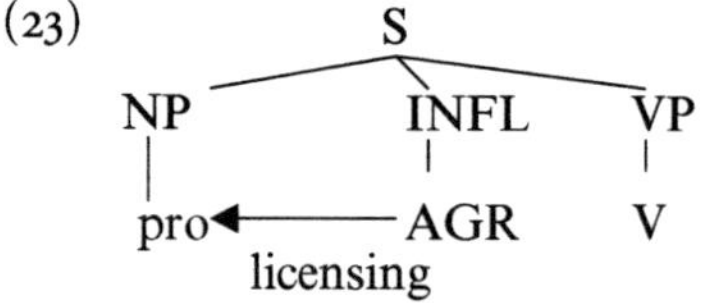

[6] The following discussion draws to a large degree on the overviews in Gilligan (1987) and Jaeggli and Safir (1989).

Chomsky's third proposal comes closest to capturing the traditional functionalist idea that subjects are optional if the auxiliary is rich enough to encode the person and number of the subject.

One evident problem for typology inherent in all three of Chomsky's proposals is that they underpredict the class of possible languages in terms of null-subject-related phenomena. In particular, they predict that if a language has null-thematic subjects it should have null non-thematic subjects, and vice versa. But as Rizzi (1982) pointed out (citing unpublished work by Paola Benincà), the Italian dialect spoken in Padua has the latter, but not the former:

(24) a. Piove 'Rains'
b. Vien Giorgio 'Comes Giorgio'
c. *Vien 'Comes'
d. El vien 'He comes'

In Rizzi's account, as in Chomsky's third account, INFL in null subject languages is [+pronominal], and in that way acts like a clitic in its ability to license an empty category. Contrary to appearances, Italian does have a *that*-trace effect, but its existence is masked by the fact that there can be extraction of a subject from a postverbal position:

(25)

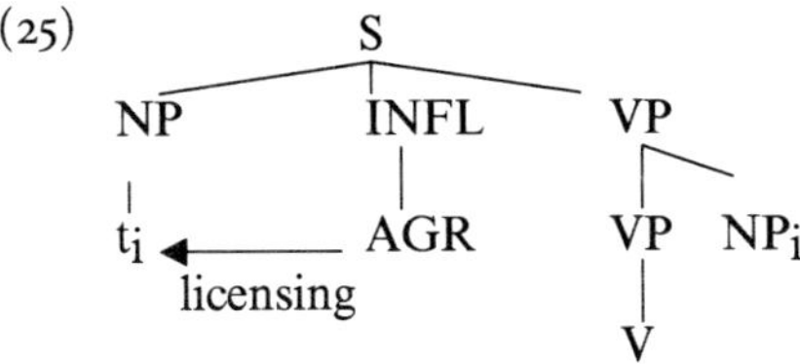

For our (typological) purposes, Rizzi's innovation was to allow pronominal INFL to be ± referential. A referential INFL licenses null thematic subjects, whereas a non-referential INFL (as in Paduan) does not do so. Hence Rizzi predicts the following possible clustering of features:[7]

(26)

NULL TS	NULL NTS	SI	THAT-T
yes	yes	yes	yes
no	yes	yes	yes
no	no	no	no

But still other language types exist, or at least appear to. In particular, we find languages such as Brazilian Portuguese (Chao 1981) and Chinese (Huang 1982, 1984) that have null subjects, but not subject inversion. Taking such language types into account, Safir (1985) broke the Null Subject Parameter into three parts,

[7] In this and in the following examples, the following abbreviations are used: NULL TS = Null thematic subjects; NULL NTS = Null non-thematic subjects; SI = subject inversion; THAT-T = the possibility of *that*-trace filter violations.

dissociating null non-thematic subjects, null thematic subjects, and subject inversion, thereby predicting a wider set of languages than did Rizzi, namely the following:

(27)

NULL TS	NULL NTS	SI	THAT-T
yes	yes	yes	yes
yes	yes	no	no
no	yes	yes	yes
no	no	yes	yes
no	no	no	no

Rizzi's and Safir's predictions were put to the test by Gilligan (1987), who worked with a sample of 100 languages, which he attempted to correct for areal and genetic bias.[8] Gilligan devotes many pages of discussion of the problems involved in determining whether a language manifests one of the four properties or not. His final determination was often based on the results of then-current generative analyses, rather than on mere surface facts about the language in question. For example, he excluded Chinese, Thai, Indonesian, Burmese, and other languages that lack agreement morphology from the ranks of those permitting null thematic subjects on the basis of the analysis of Chinese in Huang (1984), which takes the empty subject in that language to be a null topic, rather than a pro. Gilligan found the following correlations of properties in his sample (languages for which there was not sufficient data are excluded):

(28)

	yes–yes	yes–no	no–yes	no–no
NULL TS - NULL NTS	24	0	15	2
NULL TS - SI	22	49	11	15
NULL TS - THAT-T	5	3	2	1
NULL NTS - SI	14	25	1	1
NULL NTS - THAT-T	7	2	0	1
SI - THAT-T	4	0	3	4

According to Gilligan, the data in (28) reveal that the only robust correlations among the four features are the following:

(29) a. NULL TS → NULL NTS
b. SI → NULL NTS
c. SI → THAT-T
d. THAT-T → NULL NTS

These results are not very heartening for either Rizzi's theory or for Safir's, nor, indeed, for any which sees in null subject phenomena a rich clustering of properties. In three of the four correlations, null non-thematic subjects are

[8] The most extensive published discussion of Gilligan's work that I am aware of is found in Croft (2003: 80–4).

entailed, but that is obviously a simple consequence of the virtual non-existence of languages that manifest *overt* non-thematic subjects. Even worse, five language types are attested whose existence neither theory predicts.

Jaeggli and Safir (1989), which was published after Gilligan's study, returned to the question of null subjects and rich agreement. Spanish provides the best example of the correlation between the two:

(30) habl-o 1S (Spanish)
habl-as 2S
habl-a 3S
habl-amos 1PL
habl-áis 2PL
habl-an 3PL

German has no null thematic subjects, though it has null expletive subjects:

(31) Es ist möglich, dass — getanzt wurde
It is possible that — danced was
'It is possible that there was dancing'

German is inflected for person, number, and tense, so on that basis one might predict that it should be (fully) null subject:

(32) (ich) arbeit-e 1S
(du) arbeit-est 2S
(er/sie) arbeit-et 3S
(wir) arbeit-en 1PL
(ihr) arbeit-et 2PL
(sie) arbeit-en 3PL

Jaeggli and Safir noted that some forms in the German inflectional paradigm are identical and suggested tentatively that for that reason German is not fully null subject. But they go on to point to Irish (McCloskey and Hale 1984), which has synthetic forms inflected for tense, person, and number (33a) and analytic forms inflected only for tense (33b). Null subjects are licensed in the synthetic paradigm, even though some forms are identical:

(33)

	a. 'would put'	b. 'put'
1S	chuirf-inn	cuir-im
2S	chuirf-ea	cuir-eann
3S	chuirf-eadh	cuir-eann
1PL	chuirf-imis	cuir-eann
2PL	chuirf-eadh	cuir-eann
3PL	chuirf-eadh	cuir-eann

On the other hand, Japanese and Chinese have no number-person inflection, yet are null subject. In other words, no theory of null subjects can be based directly on the richness of inflectional morphology (a conclusion also reached in Chung 1984 and Webelhuth 1992). Jaeggli and Safir (1989) conclude with the suggestion that null subjects are permitted exclusively in languages with morphologically uniform inflectional paradigms, that is, in all languages in which all forms in the paradigm are complex, or none are (see also Jaeggli and Hyams 1987). So we have:

(34) a. No complex forms: Chinese, Japanese
b. All complex forms: Spanish, Italian, Irish, German
c. Some complex forms: English (*talk*, but *talk-s*); French (*parl*, but *parl-õ*)

Jaeggli and Safir go on to provide an account of the fact that German (and Icelandic) are null subject with expletives, not with thematic subjects.

Jaeggli and Safir's proposal has been seemingly refuted by the facts obtaining in Old French (Roberts 1993b), Swedish and Russian (Speas 1994), Brazilian Portuguese (Rohrbacher 1994), and the Häme dialect of Colloquial Finnish (Vainikka 1989). Roberts (1993b), Speas (1994; 2000), and Vainikka and Levy (1999) propose more empirically adequate approaches than Jaeggli and Safir's, though at the same time ones involving many more abstract mechanisms (and therefore difficult to evaluate without at the same time making a host of controversial subsidiary assumptions). For example, Speas (1994) bases her analysis on whether Spec, AgrP is required to satisfy any grammatical conditions: in Italian-type languages, the AGR head contains phonetic material, so the specifier is not called upon to fulfill conditions, while Chinese-type languages have no AGR at all. Hence these two language types are null subject. English-type languages cannot omit subjects, since no agreement morpheme is base-generated in AGR. Somewhat similarly, Vainikka and Levy posit that UG allows for a particular agreement-related feature bundle to occupy either the AGR position or the subject position. If the features occupy subject position, the language is null subject; otherwise not.

It is very difficult for me to imagine how the child could ever come to set this particular parameter, given any of the proposals discussed in the above paragraphs. Presumably it would have to have its inflectional morphology fully in place before it could decide whether it was safe to omit subjects or not. That order of development seems to me to be quite implausible. Significantly for our interests, Jaeggli and Safir and the subsequent work mentioned above all but omit discussion of the rich constellation of syntactic properties, whose unification under the aegis of a single parameter only a few years earlier had been heralded as the great success of the parametric approach to typology. As stressed in Haider (1994), the Null Subject Parameter is no more.

Some differences between English and French To take another example of a failed prediction of clustering within the envelope of parametric theory, Kayne (1984) links parametrically the following four properties of French, all of which differ from their English counterparts:

(35) a. The assigning of oblique case by prepositions (as opposed to objective case) (*avec lui/*le*)
b. The impossibility of P-stranding (**Qui as-tu parlé à?*)
c. The impossibility of Exceptional Case Marking (**Je crois Jean être sage*)
d. The impossibility of Dative Shift (**J'ai donné Marie un livre*)

But Kayne's parameter appears to make incorrect predictions cross-linguistically. For example, according to Derek Bickerton (personal communication) many English-based creoles lack stranding (36a-b illustrate with data from Sranan):

(36) a.

nanga	san	u	koti	a	brede?
with	what	you	cut	the	bread

b.

*san	u	koti	a	brede	nanga?
what	you	cut	the	bread	with

Yet, in such creoles there is no evidence for distinguishing objective from oblique case. Also, such an account does not distinguish elegantly Icelandic, a case-rich stranding language, from German and some Slavic languages, also case-rich, but non-stranding. Chinese and Indonesian have Dative Shift, but no stranding, while Prince Edward Island French has stranding but no Exceptional Case Marking. Also, there is experimental work by Karin Stromswold (1988, 1989) that shows that acquisitional data do not bear out the idea that one parameter is implicated in these processes.

Now, one must be clear that the facts discussed in this and in the previous subsection do not in and of themselves 'logically' refute either Rizzi or Safir on the one hand or Kayne on the other. It is possible that the cases of non-predicted subject inversion, for example, are the result of something other than the Null Subject Parameter. As Gilligan himself points out: 'Perhaps the Rizzi hypothesis is correct but its effects are obscured in [Brazilian Portuguese and Mandarin—two languages with a cluster of properties predicted not to exist] because of some as yet unanalyzed aspect of these languages' (1987: 90). Or, perhaps we have a sampling problem, which, if corrected, would bear out Rizzi or Safir. Or perhaps, as suggested in Pica (2001), the Null Subject Parameter itself is an epiphenomenon, whose effects are to be attributed to the interaction of other parameters. Nevertheless, the fact that even the most extensively investigated generative parameters appear to lack typological support makes one wonder what the status would be of the myriad of others, were they put to a similar test.

On the robustness of clustering in general An interesting question is how robust the cross-linguistic clustering of any set of particular morphosyntactic features is *in general*. The most thoroughly investigated set of typological features are the Greenbergian correlations, relating basic order of subject, verb, and object to other morphosyntactic properties. Table 3.3, gleaned from Dryer (1991), presents the correlates of verb finality, SVO order, and verb initiality for thirteen properties.

Table 3.3. *Percentage of V-final, SVO, and V-initial languages manifesting particular properties (Dryer 1991)*

Property	V-final	SVO	V-initial
Postpositional	96	14	9
Relative-Noun	43	1	0
Standard of comparison-Adjective	82	2	0
Predicate-Copula	85	26	39
Subordinate clause-Subordinator	70	6	6
Noun-Plural word	100	24	13
Adpositional phrase-Verb	90	1	0
Manner Adverb-Verb	91	25	17
Verb-Tense/Aspect aux verb	94	21	13
Verb-Negative auxiliary	88	13	0
Genitive-Noun	89	59	28
Sentence-Question particle	73	30	13
Wh-in situ	71	42	16

What we observe is that SVO languages are in general intermediate in their properties between those in which the verb is on the right margin or on the left margin. But the extent to which they are intermediate differs significantly for each property. A simple 'Head Parameter' would therefore make crashingly incorrect predictions, among other things attributing to a majority of V-final languages the incorrect ordering of relative and noun and failing to explain why V-initial languages are more likely than SVO languages to manifest predicate-copula order. Needless to say, one cannot rule out *a priori* the possibility that there exists a complex set of abstract parameters from which the percentages in Table 3.3 can be derived. However, I would say that skepticism is in order here and that the radically different percentages suggest that the different properties in the table are best handled by distinct rules.

As pointed out in Pintzuk, Tsoulas, and Warner (2000: 7), the MP notion that parameters are expressed as features on functional entities within the lexicon entails that 'the grammatical coverage of a single parameter is therefore constrained and may be less wide-ranging in nature.' These authors suggest that it is 'not yet clear' whether the reduction in the scope of the notion 'parametric difference' will impede the effort to apply parameter theory to capturing clusters of surface differences. It seems to me, on the other hand, that it is completely clear that this aspect of the MP makes it all but impossible to predict any significant degree of clustering. The evident *lack* of clustering, then, might be taken as an argument in favor of the MP (over GB), though at the same time it leads inevitably to scaling back the arguments for a parameter-based approach over a rule-based approach.

Some consequences of the Lexical Parameterization Hypothesis Not only have there been few examples of demonstrable cross-linguistic clustering resulting from a particular abstract parameter setting, but, as noted in the previous chapter, it has become increasingly clear that one must abandon the idea that the notion 'setting for a particular parameter' holds for individual languages. The original vision of parameters was an extremely attractive one, in that the set of their settings was conceived of as a checklist for a language as a whole. But the Lexical Parameterization Hypothesis (LPH), the idea that values of a parameter are associated not with particular grammars, but with particular lexical items (see Chapter 2, §2.3.8), has put an end to this vision. The great promise of parametric theory was its seeming ability to provide a generative approach to language typology, that is, its being able to characterize the difference from one language to the next by means of differences in parameter settings. The LPH (no matter how well motivated it might be) dashes all hope that this promise might be fulfilled. As Safir has observed:

> If lexical entries within a language L can have different parameter values for different lexical items in L, then parametric theory does not compare L and another language L', but rather the lexical items of L' are compared with lexical items of L. To put it another way, it is not so meaningful to talk about a language typology so much as a cross-linguistic lexical typology. (Safir 1987: 80)

Puzzlingly from my point of view, the relocation of the site of parametric variation from grammars of entire languages to functional heads is often portrayed as a major step forward. For example, Pica (2001: vi) writes that this move 'allows a radical simplification of the nature and design of UG yielding a model where the notion of "level" is largely reduced to S-structure whose semantics and phonological properties are built derivationally.' But the price paid for this 'radical simplification' is both an explosion in the number of functional categories needed to be posited within UG and, more seriously, the transfer of the burden for accounting for language-particular differences from properties of UG per se to idiosyncratic properties of lexical entries in particular languages.[9] In earlier versions of P&P syntax (and in current versions such as that of Baker 2001), a given language L was posited to have a particular setting for the Head Directionality Parameter, the Serial Verb Parameter, and so on. But now, in principle, individual lexical items in L must be specified as to how they relate to head directionality, serial verbs, and so on.[10] I certainly agree that 'twenty years of intensive descriptive and theoretical research has shown [that] metaparameters

[9] It should be noted in passing that in no framework ever proposed by Chomsky has the lexicon been as important as it is in the MP. Yet in no framework proposed by Chomsky have the properties of the lexicon been as poorly investigated.

[10] One is reminded of early versions of transformational grammar (e. g. Lakoff 1965/1970), in which each verb was marked for which transformations it 'governed.'

do not exist' (Pica 2001: v–vi). But we must regard that conclusion as a cause for disappointment, not rejoicing.[11]

The idea of parameter settings being properties of grammars of entire languages is further challenged by the fact that a putative language-wide parameter might have to be set differently for different structures in the same language. Consider, for example, the distinction between strong and weak islands (Szabolcsi and den Dikken 1999). English is practically as permissive as Italian with respect to extraction when the extracted *wh*-element is a direct object, especially if the lowest clause is non-finite (37a-d) and Grimshaw (1986) has called attention to a dialect of English where the facts seem to be identical to those which led Rizzi to propose S' as a bounding node for Italian (38a-d):

(37) a. This is the car that I don't know how to fix.
b. ?This is the car that I don't know when they fixed.
c. *Tell me how you wonder which car they fixed.
d. *Tell me how you wonder which car to fix.

(38) a. Which book did the students forget who wrote?
b. Which book did the TAs tell the students that they shouldn't forget who wrote?
c. *Which book did the student forget who told them that Dorothy Sayers wrote?
d. *Which book did the students forget who asked/told them who wrote?

It is by no means clear how to handle examples like (37) and (38) in any approach, though they seem to provide fairly conclusive evidence against a macroparameter like Subjacency. Indeed, that is now Rizzi's opinion as well (see also Rizzi 2004):

> The S/S' case is of some historical significance, as it was the first concrete instance of language variation treated in terms of the parametric approach.... But seen in retrospect, this case looks quite atypical.... First, no other major property seems to be clearly related to the extractability from *wh*-islands... so one does not find the clustering of properties... Second, judgments vary considerably among speakers... Third, unlike the major familiar cases of parameters, this one does not seem to be reducible to a property of a head. (Rizzi 1989: 355)

Along the same lines, there can be no macroparameter for serialization. The parameters proposed by Baker and Collins (see Chapter 2, §2.4.1) imply that a language should be fully serializing or fully non-serializing. But as pointed out by Larson (1991), every serializing language also has non-serial constructions. And even English, a non-serializing language par excellence, has constructions like

[11] Snyder's (2001) study of the cross-linguistic correlation of endocentric compounds and resultatives (see Ch. 2, §2.3.4) was explicitly offered, however, as a *refutation* of the idea that parameters are lexically based and 'micro' in nature. I know of no studies testing the predictions of his Compounding Parameter on a wider variety of languages than those discussed in his article.

(39a-b) with many of the properties of serial verbs (for discussion, see Shopen 1971 and Pullum 1990):

(39) a. Come help me.
  b. Are you going to go get the wrench?

Again, the conclusion that we have to abandon macroparameters like the one for Subjacency and the serial verb construction is regrettable, rather than laudable.[12] Be that as it may, however, their abandonment effectively negates the argument against the positing of language-particular rules. I see no empirical difference between the statement 'In language L some head H has the parametric property of licensing functional category F (with feature content F')' and the statement 'Language L has a rule R specifying the existence of functional category F (with feature content F').'

On the typological predictions of Kayne's antisymmetric program The centerpiece of the antisymmetric program of Kayne (1994)—the hypothesis from which many others are derivative—is that all languages are underlyingly Specifier-Head-Complement (see Chapter 2, §2.4.2). Interpreted as a typological prediction about observed ordering in the world's languages, it is empirically deficient. Counting languages, VO and OV are equally common (Greenberg 1963; Hawkins 1983; Tomlin 1986; Nichols 1992). However, counting 'genera' (subfamilies of roughly equal time depth),[13] OV order is significantly more widespread than VO order. Dryer (1989b) has determined that in 111 genera (or 58 per cent of the total), OV order predominates (see Table 3.4).

So whether one counts languages or genera, there is no support for the idea that cross-linguistically there is a tendency for heads to precede complements. Consider some other findings from Dryer (1992). It turns out that in 119 genera out of 196, postpositionality predominates; in 76 out of 127, the predicate precedes the copula; and in 78 out of 128 the adverb precedes the verb. All of these facts challenge the antisymmetric program, to the extent that it entails the

TABLE 3.4. *Breakdown of genera in terms of basic word order, by area (Dryer 1989b)*

	Afr	Eura	A-NG	NAm	SAm	Total
SOV	22	26	19	26	18	111
SVO	21	19	6	6	5	57
VSO	5	3	0	12	2	22

[12] Rizzi (2004: 332), while acknowledging the problems inherent in a macroparametric approach to bounding, has remarked that the distinction between macro- and microparameters bears no theoretical import and has offered the opinion that there is 'no sound basis' for rejecting the idea that 'a single parameter may be responsible for a complex cluster of properties.'

[13] Counting genera instead of languages insures that families with large numbers of languages will not be overcounted, nor families with small numbers of languages undercounted.

idea that there is a robust tendency for heads to precede complements. It remains to be seen whether the bulk of the typological predictions that fall out from the antisymmetric hypothesis can stand the test of time.

Summary In summary, the phenomena discussed in the above subsections suggest that the original vision of (macro)parameters was overly ambitious. A parametric theory would receive enormous support if unexpected correlations of properties followed from the positing of an abstract parameter. In such a situation, parameters would differ fundamentally from language-particular rules. Unfortunately, however, two decades of intensive research has failed to reveal the existence of the hoped-for correlations.[14] Given the LPH on the other hand, parameter settings seem to differ little in their degree of generality from language-particular rules. Arguments against a model incorporating (2b)—one in which language-particular rules are central—lose their force when one focuses on microvariation in the properties of functional heads.

3.2.2.6 Innateness/Universality

It is important to stress that a rejection of parametric theory does not in and of itself entail a rejection of innate UG principles per se. The poverty of the stimulus-based arguments for the innateness of one or another constraint still need to be evaluated on their own merits. Let us take the extraction of *wh*-elements, for example, and, for purposes of argument, hypothesize that typological differences among languages are characterized in terms of clearly defined macroparameters. Now how might UG play a role in explaining how languages may differ in their bounding possibilities? As we have seen, GB assumed that UG provides the set of possible bounding nodes (i.e. S and NP; S' and NP; S, S', and NP; and so on), each set corresponding to a parametric choice that the child makes based on positive evidence. Later work has pointed to the specifier system of CP and IP as the crucial factor in determining how bounding works cross-linguistically. But the assumption that the set of possible bounding nodes or the set of the possible number of specifiers of CP and IP is provided in advance by an innate UG seems entirely gratuitous. If, as we have hypothesized, children know innately that general conditions on extraction exist and, as surely must be the case, positive evidence is available to pin down the specific conditions for any particular language, what reason have we for the additional assumption that UG preselects the set of possible bounding nodes or the number of possible specifier positions? I have never seen a poverty of the stimulus-based argument for such an assumption and doubt that one can be constructed.

[14] Analogously, the hypothesized subset relationship among binding domains (Manzini and Wexler 1987) referred to above in §3.2.2.2 is apparently spurious (Bondre 1993). There is no hope for interpreting binding domains in terms of a complex parameter, whereby it would follow that the conditions for long-distance domains are fulfilled automatically if the conditions for smaller domains are fulfilled.

In other words, replacing parameter settings by rules has no effect one way or the other on the innateness of grammatical principles.

3.2.2.7 Learnability

Most work in the generative tradition takes as a starting assumption the idea that first language acquisition is shaped by UG, an idea that I feel is amply supported by empirical evidence. However, most work goes on to make the additional assumption that the principal mechanism by which UG-shaped acquisition takes place is parameter setting. That is, it takes parameters as a given and raises questions such as: 'Do parameters have default values?', 'Can parameters be reset in the course of acquisition?', and so on. Yet a number of factors suggest that a parameter-setting strategy for first language acquisition is far from the simple task that it is portrayed in much of the literature.

Several of the problems for parameters result from the fact that what the child hears are sentences (or, more correctly, utterances), rather than structures. But any given utterance is likely massively to underdetermine the particular structural property that the child needs to set some particular parameter. The greater the number of parameters to be set, the greater the problem, particularly given that few of the parameter settings appear to have unambiguous triggers. How might a child come to know, for example, in which of the thirty-two IP projections some particular adverb might find its proper place? Citing Clark (1994), Janet Fodor points out that there is an 'exponential explosion from the parameters to the number of learning steps to set them... If so, the learner might just as well check out each grammar, one by one, against the input; nothing has been gained by the parameterization.... [to] set one parameter could cost the learner thousands or millions of input sentences' (Fodor 2001b: 736). What makes the problem even more serious is the fact that children are obviously not born with the ability to recognize triggers for any one particular language. English-speaking, Chinese-speaking, and Japanese-speaking children all need to arrive at a negative setting for the Ergativity Parameter, given its existence, but it is by no means obvious what feature common to the three languages would lead the very young child to arrive at that particular setting.

In other words, the fundamental problem is that parameter setting presupposes some non-negligible degree of prior structural assignment. To illustrate the problem, Hyams (1986) speculates that a child sets the Null Subject Parameter with a negative value when it hears an expletive. But how can the child know what an 'expletive' is without already having a syntax in place? 'Expletive' is not an *a priori* construct available to the newborn, but is interpreted only with respect to an already existing grammar. But if the grammar is already in place, then why do we need parameters at all?[15]

[15] For similar arguments, see Nishigauchi and Roeper (1987); Haider (1993); Valian (1990); and Mazuka (1996).

Given the hypothesis that parameters are complemented by rules in the marked periphery, the learner's task is not simplified by the positing of parameters. As pointed out by Foley and Van Valin (1984: 20), it is made more complicated. Since learners have to acquire rules anyway, they have a double burden: acquiring both rules and parameter settings and figuring out which phenomena are handled by which. And one would assume (along with Culicover 1999: 16) that any learning mechanism sophisticated enough to acquire the 'hard stuff' in the periphery would have no trouble acquiring the 'easy stuff' at the core, thereby rendering the notion 'parameter' superfluous.

Along the same lines, there is no evidence that 'peripheral' knowledge is stored and/or used any differently from that provided by the system of principles and parameters per se. When head-directionality or V2-ness are at stake, do German speakers perform more slowly in reaction time experiments than do speakers of head-consistent non-V2 languages? Do they make more mistakes in everyday speech, say by substituting unmarked constructions for marked ones? Do the marked forms pose comprehension difficulties? In fact, is there any evidence whatsoever that such knowledge is dissociable in some way from more 'core' knowledge? As far as I am aware, the answers to all of these questions are 'no.' As Janet Fodor has stressed: 'The idea that there are two sharply different syntax learning mechanisms at work receives no clear support that I know of from theoretical, psychological, or neurological studies of language' (Fodor 2001a: 371).

Finally, there is little credence to the idea that there is a robust correlation between the order of acquisition of some feature and its typological status, a fact which casts into doubt the idea that parameters are organized in an implicational hierarchy. Some late-acquired features are indeed typologically relatively rare, as appears to be the case for the verb raising that derives VSO order from SVO order (see Guilfoyle 1990 for Irish; Radford 1994 for Welsh; Ouhalla 1991b for Arabic). But other grammatical features appear to be acquired relatively late, without being typologically rare (see Eisenbeiss 1994 on scrambling in German).

In general, however, children acquire the relevant structures of their language quite early, regardless of how common that structure is cross-linguistically. Hence English-speaking children acquire P-stranding before pied-piping (Karin Stromswold, personal communication). French-speaking children have verb raising from the earliest multiword utterances (Déprez and Pierce 1993; Pierce 1992; Meisel and Müller 1992; Verrips and Weissenborn 1992). English-speaking children never manifest verb raising (Stromswold 1990; Harris and Wexler 1996). There is no period during which the grammars of German-speaking children lack V2 (Meisel 1990; Clahsen and Penke 1992; Verrips and Weissenborn 1992; Meisel and Müller 1992; Poeppel and Wexler 1993). Furthermore, children figure out very early whether their language is null subject or not (Valian 1991) and children acquiring English, German, and French evidence strong knowledge of locality in *wh*-extraction domains at early ages (Roeper and De Villiers 1994).[16]

From all of the above we conclude that a parameter-setting model provides no more insight into the process of language acquisition than a rule-based model.

3.2.2.8 Parametric change

Does parametric change tend to progress from marked to unmarked settings, as is implied in Roberts (1999)? In the strongest interpretation of such a position, one would be forced to posit an overall directionality to language change. There have certainly been proposals in the literature to that effect. Charles Li has remarked that, 'with the exception of the Chinese case which has developed certain verb-final constructions while the language is still SVO, . . . the only documented types of word order changes that are not due to language contact are SOV to (VSO) to SVO' (Li 1977: xii–xiii). A dozen different scholars for a dozen different reasons have suggested that verb-final languages are more likely to develop into verb-medial languages than vice versa, possibly suggesting a progressive decline in the overall percentage of verb-final languages (see, for example, Vennemann 1973; Givón 1979; Beaken 1996; Aske 1998; Newmeyer 2000a; Bichakjian 2002). However, such conclusions seem premature. Harris (2000) argues that the shift in Georgian from VO to OV order was not due, as might be supposed, to contact with OV Turkish. In any event, Georgian has probably been even more influenced by VO Greek. And Claudi (1994) not only argues that the Mande languages have developed OV order, but provides an (internal) functional explanation on how and why this change took place.

Nor does there appear to be any overall drift towards analytic structure. Hodge (1970) notes that in its 5000-year recorded history, Egyptian has cycled from synthetic to analytic and back again to synthetic in its evolution to modern Coptic. Similar cyclic changes have been observed or reconstructed on a smaller scale in Tibeto-Burman languages (DeLancey 1985) and Paamese (Crowley 1982). And despite the assertion in Bichakjian (2002) that ergative languages represent a less evolved stage of development than nominative–accusative languages, shifts from the latter to the former are about as common as shifts from the former to the latter (for discussion of the mechanisms by which ergative languages arise, see Anderson 1977; Crowley 1994: 140–3; and Dixon 1994: 187–8).

In other words, one would assume that if parametric change were directional, there would have to be counterbalancing non-parametric change to keep the balance of typological features in stasis (assuming that stasis is indeed the case).[17]

[16] On the other hand, a number of language acquisition researchers continue to provide evidence for the idea, first articulated in Borer and Wexler (1987), that principles of grammar 'mature' with age (see, for example, Babyonyshev, Ganger, Pesetsky, and Wexler 2001). For an interesting, albeit brief, overview of the issues involved, see Smith and Cormack (2002).

[17] Partisans of the idea that grammaticalization unidirectionally increases the grammatical content of an item while reducing its lexical content generally posit a cycling process creating new lexical

But the idea, implicit in Roberts (1999) and Roberts and Roussou (2002), that one would expect more languages to eliminate overt movements than to add them, simply cannot be correct. We know that at least *some* languages have developed VO order from OV order. Yet a standard observation about the typological differences between SVO and SOV languages is that the former tend to be far more permissive than the latter in allowing grammatical elements to occur displaced from their subcategorized position. Once again, Dryer (1991) has found that 71 per cent of verb-final languages are '*Wh-in situ*,' that is, they lack a rule of *Wh*-Movement, while only 42 per cent of SVO languages lack such a rule, and even fewer—16 per cent—of verb-initial languages are without *Wh*-Movement. Along the same lines, rules that move elements to argument position are far more difficult to motivate for rigid verb-final languages than for other types of languages (for discussion, see Müller-Gotama 1994). The best motivated A-movement for Japanese is Passive, but this rule in Japanese (as in other languages) morphologically marks its subcategorizationally displaced argument, and thereby betrays its original thematic role (see Miyagawa 1989 for discussion). Other NP movements might well be completely absent in that language. Indeed, it is by no means out of the question that rigid SOV languages have no overt (i.e. non-LF) instantiations of Move-α at all. Even the 'scrambling' of the subject, object, and verb into non-basic orders, which is common in SOV languages, is not necessarily the result of movement. A number of linguists have put forward arguments, quite strong ones in my opinion, that the repositioning that we find in scrambling lacks many of the hallmarks of a transformational rule (see Lee 1992; Bayer and Kornfilt 1994; Kiss 1994; Neeleman 1994).[18]

It also seems unlikely that one can compare parameter settings of related languages to reconstruct a 'proto-parameter setting,' as suggested in Roberts (1998). The problem, as pointed out in Lightfoot (2002), is that parameter settings do not 'correspond' in the way that cognates do. We can reconstruct *pater* as the ancestor of *père* and *padre* because the similarities of form and meaning that have been passed down for 2000 years allow us to conclude that in some relevant sense they are all the 'same' form. Nothing like that can be concluded from the fact that two languages, related or not, share the same value for, say, the Ergativity Parameter.

Turning to other claims that have been made about parameters and change, Lightfoot's six diagnostics distinguishing parametric change from rule-based change (Ch. 2, §2.6 and (8h) above) have not been found reliably to partition the class of attested diachronic developments (Harris and Campbell 1995: 37–45). But equally seriously from our perspective, his diagnostics are not easily reconciled

categories (Givón 1979). If there were not one, many full lexical items by now would have been grammaticalized out of existence (for discussion of the issues involved, see Newmeyer 1998b: ch. 5).

[18] In particular, the change in position of the 'scrambled' elements does not lead to changes in binding relations or negative polarity interpretation, as one would expect if scrambling were an instantiation of Move-α.

with claims that have been made by other generative-oriented historical linguists about language change. In particular, grammaticalization-related changes have been analyzed as falling squarely within the orbit of parametric theory (see especially Roberts 1993a; Roberts and Roussou 1999). Furthermore, some of the particular changes that Lightfoot attributes to parametric change seem incompatible with current views on the nature of parameters. For example, he cites as an instance of parametric change the reanalysis of a preposition with an adjacent verb, thereby creating a complex verb that can properly govern the trace of movement (and thereby licensing stranding of the preposition), as shown in (40a–b):

(40) a. You talked [$_{PP}$ to who] > You [$_V$ talked to] who > Who$_i$ did you [$_V$ talk to] e$_i$?
b. e was spoken [$_{PP}$ to Mary] > e was [$_V$ spoken to] Mary > Mary$_i$ was [$_V$ spoken to] e$_i$

It is not at all obvious how such a change could be located in some functional projection, as is required by most current approaches to parameters.

The MP conception that parameters are lexically based makes it harder to distinguish the two types of changes (and their typological implications) that have been at the center of Lightfoot's historical work. After all, grammaticalization-based changes, morphological changes, and so on are examples of lexical change par excellence. It is not clear that the MP provides enough in the way of theoretical machinery to characterize any clear-cut distinction (if indeed, such a distinction exists) between parametric and non-parametric change. Perhaps for this reason 'much recent work in historical syntax has moved away from a focus on abrupt parametric change toward an emphasis on synchronic syntactic variation and the implications of gradual syntactic change as they can be interpreted within the Principles-and-Parameters paradigm' (Pintzuk, Tsoulas, and Warner 2000: 10).

3.2.2.9 Summary

Despite the importance attributed to them in the past two decades of work in generative grammar, there is little reason to believe that parameterized principles play a role in the theory of UG.

3.3 The irrelevance of typology for grammatical theory

I confess to have chosen a deliberately provocative title for this section. While it conveys a conclusion that I will stand by and defend—the conclusion that typology *is* irrelevant for grammatical theory—it may have connotations that I feel obligated to disassociate myself from immediately. The first is the possible implication that there is no need for grammatical theorists to undertake the intensive investigation of as many languages as possible. Indeed, as Wunderlich (2004) has stressed, there is such a need, both for an appreciation of the range of processes that the languages of the world can manifest and for testing candidate universals that have been mooted on the examination of one or a small number of languages. After all, no investigation of a single language, no matter how thorough, could answer the question of whether overt *Wh*-Movement in general is subject to locality conditions if that language happens not to have overt *Wh*-Movement.

Second, I am not going to argue that typology lacks theoretical interest or importance. If a particular feature is manifested in 90 per cent of languages in a properly constructed sample, then that is a fact in need of explanation. If feature A is correlated with feature B significantly greater than chance would predict, then that too is a fact in need of explanation. But crucially, it does not follow that the explanation of such facts needs to reside within grammatical theory. That is, it might be wrong to derive the overwhelming preference for the feature that shows up in 90 per cent of all languages from a principle, or set of interacting principles, within generative grammar. And similarly, the implicational relationship between A and B could fall out from the interaction of the grammatical module with others involved in the totality of language, rather than from the internal structure of grammatical theory itself.

And indeed, that is precisely what I will argue. It will be my conclusion that grammars do not encode typological generalizations, either directly or indirectly. Let us take, for example, some robust generalization, such as verb-final order tending to be associated with postpositions, rather than prepositions. I will argue that there is nothing in the theory of UG in which this correlation is either stated directly or is derivable from its interacting principles. As a corollary to this claim, I will suggest that typological generalizations are not deducible from the inspection of the grammar of any individual language. Take Japanese, for example, which upholds the above-mentioned correlation and German, which violates it. The grammar of neither language encodes, directly or indirectly, the information that the former language is typologically consistent and the latter inconsistent. Likewise, there is no grammatical provision of the information that the state of affairs represented by Japanese is relatively common cross-linguistically and that represented by German relatively rare.

It follows then that a grammar's fidelity to typological generalizations can play no part in its *evaluation*. Let us imagine two otherwise identical candidate grammars of German that differ only in how directly the typological mixedness of that language is expressed. All other things being equal, there is no reason, I will claim, to value the grammar with the more direct characterization of this state of affairs over the one that represents it less directly.

In pursuing such a line of argumentation, I will, as we have seen, be going against quite the opposing trend in the community of generativist scholars. To be explicit, I will claim that the model should not be expected to explain why typological generalizations exist. In one pithy sentence, UG tells us what a *possible* human language is, but not what a *probable* human language is.

In §3.3.1, I note that the notions 'typologically significant generalization' and 'linguistically significant generalization' have generally been equated. The following three sections make the case that this equation is incorrect: Section 3.3.2 argues that some robust sets of typological correlations do not follow from anything intrinsic to theory; in §3.3.3 evidence is presented that the Greenbergian correlations hold better at surface, rather than at deep, levels of grammar; and §3.3.4 shows that for one well-studied phenomenon, the maximally 'simple' analysis makes the wrong typological predictions. The final section, §3.3.5, argues that typological generalizations could not possibly form part of I-language.

3.3.1 *Typologically and linguistically significant generalizations*

As any generative theoretician would freely acknowledge, typological distribution cannot serve *in and of itself* as a factor determining the principles of UG and the relative markedness of rules and principles provided by UG. Typological generalizations belong to the domain of E-language, that is, aspects of language 'understood independently of the properties of the mind/brain' (Chomsky 1986b: 20). Our minds/brains, after all, have no clue as to the typological status of any aspect of any element of our mental grammars. The relationship between typological generalizations and I-language is therefore necessarily quite indirect.

Nevertheless, there has been a guiding assumption that there is no significant gap between the notions '*typologically* significant generalization' and '*linguistically* significant generalization.' That is, generative grammarians have generally taken it for granted that if investigation of the grammatical properties of a reasonably large set of languages leads to the discovery of a pervasive and profound structural pattern in those languages, then there is probably something mentally 'preferable' about that pattern, and this mental preference should be reflected by UG being organized to 'favor' that pattern.

A case in point is the X-bar schema, proposed in Chomsky (1970) and given its greatest development in Jackendoff (1977). It soon became apparent that many of the generalizations expressed by X-bar theory (which was initially formulated on the basis of English data) were borne out typologically: languages tend to favor a consistent ordering of their heads and complements. And moreover, grammars violating X-bar principles (and the Head Parameter which developed out of them) did indeed seem to be more complicated than languages in which heads are all on the same side as their complements.

It has become fairly uncontroversial, then, to the great majority of generative grammarians that the following hypotheses linking typological generalizations to aspects of I-language are well motivated:

(41) a. UG is 'well designed' for the capturing of typological generalizations.
b. Typological generalizations hold better at more abstract levels of grammar than at surface levels.
c. Cross-linguistically frequent properties of language are reflected by correspondingly simple (unmarked) properties of grammars.

The following sections will challenge all three propositions in (41).

3.3.2 *Robust typological generalizations do not fall out from UG principles*

Let us return to a typological generalization discussed at some length in the previous chapter: the fact that verb-final languages are much less likely to exhibit *Wh*-Movement than VO languages, but much more likely to have sentence-final question particles. As noted, recent attempts to integrate this generalization into current theory involve the idea that head-final languages lack a Specifier for COMP (Fukui 1986); that the analogs of *wh*-elements in movementless languages are actually quantifiers (Kim 1990); that a language must choose one of two methods of 'typing' questions: a final question particle or overt movement (Cheng 1991/1997); and that a SPEC, CP occupied by a moved IP denies a moved *wh*-phrase a landing site (Kayne 1994).

The problem with all of these accounts, as far as explaining the typological generalizations in question are concerned, is that they are highly stipulative. Why should a set of languages that are typologically similar in respects that do not involve COMP lack a specifier for that category? Why should OV languages differ from VO languages in the distribution of their quantifiers? Why, given the clausal typing hypothesis, should final Q-particle/*wh-in-situ* languages be overwhelmingly OV and movement languages overwhelmingly VO? Furthermore, why do languages that have *Wh*-Movement for questions often have it for other processes (relatives, clefts, and so on), a fact that would seem not to follow at all from the clausal typing hypothesis? The accounts just mentioned thus take the correlations essentially as primitives of theory, rather than as consequences that fall out from independently motivated principles. Kayne's account does indeed derive the correlation between OV order and lack of *wh*-fronting from independent assumptions, but here another problem arises. Since all languages start out Specifier-Head-Complement for Kayne, the null hypothesis is that that ordering would predominate cross-linguistically. But that is not the case. As we have seen, once corrections are made for genetic and areal bias, Complement–Head ordering predominates in the languages of the world.

The MP has made the correlations even more difficult to explain non-stipulatively, as far as I can tell. Basic clause structure is assumed to be universal, with differences in surface order due to differences in the strength (or, now, interpretability) of particular features. But the problem is to explain why a weak *wh*-feature on C (preventing overt *wh*-fronting) would correlate with whatever feature or combination of features are responsible for surface SOV order. None comes to mind. The problem of the typological associates of *Wh*-Movement is particularly difficult to explain vis-à-vis surface VSO languages. As Table 3.3 shows, verb-initial languages are far more likely to have *Wh*-Movement than SVO languages. Why should this be? Since Emonds (1980), the predominant position has been that such languages 'start out' as verb-medial, but have a raising of the verb (for a recent account, see McCloskey 1996). Let us say, following the account presented in Marantz (1995: 372–3), that such movement is driven by strong V-features of T and/or AGR in the context of weak N-features for these functional heads. The question then is why this constellation of features would correlate *even more strongly* with strong *wh*-features on C (thereby guaranteeing overt *Wh*-Movement) than with the alternative feature strengths associated with T and AGR that 'preserve' SVO order. I cannot imagine how such a correlation might be derived, given any mechanisms accepted as intrinsic to generativist theory.

The correlation between *wh*-fronting and word order is at least imaginably captured by combinations of parameter settings. For other typological generalizations, there is no obvious way that parameters or any other device intrinsic to a UG-based approach might work. To illustrate, let us consider another cross-linguistic regularity, what Hawkins (1983) has called the 'Prepositional Noun Modifier Hierarchy':

(42) Prepositional Noun Modifier Hierarchy (PrNMH; Hawkins 1983)
If a language is prepositional, then if RelN then GenN, if GenN then AdjN, and if AdjN then DemN.

In short, if a language allows structurally complex categories to intervene between a preposition and its object, then it allows categories of less structural complexity. This hierarchy predicts the possibility of prepositional phrases with the structures depicted in (43) (along with an exemplifying language):

(43) a. $_{PP}$[P $_{NP}$[—N . . .] (Arabic, Thai)
b. $_{PP}$[P $_{NP}$[—N . . .];$_{PP}$[P $_{NP}$[Dem N . . .] (Masai, Spanish)
c. $_{PP}$[P $_{NP}$[—N . . .];$_{PP}$[P $_{NP}$[Dem N . . .];$_{PP}$[P $_{NP}$[Adj N . . .] (Greek, Maya)
d. $_{PP}$[P $_{NP}$[—N . . .];$_{PP}$[P $_{NP}$[Dem N . . .];$_{PP}$[P $_{NP}$[Adj N . . .];
$_{PP}$[P $_{NP}$[PossP N . . .] (Maung)
e. $_{PP}$[P $_{NP}$[—N . . .];$_{PP}$[P $_{NP}$[Dem N . . .];$_{PP}$[P $_{NP}$[Adj N . . .];
$_{PP}$[P $_{NP}$[PossP N . . .];$_{PP}$[P $_{NP}$[Rel N . . .] (Amharic)

However, no language allows, say, a relative clause to intercede between a preposition and its noun complement, but not an adjective.

One could, of course, simply incorporate hierarchy (42) as a primitive of UG. But the generalization crucially involves a notion that generativists, for good reason, have been loath to appeal to as a grammar-internal construct—relative structural complexity. As we will see below, the PrNMH lends itself to a simple performance-based explanation, that is, one outside of the domain of formal grammar.

3.3.3 *Typological generalizations are not reliably D-structure generalizations*

One of the strongest pieces of support that could be adduced for the idea of explaining typological generalizations by means of UG-based principles would be to demonstrate that constructs internal to generative grammar are crucially involved in their explanation. In particular, it would involve demonstrating that levels of grammar more abstract than s(urface)-structure or PF are relevant to stating the generalization. And in fact, that is what was generally assumed, at least until very recent minimalist work (see Chapter 2, §2.2.2 and §2.3.3, and the discussion at the end of this section). For example, it was at D-structure that X-bar principles or the parameters governing directionality of heads and complements were generally assumed to be stated. Typological consistency, in this view, is associated with simplicity at that deep level, typological inconsistency with complexity at that level. However, upon close examination, D-structure is no more relevant than S-structure for typology. Some typological generalizations do indeed seem to be generalizations at D-structure, while others do not.

The most interesting argument that I have found in support of the idea that languages are more typologically consistent at D-structure than at S-structure is provided by Gilligan (1987) and involves the order of the adjective and the standard of comparison in comparative constructions. Greenberg (1963: 89) was probably the first to take on this question and formulated his 'Universal 22' as follows:[19]

(44) Universal 22. If in comparisons of superiority the only order, or one of the alternative orders, is standard–marker–adjective, then the language is postpositional. With overwhelmingly more than chance frequency if the only order is adjective–marker–standard, the language is prepositional.

Gilligan argued that the statistical universal in (44) could be strengthened to the biconditional (45), by correlating adjective–standard ordering with verb–object ordering, rather than with adpositionality, as did Greenberg for Universal 22:

(45) OV $\Leftrightarrow$ StdA

Gilligan attempted to demonstrate that for at least some OV languages that admit (typologically inconsistent) adjective–standard (henceforth AStd) ordering, that ordering can be argued to be transformationally derived, rather than obtaining at D-structure. Such is the case in Persian and Latin, both uncontroversially OV languages, in which clausal standards of comparison follow the adjective:[20]

(46) a. Persian (Boyle 1966)
u bistar asb darad ta man (daram)
he more horse has than I have
'he has more horses than I do'

[19] In a sentence like *Mary is smarter/more intelligent than Paul*, *smart* and *intelligent* are adjectives, the marker (of comparison) is *than*, and the standard (of comparison) is *Paul*. Hence English, a prepositional language, exemplifies the second clause of Universal 22.

[20] Hankamer (1973) argues that the *quam* comparative in Latin is clausal.

b. Latin (Andersen 1983)
non callid-ior es quam hic
NEG cunning-CMPR are than he
'you are not more cunning than he'

Gilligan argues that in Persian and Latin there is ample evidence that all sentential complements are extraposed from pre-head position. Hence, if we assume that if in (46a-b) the standards are generated before the adjective, as we would expect from a typologically consistent language, they could be extraposed by means of an independently motivated rule.

But a problem arises with another SOV language, Dutch. To a certain extent Dutch appears to work like Persian and Latin. That is, clausal standards follow the adjective and a rule can be motivated creating AStd as a derived order. But problematically, non-clausal comparatives also manifest AStd order:

(47) a. de jongen is groter dan ik
the boy is taller than I
'the boy is taller than I'

b. ik vind hem aardiger dan jou
I find him nicer than you
'I find him nicer than you'

Here there is no independent motivation for positing a rule extraposing the standard phase. Hence Dutch can be regarded as typologically consistent at D-structure only by positing an unnecessary movement rule.

English in some ways provides confirmation of the idea that typological consistency holds at an abstract level and in other ways does not. Virtually everybody agrees that English is an underlyingly SVO language and that it manifests most of the Greenbergian VO correlations: it is uncontroversially PN, N-Rel, C-S, and so on. Yet, as noted above in §3.2.2.1, there are constructions in English where we do not find SVO order:

(48) a. The last lecture Mary really hated. (OSV)
b. Drink the whole bottle, John never would. (VOS)
c. Away ran John. (VS)

It is easy to argue, however, that (48a-c) are underlyingly SVO, SVO, and SV respectively (Radford 1988). In other words, English is a more rigidly SVO language at D-structure than at S-structure.

But there are cases in which English fails to some significant degree to accord with the Greenbergian correlations. One example of such a situation involves the order of the genitive and the noun, since the former can both precede and follow the latter:

(49) a. John's book
b. the leg of the table

Given that English is VO, we would expect (49b), but not (49a). Is English consistently NGen at an abstract level? Put another way, is there evidence that in sentences like (49a), the possessive phrase *John* has been preposed from post-head position? That has not been the standard analysis for many years. Rather, it is generally assumed that the possessive phrase is generated in Spec, NP position and raises to Spec, DP (see Bernstein 2001 for discussion):

(50)

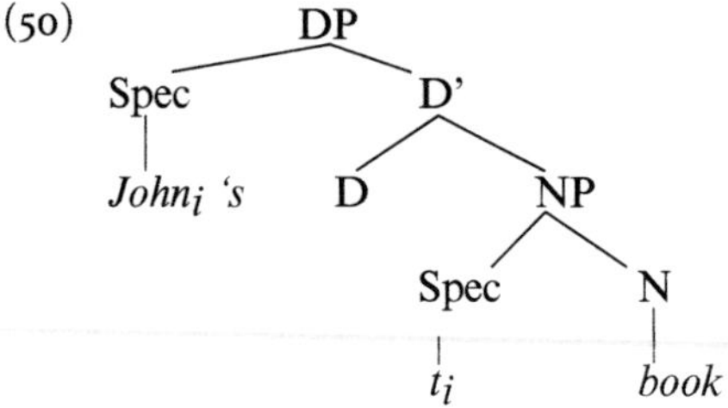

Note that at no point in the derivation is the genitive in post-head position. In other words, for English the Greenbergian correlation VO & NGen does not hold at an underlying level.

Let us now examine German and Dutch. These languages are typologically peculiar in two different ways. First, while virtually all generativists agree that they are underlyingly head-final in VP (see Chapter 2, §2.2.2), they are uncontroversially head-initial in other phrases. Second, a 'V2 rule' is responsible for VO order in main clause declaratives, leaving OV order intact in embedded sentences. What this means is that in German and Dutch we find greater typological consistency at the surface, where VO order dominates by far in actual discourse (given the frequency of main clause declaratives), than at D-structure, where OV order clashes with post-head complements for N, P, and A.

Another interesting case in point is Amharic. The surface order of this language is clearly SOV. As discussed in Chapter 2, §2.2.2, Bach (1970) presented a series of arguments based on grammar-internal regularities that Amharic is a VO language in deep structure, with a rule of verb shift creating the verb-final surface order. And as we have seen, Bach did point to a few correlates of VO order in Amharic. Bach might well have been correct that this language is underlyingly VO. However, its typological properties seem to be at least as much in accord with the OV word order that predominates on the surface than with VO order. For example, as Bach himself noted, auxiliary verbs follow the main verb, rather than precede it—behavior that we would expect from an OV language. Bach went on to note other correlates with OV syntax, such as the genitive expression always preceding the governing noun, the order in comparatives being standard–marker–adjective, and the relative construction usually preceding the modified noun. Even Amharic's prepositionality, a generally reliable marker of VO syntax, is not exceptionless. Bach pointed to a number of postposed elements denoting spatial relations ('inside,' 'top,' etc.). The other correlates of VO syntax cited by

Bach are highly controversial (for example, gapping behavior) or are of unclear grammatical relevance (e.g. the positioning of honorifics).

The best examples in support of the idea that deep order correlates with typologically consistent order involve structures generated by movements that seem motivated (intuitively speaking) by discourse or parsing considerations—that is, movements to a topic or focus position or those whose principal function seems to be to place 'heavy' elements at the periphery of the clause. But if we look at other disparities between deep and surface orders, things are not so clear. It is my impression that deeply inconsistent languages overwhelmingly allow variant surface orders that fulfill the Greenbergian correlations. Consider Persian. That language is deeply inconsistent in the same sense that German is—of the four major phrasal categories, only VP is head-final. However, on the surface Persian allows a number of reorderings of S, V, and O, subject to purely grammatical conditions. For example, a direct object followed by the specificity marker *râ* can move freely within the verb phrase (for full discussion, see Karimi 1989). In other words, Persian does have head-initial VPs on the surface, as we would expect of a prepositional language with Noun–Genitive ordering.

There are, of course, any number of languages for which controversy exists as to their underlying order or for which no intensive investigation of this feature has been undertaken. Many such languages allow a variety of surface orders of subject, object, and verb determined largely by discourse considerations. As it turns out, as far as the Greenbergian correlations are concerned, their underlying word order, whatever it might be, is irrelevant. In an important study, Matthew Dryer (1989a) has shown that languages with discourse-governed word order often exhibit the word-order characteristics associated with *the most frequent surface word order* in the language. Table 3.5 illustrates Dryer's findings for ten such languages.[21]

In other words, the D-structure order of elements in such languages seems irrelevant to determining their typological properties. And finally, convincing arguments exist that there is a set of languages which lack any underlying order of subject, object, and verb (see, for example, Kiss 1987 on Hungarian and Hale 1992 on Warlpiri). It goes without saying that in such languages, relations among D-structure elements could not bear on the Greenbergian correlations.

The above discussion has presupposed an approach to syntax containing a level of D-structure over which grammatical generalizations can be formulated. The MP, which does not provide such a level, has essentially two options for capturing typological generalizations. One would be to assume that they are captured in the 'narrow syntax,' that is, in the mapping to LF by means of the

[21] Dryer calls attention to a few languages in which his generalization does not appear to hold: Papago (higher frequency of VO, but typologically mixed), Yagua (VO more frequent, but GenN and postpositional), Hanis Coos (VO more frequent, but GenN more common than NGen), and Cree (VO more frequent, but postpositional). Dryer notes the (possibly) troublesome fact that in all of his instantiating languages, OV order is more common than VO and the languages exhibit OV characteristics.

TABLE 3.5. *Frequency of OV order and OV characteristics (Dryer 1989a)*

	Frequency of OV	OV characteristics
Ute	72%	GenN, Po
Tlingit	67%	GenN, Po, RelN
Huallaga Quechua	69%	GenN, Po, RelN
Trumai	65%	GenN, Po
Koryak	66%	GenN, Po
Tacana	86%	GenN, Po, Clause-final subordinator
Takelma	85%	GenN, Po
Hupa	53%	GenN, Po
Cherokee	(more frequent)	GenN, Po
Korana	89%	GenN, Po, Clause-final Q, etc.

processes of Merge and Move. In that case, the MP would presumably capture cross-categorial generalizations (and exceptions to these generalizations) by means of relations holding among feature strengths or other properties of functional heads. So the Greenbergian correlations might be derived from correlations among the features that check object case. Under one realization of this possibility, if the case features of N, V, A, and P are weak, we would get head–complement order; if strong, then complement–head order. Marked inconsistency might be derivable by allowing the features associated with the functional projections of these categories to differ (e.g. a strong feature for N, but a weak one for V).

There are two problems with such an approach relevant to our concerns, one identical to those faced by models containing a level of D-structure and one unique to the structure of minimalism. As far as the former is concerned, if any argument for a D-structure order of elements in GB carries over to an argument for a derivationally prior order in the MP, as I assume that it does, then the MP fails as well to capture the generalization that surface order, rather than deep order, is the best predictor of the Greenbergian correlations. But another problem arises in the MP as a result of its difficulty in making a theoretical distinction between base orders of grammatical elements from transformationally derived orders. Consider a language which manifests all the Greenbergian correlations with OV order and to which a principled GB account would, indeed, assign an SOV D-structure order. Let's say that this language allows SVO order as a variant under extremely restrictive grammatical conditions. In GB the rare order would probably be transformationally derived and hence theoretically distinguishable from the basic SOV order. But there is no mechanism internal to the MP (novel stipulations aside) that would distinguish the feature-driven SOV order from the equally feature-driven SVO order. Hence the MP would fail to capture the 'essential SOV-ness' of this language.

On the other hand, the task of capturing generalizations about head directionality and other phenomena centering around word order might be ascribed to PF, as in the approach of Fukui and Takano (1998) and other work in the MP. As was noted in the previous chapter, such an idea is suggested in part by the fact that whether a verb precedes or follows its object, say, is of no relevance to interpretation at LF. The problem with that approach is that we would be left with some generalizations being captured in the narrow syntax and some in the P-syntax, with no evident principle determining which belongs where and how typological correlations involving elements from the two domains might be captured. So presumably *wh*-fronting applies in the narrow syntax, if anything does. If linearization (and hence head directionality) is a PF phenomenon, then how would one go about formulating the generalization that the possibility of *wh*-fronting correlates with the degree of frontedness of the verb at PF? I have to agree with Kayne (2000a: 44) that 'UG should not contain two classes of otherwise similar movement operations distinguished in principle by having or not having an effect on interpretation.'

3.3.4 *Simpler grammars are not necessarily more common grammars: The case of preposition-stranding*[22]

There is no theory-independent way of characterizing one proposed grammar of a language as being 'simpler' than another. However, we can make the reasonable assumption that it is possible to compare two grammars (or at least corresponding subparts of two grammars) in terms of simplicity, so long as both are formulated within the same set of theoretical assumptions. The more complex grammar will have an extra rule of some sort, the same number of rules, but with more of them requiring complex statement, and so on. And as we have seen, a number of linguists go on to hypothesize that the more complex grammar will represent a cross-linguistically rarer state of affairs.

For one reasonably well-studied phenomenon, this prediction is false. The simpler grammar is far rarer cross-linguistically than the more complex one. The phenomenon is 'preposition-stranding,' illustrated in (51a-b) for English. In (51a) *Wh*-Movement has extracted and fronted the object of *to*, leaving the bare preposition behind. In (51b) NP-movement has taken *Mary*, the underlying object of the preposition *to*, and moved it into subject position, stranding the preposition:

(51) a. Who did you talk to?
 b. Mary was spoken to.

Stranding is extremely rare cross-linguistically. To my knowledge, it is attested only in the Germanic family (though not in German itself) and in some varieties of French. Surely, then, if a typologically rare state of affairs were to be represented by a more complex grammar, we would expect a grammar with stranding to be vastly more complicated in relevant respects than one without. Such is not

[22] The remarks in this section are developed in considerably more detail in Newmeyer (1998c).

the case, however. In GB terms, grammars without stranding can be captured by generalization (52a), those with stranding by (52b):[23]

(52) a. NON-STRANDING LANGUAGES: The lexical categories N, V, and A are proper governors. The lexical category P is not a proper governor.
b. STRANDING LANGUAGES: All four lexical categories are proper governors.

When P is not a proper governor, extraction of its object is impossible, since the resultant trace would be ungoverned. A properly governing preposition, however, allows extraction and may therefore occur stranded on the surface.

It is difficult to imagine how a grammar incorporating (52a) could be regarded as simpler than one incorporating (52b). Aside from the pure (and non-explanatory!) stipulation that it is the unmarked state of affairs in UG for P not to properly govern, there is no natural reason why P should be exceptional in this respect. Like other lexical categories, it assigns theta-roles, Case, and along with N, V, and A, it has been characterized by the distinctive features $\pm$ N, $\pm$ V.

To be sure, there is no dearth of analyses of stranding that *do* complicate the grammars of languages that have it. For example, in one popular approach (Hornstein and Weinberg 1981), P is never a proper governor. In languages that allow stranding, prepositions have the ability to overcome this defect by undergoing reanalysis with an adjacent verb, thereby creating a complex verb that can properly govern the trace of movement, as shown in (40) and repeated in (53a-b):

(53) a. You talked $_{PP}$[to who] > You $_{V}$[talked to] who > Who$_i$ did you $_{V}$[talk to]e$_i$?
b. e was spoken $_{PP}$[to Mary] > e was $_{V}$[spoken to] Mary > Mary$_i$ was $_{V}$[spoken to] e$_i$

The reanalysis approach to preposition-stranding is riddled with problems, however. A number of tests show that, in general, the reanalyzed material does not behave as a single lexical item. For example, reanalysis would have to be assumed to create utterly implausible lexical items, such as *walk across Europe in* and *pay twice for*, as in (54a-b):

(54) a. Which shoes did you [walk across Europe in] ___? (Jones 1987)
b. Which of the two knives did you [pay twice for] ___? (Inada 1981)

Furthermore, as noted in Koster (1986), Gapping does not treat the verb–preposition complex as a verb (55a-b), nor does Heavy NP Shift (56a-b). Even more problematically, reanalysis demands the possibility of Extraposition out of a lexical item, as in (57) (Levine 1984), and, as pointed out by Hornstein and Weinberg (1981), in the very article in which reanalysis was first proposed, it

[23] I am not aware of any MP analyses of stranding, though I have no reason to believe that applying the mechanisms of the MP would lead to different conclusions from those argued for here.

demands mutually incompatible analyses, as in (58a-b), where *Wh*-Movement and Passive have applied in the same sentence:

(55) a. *John looked at Mary and Bill ___ Sue.
b. John looked at Mary and Bill ___ at Sue.

(56) a. John looked at [the woman he loved] very often.
b. John looked very often [at the woman he loved].
c. *John looked at very often [the woman he loved].

(57) What did you [talk to that guy ___ about] ___who was here yesterday?

(58) a. Which problems has Harry been [[talked to] e about] e?
b. Who would you like to be [[sung to] e by] e?

Let us therefore abandon a reanalysis approach to stranding and adopt in its place the proposal first put forward, I believe, in Jones (1987) that P is a proper governor in English and other stranding languages. If such is correct, it is predicted that within V′, V and P need not be adjacent. As the sentences of (59) illustrate, this is indeed the case:

(59) a. Who did you give all those books about golf to?
b. Which burner did you leave the pot on?

The most interesting prediction of this analysis is that stranding should be possible with the extraction of NP from PP *adjuncts* to VP, i.e. in situations like (60):

(60)

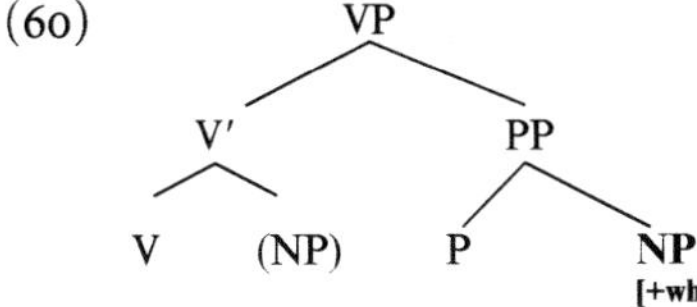

Extraction of the boldfaced *wh*-phrase leads to the crossing of only one barrier, the PP itself. As predicted, then, sentences like (61a-d) are grammatical:

(61) a. Which shoes did you walk across Europe in?
b. Which ball park did Ruth hit the most home runs in?
c. Which knife shall we use to cut the turkey with?
d. Which red-headed man is Mary standing beside?

Now it is a curious fact that many previous analyses of stranding have deemed analogous sentences *un*grammatical. For example Hornstein and Weinberg (1981) point to the famous ambiguity of (62a), which they contrast to the putative non-ambiguity of (62b):

(62) a. John decided on the boat.
b. What did John decide on?

In their view, the adjunct (i.e. locative) reading is impossible in (62b). This supposed ungrammaticality follows, in their theory, from the restriction of reanalysis to subcategorized complements of V. But in fact, it is not hard to construct a sentence with just such a reading. Consider (63), imagining a situation in which John has been going from floor to floor in a department store specializing in vehicles of all sorts, trying to decide whether to buy a boat or a car. The sentence is impeccable:

(63) Which floor did John decide on the boat on?

Clearly we would not want to say that (62b) is unambiguous.

One might object that if prepositions are proper governors, many sentences of dubious acceptability are predicted to be grammatical. For example, consider (64a-b):

(64) a. Who did you read a book about?
b. ?Who did you destroy a book about?

There have been a number of attempts to treat the deviance of (64b) in the grammar itself by devising grammatical operations to rule it out (Bach and Horn 1976; Chomsky 1977b). That strikes me as entirely the wrong move. (64b) is in fact fully grammatical, as is suggested by the well-formedness of sentences like (65):

(65) Which old Bolshevik did Stalin destroy more books about: Trotsky or Bukharin?

Destroying books is not a normal activity. If we create a discourse context in which we make it one—that is, if we make the extracted phrase the center of attention—extraction from the complement of *destroy* creates no problems.

To summarize, preposition-stranding does not pay for its rarity by requiring complex rules for its formulation in grammars that license it. Even within the same general framework of theoretical assumptions, the more complex grammar is not necessarily the more cross-linguistically rare grammar.

3.3.5 *Typological generalizations and 'knowledge of language'*

This section argues that the very nature of typological generalizations renders them all but irrelevant to the construction of a theory of UG. We can begin by considering the types of typological data that might in principle be of value for the construction of such a theory. The first type are absolute universals, that is properties that all languages share or that no languages allow. The second type are implicational universals, namely statements of the form: 'If a language has property X, then it will have property Y.' The third type are simple statements of (relative) frequency, such as: '75 per cent of languages have property X and 25 per cent have property Y' or merely: 'More languages have X than Y.'

Now, absolute universals might well be relevant to UG, since the non-existence of some property might (in principle) result from the initial state of I-language being such that a grammar containing that property is literally unobtainable. However, the second and third types of typological evidence are irrelevant to UG theory. I take it as a working hypothesis that the child constructs his or her grammar by means of an interplay between what is innately provided by UG and 'environmental' evidence to which he or she is exposed. How might implicational and frequency-based typological generalizations be located with respect to these two dimensions? Certainly, we can rule out without further discussion that evidence bearing on them could be 'environmental.' No child is exposed to cross-linguistic generalizations. More children in more speech communities are exposed to the correlation of VO order and prepositionality than to the correlation of VO order and postpositionality. But English-acquiring children have no way of knowing that they are following the majority in this respect and Finnish-acquiring children have no way of knowing that they are in the minority.

Do implicational and frequency-based generalizations follow directly then from an innate UG? As we have seen, Chomsky and Baker make precisely that claim. If they are correct, then knowledge of the second and third types of typological generalizations must be hard-wired into the child. The only place that 'evidence' enters into the picture is where the linguistic data presented to the child helps him or her to determine the setting of a particular parameter and (although the issue is not discussed by Chomsky or Baker) in what respects the language being learned is in violation of some innately provided typological generalization.

I am extremely skeptical that implicational and frequency-based typological generalizations are part of our innate genetic inheritance and the remainder of this section is devoted to elucidating the grounds for my skepticism. Most problematically, typological generalizations tend to be stochastic. That is, they are not of the type that can be represented by the either-or (or yes–no) switch settings implied by Chomsky and Baker.[24] Consider the fact that VO languages tend to have (overt) *Wh*-Movement and OV languages tend not to. Could we say that the parameter setting for *Wh*-Movement is linked in some way to the setting for the Head Directionality parameter? No, because the facts are more complicated than that. Consider again the generalizations enumerated in Table 3.3 above. What we observe is that according to thirteen criteria, SVO languages are intermediate in their typological properties between V-final and V-initial

[24] We cannot rule out *a priori*, of course, the possibility of implicational, yet absolute, universals; that is, generalizations of the form: 'If a language has property X, then it must have property Y.' A language with X, but not Y, then, would be impossible and hence a candidate for being excluded by UG. It remains to be seen whether any (non-trivial and non-accidental) universals of this form actually exist. An anonymous reviewer suggests two universals of this form: the Relative Clause Accessibility Hierarchy (Keenan and Comrie 1977) and the generalization that any language that has subject-verb inversion in yes–no questions will necessarily have this same inversion in *wh*-questions, but not vice versa (essentially Universal #11 of Greenberg 1963). But the former universal is well known to have exceptions (see Newmeyer 1998b), while the latter has not been investigated thoroughly enough to determine its status with any degree of certainty.

languages. In other words, in informal terms, one can say that the closer the verb is to the front of the clause, the more likely some other property will also be manifested. That sort of statistically framed generalization cannot be stated by means of parameter settings, and is incompatible with the 'algebraic' nature of UG, as it has generally been conceived. In other words, incorporating the generalizations of Table 3.3 into a theory of UG would necessitate a profound rethinking of UG theory—and one that would lead in a direction that one would have to assume to be uncongenial to the great bulk of UG theorists.

Baker (2001a) attempts to circumvent this problem by attributing deviance from the pure algebraic nature of his Parameter Hierarchy to extragrammatical causes, just as physicists attribute to extraneous factors such as air resistance the fact that objects are not observed to fall to earth at the theoretically predicted rate of 9.8 meters per second squared. He goes on to write:

> Languages that are close to the ideal types are much more common than languages that are far from them. According to the statistics of Matthew Dryer, only 6 per cent of languages that are generally verb final are like Amharic in having prepositions rather than post-positions.... The conflict of historical and geographical influences could partially explain why Amharic is a mixed case. (Baker 2001a: 82–3)

As an initial point to make in response to this quote, Baker's '6 per cent' is somewhat misleading, perhaps inviting the reader to conclude that 94 per cent of languages behave in accord with the predictions of the PH. But when the totality of the typological generalizations predicted by the PH (and other UG-based approaches to typology) are taken into account, very few, if any, languages manifest its full set of predictions. As observed in Smith (1981: 39), 'there is virtually no typological implicational statement that does not have exceptions.' In fact I agree with Baker's larger point, namely that historical and geographical influences are at the root of much typological inconsistency (see Chapter 5 for discussion). But the analogy between Amharic's having prepositions and leaves not falling to earth at the predicted rate seems far-fetched. Principles that predict the rate of falling bodies and those that predict the effects of air resistance belong to two different physical systems. Is there any evidence that an Amharic speaker's knowledge that auxiliaries follow verbs in that language (as predicted by the PH) and that it is prepositional (as not predicted by the PH) belong to two different *cognitive* systems? No, there is absolutely no evidence whatsoever for such an hypothesis.

Since typological generalizations are not conceivably learned inductively by the child and are implausibly innate, one must conclude that they are not part of knowledge of language at all. Upon further reflection, it is not difficult to understand why it is not within the province of generative theory to account for typological generalizations. Grammatical generalizations and typological generalizations belong to two different domains. Generative grammar provides a theory of mental representations of abstract grammatical structure and the operations that can be performed on that structure. But typological generalizations are frequency effects and implicational relationships pertaining surface configurations. That is, they belong to the domain of E-language, not of I-language. We have no more reason to think that a theory of UG should tell us, say, why there are more SVO languages than VSO languages in the world than that it should tell us why some languages have more honorific expressions than others or why some languages contain more borrowed lexical items than others.[25]

In the next section we turn to a theory that *can* explain some central facts about the cross-linguistic distribution of grammatical elements, namely one based on principles governing performance.

3.4 Hawkins's processing-based explanation of cross-linguistic variation

This section will be as positive in its outlook as the previous ones were negative. I have argued at length that it is not the task of formal grammar to account for the typological variation that we find across languages. This section, on a more positive note, outlines how a theory of performance—in particular, that aspect of performance devoted to online processing—is well designed to handle this variation. Here I rely to a considerable extent on the work of John A. Hawkins (in particular, Hawkins 1994, 2004a). Since I will be presenting the easily accessible work of another scholar, that is to say, work that I cannot claim as my original contribution to the field, I will summarize his results, but not go into great detail on the mechanisms that he proposes.

Section 3.4.1 sketches the hypothesis, central to Hawkins's approach, that much of grammar can be thought of as a conventionalization of performance preferences and §3.4.2 sketches those principles, which are derived from performance pressure to maximize efficiency and reduce complexity.

3.4.1 Grammar as a conventionalization of performance preferences

The central organizing principle of Hawkins (2004a) (and earlier work) is the 'Performance-Grammar Correspondence Hypothesis':

(66) Performance-Grammar Correspondence Hypothesis (PGCH)
Grammars have conventionalized syntactic structures in proportion to their degree of preference in performance, as evidenced by patterns of selection in corpora and by ease of processing in psycholinguistic experiments (Hawkins 2004a: 3).

[25] As both Anette Rosenbach and Martina Penke have pointed out (personal communication), there is an evolution-based argument against typological generalizations being encoded in UG. If UG is related to a specific genetic endowment of our species and goes back to some type of protolanguage capacity humans had before spreading out from Africa (see Wunderlich 2004), then it seems implausible that the typological variation which originated afterwards could be part of this universal language capacity. Also, if we assume a gradual evolution of the language capacity triggered by evolutionary principles, how could there be a selection for an option or a selection for a parameter value that one's language does not realize?

The PGCH is manifested in a number of ways. For example, one might find a language or languages in which speakers have different structural means for expressing the same content. It is very often the case that one of the alternatives is more frequently chosen than the other. If the PGCH is correct, then languages *without* these structural alternatives will more often than not grammaticalize the preferred alternative. Or one notes that, given a group of semantically related constructs, speakers more often make reference to some of these constructs than to others. The PGCH predicts that more languages will grammaticalize the more frequently appealed-to constructs than the less frequently appealed-to ones. To be more explicit, the PGCH makes the following predictions:

(67) Grammatical predictions of the PGCH
    (a) If a structure A is preferred over an A′ of the same structural type in performance, then A will be more productively grammaticalized, in proportion to its degree of preference; if A and A′ are more equally preferred, then A and A′ will both be productive in grammars.
    (b) If there is a preference ranking A>B>C>D among structures of a common type in performance, then there will be a corresponding hierarchy of grammatical conventions (with cut-off points and declining frequencies of languages).
    (c) If two preferences P and P' are in (partial) opposition, then there will be variation in performance and grammars, with both P and P′ being realized, each in proportion to its degree of motivation in a given language structure (Hawkins 2004a: 6).

(67a) can be illustrated by the tendency of heads to precede complements or to follow complements consistently. One might be tempted to simply declare a head parameter provided by Universal Grammar and leave it at that. Descriptively adequate grammars certainly must express this generalization in languages in which it applies, even if a UG-provided head parameter does not enter into the picture. But there is a lot more to the story. Consider a VO language like English, where heads typically precede complements:

(68) V-NP, P-NP, A-of-NP, N-of-NP

In each case a 'lighter' head precedes a 'heavier' complement. But the light-before-heavy tendency in the grammar involves far more than the head–complement relation. For example, the canonical order of VP constituents is relentlessly lighter-to-heavier:

(69) $_{VP}$[V - NP - PP - CP] (*convince my students of the fact that all grammars leak*)

Also notice that single adjectives and participles can appear in pre-head position:

(70) a. a silly proposal
    b. the ticking clock

But if these adjectives and participles themselves have complements, the complements have to appear in post-head position:

(71) a. *a sillier than any I've ever seen proposal
b. a proposal sillier than any I've ever seen

(72) a. *the ticking away the hours clock
b. the clock ticking away the hours

Many more examples of this phenomenon could be provided. These generalizations reflect the PGCH.[26] Evidence for its performance basis is simple. Where speakers have a choice in a VO-type language, they tend to put shorter before longer constituents. So, except for cases in which there is a strong lexical relation between V and P, PPs can typically occur in any order after the verb:

(73) a. Mary talked to John about Sue.
b. Mary talked to Sue about John.

But all other things being equal, the greater the length differential between the two PPs, the more likely speakers will be to put the shorter one first.[27] Interestingly, Hawkins's approach makes precisely the opposite length and ordering predictions for head-final languages. And to be sure, there is a heavy-before-light effect in those languages, both in language use and in the grammar itself. So there is no question in my mind that grammars have been shaped by processing considerations—that is, by language in use.

(67a) can also be illustrated with an example provided by Givón (1979). English allows referential indefinites both in subject position and in the existential construction, as in (74a-b):

(74) a. A man in the yard is asking for you.
b. There's a man in the yard (who's) asking for you.

However, speakers are vastly more likely to say something like (74b) than (74a). And as suggested by the PGCH, in the majority of languages referential indefinite subjects are banned outright.

To illustrate (67b), text counts show that speakers more often make reference to single entities than to multiple entities and more often to multiple entities than to precisely two entities. In keeping with the PGCH, there is an implicational hierarchy: if a language has a distinctive dual form, then it will have a distinctive plural form. And it is virtually never the case that a language requires more

[26] English allows 'heavy' sequences of adjectives in prenominal position: *the big, black, hairy, ferocious dog*. In fact, Hawkins's approach predicts that the short-before-long effect will be much less pronounced if the elements that contribute to pre-head heaviness are all of the same grammatical category. Seeming pre-head phrases such as *easy to please* in *an easy-to-please client* are actually complex lexical items (Nanni 1978; Roeper and Siegel 1978).

[27] The discourse status of the elements involved also plays a role in ordering (see Arnold, Wasow, Losongco, and Ginstrom 2000).

morphosyntactic complexity to express singularity than plurality (Greenberg 1966).

Now let us turn to (67c). Speakers have two measurable preferences: P (75a) and P' (75b):

(75) a. P: Verbs should be adjacent to their complements.
b. P': Verbs should be adjacent to their adjuncts.

These preferences exist because there are combinatorial and/or dependency relations between both verbs and their complements and between verbs and their adjuncts and there is a measurable performance preference for structures where such relations are stated between adjacent elements. Assuming that complements and adjuncts are on the same side of the verb (a typical state of affairs whose explanation we can pass over for the sake of the exposition), P and P' are in opposition for any case in which a verb occurs with at least one complement and one adjunct. However, in the greater percentage of cases, it is the complement that is closer than the adjunct. Why should this be? Because there are *more* combinatorial and/or dependency relations that link complements to their heads than link adjuncts to their heads. Complicating matters, another motivation for grammatical structure is the reduction of the amount of phrase structure that needs to be processed online. In a VO language, such reduction translates as a preference for short constituents preceding long constituents. Hence the prediction that languages that allow adjuncts to intervene between verbs and their object complements will be more likely to do so for short adjuncts than for long adjuncts. As we can see below, the prediction is fulfilled for French:

(76) a. J'admire souvent la gloire de mon père
'I admire often the glory of my father'
b. *J'admire la gloire de mon père souvent
'I admire the glory of my father often'

(77) a. * J'admire quand je regarde à la télé des films sur la Seconde Guerre mondiale la gloire de mon père
'I admire when I watch on the TV films about the Second World War the glory of my father'
b. J'admire la gloire de mon père quand je regarde à la télé des films sur la Seconde Guerre mondiale
'I admire the glory of my father when I watch on the TV films about the Second World War'

3.4.2 *Efficiency and complexity in grammar*

The central question, of course, is *why* speakers should prefer one structure over another. If we look at individual speakers in individual speech situations, then there can be a myriad of reasons. However, if we confine ourselves to the big picture, one factor greatly overrides all others in importance: speakers attempt to increase efficiency by reducing structural complexity. Efficiency can be increased in three ways: first, by minimizing the domains (i.e. the sequences of linguistic forms and their conventionally associated properties) within which certain properties are assigned; second, by minimizing the linguistic forms themselves (phonemes, morphemes, etc.) that are to be processed; and third, by selecting and arranging linguistic forms so as to provide the earliest possible access to as much of the ultimate syntactic and semantic representation as possible.

Concretely, Hawkins proposes three efficiency principles:

(78) Minimize Domains (MiD)

The human processor prefers to minimize the connected sequences of linguistic forms and their conventionally associated syntactic and semantic properties in which relations of combination and/or dependency are processed. The degree of this preference is proportional to the number of relations whose domains can be minimized in competing sequences or structures, and to the extent of the minimization difference in each domain (Hawkins 2004a: 31).

(79) Minimize Forms (MiF)

The human processor prefers to minimize the formal complexity of each linguistic form F (its phoneme, morpheme, word or phrasal units) and the number of forms with unique conventionalized property assignments, thereby assigning more properties to fewer forms. These minimizations apply in proportion to the ease with which a given property P can be assigned in processing to a given F (Hawkins 2004a: 38).

(80) Maximize Online Processing (MaOP)

The human processor prefers to maximize the set of properties that are assignable to each item X as X is processed, thereby increasing O(nline) P(roperty) to U(ltimate) P(roperty) ratios. The maximization difference between competing orders and structures will be a function of the number of properties that are misassigned or unassigned to X in a structure/sequence S, compared with the number in an alternative (Hawkins 2004a: 51).

Let us now have a glimpse at how an interesting typological prediction follows from each of these principles, beginning with MiD. This principle encompasses that of Early Immediate Constituents, which formed the centerpiece of Hawkins (1994) and was given an overview presentation in Newmeyer (1998b: ch. 3, §4.2.2). The basic insight of MiD is that the processor prefers shorter processing domains than longer ones, given combinatorial and/or dependency relations between two elements within a particular domain. The more such relations, the greater the pressure for adjacency. For example, MiD explains why SVO languages tend to be prepositional and SOV languages postpositional. There are four logical possibilities, illustrated in (81a–d): SVO and prepositional (81a); SOV and postpositional (81b); SVO and postpositional (81c); and SOV and prepositional (81d):

(81) 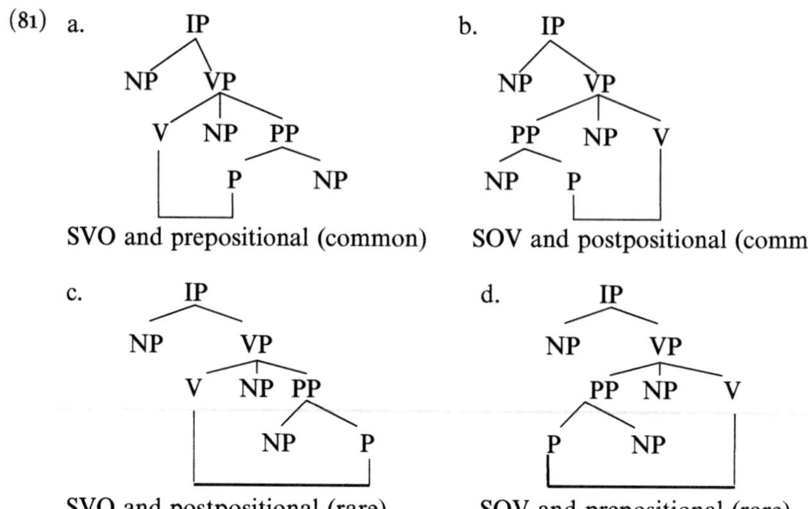

Notice that the domain necessary to identify the constituents of the VP in (81a) and (81b)—the common orderings—is the distance from P to V, with only the object NP intervening. But in (81c) and (81d)—the uncommon orderings—the object of the preposition intervenes as well. In other words, (81c) and (81d) are rarer because they are harder to process.

The Prepositional Noun Modifier Hierarchy, discussed above in §3.3.2 and repeated as (82), follows straightforwardly from MiD.

(82) Prepositional Noun Modifier Hierarchy (PrNMH; Hawkins 1983)

If a language is prepositional, then if RelN then GenN, if GenN then AdjN, and if AdjN then DemN.

The longer the distance between the P and the N in a structure like (83), the longer it takes to recognize all the constituents of the PP:

(83) 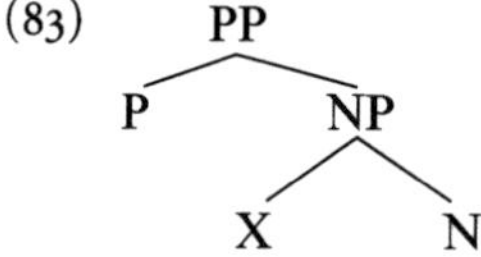

Given the idea that grammars are organized so as to reduce constituent recognition time, the hierarchy follows. Since relative clauses tend to be longer than possessive phrases, which tend to be longer than adjectives, which tend to be longer than demonstratives, which are always longer than 'silence,' the hierarchy is predicted on parsing grounds.[28] Again, it is not by any means clear how

[28] Importantly, there is no possibility of abandoning structural categories such as PP, N, etc., in the statement of the PrNMH in favor of merely quantitative notions such as 'length' or 'weight.' Long

the generalization captured by the PrNMH could be handled by means of parameters.

For another example supporting MiD, consider the Accessibility Hierarchy for relativization (see Chapter 1, §1.4 for discussion). If a language can relativize a direct object (NP_2 in the tree below), it can relativize the subject (NP_1). If it can relativize the indirect object (NP_3), it can relativize both the subject and the direct object. And so on for more 'oblique' grammatical relations:

(84)

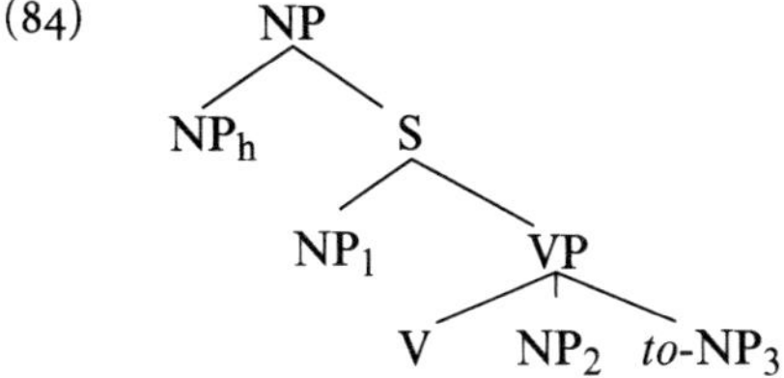

Note that the domain encompassing the head noun (NP_h) and NP_1 is shorter/less structurally complex than the NP_h-NP_2 domain, which in turn is shorter/less structurally complex than the NP_h-NP_2 domain. In other words, the more processing involved, the rarer the structure.[29]

MiF embodies the insight that there is an inverse relationship between familiarity and/or frequency and complexity. Hence, as mentioned above, it is almost unknown for a language to have a form expressing plurality that is shorter or less complex than the singular form. Another example is illustrated by what Givón (1991) and earlier work (Givón 1983a, 1985) calls the 'quantity principle.'[30] He argues that speakers will choose longer or more prominently stressed structures to encode 'information that is either semantically larger, less predictable, or more important' (Givón 1991: 87). Hence, zero anaphora will be chosen when a referent is fully predictable, unstressed lexical pronouns when it is somewhat less so, followed by stressed lexical pronouns, definite NPs, and modified definite NPs. As the contributions to Givón (1983b) indicate, this generalization appears to hold cross-linguistically.

MaOP predicts that a structure or sequence will be dispreferred in proportion to the number of properties that are unassignable to it online. Put simply, as far as processing is concerned, the sooner the better.

adjectives position in the hierarchy the same as short adjectives, while short possessive phrases position themselves in the same way as long possessive phrases.

[29] For a largely compatible processing-based account of the Accessibility Hierarchy, see Kirby (1997).

[30] The quantity principle seems to me to be an instantiation of Grice's maxim of quantity: 'Make your contribution as informative as required (for the current purposes of the exchange)' (Grice 1975: 54). Hawkins notes that this maxim is subsumed under MiF. For other approaches to the grammatical correlates of predictability or familiarity of information content, see Prince (1981, 1985); and Gundel, Hedberg, and Zacharski (1990).

This principle accounts for a wide variety of well-known typological generalizations involving left–right asymmetries, among which are the following:

(85) Asymmetries predicted by MaOP:
  a. Fillers tend to precede gaps
    i. *Wh*-questions
    ii. Relative clauses
    iii. Control structures
    iv. A wide variety of 'deletion' constructions
  b. Antecedents tend to precede anaphors
  c. Topics tend to precede predications (cf. Japanese *wa*)
  d. Restrictive relative clauses tend to precede appositives
  e. Agents tend to precede patients
  f. Quantifiers/operators tend to precede elements within their scope

Why should *wh*-phrases tend cross-linguistically to precede, rather than follow, their extraction sites? MaOP provides an answer. Fodor (1983) observed that given an obvious filler (say, a *wh*-phrase in non-canonical position), the hearer is primed to search for a coreferential gap, but a gap is simply the absence of something—its existence could easily go unobserved by the hearer. MaOP provides a concretization of this insight. Note that more *properties* are immediately assignable to a lexical *wh*-phrase than to a gap. The other asymmetries outlined in (85) are explained by MaOP in parallel fashion.

But not every relation between grammatical elements is an asymmetrical one. For example, there are about equal numbers of VO and OV languages. Such symmetries occur when the two elements depend on each other for property assignments. So the direct object depends on the verb for case, for thematic role, and for the construction of the VP mother node. And the verb depends on the object for selection of the intended syntactic and semantic co-occurrence frame (e.g. transitive versus intransitive *run* as in *John ran* versus *John ran the race*), and for the intended semantics of V from among ambiguous or polysemous alternatives (*ran the race/the water/the advertisement)*.

Again, it is not my intention here (nor would it be appropriate) to present and motivate the dozens, if not hundreds, of typological generalizations that are explained by the processing principles in Hawkins (1994) and Hawkins (2004a). Suffice it to say that they provide a convincing alternative to the idea that such generalizations should be accounted for internally to grammatical theory. If such is correct, there is no need for UG-provided parameters.

3.5 Conclusion

This chapter has argued that it is not the job of generative theory to account for typological generalizations. Attempts to do so by means of parameterized principles have been failures. Such generalizations belong to the domain of performance, rather than to the domain of formal grammar and, as a consequence, Universal Grammar itself can be relieved of the responsibility of accounting for them. While I am certain that some formal linguists will take this conclusion negatively, in my view it is an entirely positive development. The principles proposed by Hawkins have an obvious basis in pressure for efficiency in language processing and it is always a good thing to be able to derive the unknown from the known. Stefan Frisch has expressed my sentiments on this issue better than I could in my own words:[31]

> For the traditional formalist, it is actually desirable for some linguistic patterns, especially those that are gradient, to be explained by functional principles. The remainder, once language processing influences are factored out, might be a simpler, cleaner, and more accurate picture of the nature of the innate language faculty and its role in delimiting the set of possible human languages. (Frisch 1999: 600)

The question to which we turn in the next chapter is whether, given that grammars are such obvious responses to performance considerations, we should abandon the formal grammar project altogether. I argue that we should not do so.

[31] For a similar sentiment expressed over twenty-five years ago, see Kuno (1978).

4

In Defense of the Saussurean View of Grammar

4.1 Introduction

The previous chapter was highly critical of formal accounts of cross-linguistic variation and suggested instead that such variation is more properly handled by a theory of performance. The net result, of course, is a diminished role for formal grammar, insofar as accounting for the full nature of language is concerned. One might be tempted, then, to throw the baby out with the bathwater and to suggest that there is *no* role for purely structural principles at the heart of language. That is, one might conclude that the explanation of the grammatical properties of an individual language or of language in general is based entirely on performance factors. This chapter is devoted to dispelling that idea. I argue at length that Saussure (and Chomsky after him) were correct in distinguishing language knowledge from language use.

The bulk of the chapter, then, will be devoted to arguing in favor of the classical Saussurean position with respect to the relationship between knowledge of language and use of language, providing evidence in support of the idea that the mental grammar contributes to language use, but that usage, frequency, and so on are not represented in the grammar itself.[1] Sections 4.2 and 4.3 describe current anti-Saussurean 'usage-based models' and attempt to account for their popularity. The following three sections defend the classical position with arguments based on the compatibility of formal grammar and functional explanation (§4.4), the failure of connectionism to provide an alternative to formal grammar (§4.5), and the fact that speakers mentally represent full argument structure (§4.6). Section 4.7 points out that the mental grammar is only one of many systems that drive usage, §4.8 argues that grammars are not well designed to meet language users' 'needs,' and §4.9 that pressure to reduce ambiguity is not an important factor in language. The following two sections argue against stochastic

[1] The position to be defended here hence encompasses what in Newmeyer (1998b) I called 'The autonomy of knowledge of language with respect to use of language' ('AUTOKNOW') and 'The autonomy of grammar as a cognitive system' ('AUTOGRAM'). This chapter has nothing new to add in support of the third autonomy hypothesis, namely 'The autonomy of syntax' ('AUTOSYN').

grammars (§4.10) and the idea that grammars are fragile temporary objects (§4.11). Section 4.12 proposes an evolutionary scenario that makes sense of the grammar-use distinction, while §4.13 is a brief conclusion.

4.2 Usage-based models of grammar

The late 1960s witnessed the birth of the approach to grammar called 'generative semantics.' This approach promised to revolutionize the field of transformational generative grammar, itself barely a decade old at the time. With each passing year, generative semanticists declared that some seemingly well-established boundary was nothing but an illusion. The framework began in 1967, when George Lakoff and John R. Ross challenged the existence of the level of deep structure, and with it the boundary between syntax and semantics (Lakoff and Ross 1967/1976). The following year McCawley (1968) argued that syntactic and lexical structures were formal objects of the same sort. Then in quick succession, the dividing line between semantics and pragmatics (Lakoff 1970/1972), grammaticality and ungrammaticality (Lakoff 1973), category membership and non-membership (Ross 1973a,b), and, finally, grammar and usage (Lakoff 1974) were all cast into doubt. At the same time, many sociolinguists were proposing models in which statistical facts about the speech community were incorporated into grammatical rules (Labov 1969, 1972). By the late 1970s, however, generative semantics, for reasons I have discussed elsewhere (see Newmeyer 1986), had all but disappeared. Most syntacticians had re-embraced the boundaries whose demise had been heralded only a few years earlier.

The last decade has seen the resurgence of many of same ideas that were the hallmark of generative semantics. In particular, most of the ways of looking at form and meaning that fall under the rubric of 'cognitive linguistics' have reasserted—albeit in different form—the bulk of the ideas that characterized generative semantics. Langacker (1987: 494) coined the term 'usage-based model' to refer to those approaches that reject a sharp distinction between language knowledge and language use. My impression is that more linguists around the world do cognitive linguistics than do generative grammar. Many functional linguists share the view of a usage-based model; indeed, the dividing line between cognitive linguistics and functional linguistics has never been sharp. The following quotation from two prominent functionalists gives the flavor of what is implicit in a 'usage-based model':

> Increasingly, then, in many quarters structure has come to be seen not as a holistic autonomous system but as something more fluid and shifting. An influential concept here has been that of emergence (Hopper 1987, 1988, 1998), understood as an ongoing process of *structuration* (Giddens 1984)... [E]mergent structures are unstable and manifested stochastically... From this perspective, mental representations are seen as provisional and temporary states of affairs that are sensitive, and constantly adapting themselves, to usage. 'Grammar' itself and associated theoretical postulates like 'syntax'

and 'phonology' have no autonomous existence beyond local storage and real-time processing... (Bybee and Hopper 2001b: 2–3)

Some of these ideas have been adopted by syntacticians working in the generative tradition. In particular, language-particular and cross-linguistic statistical regularities have been incorporated into stochastic implementations of Optimality Theory:

The same categorical phenomena which are attributed to hard grammatical constraints in some languages continue to show up as statistical preferences in other languages, motivating a grammatical model that can account for soft constraints... [T]he stochastic OT framework can provide an explicit and unifying framework for these phenomena in syntax. (Bresnan, Dingare, and Manning 2001: 32; see also the discussion in Wasow 2002)

I believe it to be the case that the great majority of psycholinguists around the world consider the competence–performance dichotomy to be fundamentally wrong-headed. Usage-based approaches have swept natural language processing as well. I am quite sure that Christopher Manning is right when he writes that:

[d]uring the last fifteen years, there has been a sea change in natural language processing (NLP), with the majority of the field turning to the use of machine learning methods, particularly probabilistic models learned from richly annotated training data, rather than relying on hand-crafted grammar model. (Manning 2002b: 441)

4.3 The appeal of usage-based models

The obvious question to ask is why there has been a change of mind among many theoretical linguists. If the ideas that characterized generative semantics were laid to rest in the 1970s, then why are they back again? There are several reasons. First and most importantly, there is the evidence that has mounted in the past quarter-century that significant aspects of grammars are motivated by considerations of use. Functional linguists and generative linguists with a functional bent have provided (to my mind) incontrovertible evidence that grammars are shaped in part by performance considerations. Well before the Hawkins work described in the previous chapter, publications such as Hopper and Thompson (1980); Bybee (1985); Comrie (1989); Heine and Claudi (1986); Croft (1990); and Haspelmath (1993) demonstrated that grammars are in part responses to the behavior and cognitive make-up of language users.[2]

Related to work showing that grammars are externally motivated is the increasing realization that language users are sensitive to the *frequency* of grammatical forms (see especially the papers in Bybee and Hopper 2001a). This notion has in fact been put forward for well over a century in the domain of phonological

[2] For detailed discussion of the mechanisms by which performance considerations can lead to changes in grammatical competence and of the scale at which the interaction takes place, see Newmeyer (1998b).

change, dating from at least Schuchardt (1885/1972), though the exact way in which word frequency interacts with sound change is controversial.[3] In a somewhat parallel fashion, though not necessarily the reflection of a sound change per se, my own pronunciation of words with orthographic <o> between or next to consonants varies in a way connected to a word's frequency, even when the same consonants are involved. Table 4.1 illustrates.

Frequency effects have been pointed to at levels higher than the phonological. Hawkins's principle Minimize Forms is based on the long-established fact that frequently occurring forms tend to be shorter than less frequently occurring ones (Zipf 1935, 1949; Horn 1984, 1993). And a crucial component of David Lightfoot's analysis of the rise of VO word order in Middle English is language-learner sensitivity to declining token frequency of OV order (Lightfoot 1991). Again, such facts might be taken to suggest that grammar and use are too intertwined to be separated one from the other.

Reinforcing skepticism about classical generative models is the disparity between sentences generated by these grammars and actual utterances produced by language users. This disparity has led some linguists to conclude that grammar itself bears no relation to the proposition-like structures posited by formal linguists; structures specified by formal rules that take the sentence to be the basic unit of grammar, where sentences are in a rough mapping with propositions, verbs with predicates, and noun phrases with logical arguments. The priority of the sentence is dismissed by some critics of the generative program as a carry-over from the Western logical tradition, reinforced by the conventions of written language (see especially Harris 1980, 1981; Linell 1982; Miller and Weinert 1998).

Why would anyone draw that conclusion? Well, the argument goes that in *actual speech* speakers rarely utter sentences with a subject, a verb, and an object, where the two arguments are full lexical items, even though that is what gram-

TABLE 4.1. *Some vowel contrasts in the author's English*

/ɔw/	/a/
on, off	honor, offal, don, doff, Goth
dog	frog, log, bog
loss, boss	floss, dross
strong, song, wrong	gong, tong
cost, frost	Pentecost

[3] Studies of lexical diffusion are relevant here (see Wang 1969, 1977; Chen and Wang 1975 for discussion and references), though there is controversy as to whether frequent items are affected first or last, as discussed by Phillips (1984). There are some linguists who even doubt the existence of lexical diffusion as it pertains to sound change, though they recognize a diffusionary effect in the spread of pronunciation changes (e.g. Joseph 2001).

mars generate. Rather, what one finds the most is what Du Bois (1987) calls 'preferred argument structure.' Most clauses consist of a verb with one full argument, which is either the subject of an intransitive verb or the object of a transitive verb. Other arguments are either reduced to clitic or affix status, or omitted entirely. Examples are provided in Table 4.2.

TABLE 4.2. *Some examples of preferred argument structure*

Language	Genre	Finding	Source
Cayuga (Iroquoian)	texts	1–2% of clauses contain 3 major constituents	Mithun (1987)
Chamorro (Austronesian)	narratives	10% of transitives have 2 lexical arguments	Scancarelli (1985)
Coos (Penutian)	texts	2–3% of clauses contain 3 major constituents	Mithun (1987)
French (Romance)	long corpus of conversations among family members	3% of clauses contain lexical subjects (French preferred clause structure is [(COMP) clitic+ Verb (X)])	Lambrecht (1987)
German (Germanic)	spoken discourse	ditransitive verbs tend to follow preferred argument structure	Schuetze-Coburn (1987)
Gooniyandi (Bunaban, Australian)	narratives	3% of clauses have 2 lexical arguments	McGregor (1999)
Hebrew (Semitic)	narratives	93% of transitive clauses lack a subject NP	Smith (1996)
Huallaga Quechua (Andean)	texts	8% of sentences contain both a noun subject and a noun object	Weber (1989)
Inuktitut (Eskimo-Aleut)	child language	.04% of clauses have 2 lexical arguments	Allen and Schroeder (2003)
Korean	children's speech	5–6% of clauses have 2 lexical arguments	Clancy (2003)
Malay (Austronesian)	written text	no clause has both a full agent NP and a full patient NP	Hopper (1988)
Mam (Mayan)	narratives	1% of clauses have 2 lexical arguments	England (1988)

Table 4.2. *(cont'd)*

Language	Genre	Finding	Source
Nepali (Indic)	narratives	11% of clauses have 2 lexical arguments	Genetti and Crain (2003)
Ngandi (Australian)	texts	2% of clauses contain 3 major constituents	Mithun (1987)
Old French (Romance)	texts	7% of clauses have 2 lexical arguments	Ashby and Bentivoglio (2003)
Old Spanish (Romance)	texts	5% of clauses have 2 lexical arguments	Ashby and Bentivoglio (2003)
'O'odham = Papago (Uto-Aztecan)	texts	9% of transitives have 2 overt arguments	Payne (1992)
Rama (Chibchan)	text	transitive clauses with 2 NPs are rare	Craig (1987)
Sacapultec (Mayan)	connected discourse	1.1% of clauses have 2 lexical arguments	Du Bois (1985, 1987)
Yagua (Peba-Yaguan)	corpus of 1516 clauses	3% contain both a noun subject and a noun object	Payne (1990)

Even English, which is non-null subject and considered rigidly SVO, manifests preferred argument structure. A corpus of 20,794 sentences (from telephone conversations) included only 5,975 (29 per cent) that were SVO (see Godfrey, Holliman, and McDaniel 1992 and the discussions in Francis, Gregory, and Michaelis 1999 and Dick and Elman 2001; see also Kumagai 2000 and Thompson and Hopper 2001 for similar figures).

Thompson and Hopper (2001) conclude from such facts that if real speech is not propositional, then grammars should not be either. They appeal to preferred argument structure data to conclude that full argument structure (i.e. the structurally manifested relationship between a predicate and its arguments) is not a central concept in linguistic theory. In their view:

> [T]he apparent importance of [full argument structure] facts may be an artifact of working with idealized data. Discussions of [full] argument structure have to date been based on fabricated examples rather than on corpora of ordinary everyday talk... (Thompson and Hopper 2001: 40)

They go on to claim that theories of full argument structure have been based on verbs that are little used in conversation, such as *elapse, swarm, spray,* and so on. They claim that 'the more frequent a verb is, the less likely it is to have any fixed number of "argument structures"' (p. 49), a claim which they illustrate with the verb *get,* which has no 'easily imagined obvious argument structures, precisely because it is used in so many lexicalized "dispersed" predicates and specific constructions' (p. 49), among which are the following:[4]

(1) a. got sick
 b. don't get wet
 c. you guys are getting ashes all over me
 d. getting a good rest
 e. we gotta get a picture
 f. get that out of my mouth
 g. I don't think that you'll be getting much out of that one

Citing Biber, Johansson, Leech, Finegan, and Conrad (1999), they claim that the next most frequent eight verb forms in English conversation (*say, go, know, think, see, come, want,* and *mean*) behave the same way. They conclude that

> '[full] argument structure' needs to be replaced by a greatly enriched probabilistic theory capturing the entire range of combinations of predicates and participants that people have stored as sorted and organized memories of what they have heard and repeated over a lifetime of language use. (Thompson and Hopper 2001: 47)

Miller and Weinert (1998) concur, pointing out that it is not just full argument structure that is lacking in everyday speech, yet central to formal grammars. They argue that normal discourse lacks dozens of construction types that have loomed large in generative research, including gapping, indirect questions, conditional clauses signaled by subject–auxiliary inversion, gerunds with possessive subjects, initial participial clauses, and much more.

It is worth noting that the rejection of the idea that verbs are represented along with their subjects and objects poses a challenge not just to generative approaches to language, but to traditional views central to linguistic typology as well. Virtually all scholars agree that it was Joseph Greenberg's seminal 1963 paper that laid the basis for modern functional-typological linguistics. Greenberg proposed a six-way classification of the languages of the world according to the relative position of their subjects, verbs, and objects:

(2) Greenberg's six-way classification: VSO, SVO, SOV, VOS, OSV, OVS

Greenberg was not explicit as to his criteria for assigning a basic order to a language, but it appears that he was motivated primarily by that language's canonical order of arguments. For example, his first universal appealed to 'declarative sentences with nominal subject and object' (1963: 77) and he classified German and Chinese as SVO, the most frequent order in those languages in main clause declaratives, despite the fact that those languages also manifest SOV order. In any event, '(full) argument structure' has traditionally been a notion as central to typology as to formal grammar.

[4] For more on *get* leading to the same conclusion, see Fox (1994).

Finally, I think that the appeal of usage-based models is based in part on the rise in the past fifteen years of an approach to the human mind that seems to allow no place for the algebraic autonomous grammars of classical generative grammar. I am referring of course to connectionism (PDP models). If all that we have are stored activation weights, which themselves are no more than predispositions to behave, and connections among them, then 'usage-based' approaches to grammar would seem to follow as a matter of course.

4.4 Functional explanation is fully compatible with formal generative grammar

I think that some arguments in favor of usage-based models can be dismissed right away. Most importantly, one that can be laid to rest is based on the fact that since properties of grammars are functionally motivated, grammar and use are necessarily inextricable. Such a view seems to assume that once a system is characterized as discrete and algebraic, a functional explanation of that system (or its properties) becomes impossible. But that is simply not true. Indeed, it seems only to be linguists who have this curious idea. In every other domain that I am aware of, formal and functional accounts are taken as complementary, rather than contradictory.

The point can be illustrated with a look at a couple other systems (which are discussed in more detail in Newmeyer 1998b: ch. 3). Consider the game of chess. One could not ask for a better formal system. There exists a finite number of discrete rules; given the layout of board, the pieces and their moves, every possible game of chess can be 'generated.' But functional considerations went into the design of system. Presumably it was designed in such a way as to make it a satisfying pastime. And external factors can change the system. However unlikely, a decree from the International Chess Authority could change the rules for castling. Furthermore, in any game of chess, the moves are subject to the conscious will of the players, just as in the act of speaking, the conscious decision of the speaker plays a central role. So chess is a formal system and explained functionally.

A more biological analogy can be provided by any bodily organ. The liver, say, can be described as an autonomous structural system. But still it has been shaped by its function and use. This organ evolved in response to selective pressure for a more efficient role in digestion. And it can be affected by external factors. A lifetime of heavy drinking can alter its structure. So I simply do not see any merit in pointing to functional explanation as a wedge against the classic view of what grammars are like.

By the way, I regard the assumption that much of grammatical structure is motivated by external functional pressure as being a fairly uncontroversial one, even among the most doctrinaire formal linguists. Certainly Chomsky has never questioned it. As long ago as 1975 he wrote:

Surely there are significant connections between structure and function; this is not and has never been in doubt.... Searle argues that 'it is reasonable to suppose that the needs of communication influenced [language] structure'. I agree. (Chomsky 1975: 56–8)

More recently, in the *Minimalist Program* book (Chomsky 1995) and in subsequent work (Chomsky 2000, 2001), he suggests that displacement phenomena—that is movement rules—probably exist to facilitate language use, both in terms of parsing needs and the demands of information structure. So the issue is not whether grammars have functional motivation, but where and how much, and the centrality of focusing on this motivation in one's research program.[5]

4.5 Connectionism and usage-based models of grammar

As far as connectionism is concerned, there is not much to say. We have come a long way from the days when connectionism was little more than behaviorism on the computer. To be sure, the very earliest connectionist models from the 1980s and early 1990s (e.g. Rumelhart and McClelland 1986) were hopeless at capturing even the most basic aspects of grammar, such as long-distance dependencies, category-sensitive processes, structure dependence, and so on. The problem is that now anything can be called 'connectionist,' as long as it involves modeling on a network. In particular, current connectionist models have no trouble implementing rules, and even, by virtue of prespecified connection weights, they can mimic a rich innate component to grammar. I take that point as being uncontroversial. Consider what some connectionists themselves say (or those who are in general sympathetic to the endeavor):

Connectionist models do indeed implement rules. (Elman, Bates, Johnson, Karmiloff-Smith, Parisi, and Plunkett 1996: 103)

Thus a commitment to the PDP Principles ... does not *per se* constitute a commitment regarding the degree to which discreteness, modularity, or innate learning bias applies to human cognition. (Smolensky 1999: 592)

The emphasis in the connectionist sentence-processing literature on distributed representation and emergence of grammar from such systems can easily obscure the often close relations between connectionist and symbolist systems.... Connectionism is no more intrinsically non-modular than any other approach, and many connectionists ... have explicitly endorsed modular architectures of various kinds. (Steedman 1999: 615)

And despite that, connectionist modeling still has little to show for itself when it comes to handling grammatical facts. Again, I let sympathizers speak for themselves:

The [connectionist] approach [to language] is new and there are as yet few solid results in hand. (Seidenberg 1997: 1602)

[5] For Chomsky, of course, such a focus has zero centrality.

And this was after a decade of PDP work on language!

> I realize how enormous the gap is between existing PDP models and a system that would approximate the actual complexity of linguistic structure, even in limited domains. (Langacker 2000: 6)

> Despite these grand pretensions, the reality of connectionist modeling is more sober and modest. In fact, much of the work to date has focused on the learning of narrow aspects of inflectional morphology in languages like English and German. (MacWhinney 2000: 125)

So for various reasons, I do not think that one needs to dwell on the achievements of connectionism as somehow tipping the scales in favor of usage-based models.

4.6 Full grammatical structure is cognitively represented

Let us now turn to what I take to be greater challenges to the classical Saussurean position. Consider the disparity between what formal grammars generate (and are therefore, by definition, 'grammatical sentences') and the sorts of utterances that speakers actually make. As we have seen, this disparity has led to the conclusion that full argument structure is irrelevant to actual language use and that, therefore, generative grammarians are fundamentally misguided in their construction of grammars generating sentences that represent full argument structure. A methodological point needs to be made at the outset, however. The goal of generative grammar is to characterize grammar as a cognitive phenomenon. Not everybody shares those goals, nor should they be expected to. The object of research for Miller and Weinert (1998: 380), for example, is 'spontaneous spoken language.' That is a totally reasonable object of investigation and one which has led to interesting insights about human communication. But for Miller and Weinert there is evidently a *conflict* between the generative goal of 'generat[-ing] all and only the correct [*sic*] sentences of a given spoken language' and their goal of 'generat[ing] the typical sentences' (p. 380). If they feel that insight will be achieved by carrying out their goal, then they should do it, but with the understanding that it is conceptually independent of the generative goal.[6]

The following subsections defend that idea that full argument structure is mentally represented. Section 4.6.1 presents some typological evidence for the cognitive representation of full argument structure. Section 4.6.2 reinforces this point, arguing that Greenberg was correct in characterizing languages in terms of the position of their subjects, verbs, and objects. Sections 4.6.3 through 4.6.6 respectively bolster the arguments against usage-based models by appealing to properties of the English verb *get*, elliptical sentences, facts about child speech, and our knowledge of the properties of sentences that are rarely used in actual discourse.

[6] But I have to say that I am puzzled by why anybody would want to write a grammar that generates only the typical sentences. What would be the point? I am reminded of a colleague who, some decades ago, was engaged in writing a set of rules that generated the names of every restaurant in Paris. Fine, if that is what one wants to do, but why would one want to do that?

4.6.1 *A typology-based argument for full argument structure*

We begin with some typological evidence that subjects, verbs, and objects are fully represented cognitively, even if actual utterances are pared down. Since Greenberg (1963) it has been customary to divide languages into their basic ordering of subject, verb, and object. From this ordering, certain predictions tend to follow. For example, SOV languages are more likely to have postpositions than prepositions. SVO languages are more likely to have *Wh*-Movement than SOV languages and VSO languages are even more likely to have it than SVO languages. But as we have seen, very few clauses in spoken natural language actually have the full subject, verb, and object. If speakers do not mentally represent the full propositional structure, then the prediction follows that the ordering of full subject, verb, and object should be irrelevant to typology. But that prediction is false, as a look at French indicates. French is SVO when the object is lexical, but SOV when the object is pronominal:

(3) a. Je vois Jean.
    b. Je le vois.

Text counts show that VO sentences like (3a) occur only in two-thirds of the cases; fully one-third are OV like (3b) (Ashby and Bentivoglio 1993). But French is archetypically a VO language in its typological behavior. In other words, it is irrelevant to typology that in actual discourse a third of objects are pronominal. It is interesting to compare 'typologically consistent' French with 'typologically inconsistent' languages like German, Chinese, and Amharic. For the latter languages, typological inconsistency reflects variation in the placement of full lexical arguments. For French, on the other hand, the fact that a third of objects are preverbal does not result in typological inconsistency, because these objects are pronominal, rather than fully lexical.

The psychological underpinnings for the differences between French and the other three languages cited derive from the fact that full argument structure is called upon in speech production. According to Levelt (1989), still the major work on this topic, a central part of planning a speech act involves retrieving lexical information, what he calls 'lemmas,' essentially predicates and their argument structure. In other words, for transitive verbs like *hit*, *know*, *eat*, and so on, the speaker has a mental representation of the full argument structure of the sentence:

> Lemma structure plays a central role in the generation of surface structure. In particular, the main verb dictates what arguments have to be checked in the message, and which grammatical functions will be assigned to them. (Levelt 1989: 244)

The 'formulator,' the formulating component of speech production, takes this information as input. Because of that, sentences with full argument structure are psychologically more basic than others. Where full argument structure varies in discourse, typological properties vary. Where full argument structure alternates with a structure in which one of the arguments is pronominal, typological properties are consistent.

4.6.2 *Matthew Dryer on the question of canonical word order*

Dryer (1991, 1997a) proposes replacing Greenberg's word-order typology, which appeals to the basic ordering of S, V, and O for each language, with two two-way parameters, SV versus VS and OV versus VO. Since sentences with just V and S or just V and O are common in discourse, Dryer points out that his system does not rely on discourse-rare sentence types with all three arguments expressed. In other words, he poses another—and rather different—challenge to the idea that full argument structure is mentally represented. In this section, I outline his revised typology and attempt to show that it is not successful.

Dryer (1997a) gives eight arguments for his SV-VS / OV-VO system, namely (4a–h), one of which—(4d)—appeals directly to the fact that most clauses manifest preferred argument structure, rather than full argument structure:

(4) Arguments for two two-way typological parameters (Dryer 1997a)
  a. A number of languages are indeterminately VSO or VOS—the revised typology classifies them identically (i. e. VO and VS).
  b. VSO and VOS languages are now predicted (correctly) to have the same typological properties.
  c. We now have an explanation for the fact that VSO and VOS languages readily change historically from one order to the other.
  d. Cross-linguistically, clauses are rare with both an N subject and an N object.
  e. Some languages can be classified by the revised typology, but are too 'inconsistent' with respect to the six-way typology.
  f. Some languages can be classified with respect to SV/VS, but not by OV/VO, or vice versa. Therefore, it is correct to separate out the two parameters.
  g. It is the OV/VO parameter that is central for typological predictions (i.e. the position of the subject is not an important consideration).
  h. The six-way typology does not distinguish between transitive subjects and intransitive subjects, yet they often behave differently (e.g., Spanish is typically SVO, but VS).

I will now argue that Dryer's attempt to replace the Greenbergian six-way classification by his dual two-way classification is unsuccessful. Let us begin with (4g). How similar typologically are VSO and SVO languages? Consider Table 4.3, which was of interest to us in the previous chapter in a different context.

One notes that SVO and VSO languages do indeed behave a lot more like each other than either behaves like SOV languages. But one notes also the striking fact that by only one test out of thirteen are V-initial languages intermediate between V-final and SVO. For all the others, SVO languages are intermediate and by the last three tests on the table, SVO languages are strikingly intermediate. In other words, VSO languages *are* different from SVO, and hence the position of the subject is relevant for typological purposes.

TABLE 4.3. *Percentage of V-final, SVO, and V-initial languages manifesting particular properties (Dryer 1991)*

Property	V-final	SVO	V-initial
Postpositional	96	14	9
Relative-Noun	43	1	0
Standard of comparison-Adjective	82	2	0
Predicate-Copula	85	26	39
Subordinate clause-Subordinator	70	6	6
Noun-Plural word	100	24	13
Adpositional phrase-Verb	90	1	0
Manner Adverb-Verb	91	25	17
Verb-Tense/Aspect aux verb	94	21	13
Verb-Negative auxiliary	88	13	0
Genitive-Noun	89	59	28
Sentence-Question particle	73	30	13
Wh-in-situ	71	42	16

In fact Dryer's system can characterize the difference between VSO and SVO languages as illustrated in (5–6):

(5) VSO languages are VS and VO

(6) SVO languages are SV and VO

But as I argue now, his system cannot *explain* the difference. Such requires an appeal to structural relations in the entire tree, i.e. to the relative positions of (all of) the subject, the verb, and the object. Trees (7a) and (7b) represent an SVO language (English) and a VSO language (Irish) respectively:

(7) a.

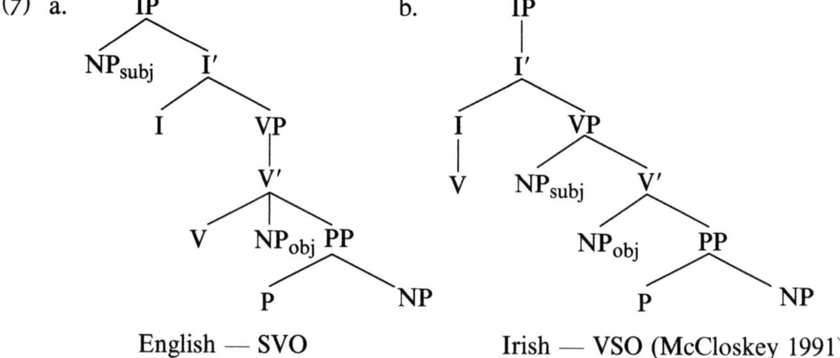

English — SVO   Irish — VSO (McCloskey 1991)

As an inspection of the two structures reveals, VSO Irish is more consistently right-branching than SVO English. In English, unlike in Irish, the subject is on the left branch of the structural path leading to the verb node. Given the principle of Minimize Domains (Hawkins 2004a), discussed in Chapter 3, §3.4.2, there is a processing advantage for constituents of the same subpart of a tree to branch in the same direction. Since VSO languages are right-branching both in subject position and in object position, subparts of both subjects and objects will favor right-branching. On the other hand, since SVO languages are left-branching in subject position, they would favor left-branching subconstituents in that position. So take the ordering of genitive and noun as an example. For SVO languages, there is actually a processing advantage for genitive-noun orders in subject position. Hence, Hawkins's theory explains why VSO languages are so much more strongly noun-genitive than SVO languages. For prepositionality and postpositionality we would, all other things being equal, expect the same situation, namely, a more robust degree of prepositionality for VSO languages than for SVO languages. However, as Table 4.3 illustrates, this prediction is not met—VSO languages are only slightly more prepositional than SVO languages. The explanation for this fact is a simple one—adpositional phrases are much less likely to *appear* in subject position than in object position (John A. Hawkins, p. c.).

The facts discussed in the preceding paragraph could be handled in Dryer's system, since they involve considering the relationship between V and S separately from the relationship between V and O. But other facts require taking into consideration structural relations in the *entire* tree. First, attention should be called to a factor which conspires to increase the prepositionality of VSO languages. As (7b) illustrates, in VSO Irish both the subject and the object intervene between the verb and the subcategorized PPs of the verb. This circumstance leads to more pressure for the early recognition of those PPs by using prepositions. In other words, the structural relations in the entire sentence are relevant, not just the information about whether the language is VS/SV or VO/OV.

For another example, consider dependent (essentially, case) marking. As Table 4.4 (which was also called upon in the previous chapter in a different context) illustrates, V-initial languages are actually intermediate between V-medial and V-final languages in that regard.

Why should such be the case, particularly given the fact that it is usually V-medial languages that are intermediate? The functional explanation for the reduced case marking for SVO languages is well known—in such languages the medial verb keeps the subject and object separated, minimizing the need to distinguish them by a special marking. That is, SVO languages *don't need* case

TABLE 4.4. *Percentage of languages of each type with explicit dependent (case) marking (Siewierska and Bakker 1996)*

V-initial	V-medial	V-final
42	30	64

marking the way the other orderings do. And they don't need it, not because they are SV and VO, but because they are SVO! The functional explanation appeals to both arguments and to the verb at the same time, thereby supporting the Greenbergian classification scheme.[7]

Let us now turn to the differences between VSO and VOS languages. Dryer's (4a,b,c) capitalize on the fact that his two-way classification treats VSO and VOS the same as far as their typological properties are concerned.[8] Such is a desirable result, according to Dryer, because he considers them *to be* the same typologically. But are they the same? It is not obvious from the figures that Dryer himself gives. Consider Table 4.5. Dryer contrasts VSO and VOS languages with respect to ten properties and for all but two of them, VOS languages are either more 'extreme' in their head-initial-related properties, or manifest no difference in that respect.

Why should this be? Again, Hawkins's processing theory has an explanation. A typical VOS language has the surface structure in (8), where the PP is extraposed to the right of the subject:[9]

TABLE 4.5. *Word-order characteristics of VSO and VOS languages (Dryer 1997a: 77)*

	VSO			VOS		
	With property	With opposite property	% with property	With property	With opposite property	% with property
Prep	20	4	83	12	0	100
NGen	24	3	89	11	3	79
NRel	22	0	100	6	0	100
ArtN	14	3	82	7	0	100
NumN	19	5	79	8	1	89
V-PP	20	0	100	8	0	100
NegV	23	1	96	10	0	100
AuxV	16	6	73	5	1	83
Initial Q	12	7	63	3	0	100
Initial *wh*	19	5	79	6	2	75

[7] Matthew Dryer (p. c.) has suggested that in order to explain the diminished need for case marking in SVO languages it is not necessary to consider clauses with both a subject and an object expressed directly. As he notes, for a sentence like *The man saw the woman*, the SV relation will be *the man saw* and the VO relation *saw the woman*. S and O are thus distinguished by position and so case marking serves no functional role. But such an analysis presupposes a 'simultaneous' look at the SV and VO relations, thereby effectively undermining the idea, central to the double two-way typology, that SV/VS and VO/OV are independent parameters.

[8] For interesting theoretical discussion on the differences between VSO and VOS languages, see Polinsky (1997).

[9] Matthew Dryer (p. c.) informs me that of the nine VOS languages in his database, seven are VOSX (as in (8)), one is VOXS, and one has both orderings.

(8)

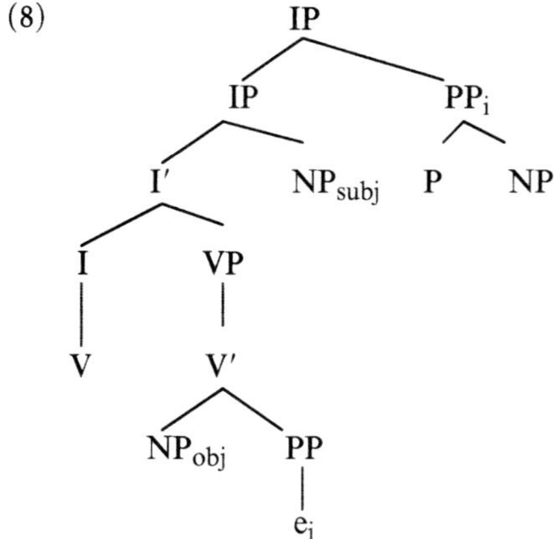

A typical VOS language

The extraposed PP helps to reduce the heaviness of the pre-subject constituent. But a side consequence is to make the structural distance between V and its complements and adjuncts greater than for VSO languages. Hence there is even more pressure for a VOS language to be prepositional than there is for a VSO language.

There is another—more serious—problem with Dryer's dual two-way contrast as opposed to the traditional Greenbergian six-way classification. Consider what it means to label a language as 'SVO,' 'SOV,' and so on. Such labels are merely shorthand ways of talking about *structure.* To say that a language is SVO, for example, is to say that it has a structure something like the simplified representation in (9):

(9)

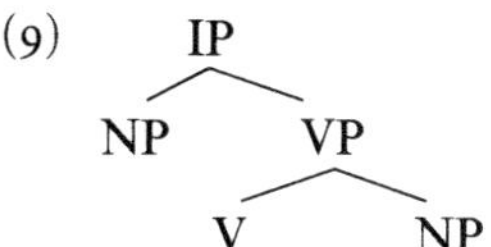

Subjects and objects are identified by their structural positions. Now consider Dryer's two-way split hypothesis—SV/VS and OV/VO. How would a speaker know if his or her language is SV, VS, or whatever? One possibility would be simply that they read off that bit of knowledge from a tree like (9). But that would simply be to admit that speakers *have* a gestalt of a representation with subject, verb, and object—the very point that I am arguing. The other possibility would be to argue that speakers have no internalized representation like (9), a position that amounts to saying that subjects and objects are either primitive notions or defined in semantic or discourse terms. But the adoption of that possibility undercuts the processing explanation for the correlations between subject and object position and a host of other properties. Here is what I mean. (10a) and (10b) give the representations appropriate to an SVO language in a theory in which subjects and objects are not read off of a full sentential P-marker, as in (9):

(10) a. subject - V b. V - object

Now, we know that SVO languages tend to be prepositional, that is, that adpositions and their objects pattern like (10b). But why should that be? As far as I can tell, in any theory that bypasses the idea that speakers have a gestalt of the entire sentence—with subjects and objects in particular structural slots—there is no more reason to expect an SVO language to be prepositional than to expect it to be postpositional.

In summary, the Greenbergian six-way classification, which appeals in effect to full argument structure, is motivated.

4.6.3 Get *again*

Recall the conclusion of Thompson and Hopper (2001), discussed above, that the notion 'full argument structure' should be dispensed with on the basis of the properties of the verb *get.* But their examples, rather than challenging the notion, actually support it. *Get* does indeed occur in a variety of frames, but there is nothing hard to pin down about their precise nature. I repeat their examples from (1), with the complements of *get* that Thompson and Hopper provide in boldface, followed by a few other examples in italics illustrating *get* occurring in the same frame.

(11) a. got **sick** / *well* / *unhappy* / *envious*
b. don't get **wet** / *tired* / *overexcited* / *too confident*
c. you guys are getting **ashes all over me** / *crumbs on the table* / *rashes on your noses*
d. getting **a good rest** / *a snapshot* / *a close look* / *an overall picture*
e. we gotta get **a picture** / *a toothbrush* / *a signature* / *a promise*
f. get **that out of my mouth** / *the baby away from the cliff* / *the whatzit into the thingy*
g. I don't think that you'll be getting **much out of that one** / *golden eggs out of that goose* / *a lot that's useful out of your linguistics courses*

In other words, *get* occurs in the frames +___ AP (11a–b); +___ NP PP (11c,f-g); +___ NP (11d-e). Does *get*, then, occur in any imaginable frame? Certainly not. There is no way in spoken (or any other kind of) English that *get* can occur as a bare intransitive, before an *-ly* adverb, or before a *that*-complement:

(12) a. *I got
b. *I got rarely
c. *I got that you would be admitted for free

The only way that *get* differs from the scorned verbs *elapse*, *swarm*, and *spray* is that it occurs in more frames than they do—a not very interesting fact.

4.6.4 *Ellipsis and full argument structure*

The way that elliptical utterances are processed also points to the idea that we have mental representations of full sentence structure, as has been established by a long tradition of work beginning with Pope (1971) and Morgan (1973), and culminating with Merchant (2004). Consider some possible answers to the question in (13):

(13) Who does John_i want to shave?

Those in (14a–c) are possible, but not those in (14d–e):

(14) a. Himself_i
b. Him_j
c. Me
d. *Myself
e. *Him_i

The generalization, of course, is that the possible pronoun corresponds to the one usable in full sentences, with all arguments expressed:

(15) a. John_i wants to shave himself_i.
b. John_i wants to shave him_j.
c. John_i wants to shave me.
d. *John_i wants to shave myself.
e. *John_i wants to shave him_i.

In other words, whatever one might do in actual speech, one's cognitive representation embodies all the arguments and the principles for assigning the proper pronominal form to the direct object.[10]

As Merchant (2004) has demonstrated, the anaphoric dependencies that are mentally represented can be quite complex. For example, the Greek anaphor *o idhios* (lit. 'the same') can be bound across a finite clause-boundary, but cannot itself c-command a co-indexed DP. Hence it can occur as an embedded subject in the sentential answer in (16c) to the question in (16a) and as a fragment

[10] Richard Oehrle notes (p. c.) that *Clinton* can be understood as the antecedent of *himself* in (ib), even though the coreference depicted in (ii) is impossible:

(i) a. Who did Clinton say that Cuomo planned to nominate?
b. Himself.

(ii) * Clinton_i said that Cuomo planned to nominate himself_i.

While it is certainly true that (ii) is a violation of Principle A of the classic Binding Theory (Chomsky 1981), I wonder if it is really the case that such sentences do not occur in natural discourse. Unfortunately, I know of no corpus-based studies on the subject. Sentence (ii) does in fact seem (marginally) possible to me, particularly with heavy stress on the anaphor. Long-distance anaphoric relationships are fine, of course, in many (perhaps most) of the world's languages.

answer in (16b). In contrast, *o idhios* cannot occur as a matrix subject in a sentence like (17c); it is likewise impossible as a fragment answer over that position in (17b):

(16) a. Pjos nomizi o Giannis oti tha pari tin dhoulia?
who thinks the Giannis that FUT gets the job
'Who does Giannis think will get the job?'
b. O idhios.
the same
'Him.' (= Giannis$_1$ thinks that he$_1$ will get the job.)
c. O Giannis$_1$ nomizi oti tha pari tin dhoulia o idhios$_1$.
the Giannis thinks that FUT gets the job the same
'Giannis$_1$ thinks that he$_1$ will get the job.'

(17) a. Pjos nomizi oti tha pari tin dhoulia o Giannis?
who thinks that FUT get the job the Giannis
'Who thinks Giannis will get the job?'
b. *O idhios.
the same
c. *O idhios$_1$ nomizi oti tha pari tin dhoulia o Giannis$_1$.
the same thinks that FUT gets the job the Giannis

One concludes that speakers of Greek mentally represent full sentences with all of their anaphoric dependencies, even if they utter only fragments.

Merchant (2004) has also demonstrated, pointing to evidence from seven different languages, that the correct morphological case manifests itself in fragments as well. Merchant gives the full paradigm only for Greek, but remarks that the facts are parallel for other languages:

Greek:

(18) Q: Pjos idhe tin Maria?
who.NOM saw the Maria
'Who saw Maria?'
a. A: O Giannis.
the Giannis.NOM
b A: *Ton Gianni
the Giannis.ACC

(19) a. A: O Giannis idhe tin Maria.
the Giannis.NOM saw the Maria.ACC
'Giannis saw Maria.'
b. A: *Ton Gianni idhe tin Maria.
the Giannis.ACC saw the Maria.ACC
'Giannis saw Maria.'

(20) Q: Pjon idhe i Maria?
who.ACC saw the Maria
'Who did Maria see?'
a. A: *O Giannis..
the Giannis.NOM
b. A: Ton Gianni
the Giannis.ACC

(21) a. A: *I Maria idhe o Giannis.
the Maria.NOM saw the Giannis.NOM
'Maria saw Giannis.'
b. A: I Maria idhe ton Gianni.
the Maria.NOM saw the Giannis.ACC
'Maria saw Giannis.'

German (parallel to examples in Hankamer 1971/1979: 394):

(22) Q: Wem folgt Hans?
who.DAT follows Hans
'Who is Hans following?'
a. A: Dem Lehrer.
the.DAT teacher
b. A: *Den Lehrer.
the.ACC teacher

(23) Q: Wen sucht Hans?
who.ACC seeks Hans
'Who is Hans looking for?'
a. A: *Dem Lehrer.
the.DAT teacher
b. A: Den Lehrer
the.ACC teacher

Korean (from Morgan 1989):

(24) Q: Nu-ka ku chaek-ul sa-ass-ni?
who-NOM this book-ACC bought
'Who bought this book?'
a. A: Yongsu-ka
Yongsu-NOM
b. A: *Yongsu-rul
Yongsu-ACC

(25) Q: Nuku-rul po-ass-ni?
who-ACC saw
'Who did you see?'

a. A: *Yongsu-ka.
Yongsu-NOM
b. A: Yongsu-rul.
Yongsu-ACC

English:

(26) Q: Whose car did you take?
a. A: John's.
b. A: *John.

Hebrew (from Ginzburg and Sag 2000: 299):

(27) Q: Et mi shibaxt?
DEF.ACC who you.praised
'Who did you praise?'
a. A: Et Moti.
DEF.ACC Moti
b. A: *Moti.

Russian:

(28) Q: Komu pomogla Anna?
who.DAT helped Anna
'Who did Anna help?'
a. A: Ivanu.
Ivan.DAT
b. A: *Ivan/ Ivana.
Ivan.NOM / Ivan.ACC

Urdu:

(29) Q: Kis-ne Gautam se baat kii thii?
who-ERG Gautam with talk do.PFV PAST
'Who talked to Gautam?'
a. A: Samira-ne.
Samira-ERG
b. A: *Samira.
Samira-ABS

Consider now some English examples (from Morgan 1973) involving complementizer choice. The verb *think* takes a finite complement, but not a gerundive or infinitival one:[11]

[11] Thomas Wasow has pointed out to me (p. c.) that in response to *What did you talk about?* one can say *That war is imminent*, even though the sentence *We talked about that war is imminent* is ungrammatical. The analysis presented in Merchant (2004) accounts for that fact, though space does not allow discussion here.

(30) a. Mary thinks that Sue has finally solved the problem.
b. *Mary thinks Sue's having finally solved the problem.
c. *Mary thinks Sue to have finally solved the problem.

Notice the possible answers to (31):

(31) What does Mary think?

Only (32a) is possible, not (32b) or (32c):

(32) a. Sue has finally solved the problem.
b. * Sue's having finally solved the problem.
c. * Sue to have finally solved the problem.

The internal structure of NP arguments has to be preserved as well, as (33a–c) show:

(33) a. Does Alice like the soprano?
b. No, the tenor.
c. *No, tenor.

These observations all lead to the conclusion that speakers mentally represent the full grammatical structure, even if they utter only fragments.

4.6.5 *Evidence against usage-based models from child speech*

It is worth pointing out that the disparity between knowledge of grammar and actual usage is taken for granted by most researchers of infant and child speech. Clearly infants know more about grammar than is reflected by their utterances. This has been demonstrated by series of experiments carried out by Hirsh-Pasek and Golinkoff:

(34) Some findings reported in Hirsh-Pasek and Golinkoff (1996):
a. One-word speakers between thirteen and fifteen months know that words presented in strings are not isolated units, but are part of larger constituents.
b. One-word speakers between sixteen and nineteen months recognize the significance of word order in the sentences that they hear.
c. Twenty-eight-month-old children who have productive vocabularies of approximately 315 words and who are speaking in four-word sentences can use a verb's argument structure to predict verb meaning.

The grammatical principles that very young children have assimilated can be extremely complex and abstract. Consider the acquisition of anaphoric binding. Crain and McKee (1986) have shown that even children as young as two years old understand the coreference possibilities in (35a-d):

(35) a. The Ninja Turtle danced while he ate pizza.
b. While he danced, the Ninja Turtle ate pizza.
c. His archrival danced while the Ninja Turtle ate pizza.
d. He danced while the Ninja Turtle ate pizza.

They recognize that in (35a–b) *he* can be coreferential with *the Ninja Turtle*, in (35c) *his* can be coreferential with *the Ninja Turtle*, but that in (35d) *he* and *the Ninja Turtle* cannot corefer.

Examples like (34) and (35) are often given to support the idea that much of grammar is innate. They might very well support that idea, but that is not my purpose for giving them here. This chapter has nothing to contribute to the issue of innateness. The importance of such examples is that they support a much weaker claim than the innateness of grammatical structure, though still a controversial one. They indicate quite clearly that the understanding of knowledge of grammar involves going beyond an examination of language in use.

4.6.6 Evidence against usage-based models from little-used sentences and from introspective judgments

Let us consider another piece of evidence that language users have representations that are not predictable from usage-based facts about language. Generative grammarians have long been castigated by other linguists for working with sentences that they make up out of their heads, rather than those taken from actual texts.[12] Now, there are many pros and many cons to the use of introspective data and it is not the purpose of this chapter to review them here (for a good discussion, see Schütze 1996). However it is worth pointing out a remarkable fact about the human language faculty that would never have been unearthed if one just confined one's attention to usage. Speakers have the remarkable ability to make reliable judgments about sentence types that they only rarely hear or utter. Take sentences with parasitic gaps, as in (36):

(36) This is the paper$_i$ that I filed $\_\_\__i$ before reading $\_\_\__i$

I believe that these are rare in actual speech, though I do not know of any statistical studies to confirm that claim. But I doubt that there exists an adult speaker of English who does not know that (36) is a better sentence than (37a-b), despite their superficial similarities:

(37) a. *I filed the paper$_i$ before reading $\_\_\__i$
b. *This is the paper$_i$ that I filed the notes before reading $\_\_\__i$

[12] Not all sentences used in generative research are derived introspectively, of course. Any generative account of a no longer spoken language necessarily involves textual material, and a number of generative studies have appeared on the syntax of specific genres, where the data are taken from newspaper articles, books, radio broadcasts, etc. (see, for example, Haegeman 1987, 1990; McCloskey 2004). There is also a trend among formal syntacticians to use the web to search for attested examples of rare construction types (as in Newmeyer forthcoming).

'Useless' as it is to know the facts surrounding (36) and (37), we know them anyway. Recent experimental work has confirmed that speakers can make reliable introspective judgments, even about rarely occurring sentence types. Cowart (1997) took some constructions that have loomed large in theoretical discussions (the examples of (38) to (40)) and found a stable pattern of response to them among his subjects.

Subjacency:

(38) a. Why did the Duchess sell a portrait of Max?
  b. Who did the Duchess sell a portrait of?
  c. Who did the Duchess sell the portrait of?
  d. Who did the Duchess sell Max's portrait of?

That-trace phenomena:

(39) a. I wonder who you think likes John.
  b. I wonder who you think John likes.
  c. I wonder who you think that likes John.
  d. I wonder who you think that John likes.

Coordination and binding theory:

(40) a. Cathy's parents require that Paul support himself.
  b. Paul requires that Cathy's parents support himself.
  c. Cathy's parents require that Paul support himself and the child.
  d. Paul requires that Cathy's parents support himself and the child.

These are not particularly common sentence types in use, and yet experimental subjects are quite consistent as to how they judge them.[13]

Along the same lines, McDaniel and Cowart (1999) found that subjects can reliably rate sentences like (41) and (42) in terms of degree of acceptability.

Resumptive pronouns:

(41) a. That is the girl that I wonder when met you.
  b. That is the girl that I wonder when she met you.

(42) a. That is the girl that I wonder when you met.
  b. That is the girl that I wonder when you met her.

These results indicate that there is a lot more to grammar than can be predicted from use in naturally occurring discourse. More importantly, they suggest that the human language faculty is designed—at least in part—for something other than communication, a point to which we return below.

[13] The results reported by Cowart do not always support the grammaticality assignments found in the generative literature, but that is another story.

4.7 The mental grammar is only one of many systems that drive usage

No generative grammarian ever claimed that sentences generated by the grammar should be expected to reveal directly what language users are likely to say. This must be true for an obvious reason, namely that knowledge of grammatical structure is only one of many systems that underlie usage. So it will not do as a refutation of formal grammar to find some generalization that the grammar does not encompass. The explanation of that generalization might lie somewhere else. Lakoff and Johnson's mistake in their book *Philosophy in the Flesh* (Lakoff and Johnson 1999) was to assume that any generalization about usage is necessarily a matter for grammar to handle. They pointed out that deictic locatives and rhetorical questions like (43a-b) have traditionally been assumed to occur only as main clauses:

(43) a. Here comes the bus! (Deictic Locative)
 b. Who on earth can stop Jordan? (Rhetorical Questions)

They show, however, that such sentences occur in subordinate clauses introduced by *because* (44a–b), though not in those introduced by *if* (45a-b):

(44) a. I'm leaving because here comes my bus.
 b. The Bulls are going to win because who on earth can stop Jordan?
(45) a. *I'm leaving if here comes my bus.
 b. *The Bulls are going to win if who on earth can stop Jordan?

Lakoff and Johnson's reasonable generalization is that deictic locatives and rhetorical questions can occur in certain subordinate clauses because they convey statement speech acts. Since *because*-clauses express a reason and the statement speech act *is* the reason, deictic locatives and rhetorical questions can occur after *because*. Lakoff and Johnson conclude that since a pragmatic generalization unites the syntactic constructions, it is wrong-headed to dissociate grammar from usage. But their solution is too limited and construction-specific. What we have here is a generalization about what constitutes a coherent discourse. Notice that (46a) is as good as (44a) (and for the same reason), while (46b) is as bad as (45a) (and for the same reason):

(46) a. I'm leaving. Do you know why? Here comes my bus.
 b. #I'm leaving if the following condition is met. Here comes my bus.

In other words, we are not dealing with a grammatical generalization at all. English grammar does not distinguish between *because* and *if* clauses with respect to the issues that concern us. A condition (presumably universal) on coherent discourse is at work here.[14]

[14] Given the fact that there are more grammatical restrictions obtaining in subordinate clauses than in main clauses (Ross 1973c; Emonds 1976), some well-formed sequences of simple sentences will

When one thinks about the nature of speech, it is pretty obvious why other systems besides grammar per se have to take over a big part of the job of communication. The transmission rate of human speech is painfully slow. According to Bill Poser (cited as a personal communication in Levinson 2000: 382), it is less than 100 bits per second—compared to the thousands that the personal computer on one's desk can manage. A consequence is that speakers have to pack as much as they can in as short a time as they can, leading to most utterances being full of grammatical ambiguity. For example, sentence (47) was calculated by Martin, Church, and Patel (1987) to have 455 parses:

(47) List the sales of products produced in 1973 with the products produced in 1972.

For that reason, humans have developed complex systems of inference and implicature, conveyed meanings, and so on. Grammar is such a poor reflection of usage because we have many more meanings to convey than could ever be supported by our grammatical resources in a reasonable period of time. Stephen Levinson phrased it beautifully:

> [I]nference is cheap, articulation expensive, and thus the design requirements are for a system that maximizes inference. (Levinson 2000: 29)

4.8 Grammars are not tailor-made to serve language users' 'needs'[15]

The role played by extragrammatical systems in communication means that grammar per se is not always going to tailor itself to our communicative needs. But a standard assumption in a lot of functionalist writing is that grammar *does* oblige itself in that way. This assumption has been enshrined in a famous dictum from Jack Du Bois:

> Grammars provide the most economical coding mechanism ... for those speech functions which speakers most often *need* to perform. More succinctly: Grammars code best what speakers do most. (Du Bois 1985: 362–3; emphasis added)

That is much too strong a position. The problem is that appeals to 'need' have a post-facto feel to them. One observes a generalization and comes up with a plausible story to account for it. But there is nothing *predictive* about accounts

correspond to ungrammatical sentences with subordinate clauses. An example is the following, pointed out to me by Richard Oehrle (p. c.):

(i) *Because here comes my bus, I'm leaving.
(ii) Here comes my bus. I'm leaving.

For additional arguments that there is no conflict between the idea of an embedded speech-act denotation and the general program of generative grammar (and formal semantics), see Krifka (2001) and McCloskey (2004).

[15] I am indebted to Martin Haspelmath for taking the time to discuss with me the issues raised in this section and the following one, without thereby wishing to imply that he agrees with what I have written there.

that say that grammars encode whatever because that is what speakers need grammars to do. One can imagine any number of things that it would be useful for grammars to do, but which they never do. We need a theory, which is now lacking, of why some seemingly needed features result in grammatical coding, and some do not.

It is worth providing a few examples of how we rely on extragrammatical systems to take over the job of conveying meaning, thereby exempting the grammar from the burden of meeting our 'needs.' Consider first the clusivity distinction (sometimes called the 'inclusive/exclusive pronoun distinction'):

(48) The clusivity distinction in Washo (Jacobsen 1980)

	Sg.	Dual	Pl.
1st exclusive	lé	léši (= I and one other)	léw (= I and others)
1st inclusive		léšiši (= I and you [sg.])	léwhu (= I and you [pl.])

According to Nichols (1992), only a minority of languages (about 42 per cent) make this distinction. And it is heavily areal—only in Australia, Oceania, and South America do more than 60 per cent of languages manifest it. Yet the distinction seems like quite a 'useful' one. We all have been in situations where we or someone else has said 'We are going to do X, Y, and Z' and it has not been clear whether the person addressed was included in the 'we' or not. So a distinction that one might suggest that we 'need' is not generally lexicalized. The only way that usefulness enters the picture with respect to clusivity is with respect to an implicational relationship: if a language has a clusivity distinction at all, it will have it at least in the first person, presumably because it is more useful there than in the second person.

One could make the same point about the falling together of second-person singular and plural pronouns in English (where it is total) and in other European languages (where it affects the polite form). How does that phenomenon play to our needs? Consider also the fact that a majority of the world's languages are null subject (Gilligan 1987). That might make language faster to use, even though it opens up the potential for user confusion. Or take deictic systems. They do not seem particularly designed to meet language users' needs either. They are typically organized in terms of distance from speaker or hearer. The height of an object in relation to the speech participants seems like a useful distinction for grammars to make. But according to Anderson and Keenan (1985), only a small handful of languages encode this distinction grammatically. Speakers might also benefit from a grammatical marker specifying whether an object is on their left side or their right side. However Hawkins (1988) writes that no language grammaticalizes this distinction. I have no doubt that one could construct an argument that distance distinctions are more useful to make than height distinctions, which in turn are more useful to make than position distinctions. But I am highly skeptical that 'usefulness' and 'need' are sufficiently well-defined concepts to merit the status of explanatory factors in grammar organization.

A final striking fact, reported in Talmy (1985/2000), is that no language has grammatical means (inflectional morphology, incorporations, etc.) for encoding an event structure that is independent of that encoded by the lexical categories in the sentence. In other words, no matter how useful it would be to provide grammars with the possibility of sentences like (49) with meanings like (50a-b), no language allows that possibility:

(49) The chair broke-ka

(50) a. The chair broke and I'm currently bored.
b. The chair broke and it was raining yesterday.

4.9 Pressure to reduce ambiguity is not an important factor in language

It is a good question whether the drive to reduce ambiguity, as 'useful' as it might be to languages users—and therefore language use—is ever much a driving force in grammatical change.[16] Labov (1994) has explicitly argued that it is not. He has based his conclusion on the observation that in actual speech one variant is rarely chosen over another for paradigmatic reasons, that is, in a fashion designed to preserve information. The choice is mechanical and syntagmatic—for example, phonetic conditioning and repetition of the preceding structure. Bill Croft has argued along similar lines in his book *Explaining Language Change.* He also stresses syntagmatic over paradigmatic change, as the following quote illustrates:

> Form-function reanalysis [one of Croft's principal mechanisms of change—FJN] is syntagmatic: it arises from the (re)mapping of form-function relations of combinations of syntactic units and semantic components. The process *may nevertheless have an apparently paradigmatic result,* for example, a change of meaning of a syntactic unit... (Croft 2000: 120; emphasis added)

In support of Labov and Croft, I discuss examples of what look on the surface like compelling examples of paradigmatic pressure on morphosyntax to reduce ambiguity and show how the facts can be reanalyzed in syntagmatic terms. The following two subsections treat the reflexive-person generalization (§4.9.1) and differential object marking (§4.9.2). Section 4.9.3 argues that if language users were ambiguity reducers, then objects would typically precede subjects. Section 4.9.4 calls attention to fully acceptable ambiguity in Modern Irish and §4.9.5 is a brief summary.

[16] Laury and Ono (2005: 222) have remarked that 'Ambiguity reduction was a popular topic in functional research some two decades ago, but has lost some of its appeal since then. We think this shift in research focus is partly due to the realization by researchers actively involved in discourse-functional linguistics that ambiguity reduction plays a relatively minor role in actual interaction...' I have no doubt that they are correct. Nevertheless, functional explanations appealing to ambiguity reduction continue to be proposed (see below and Haspelmath 1999b; Jäger 2005; Keller 1994), so it is well worth taking on the issue.

4.9.1 *The reflexive-person generalization*

Faltz (1977/1985) and Comrie (1998) point out that if a language has first- and second-person reflexives, it also has third-person reflexives, as (51) illustrates:

(51) Occurrence of distinctive reflexives

	Third Person	*First/Second Person*
English	yes	yes
Old English	no	no
French	yes	no
*	no	yes

Faltz's and Comrie's explanation for (51) is based on the idea that first- and second-person referents are unique, but third-person referents are open-ended. In principle, a third-person referent could be any entity other than the speaker or the hearer. So it would seem to be more 'useful' to have third-person reflexives, since they narrow down the class of possible referents. Hence it appears that grammars are serving our needs by reducing potential ambiguity.

I can offer a syntagmatic explanation of these facts, that is, an explanation that does not involve problematic appeals to ambiguity reduction. In languages that have reflexive pronouns in all three persons, third-person reflexives are used more frequently than first and second. Consider English. In a million-word collection of British English texts, third-person singular reflexives were 5.8 times more likely to occur than first person and 10.5 times more likely to occur than second person (Table 4.6 gives the facts).

It is not just the absolute number of third-person reflexives that is greater than first and second person. The relative number of third-person reflexives is greater too, as the following figures, also from Johansson and Hofland, reveal:

(52) Johansson and Hofland (1989):
a. I 7620 myself 169 = 2.2%
b. he 9068 himself 511 = 5.6%

TABLE 4.6. *Reflexive pronoun occurrence in a million-word collection of English texts (Johansson and Hofland 1989)*

Reflexive pronoun	Number of occurrences in corpus
myself	169
yourself	94
himself	511
herself	203
itself	272
TOTAL 3rd PERS. SG.	986

Similar results obtain in spoken language corpora, though the differences are not so dramatic (Table 4.7).

Language users (for whatever reason) more frequently use identical subjects and objects in the third person than in the first or second. Given that more frequently appealed-to concepts are more likely to be lexicalized than those that are less frequently appealed to, the implicational relationship among reflexive pronouns follows automatically. There is no need to appeal to ambiguity-reducing 'usefulness.' Also, it is worth asking how much ambiguity is reduced by a third-person reflexive anyway. It eliminates one possible referent for the object, leaving an indefinite number of possibilities remaining.

4.9.2 *Differential object marking*

A second example of supposed ambiguity reduction that has left its mark on morphosyntax involves the phenomenon of differential object marking (DOM). Some languages overtly case-mark direct objects and some do not. In many languages, whether they do or not is a function of the degree of animacy or definiteness of that object. The higher in the hierarchies of animacy and/or definiteness (see 53 and 54) the object is in such languages, the more likely it is to be case-marked in a particular language:

(53) Animacy: Human > Animate > Inanimate
(54) Definiteness: Personal Pronoun > Proper Noun > Definite NP > Indefinite Specific NP > Non-specific NP

The functionalist account of DOM has generally been one based on ambiguity reduction (see, for example, Silverstein 1981; Croft 1988; Comrie 1989). As Table 4.8 (from Jäger 2004) illustrates, subjects of transitive sentences are overwhelmingly animate and definite, while direct objects are overwhelmingly inanimate and are definite to a much smaller degree than subjects.

Hence, it is argued, marking the less prototypical animate and/or definite direct objects reduces ambiguity by preventing them from being confused with subjects. As Judith Aissen has noted:

TABLE 4.7. *Reflexive pronoun occurrence in the 1,848,364-word Michigan Corpus of Academic Spoken English (http://www.hti.umich.edu/m/micase/)*

Reflexive pronoun	Number of occurrences in corpus
myself	151
yourself	189
himself	129
herself	43
itself	296
TOTAL 3rd PERS. SG.	468

TABLE 4.8. *Frequencies in the Samtal i Göteborg corpus of spoken Swedish*[17]

	NP	+def	−def	+pron	−pron	+anim	−anim
Subj	3151	3098	53	2984	167	2948	203
Obj	3151	1830	1321	1512	1639	317	2834

> An intuition which recurs in the literature on DOM is that it is those direct objects which are most in need of being distinguished from subjects that get overtly case-marked. This intuition is sometimes expressed as the idea that the function of DOM is to disambiguate subject from object.... In a weaker form, the intuition can be understood in the following terms: the high prominence which motivates DOM for objects is exactly the prominence which is unmarked for subjects. Thus it is those direct objects which most resemble typical subjects that get overtly case-marked. (Aissen 2003: 437)

Again, a purely syntagmatic frequency-based explanation will suffice. All that one needs to adopt is the well-established hypothesis that within a given domain, more frequent combinations of features require less coding than less frequent ones. There is no need to appeal to ambiguity reduction to explain the phenomenon of DOM. This is a welcome result, since, as noted by Aissen, it is 'clear that DOM is required in many instances where the absence of case-marking could not possibly lead to ambiguity' (Aissen 2003: 437).

4.9.3 *Subject–object ordering*

If speakers were looking ahead to reduce ambiguity, language typology would look very different. By way of example, consider subject–object ordering in the world's languages. In the three rarest orders, the object precedes the subject (Tomlin 1986). Only a couple of per cent of languages are VOS, OVS, or OSV:

(55) SVO/SOV > VSO > VOS/OVS > OSV

If speakers were driven to reduce ambiguity, however, object-initial languages would predominate. Here is why. A central property of subjects vis-à-vis objects is their relative obligatoriness. Virtually every sentence has a subject, whether overt or covert. But not every sentence has an object, only (by definition) those whose verb is transitive. In other words, from the occurrence of a subject, nothing can be predicted about the argument structure of the sentence. All other things being equal, the verb could be as easily transitive or intransitive. However, the occurrence of an object (identifiable as such, say, by case marking) predicts the existence of both a verb and a subject. So if speakers were really driven to reduce

[17] The 'Samtal i Göteborg' corpus was originally used as a basis for Löfström (1988) and was tagged by Dahl (2000a). Jäger (2004) notes that the same patterns have been found in the *Wall Street Journal* Corpus by Hank Zeevat, in the CallHome corpus of spoken Japanese by Fry (2001), and in the SUSANNE and CHRISTINE corpora of spoken English by himself.

potential ambiguity, they would put the object before the subject, something that they rarely do.

One might object that the preceding argument is very weak, given that (virtually) all sentences have both subjects and verbs. That is, placing the object before the subject 'predicts' what every speaker-hearer would know anyway. However, when we look at the *specific properties* of subjects and objects, the ambiguity-reduction theory runs into difficulties that cannot be explained away so easily. Prototypically, subjects are agents and objects are patients. Cross-linguistically, in non-passivized clauses, agent objects and patient subjects are exceedingly rare. Now then, is it easier to predict the properties of the direct object of a transitive sentence, given the subject, or to predict properties of the subject, given the direct object? The latter possibility would appear to be correct. Many direct objects are largely limited in their co-occurrence options to animate agentive subjects. Examples are NPs whose meaning encodes the result of human activity, such as *the book, the garden, dinner*, and so on. Hence given such an object, central properties of the subject are predictable. But given, say, an animate or human subject, virtually nothing can be predicted about the properties of the object. That is, a human subject seems just about as likely to occur with an inanimate patient as with a human one. My suspicion is that non-prototypical (i.e. non-patient) objects are even more likely to occur with human subjects than are prototypical ones. Consider, for example, transitive sentences describing experienced events, such as *The guests/*The radiator enjoyed the meal.* In other words, given the ambiguity-reduction theory, one would expect objects to precede subjects.

Furthermore, the ambiguity-reduction theory makes precisely the wrong predictions with regard to grammatical relations and case marking. As first observed in Greenberg (1963) and stressed in every introduction to typology, subjects are the least likely grammatical relation to be overtly case-marked. Indeed, the more 'oblique' the relation, the more likely case marking is. But case marking not only reveals properties of the element case-marked, but it also reveals properties of other sentential elements, in particular the predicate. So, a benefactive marker, say, on an NP restricts severely the class of verbs possible in the sentence, namely, to those that can take benefactive arguments. The ambiguity-reduction theory, in other words, would predict incorrectly that benefactive NPs should in general occur earlier than (non-predictive because non-case-marked) subjects.

4.9.4 *Acceptable ambiguity in Modern Irish*

For any VSO language, the extraction of a subject or an object will potentially create ambiguity, given that order alone will no longer suffice to distinguish the two grammatical relations. As noted in McCloskey (1977), just such an ambiguity is found in Modern Irish:

(56) Seo an scríbhneoir a mhól na mic léinn
this the writer c praised the students
a. 'This is the writer who praised the students'
b. 'This is the writer whom the students praised'

According to McCloskey (personal communication), such ambiguous structures are easy to find in attested usage and have been tolerated by the language for centuries. There is apparently no pressure at all to 'fix the problem.'

4.9.5 Summary

The basic problem with the kind of paradigmatic explanations that I am criticizing—those that see the speaker as a formal-ambiguity reducer—is that they are psychologically implausible, in that they require the speaker to imagine the set of possible contrasting utterances and their meanings. There is no evidence that speakers actually do that.

4.10 Some arguments against stochastic grammars[18]

Because of the divergence between grammar and usage, one needs to be very careful about the use made of corpora in grammatical analysis, and particularly the conclusions derived from the statistical information that these corpora reveal. Now, for some purposes, as we have seen, statistical information can be extremely valuable. Corpora reveal broad typological features of language that any theory of language variation, use, and change has to address. Two examples are the prevalence of preferred argument structure and the predominance of third-person reflexives. And it goes without saying that facts drawn from corpora are essential for engineering applications of linguistics. But it is a long way from there to the conclusion that corpus-derived statistical information is relevant to the nature of the grammar of any individual speaker, and in particular to the conclusion that grammars should be constructed with probabilities tied to constructions, constraints, rules, or whatever.

Let us consider some arguments against stochastic grammars as models of linguistic competence. In every proposal that I am aware of, the probabilities that one finds in these models are drawn from corpora. One corpus that is widely applied is derived from the *New York Times*. But no child learns English by being read to from the *Times*! Another is the 'Switchboard Corpus,' a database of

[18] I am indebted to Brady Clark, Christopher Manning, and Gabriel Webster for their helpful discussions with me on the topic of this section and especially for their good humor in being willing to take part in an exchange with a colleague like myself whose ideas are fundamentally opposed to their own (at least as far as the former two individuals cited are concerned). The literature defending stochastic approaches to linguistic phenomena is vast—Jelinek (1997); Bod (1998); Manning and Schütze (1999); Jurafsky and Martin (2000); and Bod, Hay, and Jannedy (2003) are important recent book-length works. A comprehensive refutation of this literature is yet to be written; the brief remarks in this (necessarily) short section cannot and should not be taken as anything more than suggestive.

spontaneous telephone conversations by over 500 American English speakers (Dick and Elman 2001). The Switchboard Corpus explicitly encompasses conversations from a wide variety of speech communities. But how could usage facts from a speech community to which one does not belong have any relevance whatsoever to the nature of one's grammar? There is no way that one can draw conclusions about the grammar of an individual from usage facts about communities, particularly communities from which the individual receives no speech input.

There are a lot of non-sequiturs in the literature that arise from ignoring this simple fact. So, Manning (2002a) observes that Pollard and Sag (1994) consider sentence (57) grammatical, but that they star sentence (57b):

(57) a. We regard Kim as an acceptable candidate.
 b. *We regard Kim to be an acceptable candidate.

Manning then produces examples from the *New York Times* of sentences like (57b). Perhaps (57b) is generated by Pollard's grammar and perhaps it is not. Perhaps (57b) is generated by Sag's grammar and perhaps it is not. But we will never find out by reading the *New York Times*. The point is that we do not have 'group minds.' No input data that an individual did not experience can be relevant to the nature of his or her grammar.

There is no objection, of course, to pointing to a corpus-derived sentence like (57b) as a heuristic in gleaning grammatical generalizations. The fact that it is possible in some varieties of English might well lead us to be skeptical that it is truly impossible for Pollard and Sag. The next step therefore would be to subject these two individuals to rigorous testing to see if such is the case. But there is no 'Pan-English' grammar, one which encompasses every sentence possible in all dialects and idiolects of English.

In any event, the evidence for probabilities being associated with grammatical elements seems pretty weak. The numbers are overwhelmingly epiphenomenal. Let us examine another example from Manning (2002a):

(58) a. It is unlikely that the company will be able to meet this year's revenue forecasts.
 b. # That the company will be able to meet this year's revenue forecasts is unlikely.

Manning points out that we are far more likely to say (58a) than (58b) and suggests that this likelihood forms part of our knowledge of grammar. No it does not. It is part of our *use* of language that, for the processing reasons already discussed, speakers tend to avoid sentences with heavy subjects.[19] As a consequence, one is more likely to say things like (58a) than (58b). So there is no reason to conclude that grammars themselves reveal that likelihood.

[19] Sentence (58a) is predicted to be more frequently used than (58b), given the performance principle of 'Minimize Domains' (see Hawkins 2004a and the discussion in Ch. 3, §3.4.2).

The probability of using some grammatical element might arise as much from real-world knowledge and behavior as from parsing ease. For example, Wasow (2002) notes that we are much more likely to use the verb *walk* intransitively than transitively, as in (59a-b):

(59) a. Sandy walked (to the store).
b. Sandy walked the dog.

He takes that fact as evidence that stochastic information needs to be associated with subcategorization frames. But to explain the greater frequency of sentence types like (59a) than (59b), it suffices to observe that walking oneself is a more common activity than walking some other creature. It is not a fact about grammar. Furthermore, since we speak in *context*, the probability of what we say varies with that context. To give an example, Abney (1996) suggests that grammars have weighted probabilities for different parses of the same string. So consider phrase (60):

(60) the shooting of the hunters

It is apparently the case that overwhelmingly in structures of the form 'the gerund of NP,' the NP is interpreted as the object of the gerund, not as the subject. That is a raw fact about frequency of interpretation. But our interpretation of a structurally ambiguous string is determined in large part by real-word contextual factors that have nothing at all to do with grammar, no matter how broadly defined. If somebody says to me (61):

(61) The shooting of the hunters will shock the cruelty-to-animals people

while we are looking at men with rifles standing in front of piles of bullet-ridden deer, then I would guess that the probability of the *subject* interpretation of the gerund would jump to 99.9 per cent. One would still like to know why in general (i.e. without special context) the object reading is more natural than the subject reading. Most likely that is because there is an alternative means of expressing the subject reading where the preposition's thematic role is explicit:

(62) the shooting by the hunters

It seems to me that the most natural treatment is to say that the phrase is grammatically ambiguous and that extragrammatical factors determine which reading is both statistically preferred and likely to be preferred in a given instance.

A recent defense of stochastic grammar, Clark (2005), argues that 'the mental grammar accommodates and generates variation, and includes a quantitative, noncategorical, and nondeterministic component' (p. 207). As the paper notes, such a position entails 'mak[ing] the idealization that speakers share the same mental grammar' (p. 208). Clark's remarks echo what is perhaps the most famous (some would say 'notorious') passage in any of Chomsky's writings: 'Linguistic theory is concerned primarily with an ideal speaker-listener, in a completely homogeneous speech-community...' (Chomsky 1965: 3). That passage evoked outrage among the growing community of grammarians interested in describing and explaining linguistic variation and led, among other things, to the development of the 'variable rules' of sociolinguistics. Clark identifies his position as being within the tradition represented by the variable rules approach, but in an important respect he is mistaken.[20] Cedergren and Sankoff (1974) (one of the foundational papers on variable rules) was explicit (see p. 335) that the numerical quantities associated with the features in the environment of a variable rule are not discrete probabilities 'in the head of the speaker.' But for Clark and other modern advocates of stochastic grammar, the probabilities are very much in the head of the speaker. Indeed, Clark's stated goal in his reply is to defend 'models of mental grammar that incorporate probabilistic information' (p. 207).[21]

Clark recognizes that 'one possible objection [to stochastic grammar] is that by mixing data from different individuals together in a large data set, evidence relevant to the investigation of the mental grammar of particular individuals is potentially obscured' (p. 208). But he then dismisses the importance of the objection. Again, sociolinguists in the 1970s were well aware of the problem, which is why many considered and then rejected the formal representation of variability advocated by Clark:

> One never seems to find the 'ideal speaker-hearer [*sic*] in the perfectly homogeneous speech community'... Individuals may and do act linguistically in ways which are not reflected by group data. Berdan (1973) has shown that for a sample of Los Angeles school children, individual behavior and group behavior do not match. Similarly, Levine and Crockett (1967) showed that the high status group of white speakers is disproportionately made up of extremely high and extremely low users of post-vocalic r. When the means for groups are considered, the higher PVR users balance the low PVR users and the mean use of PVR does not differ significantly from other groups. (Anshen 1975: 6)

I had never heard a 'positive *anymore*' sentence like *We go there anymore* (in the meaning 'Nowadays we go there') until I was away at college and the first time I heard one I couldn't parse it. How could my grammar at the age of sixteen conceivably have been the same as that of an English speaker to whom the construction was native? I have never used the 'invariant *be*' construction of African American Vernacular English (AAVE) and would not know how to use it appropriately even if I wanted to. Yet the corpora upon which stochastic grammars of American English are based do not (to my knowledge) explicitly exclude spoken language samples from AAVE. And why stop at the American border? If corpora contain utterances from diverse dialects of American English, then why

[20] I do not wish to imply that I feel that variable rules are problem-free. For critical discussion, see Bickerton (1973); Kay and McDaniel (1979); and Newmeyer (1983: 77–80).

[21] At one point in his paper Clark appeals to the notion of a 'usage grammar,' which 'preserves the classical competence/performance distinction' (p. 213). Since the notion is unexplicated and derives from unpublished class lectures by Bresnan and Aissen, I am unable to comment on it here.

not from British, Australian, and Indian English as well? Questions like these challenge the foundations of the version of stochastic grammar that Clark defends.

An interesting argument for stochastic grammars is developed in Bresnan, Dingare, and Manning (2001) (see also Bresnan and Aissen 2002). They point out that phenomena that are categorical in some languages are simply a matter of statistical preference in others. So in Lummi, the person of the subject argument cannot be lower than the person of a non-subject argument. A consequence is that one never finds first- or second-person subjects of passives in that language where the agent is in the third person. In English, as it turns out, similar passives are possible, but very rare compared to passives with, say, third-person subjects. As they note, a traditional generative model would ascribe the (categorical) Lummi facts to competence and the (statistical) English facts to performance. They see this as a lost generalization. In their view, only a model of grammar allowing stochastic constraints can unite the facts in the two languages, assigning them two different points along the same continuum with respect to relations involving grammatical person.

In fact, however, there is no lost generalization in the classical (non-stochastic) approach. There is one functional force at work, which has categorical effects in some languages and non-categorical effects in others.[22] Consider an analogy. Suppose that the bubonic plague strikes Seattle, causing thousands of people to be sick and leaving hundreds dead. One does not say that a 'generalization was lost' by describing the latter as categorically dead. Certainly language users and hence indirectly their grammars are sensitive both to pressures that cause frequency differences in usage and to frequency itself.[23] But from the fact that Y is sensitive to X, it does not follow that X is part of the same system that characterizes Y. Stochastic grammar is no more defensible as an approach to language and mind than a theory of vision would be that tries to tell us what we are likely to look at.

There is a problem with stochastic approaches to syntax that does not arise with analogous approaches to phonology. (Here I am indebted to the discussion of the variable rules of sociolinguistics in Lavandera 1978.) Lavandera pointed out that the choice of phonological variants is purely a social matter. But syntactic variants often differ in the meaning that they convey. Viewed from that angle, assigning probabilities to structures or constraints seems especially problematic.

[22] Givón (1979: 26–31) had argued similarly to Bresnan, Dingare, and Manning (2001), pointing out that the dispreference for referential indefinite subjects is categorical in some languages, but only a strong tendency in others (as noted for English in Ch. 3, §3.4.1). His arguments are addressed in Newmeyer (1998b: ch. 2, §3.4.4).

[23] The sensitivity of the language learner to frequency is sometimes appealed to in order to undermine an innate basis for language acquisition. In rebuttal, Charles Yang has pointed out: 'Although infants seem to keep track of statistical information, any conclusion drawn from such findings must presuppose that children know *what kind* of statistical information to keep track of. After all, an infinite range of statistical correlations exists' (Yang 2004: 452; emphasis in original).

The probabilities may be more a function of the meaning that one wants to convey than of some inherent property of the structure itself.

And finally there is the question of genre. Surely the probability of use of whatever construction is a function of the particular genre. But there is an indefinite number of genres. Biber (1988, 1995) has discussed forty-five different registers of spoken and written English, and says that there are many more. One thinks of all the studies of the differences between the speech of men and women, gays and straights, old people and young people, and so on. Consider an example of how the multiplicity of genres cuts at the heart of stochastic grammar. Whenever one flies, one hears some bizarre (but genre-normal) syntax and lexicon from the flight crew:[24]

(63) a. We do request that you remain in your seats until the seat-belt light is turned off.
b. We are ready to depart the gate.
c. Please turn off all electronic devices and stow these devices (*them).
d. ... until you are further notified.
e. ... you$_i$ will be free to move about the cabin as required (UNDERSTOOD: by you$_i$, not *by [the flight crew]$_j$).
f. Take-off will be shortly.
g. This is the last and final call for Flight 583.
h. We hope that you will enjoy your stay in the Seattle area, or wherever your destination may take you.

What do the facts of (63) imply for our concerns? Do flight attendants have different stochastic grammars from the rest of us? Or only when they are working? Does my grammar change when I am on an airplane? Surely, it is simpler to say that part of one's training in the airline industry is in the use of otherwise ungrammatical sentence types. And those who are not airline professionals learn to interpret the meaning and appropriate use of such sentence types by appealing to their grammatical resources and world knowledge.[25]

In a reply to the above genre-based arguments, Clark (2005) suggests, following Boersma and Hayes (2001), that utterances can be characterized along a casual-to-formal continuum. If so, then the stochastic OT approach that he advocates could handle this aspect of register variation fairly neatly, it would seem. But there is so much more to genre than that! Just taking the airline industry examples, the idiosyncratic use of *do*-support by industry professionals bears no relation to the abovementioned continuum. More generally, Biber (1988) studied the relative frequency of a wide variety of categories and constructions in a wide variety of genres, from official documents to academic prose to adventure

[24] I would like to thank Ralph Fasold and Jerrold Sadock for providing me with some of these examples.

[25] Perhaps the more systematic aspects of one's extragrammatical knowledge are organized in the sort of 'user's manual' discussed by Zwicky (1999).

fiction to telephone conversations. The differences from genre to genre are dramatic, as far as frequency of particular construction is concerned. For example, past participle '*wh-is* deletions' (e.g. *the books read*) occur 3.1 times per 1000 words in press reportage, but only 0.1 times in face-to-face conversations. Berkenfield (2002) found that 28 per cent of the instances of the word *that* in news-hour transcripts were demonstrative pronouns, as opposed to 56 per cent in the broad-based Switchboard Corpus. Thompson (1988), using a corpus of more than 100 pages of transcribed natural spontaneous discourse, found 308 adjectives, only one of which occurred in a definite NP. Yet, in written texts, including Thompson (1988) itself, adjectives within definite NPs are rampant (see Newmeyer 1998b: 41). And I would be quite surprised to find a quotative inversion sentence like (64) ever occurring in a corpus of spoken English, even though I encounter them quite regularly in written text:

(64) 'Now we're in for it', declared Indiana Jones.

To sum up, probabilistic information drawn from corpora is of the utmost value for many aspects of linguistic inquiry. But it is all but useless for providing insights into the grammar of any individual speaker.

4.11 Grammars are not fragile, fluid, and temporary

One also has to take issue with the view, expressed so often by advocates of usage-based grammar, that grammars are fragile, fluid, temporary objects. To repeat part of the Bybee and Hopper quote:

> [E]mergent structures are unstable and manifested stochastically... From this perspective, mental representations are seen as provisional and temporary states of affairs that are sensitive, and constantly adapting themselves, to usage. (Bybee and Hopper 2001b: 2–3)

As Robert Levine pointed out to me (personal communication), to read such passages, one would think normal human languages are not any different from trade pidgins like Chinook Jargon, where there are hardly any rules and communication is largely based on world knowledge and context. In my view, one of the basic things to explain about grammars is their stability, at least where there is no significant language contact to complicate things. Consider some examples. I suspect that we could carry on a conversation with Shakespeare, who lived 400 years ago. And the problems we would have with him would more likely be lexical and low-level phonological, rather than syntactic. Preposition stranding survives, despite its being functionally odd, typologically rare, and the object of prescriptivist attack for centuries. Modern Icelanders can read the sagas from 1000 years ago. Spanish and Italian are close to being mutually intelligible, despite the fact that their common ancestor was spoken over 1500 years ago and there has been no significant contact between the masses of speakers of the two languages. And so on.

4.12 The evolutionary origins of grammar lie in conceptual structure, not in communication

Let us change gears fairly radically and speculate on the origins of human language. I think that the most plausible evolutionary scenario might help explain why the disparity between grammar and usage is as great as it is. Section 4.12.1 lays out the mainstream position (with which I concur) that the ultimate origins of grammar lie in conceptualization, not in communication, and §4.12.2 presents and defends a three-stage process in language evolution in which first the former and then the latter was the major influence shaping the properties of grammar.

4.12.1 *The mainstream position on the evolution of language*

When linguists started turning to questions of language origins and evolution in the early 1990s, a near consensus began to develop on a central issue. In a nutshell, the idea was that the roots of grammar lay in hominid conceptual representations and that the shaping of grammar for communicative purposes was a later development. For the most part that was taken to mean that syntax is grounded in predicate-argument structure, that is, representations embodying actors, actions, and entities acted upon, though other aspects of conceptualization were sometimes pointed to as possible antecedents of grammar. Here are some quotes from representative work, with key passages emphasized:

We could search for the ancestry of language not in prior systems of animal communication but *in prior representational systems.* (Bickerton 1990: 23)

A far better case could be made that grammar exploited mechanisms *originally used* for the conceptualization of topology and antagonistic forces [than for motor control] (Jackendoff 1983; Pinker 1989; Talmy 1983; Talmy 1988), but that is another story. (Pinker and Bloom 1990: 726)

The syntactic category system and the conceptual category system match up fairly well. In a way, the relation between the two systems serves as a partial explication of the categorial and functional properties of syntax: *syntax presumably evolved as a means to express conceptual structure*, so it is natural to expect that some of the structural properties of concepts would be mirrored in the organization of syntax. (Jackendoff 1990: 27)

The conditions for the *subsequent development* of language as a medium of communication were set by the evolution of... the level of conceptual structure... A *first step* toward the evolution of this system for communication was undoubtedly the linking up of individual bits of conceptual structure to individual vocalizations. (Newmeyer 1991: 10)

[T]he emergent ability, driven by the evolutionary appearance of C[onceptual] S[tructure], was the capacity to acquire meaningful, symbolic, abstract units... *it would be appropriate to expect adaptation-based explanations to come into play at later stages, once language came to be used preferentially as the human communicative system.* (Wilkins and Wakefield 1995: 179)

Let me summarize the reasons for the belief that the roots of grammar lie in pre-human conceptual structure rather than in pre-human communication.[26] First, we have learned that the conceptual abilities of the higher apes are surprisingly sophisticated (Cheney and Seyfarth 1990; Tomasello 2000; de Waal 1996). Each passing year leads to new discoveries about their capacity for problem solving, social interaction, and so on. Not human-level, but sophisticated nevertheless. Second, the *communicative* abilities of the higher apes are remarkably primitive (Hauser 1996). There is very little calling on their conceptual structures in communicative settings. Now let us look ahead to human language. What almost all theories of grammar have in common is a tight linkage between syntactic structure and certain aspects of conceptual structure. The basic categories of reasoning—agents, entities, patients, actions, modalities, and so on—tend to be encoded as elements of grammar. This encoding is directly built in into theories like cognitive grammar and construction grammar, which do not even allow for an independent level of morphosyntactic patterning. But it is true of standard generative models too. No one denies that the links between syntactic structure and whatever one might want to call it—conceptual structure/logical structure/semantic representation—are very direct.

Now, few linguists would deny that over time (possibly evolutionary time, but surely historical time) the needs of communication *have* helped to determine the properties of grammars. This is most evident in the shaping of grammars to allow the more rapid expression of frequently used meaningful elements than of those less frequently used ones. So, it is auxiliaries and negative elements that tend to contract in English, not full lexical nouns and verbs. Many languages have affixes for the most commonly used concepts, such as negation, causation, comparison,

[26] This position has been challenged recently by both functional and formal linguists. As far as the former are concerned, Charles Li, for example, simply *defines* the question of language evolution as one that involves the evolution of communicative behavior, pure and simple:

> The study of the origin of language, however, concerns the evolution of the communicative behavior of our hominid ancestors toward the emergence of language. (Li 2002b: 218)

Li cannot even imagine what it might mean to take the position that grammar is rooted in cognition:

> Scholars who recognize the merit of functional linguistics agree that language emerged evolutionarily first and foremost as a vehicle of human communication, *not* as an instrument of thought. The claim of language as an instrument of thought is an intuitive and *a priori* claim that defies scientific verification. (Li 2002a: 87)

It is not at all clear to me why the claim that language emerged from thought is any more 'intuitive and *a priori*' than the claim that it emerged from communication.

Turning to formal linguists, important recent work rejects, at least implicitly, the idea that the evolutionary origins of language lie in conceptual structure. For Berwick (1998) all that was needed for syntax to arise was a pre-existing lexicon and a single combinatorial operation called 'Merge.' Berwick's position is developed further in a paper co-authored by Chomsky (Hauser, Chomsky, and Fitch 2002). Chomsky's remarks in this paper represent one more example of his (to my mind, extremely troubling) retreat from advocating a richly articulated theory of Universal Grammar (for discussion, see Newmeyer 2003b).

and so on, but rarely for more complex infrequent concepts. Pressure for the rapid processing of spoken language has helped to shape grammars in other ways. We have seen some examples already. And one could make the same point about constraints. Universal or near-universal constraints seem designed—intuitively speaking—to 'help' the hearer recover pairings of fillers and gaps, antecedents and anaphors, and so on.

4.12.2 *A three-stage process in language evolution*

So let us consider a three-stage process in language evolution. First, there existed a level of conceptual structure:

(65) CONCEPTUAL STRUCTURE

Secondly came the principal evolutionary event. Conceptual structure was linked to the vocal output channel, creating for the first time a grammar that was independent of the combinatorial possibilities of conceptual structure per se, and making possible the *conveying* of thought. That is, it made vocal communication possible. Diagram (66) illustrates:

(66)

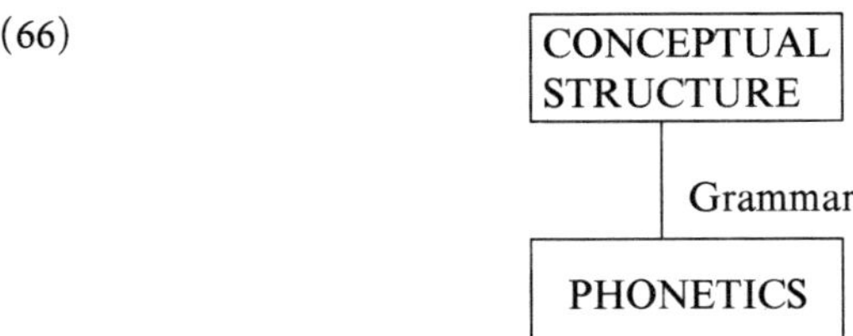

But once grammars started to be drawn upon for real-time purposes, the constraints of real-time use began to affect their properties. In particular, grammars began to be shaped to facilitate processing, the tendency for frequently used elements to become shorter began to assert itself, and so on (67).

(67)

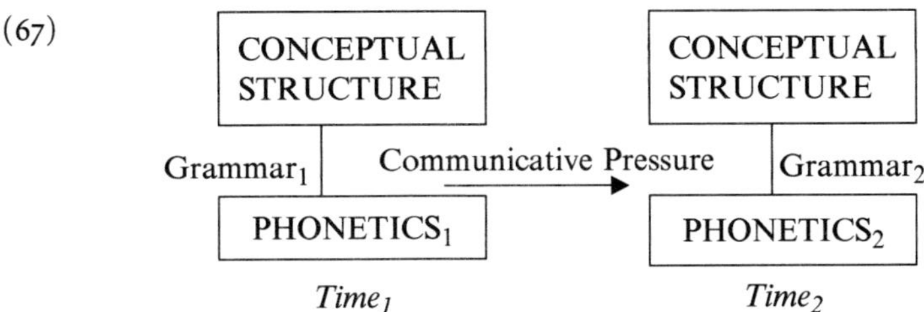

The importance of conceptual structures, that is, their antedating language per se and their forming the basis on which syntax developed, combined with the derivative appearance of language for communicative purposes, provides the evolutionary-historical basis for the disparity between grammar and usage that I have been stressing.

One of the most interesting bits of support for this model comes from the possibility of recursion in grammar, that is, sentences embedded inside of sentences inside of sentences, *ad infinitum*. For example, in principle, there is no limit to the number of times that another subordinate clause can be added in sentences like the following:

(68) Mary thought that John said that Sue insisted that Paul believed that...

Is recursion necessary for communication? Apparently, it is not. We virtually never have any reason to utter complex sentences like (68). And the desired message conveyed by simpler sentences with recursion like (69a) can easily be communicated by a sentence like (69b), employing juxtaposition of two clauses:

(69) a. Mary thought that John would leave.
b. Here is what Mary thought. John was going to leave.

Actually, everyday communication makes use of surprisingly little recursion. Givón (1979) and many others have suggested that the use of subordinate clauses increases dramatically with literacy. The major study along these lines is Kalmár (1985), which maintains that Samoyed, Bushman, Seneca, and various Australian languages rarely employ subordination. According to Kalmár:

> It is quite likely that the number of subordinate clause types grew as narrative developed and accelerated with the advent of writing. Typical is the development of subordination in Greek, which hardly existed in Homer but was well developed in the classics (Goodwin 1912). (Kalmár 1985: 159)

Mithun (1984) carried out text counts on a number of languages with respect to the amount of subordination that one finds in discourses produced in those languages. All languages manifest some subordination, but there is a strong correlation between its rare use and the pre-literate status of their speakers.[27]

It is important to stress that there exists no language for which subordination is literally impossible.[28] In fact, as societies 'modernize,' the use of subordination

[27] James McCloskey (p. c.) has expressed skepticism that subordination is rare in illiterate and pre-literate communities, suggesting that questions of genre are not sufficiently taken into account. He has worked with Irish texts collected by folklorists, the vast majority representing narratives that were recorded or taken in dictation. In texts from the nineteenth and early twentieth centuries, most narrators were illiterate or barely literate, yet, he says, complex embeddings and extractions are easy to find. An example like (i), for example, involves *Wh*-Movement out of a three-deep embedding:

(i) Aon bhliain déag is dóigh liom a
one year ten C-COP I-think C

deireadh m' athair a bhí sé nuair...
say [PAST-HABIT] my father C was he when

'It's eleven years old that I think that my father used to say that he was when...'

[28] With one possible exception, that is. Everett (2004) reports that the Amazonian language Pirahã lacks embedding. He also notes that the Pirahã people have no creation myths, no numbers and counting, no terms for quantification, no color terms, no collective memory of more than two

becomes more frequent. For example, Kalmár observes that Inuktitut is now developing subordinate clauses. The fact that every language allows the possibility of recursion suggests that it is a genuine design feature of language, there from the beginning. Why would this be the case? The obvious answer is that human thought has recursive properties, even if the manifestation of the expression of that thought in communication does not necessarily draw on those properties. As noted by Pinker and Jackendoff:

> Indeed, the only reason language *needs* to be recursive is because its funtion is to express recursive *thoughts*. If there were not any recursive thoughts, the means of expression would not need recursion either. (Pinker and Jackendoff 2005: 230; emphasis in original)

Grammarians have long stressed the importance of recursion as a distinguishing feature of human language (Hockett 1960; Hauser 1996; Hauser, Chomsky, and Fitch 2002). Charles Li, taking a frequently expressed functionalist viewpoint, attempts to deflect its importance by raising the question of whether it can be found in other species:

> In order to determine whether or not the recursive property is a unique defining feature of human language, we must find out if there is a theoretical possibility that certain animal communicative signals could also be described with a re-writing rule that is recursive. (Li 2002b: 211)

Li suggests that the vocalizations of humpback whales can be described by means of a recursive system. I have no idea if he is right or wrong about such creatures, but it hardly matters to the point under consideration, since no one, to my knowledge, has ever claimed that there is semantic significance to the recursion.

Consider now discourse markers, that is, expressions like:

(70) then, I mean, y'know, like, indeed, actually, in fact, well, . . .

According to Schiffrin (1987), they are essential to the makings of a coherent discourse. But as Traugott and Dasher (2002) have recently pointed out, they typically arise from something else. Usually they derive from conceptual meanings and uses constrained to the argument structure of the clause. In other words, they are central to communication, but derivative historically. That seemingly curious state of affairs loses some of its mystery if *vocal communication itself* is derivative. Nouns and verbs trace back to nouns and verbs, because they were there from the start. The derivative nature of discourse markers points to a time when we had structured conceptual representations, but they were not coopted yet for communication.

It is not just discourse markers that seem derivative evolutionarily speaking. By and large, elements that convey grammatical meaning, and those that supply

generations past, and after more than 200 years of regular contact with other peoples and their languages, they are monolingual. One dares to speculate the unspeculable, namely, that the Pirahã in some relevant way are genetically different from other humans.

the clause with aspectual modalities, nuances of quantification and reference, and so on derive from something else and often can be traced back in their historical lineage to nouns and verbs. Heine and Kuteva (2002) have illustrated some common pathways of the development of grammatical elements as in (71):

(71)

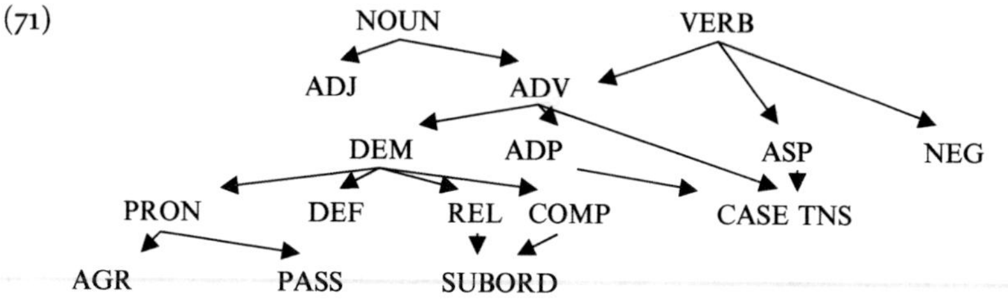

(ADP = adposition; ADJ = adjective; ADV = adverb; AGR = agreement; ASP = aspect; COMP = complementizer; DEF = definite marker; DEM = demonstrative; NEG = negation; PASS = passive; PRON = pronoun; REL = relative clause marker; SUBORD = subordination marker; TNS = tense)

Heine and Kuteva draw the reasonable conclusion that in the earliest form of human language there were only two types of linguistic entities. One denoted thing-like, time-stable entities—nouns, in other words. The other denoted actions, activities, and events—verbs, in other words. Although they themselves do not go on to suggest these facts point to a pre-communicative stage for language, the conclusion seems like a reasonable one.

While I would not want to push 'ontogeny recapitulates phylogeny' too far, it is suggestive that discourse markers, determiners, complementizers, and so on are often relatively late to appear in children's speech (Radford 1990). And this is the case despite the fact that the child is constantly exposed to them and they play a central role in communication.

4.13 Conclusion

Let us recapitulate and conclude. The disparities between what the grammar generates and both usage *by* the speaker and usefulness *to* the speaker are striking. We see this in the centrality of full argument structure to grammar, even if that full argument structure is rarely expressed. We see it in the fact that speakers can make reliable judgments about sentences they would never use. And we see it in the limited place for the drive to reduce ambiguity as a functional force affecting language. The evolutionary scenario discussed here might help to explain these facts. Pre-humans possessed a rich conceptual structure, in particular one that represented predicates and their accompanying arguments. The evolutionary 'event' that underlies human language was the forging of a link between conceptual structures and the vocal output channel—in other words, the beginnings of grammar per se. But early grammar was extremely unstable. Once it was put to use for communicative purposes, it began to be shaped by those purposes. In particular, it was shaped to allow language to be produced and comprehended as rapidly as possible. But conceptual structures did not 'go away'; they remained as part-and-parcel of every grammatical representation. They are drawn upon in every speech act, even if the actual utterance is pared down and fragmentary. At the same time, the necessarily slow rate of the transmission of human speech means that grammar has to be relieved from a big part of the job of conveying meaning in acts of language use. These considerations help explain why it makes sense to characterize grammar independently of usage.

5

The Locus of Functional Explanation

5.1 Introduction

To recapitulate, we have concluded that it is not within the purview of generative grammar per se to account for typological generalizations. Rather, such generalizations have a performance basis. But that fact in and of itself does not threaten the Saussurean conception that grammar and usage are distinct. One central question remains: how direct is the linkage between functional pressures and the typological distribution of formal elements that represents a response to those pressures? In this chapter, I will contrast two positions on the question, one of which maintains that the link between grammatical constructs and functional motivations is very close, the other that maintains that the relationship between the two is extremely indirect. I conclude that the latter position is the correct one.

Section 5.2 contrasts two views of the form–function interface, which I call 'atomistic functionalism' and 'holistic functionalism.' The former sees direct linkage between properties of particular grammars and functional motivations for those properties. The latter sees no direct linkage. Section 5.3 discusses some of the difficulties in deciding between them and §5.4 suggests that the arena of language change provides a good testing ground for doing just that. As we will see, facts about language change provide clear support for holistic functionalism. Section 5.5 raises some new difficulties for atomistic functionalism and §5.6 presents a critical discussion of the version of atomistic functionalism that links the constraints of Optimality Theory to their functional motivations. Section 5.7 is a conclusion.

5.2 Two views of the form–function interface

Broadly speaking, there are two positions with respect to the interface between form and function, which I will call 'atomistic functionalism' (AF) and 'holistic functionalism' (HF):

(1) Atomistic functionalism (AF): There is direct linkage between properties of particular grammars and functional motivations for those properties.

(2) Holistic functionalism (HF): There is no direct linkage between external functions and grammatical properties. The influence of the former on the latter is played out in language use and acquisition and (therefore) language change and is manifested only typologically.

The goal of this chapter is to argue for the correctness of HF and to point out the inadequacies of AF. As will become clear, my conclusion will have important consequences for the explanation of the typological properties of the languages of the world.

As I read the literature, much of mainstream functionalism subscribes to AF, though it is instantiated differently in different approaches. It is common to find accounts in which subparts of individual grammars are said to be functionally motivated. For example, Haiman (1983) observes that iconicity and economy are important motivating factors in grammars and goes on to attribute particular constructions in particular languages to the effects of iconicity or economy, as the case may be. For example, he notes (citing Givón 1983a) that many languages reduce subordinate clauses by omitting redundant coding, such as an embedded subject that is identical to the higher subject. Such constructions Haiman regards as manifesting economic motivation. On the other hand, subordinate clauses in Hua and other Papuan languages fail to undergo reduction, which 'is an icon of the conceptual independence of these clauses. Economy conflicts with a kind of iconicity, and economy loses' (Haiman 1983: 814). Haiman leaves no doubt that the particular functional motivations for these constructions are encoded in the grammar itself (see the remarks in Haiman 1983: 815–16 and the discussion in Newmeyer 1998b: 142–5).

Along the same lines, Dik (1989) calls attention to cross-linguistic variation in the indirect object construction. Some languages have the order represented in (3a), some the order represented in (3b), and some, like English, manifest both orders:

(3) a. Verb—Direct Object—Indirect Object
b. Verb—Indirect Object—Direct Object

Dik links the first order when it occurs in a particular language to the function of iconicity, since it reflects the movement of the object from the donor to the recipient. The second order, according to Dik, has a functional linkage as well, since it places the 'more prominent' indirect object before the 'less prominent' direct object. As Dik puts it, 'If a choice is made for iconicity, we will get a predicate frame such as [(3a)]; if the choice is in favor of prominence, the result will be a predicate frame such as [(3b)]' (Dik 1989: 215).

Likewise, any approach that attributes a degree of prototypicality to a grammatical property is an example of AF, given the standard functionalist position that prototypicality facts are motivated externally. In frameworks as otherwise disparate as George Lakoff's 'Cognitive Linguistics' (Lakoff 1987) and Paul

Hopper's 'Emergent Grammar' (Hopper 1987, 1988), categories, constructions, and processes in individual languages can be assigned a degree of prototypicality. In general, the claim is that the better functionally motivated a property is, the more prototypical it is and—therefore—the more it exhibits the characteristic behavior of members of its class. In the view of William Croft, grammatical processes in individual languages are sensitive to the degree of deviation of the elements participating in them from the typologically established prototype:

These [prototype] patterns are universal, and are therefore part of the grammatical description of any language. Language-specific facts involve the degree to which typological universals are conventionalized in a particular language; e.g. what cut-off point in the animacy hierarchy is used to structurally and behaviorally mark direct objects. (Croft 1990: 154)

Lakoff (1987) proposes a formal model in which the grammar specifies the properties of the prototypical central construction, along with the properties that minimally distinguish each of the subconstructions from it. Lakoff observes:

The result is a cognitive structure that is very much like the category structures that occur elsewhere in the conceptual system. The point is that structures like this are to be expected, given the way people normally construct categories. Prototype theory *explains* why such a grouping of constructions should exist in a language. According to traditional generative theories, such a clustering of categories is simply an anomaly. (Lakoff 1987: 482; emphasis in original)

We also find generative (or generative-influenced) approaches embodying AF. One strain of Optimality Theory (OT) links the constraints of that model to external functional motivations. Bruce Hayes, an advocate of this program for phonology, takes the position that 'constraints need not necessarily be innate [as in standard versions of OT], but only *accessible in some way* to the language learner, perhaps by inductive grounding' (Hayes 1998: 268, emphasis in original).[1] According to Hayes:

...a constraint can be justified on *functional* grounds. In the case of phonetic functionalism, a well-motivated phonological constraint would be one that either renders speech easier to articulate or renders contrasting forms easier to distinguish perceptually. From the functionalist point of view, such constraints are *a priori* plausible, under the reasonable hypothesis that language is a biological system that is designed to perform its job well and efficiently.... Given that [Optimality Theory] thrives on principled constraints, and given that functionally motivated constraints are inherently principled, the clear route to take is to explore how much of phonology can be constructed on this basis.... A theory of [phonetically driven optimality-theoretic phonology] would help close the long-standing and regrettable gap between phonology and phonetics. (Hayes 1998: 246; emphasis in original)

[1] According to Hayes, 'the formal system of grammar characteristically reflects principles of good design' (p. 276). But he is clear that not all 'good design' is necessarily 'functional'—for example, he feels that the tendency of phonological systems toward symmetry has no evident functional explanation.

Many other phonologists have argued for the phonetic grounding of constraints, either implying or stating outright that such grounding provides a motivated and preferable alternative to hypothesizing their innateness (see, for example, Kaun 1994; Jun 1995; Casali 1997; Morelli 1998; Kirchner 2000).

Recently, we have seen a similar turn in syntax. For example, Haspelmath (1999b: 187) suggests that 'the grammatical constraints [of OT] are ultimately based on the constraints on language users' and provides a list of proposed constraints, from both phonology and syntax, that seem to reflect user-functionality. Three of these from the syntactic OT literature are presented in Table 5.1.

Joan Bresnan has also expressed the idea that the constraints of OT are paired with their functional motivations:

> ... both phonologists and functional linguists have recognized that linguistic inventories also reflect universal patterns of markedness and are often functionally motivated by perceptual and cognitive constraints. I will argue in support of this conclusion by showing how different inventories of personal pronouns across languages may be formally derived by the prioritizing of motivated constraints in Optimality Theory. (Bresnan 1997: 26)

and:

> The existence of an appropriate EVAL, then, reduces to the discovery of universal constraints whose ranking generates the desired inventories of pronominal forms. We further require that these constraints be *motivated*. (Bresnan 1997: 34; emphasis in original)

TABLE 5.1. *Some OT constraints and their possible functional motivations (Haspelmath 1999b: 185)*

Name	Grammatical constraint	Corresponding user constraint
STAY (Grimshaw 1997; Speas 1997)	'Do not move'	Leaving material in canonical position helps the hearer to identify grammatical relationships and reduces processing costs for the speaker.
TELEGRAPH (Pesetsky 1998)	'Do not pronounce function words'	Leaving out function words reduces pronunciation costs for the speaker in a way that is minimally disruptive for understanding by the hearer.
RECOVERABILITY (Pesetsky 1998)	'A syntactic unit with semantic content must be pronounced unless it has a sufficiently local antecedent'	Omitting a meaning-bearing element in pronunciation makes the hearer's task of extracting the intended meaning from the speech signal very difficult unless it can be inferred from the context.

In two important papers, Judith Aissen (1999, 2003) makes crucial use of grammatical hierarchies that have, for the most part, emerged from typological research carried out by functional linguists. The first paper, which deals with different possibilities for the choice of subjects in the world's languages, points to a user-based constraint motivation in only one place, where it is noted that 'the functional motivation of [a particular local conjunction of constraints] is clear: the more marked a nominal is *qua* subject/object, the more useful it is to overtly mark its grammatical function' (1999: 703). However, the second paper has as its explicit purpose 'to develop an approach to [differential object marking] within OT which is formal *and* at the same time expresses the functional-typological understanding of [that phenomenon]' (2003: 439; emphasis in original). Not only does it incorporate functionally motivated hierarchies, but it attempts to provide functional motivation for the constraints themselves. For example, a constraint that penalizes the absence of case marking is attributed to the listener-oriented principle 'minimization of perceptual confusion.' Another set of constraints are regarded as being rooted in 'iconicity,' since they favor morphological marks for marked configurations. And a constraint that penalizes the morphological expression of case, on the other hand, is said to have an economy-based motivation, since it reduces the amount of structure that needs to be processed.

The goal of the Optimal Typology Project, which Aissen and Bresnan head, has explicitly typological aims, namely to:

> ...develop a fully explicit Optimality Theoretic approach to markedness hierarchies in syntax, and to test it against both crosslinguistic typological research and language-internal studies of syntactic structures...[to] captur[e] both the universal and the 'soft' properties of hierarchies with harmonic alignment in syntax... and the more general idea of functional/typological grounding of syntactic markedness constraints. <http://www-ot.stanford.edu/ot/#Project activities>

In HF, on the other hand, elements of grammars are not accompanied by or linked to their functional motivations. The linkage is far more indirect and can be detected only by an examination of many languages. That is, grammars as wholes reflect the 'interests' of language users, but there is no question of parceling out rules, constraints, constructions, and so on of individual grammars and assigning to them a functional motivation. In the course of this chapter, the more concrete aspects of an HF approach will become clear.

5.3 Some problems in deciding between atomistic and holistic functionalism

The choice between atomistic and holistic functionalism is clouded by the fact that it is by no means clear that there is, at present, much content to the claim that each element of grammar can be paired with a functional explanation (§5.3.1). A further complication is posed by the fact that psychologically determined preferences of language users do not always point to robust typological generalizations about grammars (§5.3.2).

5.3.1 *On the content of the claim that grammatical processes are linked to functional motivations*

A methodological problem immediately arises in trying to decide between AF and HF. This problem is derived from the dubious empirical content of the claim that every element of grammar has a functional motivation. In phonology, at least, there is a long tradition, going back to the work of the Prague School in the interwar years, pointing to the phonetic grounding of phonological rules. The 'markedness' and 'faithfulness' constraints of OT phonology have analogues in most approaches to phonology, they seem to encompass a great percentage of well-understood phonological processes, and, at the same time, seem grounded in the behavior and abilities of language users. But nobody understands or, in the foreseeable future, is likely to understand the full set of external factors that might combine to account for the properties of syntactic structure. The functionalist literature has mooted literally dozens of potential factors, ranging all the way from economy, iconicity, and parsing to love of metaphor and 'playfulness.' In short, even the plausible external motivations are so numerous, so diverse, and so open-ended that any conceivable rule or constraint in any framework could be provided with one. In the words of Gereon Müller (1999: 232), 'it is usually not hard to contrive *some* functional motivation for almost any given constraint.'[2]

To illustrate the ease with which any constraint might be 'motivated functionally,' let us consider the two constraints that Haspelmath (1999b: 186) writes would be 'the first candidates for elimination' if OT constraints had to be rephrased in terms of user-optimality:

(4) NO LEXICAL HEAD MOVEMENT: A lexical head cannot move.
(5) LEFT EDGE (CP): The first pronounced word in CP is a function word related to the main verb of that CP.

But it does not seem to be too much of a challenge to provide NO LEXICAL HEAD MOVEMENT with a functional motivation. An iconicity requirement presumably keeps heads and dependents from straying too far from each other in order to facilitate semantic interpretation.

LEFT EDGE (CP) is instantiated by the mandatory presence of the *que* complementizer in French and that of *for* initiating English infinitival complements:

[2] Müller, however, goes on to give examples of constraints which he feels lack functional motivation (see below, *n.* 9).

(6) a. Je crois que Pierre a faim.
    b. *Je crois Pierre a faim.

(7) a. I found a book for you to think about.
    b. *I found a book you to think about.

Here too there is a plausible functional motivation. LEFT EDGE (CP) aids the hearer by providing explicit information as to clause boundaries, as well as typing the clause as finite or non-finite. In other words this constraint plays a role in semantic interpretation. Hence we could add the material in Table 5.1a below to Table 5.1.[3]

By way of illustrating the ease with which any conceivable grammatical construct might be provided with some functional motivation, consider the transformational rules of pre-principles-and-parameters approaches. Even though they formed the target of functionalist assault for their abstractness and seeming divorce from anything that might be considered user-based (see, for example, Givón 1979), they too were argued by certain linguists to have functional motivations. For example, Langacker (1974) classified transformational rules in

TABLE 5.1a. *Possible functions for NO LEXICAL HEAD MOVEMENT and LEFT EDGE (CP)*

Name	Grammatical constraint	Corresponding user constraint
NO LEXICAL HEAD MOVEMENT (Grimshaw 1997)	'A lexical head cannot move'	Moving a lexical head away from its dependents makes it difficult for the hearer to pair heads and dependents.
LEFT EDGE (CP) (Pesetsky 1998)	'The first pronounced word in CP is a function word related to the main verb of that CP'	Not explicitly marking embedded clauses in terms of their boundaries and finiteness impedes rapid recognition of their meaning and role.

[3] Haspelmath has informed me (p. c.) that the lack of generality of these two constraints led him to regard them as lacking corresponding user constraints. That the constraints of Table 5.1a lack generality compared to those of Table 5.1 is certainly correct. But the reasonable conclusion from that fact is that the functional motivations for the former are weaker than those for the latter, not that the former have no functional motivations at all.

Robert Levine points out (p. c.) that it is often legitimate to move dependents away from heads, as in (i):

(i) [Rumors t] I have heard from time to time [that John was a double agent].

The extraposition in (i) does not violate NO LEXICAL HEAD MOVEMENT. Presumably it would be motivated by its role in parsing efficiency, which prefers (for VO languages) a late appearance of heavy constituents (Hawkins 2004a).

terms of whether they raise, front, or back grammatical elements and claimed that each formal operation is designed to facilitate a particular discourse function (see also Creider 1979).

5.3.2 *Atomistic functionalism and psycholinguistic experimentation*

One can imagine one possible check on runaway functional explanations for typological generalizations: namely, to demand that each hypothesized function reflect in some fairly direct way experimentally ascertained preferences of language users. Parsing and iconicity-based explanations come out pretty well in that respect. The advantage to parsing sentences rapidly can hardly be controversial. We know that parsing is fast and efficient. Every word has to be picked out from ensemble of 50,000, identified in one-third of a second, and put in the right structure. And as far as iconicity is concerned, we know that comprehension is made easier when syntactic units are isomorphic to units of meaning than when they are not. Experimental evidence has demonstrated that the semantic interpretation of a sentence proceeds online as the syntactic constituents are recognized.

Nevertheless, the link between experimentally determined preferences of users and cross-linguistic facts about language is too tenuous to narrow significantly the class of functional explanations. An example from Kirby (1998) will illustrate. There are two ways that we can talk about relative clause movement strategies in particular languages. One is in terms of the permitted grammatical relation of the moved item. We have known since Keenan and Comrie (1977) that there is a robust cross-linguistic Accessibility Hierarchy for movement, based on the grammatical relation borne by the moved element (for discussion, see Ch. 1, §1.4). Here we do have a case where psycholinguistic experiment reveals the same preference. Native speaker subjects perform in ways consistent with the cross-linguistic hierarchy (Keenan and Hawkins 1987). In other words, the more abstract parsing-based explanations for the Keenan–Comrie Hierarchy (see Hawkins 2004a) translate into concrete results in the psycholinguistic laboratory.

Now consider another way that relative clause movement can be typologized. One can speak of 'parallel function relatives' and 'non-parallel function relatives.' In parallel function relatives, the grammatical relation borne by the moved relative pronoun and the grammatical relation borne by the relative clause itself are the same. In non-parallel function relatives, they differ. Sentences (8a-d) and trees (8a′-d′) illustrate:

(8) a. [THE WOMAN *WHO* (SUB) IS WALKING IN THE HALLWAY]$_{(SUB)}$ is my friend
    b. I saw [THE WOMAN *WHO* (OBJ) JOHN KNOWS]$_{(OBJ)}$
    c. [THE WOMAN *WHO* (OBJ) JOHN KNOWS]$_{(SUB)}$ is walking in the hallway
    d. I saw [THE WOMAN *WHO* (SUB) IS WALKING IN THE HALLWAY]$_{(OBJ)}$

(8)

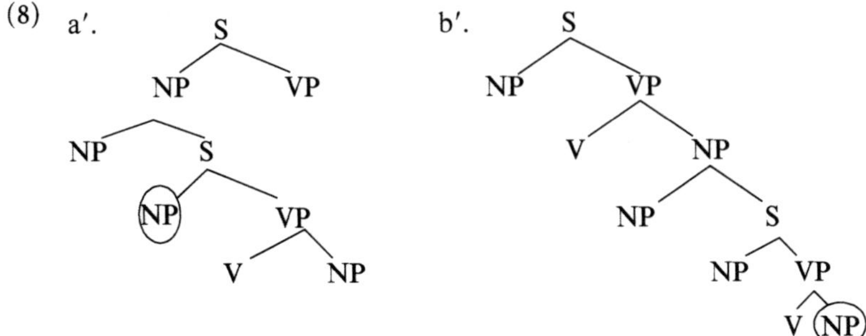

Parallel function relatives (the relativized NP is circled)

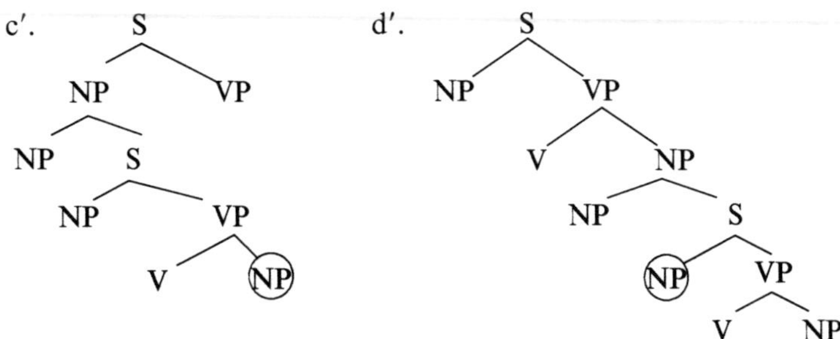

Non-parallel function relatives (the relativized NP is circled)

Kirby notes that experimental subjects overwhelmingly prefer parallel function relatives; non-parallel function relatives present considerable processing difficulty for them. One might predict then that parallel function relatives would predominate cross-linguistically over non-parallel function relatives or that there would be an implicational relationship demanding that if a language has non-parallel function relatives it necessarily has parallel function relatives. Neither is true, however. Kirby attributes this fact to properties of Universal Grammar. In his explanation, structural principles governing predication and *Wh*-Movement demand that a language user automatically acquire object–subject relatives when subject–subject relatives are acquired and subject–object relatives when object–object relatives are acquired.[4]

5.4 Language change as a testing ground for atomistic and holistic functionalism

In this section, it will be argued that facts about language change decide in favor of holistic functionalism. Section 5.4.1 explains why diachronic facts are better

[4] Things might be more complicated than are implied in this paragraph. In still unpublished work, Aldai (2003) and Hawkins (2004b) have pointed to parallel function effects at the lower end of the Accessibility Hierarchy.

suited than synchronic ones in terms of enabling a choice between the two approaches to functionalism. Sections 5.4.2, 5.4.3, and 5.4.4 make the case that studies of historical retentions, propagations, and innovations, respectively, support holistic approaches.

5.4.1 *Atomistic functionalism at the synchronic and diachronic level*

There is a means by which we can at least partly get around the problem posed by the overavailability of functional explanations for typological generalizations and the sometimes tenuous independent evidence for some of these functional explanations. That is to focus on *language change* as a testing ground for AF versus HF. Changes—at least those that are attested or reconstructed with a high degree of certainty—are more concrete and easier to study than more abstract properties of grammars. It is far easier, for example, to answer question (9a) than question (9b):

(9) a. What was the functional motivation (if any) for the appearance of 'supportive *do*' in the history of English syntax?
  b. What is the functional motivation (if any) for the presence of 'supportive *do*' in the syntax of Modern English?

Also, an understanding of (9a) helps to shed light on (9b) in a way that an understanding of (9b) is not necessarily helpful to an understanding of (9a).

Now, it seems that AF rather strongly implies a particular view of language change. If grammars are collections of properties that have functional motivations, then any *change* in a grammar is necessarily a change in the degree of functionality of one or more of those properties. Clearly, such a view embodies a default assumption about the nature of language change. It will—at least in the typical case—be in the direction of maximizing the functionality *of* those properties. If that were not the case, it is difficult to see what content AF could possibly have; indeed, it is difficult to see what interest it could possibly have. It would be an odd theory that demanded a functional motivation for each, say, grammatical rule, but disavowed the necessity for rule changes to be consequences of the maximization of function. Likewise, if some new property is added to the grammar, it will, by hypothesis, have to be functionally motivated. Such a conclusion follows automatically from the hypothesis that grammatical properties are linked to functional motivations.

As it turns out, a number of functionalists have taken the strongest possible position along these lines, namely, that individual instances of language change must be functionally motivated:

> Saying that a certain feature of linguistic design or change cannot be functionally explained is tantamount to saying that we have not yet been able to find a functional explanation for that feature. (Dik 1986: 22)

Other functionalists have taken a somewhat weaker approach to the grammar–function linkage, in that they recognize that synchronic grammars are filled with rules of dubious functional utility, but they nevertheless still uphold the idea that each instance of language change is functionally motivated. Such a view embodies a weaker version of AF that holds only diachronically. Talmy Givón argues along these lines:

> What I will argue here is that, in each instance, a *crazy* synchronic state of the grammar has arisen via diachronic changes that are highly *natural* and presumably motivated independently by various communicative factors. (Givón 1979: 235, emphasis in original)

If the weaker version of AF fails at the diachronic level, then the stronger version could hardly be correct at the synchronic level. The remainder of this section will therefore focus primarily on language change as a testing ground for AF versus HF. It will conclude that there is no diachronic support for AF.

Ever since the work of Weinreich, Labov, and Herzog (1968), it has been standard to break down the process of language change into three stages, stated in (10) in chronological order:

(10) a. innovation (the first appearance of the change)
b. propagation (the adoption of the change by the speech community)
c. retention (the transmission of the change from grammar to grammar in successive generations)

The following sections will examine each in terms of their response to external functional pressures such as parsing, iconicity, and so on. They will argue that many, but by no means all, innovations are functionally motivated in this sense, while propagations and retentions tend not to be. Hence, AF fails at the diachronic level and therefore cannot be correct at the synchronic.

For expository reasons, I will treat them in reverse chronological order: first retention, followed by propagation, and concluding with innovation.

5.4.2 *Retention*

Let us begin with a couple of simple questions about the grammar of Mary Miller, a native speaker of English. One is: 'Why do subjects precede objects?' The other is: 'Why aren't there null subjects?' We could supply very functionalist-sounding answers to those questions: 'Subjects precede objects because they have cognitive prominence over objects and cognitive prominence is iconically represented'; and 'There are no null subjects because agreement is too weak to license them.'

But those are the wrong answers. Mary Miller's grammar has those properties because the grammars of her parents and peers have them. Except in unusual historical circumstances, one's grammar reflects to an extremely high degree the grammars of those in one's speech community. The factor that best explains why a person's grammar has the properties that it has is *conventionality*. Grammars differ only slightly from generation to generation. As noted by William Croft (1995: 522), this stability in a sense has a functional motivation, since it is rooted in mental routinization and social convention. More recently, Croft has made the perspicacious observation that:

> ... a central aspect of a speaker's use of language is convention. When I say *Who did you meet yesterday?*, I put the interrogative pronoun *Who* at the beginning of the sentence because that is the convention of my speech community. I know the conventions of my speech community, and my use of language will serve its purpose best most of the time if I conform to the conventions of my speech community. It may be that the initial position of *Who* is partly motivated by pragmatic universals of information structure, or partly specified by an innate Universal Grammar. In fact, one (or both) of those factors may be the motivation for the origin of the convention. But that is not why I have put it there in that utterance. (Croft 2000: 7)

'Conforming to the conventions of one's speech community' is not, of course, the sort of functional motivation that has been claimed to underlie constraints. Models of grammar such as AF that see constraints as being tied synchronically to motivations such as parsing and iconicity are thus empirically off-base. Grammars do reflect the effects of motivations such as parsing pressure and pressure towards iconicity, of course. But these effects make themselves felt over historical time, and are not 'registered' internally to the grammars themselves. (This point is made forcefully with respect to phonology in Hale and Reiss 2000 and Buckley 2000.) In a nutshell, the forces (functional or otherwise) that bring a construction into a language are not necessarily the same ones that keep it there. To give an example in support of this claim, consider the Modern English genitive. It may either precede or follow the noun it modifies:

(11) a. GEN–N: Mary's mother's uncle's lawyer
 b. N–GEN: the leg of the table

The GEN–N ordering is unexpected, since English is otherwise almost wholly a right-branching language. So why do English-speaking children acquire the GEN–N ordering? The short—and 100 per cent correct answer—is 'conventionality.' They learn that ordering because they detect it in the ambient language of their speech community. But the long answer is very interesting and drives home the great divide between the functional explanation of a grammatical change and force of conventionality that leads to the preservation of the effects of that change.

Old English a thousand years ago was largely left-branching with dominant orders of OV and GEN–N.[5] This is the correlation that is most efficient for parsing (Hawkins 1994, 2004a). The shift to VO order in the Middle English period was matched by a shift to N–GEN order. A text count of 85 per cent N–GEN has been reported for Middle English in Kirby (1998) and Fischer (1992). We do not know details of why this happened. Lightfoot (1991) suggests that as tokens of VO order in main clauses increased, cues that English was OV declined,

[5] Lightfoot (1999: 117) notes that in limited circumstances, N-GEN order and split genitive order were possible as well.

leading English to be reanalyzed as VO underlyingly.[6] But then, after a certain time, everything started to reverse itself, with the text count of GEN–N order increasing dramatically. Why did this reversal occur? According to Kroch (1994) and Rosenbach and Vezzosi (2000), it may have been a result of the two genitives becoming 'functionally differentiated.' The GEN–N construction became favored for animates while the N–GEN construction has tended to be reserved for inanimates (see also Wedgwood 1995 and Kirby 1998). That idea has a lot to commend it, as it is well known that there is a tendency for animates to occur earlier and inanimates later. And now Rosenbach (2005) has demonstrated that the positioning of the genitive is a factor of its 'weight' (some combination of length and structural complexity), as well as its animacy.

Now, then, what would the relation be between the rules and principles that license these two orders in Modern English and the functional motivations that gave rise to them? The answer is that it is so indirect as to be uninteresting. The current state of the English genitive is a product of over a thousand years of changes, many functionally motivated when they occurred, but preserved in the language primarily by the force of conventionality. Yes, it was undoubtedly parsing pressure that led Old English to be predominately GEN–N. That pressure no longer exists, but the order does. If the need for 'functional differentiation' is part of the explanation for why that order was preserved, one challenges any advocate of AF to demonstrate that the particular functional force excludes potential structures from the grammars of English speakers today and to identify the particular constraints to which this factor is linked. Among other problems that would need to be addressed is the fact that the functional differentiation is only partial. That is, inanimates can occur in the GEN–N construction (12a is not horribly unacceptable) and animates can occur in the N–GEN construction (as in 12b):

(12) a. The table's leg
     b. The mother of the lawyer

So at least four pressures are involved in maintaining the two genitive orders in Modern English: the pressure of conventionality; the pressure to have animate specifiers and inanimate complements; pressure to place 'more weighty' elements after 'less weighty' ones; and purely structural pressure, caused by the existence of noun phrases with the structure [NP's N] and [N of NP] where there is no semantic possession at all:

(13) a. Tuesday's lecture
     b. the proof of the theorem

[6] Lightfoot (1999: 119) gives examples of split genitives in Middle English. Unlike in Old English, the element to the right in the split genitive does not have to bear a thematic relation with the element to the left, a state of affairs that Lightfoot ties to Case theory.

The point is that languages are filled with structures that arose in the course of history to respond to some functional pressure, but, as the language as a whole changed, ceased to be very good responses to that original pressure. Such facts are challenging to any theory like AF, in which the sentences of a language are said to be a synchronic product of constraints that must be functionally motivated.[7]

AF confounds what we know with how what we know *got to be* what we know. Parsing ease, desire for functional differentiation, pressure for an iconic relationship between form and meaning, and so on are indeed forces that shape grammars. These forces influence adult speakers, in their use of language, to produce variant forms consistent with them. Children, in the process of acquisition, hear these variant forms and grammaticalize them. In that way, over time, certain functional influences leave their mark on grammars. There is no place—indeed no *need*—for the functional forces to match up in a one-to-one fashion with particular constraints internal to any particular grammar.

5.4.3 *Propagation*

It is by now well established, I think, that functional utility has little to do with whether any particular innovation in language use is incorporated into the grammars of the individuals making up a particular speech community. Work such as Milroy (1987) has demonstrated that the mechanisms of propagation are social, not linguistic. That is, whether an innovation will become entrenched is for the most part a function of the social networks within the speech community.

Let us make the assumption that social forces and functional forces are independent variables—after all, one does not gain prestige over one's peers by being better than they in effecting an iconic relationship between form and meaning! What this means is that only 50 per cent of the time will the 'more functional' variant become entrenched. This fact has fairly grave implications for AF. Consider an innovation that was adopted by the speech community some generations earlier because it was used by an influential member of that community, even though its functional motivation (in the sense that grammarians use the term) was less than that of the form that it replaced. It seems that AF has two options with respect to the rule or constraint that characterizes that innovation. One would be to find some functional motivation (parsing, iconicity, etc.) that it could plausibly be said to serve and to link it to that function; the other would be to link it to the function of 'prestige enhancing,' or some such thing. Both

[7] In rebuttal to this point, Bresnan and Aissen (2002) cite work that observes that speakers of Modern English are more likely to use animate genitives than inanimates in the GEN–N construction and more likely to use inanimate genitives than animates in the N–GEN construction, and that their choice of genitive seems to reflect functionally motivated hierarchies such as those of topicality and animacy (see Hawkins 1981; Deane 1987; Rosenbach 2002, 2003). To account for these and related facts, they suggest stochastic OT constraints that penalize inanimate specifiers more than animate specifiers and penalize animate complements more than inanimate complements. The remarks in the previous chapter on stochastic approaches to grammar apply here. For comments specifically addressed to an OT approach to this phenomenon, see below, §5.6.4.2.

alternatives are unacceptable. The former simply represents a *post hoc* attempt to save the core idea of AF. The latter will, in the typical case, fail empirically—the prestige factors that led to the propagation of the form are unlikely to be responsible for its retention after several generations.

5.4.4 *Innovation*

As opposed to retentions and propagations, one can indeed make the case that many innovations are motivated by user-based external functions. This is particularly true for those that arise language-internally. For example, many tend in the direction of increasing 'iconicity,' in that they increase the degree of transparency of the mapping between form and meaning. Croft (2000) discusses a number of mechanisms by which such a change can be effected. One is what he calls 'hyperanalysis,' in which an existing irregularity in the form–meaning mapping is eliminated. An example is the loss of governed dative and genitive objects in several Germanic languages. This process began in Old English even before the loss of the case system in general. The following examples, from Allen (1995: 133, 135), illustrate a governed genitive giving way to a structurally determined accusative:

(14) a. Micel wund behofað micles læcedomes
great.NOM wound.NOM needs great.GEN leechcraft.GEN
'A great wound requires great medicine'

b. ...swa heo maran læcedom behofað
...so it greater leechcraft.ACC needs
'...so it requires better medicine'

Croft also discusses 'hypoanalysis,' in which a contextual property of a form is reanalyzed as an inherent property. The history of German umlaut provides an illustration. The umlaut process was phonemicized in the Carolingian period (from the ninth to the tenth century), morphologized in Middle High German, and became hypoanalyzed as plural marker in Early New High German. Hence we now have *Baum*/*Bäume* 'tree'/'trees', where there was never any phonetic motivation for the umlaut.

Many innovations appear to be parsing-motivated, as well. Foremost among these are those that aid parsing by making language more 'harmonic,' that is, by increasing branching-direction consistency. This often takes place by means of the reanalysis of an existing construction. For example, several scholars have remarked that languages that have developed VO order often develop harmonic PN order by reanalyzing some verbs as prepositions (Aristar 1991; Givón 1971; Heine and Reh 1984; Vennemann 1973).

Another class of parsing-motivated changes involves the reordering of existing elements. For example, Harris and Campbell (1995: 229) note that Old Georgian was SVO with SVO harmonies, while Modern Georgian is SOV with SOV harmonies. In the course of time, existing prepositions turned into postpositions, while genitives and relatives were moved in front of the head.

However, not all innovations make things easier for language users, in any obvious sense of the term 'easier.' Historical linguists with a functionalist bent tend to stress the common tendency to rule generalization in language change, that is, where an existing rule tends to broaden its scope to maximize the transparency of the link between form and meaning. We have just seen a couple of examples of this process. But the reverse is also common, that is, where we have the *shrinking* of the applicability of a rule, sometimes with consequences that run counter to any iconic relationship between form and meaning. To cite one example, Old English, like most modern Germanic languages, was a V2 language, with a productive process moving verbs from V to I to C. For reasons that have been much debated in the literature on the history of English, the I-to-C movement has become restricted to tensed auxiliaries, as (15a-b) shows:

(15) a. Have you been working hard?
b. *Worked you hard yesterday?

But bafflingly, some phrasal elements in Spec, CP still trigger this inversion and some do not:

(16) a. Under no circumstances will I take a day off.
b. *Given any possibility will I take a day off.
(17) a. So tall is Mary, she can see into second story windows.
b. *Solved the puzzle has Mary, so she can be proud of herself.

There is no way that the set of changes leading to the fragmentary instances of inversion in Modern English—all internally triggered, as far as I know—can be said to have led in the direction of greater 'functionality.'[8]

Or consider the historical changes in French negation, in particular the grammaticalization of *pas* from noun to negative particle. In Old French sentences with negative force, the negative particle *ne* was often reinforced by the use of semantically appropriate independent nouns. With motion verbs, for example, *ne* was accompanied by the noun *pas* 'step.' Other negation-reinforcing nouns included *point* 'dot, point', *mie* 'crumb', *gote* 'drop', among others. As French developed, *pas* began to accompany *ne* even where no motion was taking place, displacing its rival negation-reinforcers. Since the seventeenth century *pas* has been virtually compulsory in the negative construction. There were several innovations in this entire process, and it is hard to see how any of them led to increased 'functionality' of the process of negative formation in French. Old French negative formation could not have been simpler. Presumably, an AF-oriented theory would predict that French would have left things alone.

[8] A full treatment of inversion possibilities in the history of English would require several volumes. Oddly, some inversion triggers were historically late innovations, even while the majority of fronted phrases ceased to function as triggers. For a recent discussion, see Nevalainen (1997).

In fact, a number of linguists have claimed that the changes associated with grammaticalization are literally *dysfunctional* (see, for example, Haspelmath 1999b,c; Dahl 2000b). Table 5.2 presents some typical grammaticalization-related changes.

Are the changes depicted in the table 'functional'? That all depends on what one might mean by 'functional.' According to Haspelmath, they have their origins in what he calls 'speaker extravagance,' whereby language users make unusually explicit formulations in order to attract attention. The first Old French speakers to say *casa* instead of simply *a* were not making anything 'more functional' either for themselves or their addressees, at least not if 'functional' has something to do with maximizing economy of effort, being more semantically transparent, and so on. In fact, just the opposite is the case. Speakers were adding an unnecessary complication to the grammar for the sake of, essentially, showing off. But a sizeable percentage of well-studied instances of grammatical change are grammaticalization-related. It does not say much in favor of AF if grammars are full of words, constructions, and rules that entered the language for—essentially—anti-functional reasons.

So far, we have confined our discussion to the innovation of 'internal' changes, namely, those that do not seem to have been triggered by language contact. But a huge amount of grammatical change is contact-induced. Here, functional factors

TABLE 5.2. *Some grammaticalization changes (lexical > functional category) cited in Haspelmath (1999c: 1045)*

Category Change	Example	Discussion
N > P	Latin *casa* 'house' > French *chez* 'at (somebody's place)'	Svorou (1994); Longobardi (2001)
N > C	English *while* 'period of time' > *while* 'simultaneity'	Kortmann (1996)
ProN > Agr	Lat. *Illam video* 'I see that one' > Span. *la veo a María* OBJ. AGR.	Givón (1976)
N > Num	Chinese *men* 'class' > *-men* 'plural'	
V > P	Yoruba *fi* 'use' > *fi* 'with'	Lord (1993)
V > C	German *während* 'enduring' > *während* 'while, during'	Kortmann and König (1992)
V > Asp	Lezgian *qačuz awa* 'taking, is' > *qaču-zwa* 'is taking'	Bybee and Dahl (1989)
V > T	Greek *θélo na páo* 'I want to go' > *θa páo* 'I'll go'	Bybee, Perkins, and Pagliuca (1994)
A > P	English *like* 'equal' > *like* 'similative'	Maling (1983)
A > D	Latin *ipse* 'himself' > Sardinian *su* 'the'	
Q > Num	English *all* > Tok Pisin *ol* 'plural'	

are even more remotely at the root cause of the changes. Indeed, borrowed forms are often counter-functional from a language user's perspective. Harris and Campbell (1995: 136–42) and Campbell (1996) point to a number of contact-induced word-order disharmonies. Amharic was originally VO, like most Semitic languages, but borrowed OV and genitive–noun order from the neighboring Cushitic languages. Nevertheless, it retained prepositions. Ahom (Thai) borrowed modifier–head order from Assamese (Indo-European) or some Tibeto-Burman language. Munda languages borrowed modifier–head order from Dravidian. And Pipil, Xinca, and Copainalá Zoque borrowed VOS from neighboring Mayan languages. All of these cases led to disharmonies, resulting in decreased parsing efficiency, without any obvious gain in functionality in some other respect.

Perhaps the most dramatic example of the possible dysfunctional consequences of borrowing involves the history of English word stress. Old English word stress was very simple, and not significantly different from the Modern German rule (Moore and Knott 1965):

(18) The first syllable is stressed, except for words containing certain prefixes, in which case the root syllable is stressed.

As far as Modern English is concerned, it suffices to consult the approximately 200 pages of Chomsky and Halle (1968) devoted to this question. What was responsible for the increased complication? Most importantly, England was invaded and conquered by Old French-speaking Normans. Some of the words that entered English as a result were stressed by the Old French rule and some by the Latin rule, both of which are pretty simple (19a-b):

(19) a. Old French: The last syllable is stressed, except for words ending in schwa.
b. Latin: The penultimate syllable is stressed if it is strong, the antepenultimate if it is weak.

But the net result of the synthesis of these simple rules after hundreds of French words poured into English was the monstrosity that we have today. There is no coherent sense of the word 'functional' that would allow anybody to conclude that changes in English stress patterns have become more 'functional.'

5.5 Some further difficulties with atomistic functionalism

Other difficulties with atomistic functionalism arise from the fact that functionally motivated innovations overgeneralize beyond their functional utility (§5.5.1), that functionally motivated principles can have dysfunctional consequences (§5.5.2), and that functionally motivated principles can compete with each other (§5.5.3).

5.5.1 *The overgeneralization of functionally motivated principles*

What makes a defense of AF even more difficult—at either the diachronic or synchronic level—is the fact that functionally motivated principles tend to generalize beyond their functional need. That is, they become grammaticalized. Island constraints provide good illustrations. I have no doubt that their ultimate origins are in parsing efficiency (see Newmeyer 1991). Nevertheless, over time, their range of applicability has extended beyond those cases in which they serve an obvious function. To repeat some examples from Chapter 1, Janet Fodor (1984) has called attention to sentences that are ungrammatical because they contain constraint violations, even where there are no processing difficulties:

(20) a. *Who were you hoping for ___ to win the game?
 b. *What did the baby play with ___ and the rattle?

Along the same lines, she points to pairs of sentences of roughly equal ease to the parser, where one is grammatical and the other contains a constraint violation and is therefore ungrammatical (21a-b; 22a-b):

(21) a. *John tried for Mary to get along well with ___.
 b. John is too snobbish for Mary to get along well with ___.

(22) a. *The second question, that he couldn't answer ___ satisfactorily was obvious.
 b. The second question, it was obvious that he couldn't answer ___ satisfactorily.

Universal grammar in interaction with the structural system of English decides the grammaticality; the parser takes a back seat. Again, such examples suggest that the linkage between individual constraints in the grammar and functional motivations is rather weak.

5.5.2 *Dysfunctional consequences of functionally motivated principles*

Lightfoot (1999) has even provided an example of how a constraint can have *dysfunctional* consequences. Consider condition (23):

(23) Traces of movement must be lexically governed

This condition does a lot of work—for example, it accounts for the grammaticality distinction between (24a) and (24b):

(24) a. Who$_i$ was it apparent [e$_i$ that [Kay saw $\mathbf{e}_i$]]?
 b. * Who$_i$ was it apparent yesterday [$\mathbf{e}_i$ that [Kay saw $\mathbf{e}_i$]]?

In (24b) the word *yesterday* blocks government of the intermediate trace (in boldface) by the adjective *apparent*. Or consider phrase (25):

(25) Jay's picture

(25) is at least three-ways ambiguous: Jay could be the owner of the picture, the agent of the production of the picture, or the person portrayed (the object reading). The derivation of the object reading is depicted in (26):

(26) [Jay_i's [picture e_i]]

Notice that the trace is governed by the noun *picture*. Now consider phrase (27):

(27) the picture of Jay's

(27) has the owner and agent reading, but not the object reading, That is, Jay cannot be the person depicted. The derivation, schematically illustrated in (28), explains why:

(28) *the picture of [Jay_i's [e e_i]]

The trace of *Jay's* is not lexically governed; rather it is governed by another empty element, understood as 'picture.'

Lightfoot is quite open to the possibility that condition (23) is functionally motivated:

> ...the general condition of movement traces...may well be functionally motivated, possibly by parsing considerations. In parsing utterances, one needs to analyze the positions from which displaced elements have moved, traces. The UG condition discussed restricts traces to certain well-defined positions, and that presumably facilitates parsing. (Lightfoot 1999: 249)

However, he goes on to show that this condition—functionally motivated though it may be—has dysfunctional consequences. The problem is that it blocks the straightforward extraction of subjects:

(29) a. *Who_i do think [e_i that $\mathbf{e_i}$ saw Fay]?
b. *Who_i do you wonder [e_i how [$\mathbf{e_i}$ solved the problem]]?

Sentences (29a-b) are ungrammatical because the boldfaced subject traces are not lexically governed. Indeed, in the typical case, subjects will not be lexically governed. Nevertheless, it is safe to assume that it is in the interest of language users to question subjects, just as much as objects or any other syntactic position. In other words, the lexical government condition is in part dysfunctional.

Interestingly, languages have devised various ways of getting around the negative effects of the condition. They are listed in (30a-c):

(30) Strategies for undoing the damage of the lexical government condition:
a. Adjust the complementizer to license the extraction.
b. Use a resumptive pronoun in the extraction site.
c. Move the subject first to a non-subject position and then extract.

English uses strategy (30a):

(31) Who do you think saw Fay?

Swedish uses strategy (30b):

(32) Vilket ord$_i$ visste ingen [hur det/*e$_i$ stavas]?
Which word knew no one how it/e is spelled?
'Which word did no one know how it is spelled?'

The resumptive pronoun *det* replaces the trace, so there is no unlexically governed trace to violate the lexical government condition. And Italian uses the third strategy (30c). In Italian, subjects can occur to the right of the verb and this is the position from which they are extracted (as in 33):

(33) Chi$_i$ credi [che abbia telefonato e$_i$]?
who do-you-think that has telephoned?
'Who do you think has telephoned?'

What we see here in other words are functional patches for dysfunctional side-effects of functional principles. The whole package is, in a sense, functionally motivated— after all, it does let us communicate—but it does not make much sense to attempt to provide functional motivations for each of the component parts.

To put the issues before us somewhat differently, it is a mistake to ask questions like: 'Is this rule or constraint (or whatever) functionally motivated?' or 'Is Rule A better functionally motivated than Rule B?' No rule or constraint has a functional motivation in and of itself, but rather only within the total system in which it occurs. To illustrate further, let us consider the rule of *Wh*-Movement (34) and the constraint (or parameter setting, if you will) (35):

(34) *Wh*-Movement: Front *wh*-expressions
(35) HEAD-RIGHT: Heads uniformly follow their complements and adjuncts

Is *Wh*-Movement functionally motivated? It certainly seems to be, since it plays a role in marking scope and reserving a 'special' position for focused elements.[9] What about HEAD-RIGHT? Again, this constraint appears to be functionally motivated, since there is a parsing advantage to all heads being on same side of their complements (Hawkins 1994). But what is *dysfunctional* is for any language to have *both* of them. Most head-final languages do not have *Wh*-Movement and there is a good reason for that. *Wh*-Movement creates too much temporary ambiguity in OV languages if arguments are moved away from their subcategorized position. OV languages tend to make arguments 'toe the line': *Wh*-Movement is rare and A-movements are in general disfavored. In other words, all

[9] Müller (1999), however, argues that the OT constraint OP-SPEC (operators in Specifier position), which has the effect of licensing *Wh*-Movement, is not functionally motivated. As he points out, *wh*-phrases are not necessarily (semantic) operators, some cases of *Wh*-Movement have to be partly undone semantically, all *wh*-phrases can in principle be interpreted *in situ*, and *wh*-phrases may respect OP-SPEC by undergoing partial movement to an embedded non-scope position. It is not clear how an advocate of the idea that all constraints have functional motivations would respond to these points.

other things being equal, in grammars with *Wh*-Movement, the constraint HEAD-RIGHT is dysfunctional. But these are just two grammatical processes out of, presumably, thousands. For any pair—or triple, or quadruple, etc., etc.— of processes one can ask the degree to which that association of processes is a 'functional' one. After all, only the most ardent anti-structuralist would deny that languages are tightly connected wholes. So what place is there, then, for assigning a function to any individual part of a grammar? The root of the problem for AF is the fact that functional explanation is vastly too complex to allow individual functions to be attached to individual grammatical elements.

5.5.3 *The problem posed by competing motivations*

Complicating still further the possibility of linking processes and functions as a step toward the explanation of the cross-linguistic distribution of grammatical elements is the problem of multiple competing factors, pulling on grammars from different directions. As has often been observed, the existence of competing motivations threatens to render functional explanation vacuous. For example, consider two languages L1 and L2 and assume that L1 has property X and L2 has property Y, where X and Y are incompatible (i. e. no language can have both X and Y). Now assume that there exists one functional explanation (FUNEX1) that accounts for why a language might have X and another functional explanation (FUNEX2) that accounts for why a language might have Y. Can we say that the fact that L1 has property X is 'explained' by FUNEX1 or the fact that L2 has property Y is 'explained' by FUNEX2? Certainly not; those would be totally empty claims. Given the state of our knowledge about how function affects form, we have no non-circular means for attributing a particular property of a particular language to a particular functional factor. The best we can do is to characterize the general, *typological* influence of function on form.

But this situation is typical of what is encountered in external explanation. Consider cigarette smoking and lung cancer. We know that smoking is a cause of lung cancer. We also know that eating lots of leafy green vegetables helps to prevent it. Now, can we say with confidence that John Smith, a heavy smoker, has lung cancer *because* he smokes? Or can we say that Mary Jones, a non-smoker and big consumer of leafy green vegetables, does not have lung cancer for that reason? No, we cannot. Most individuals who smoke several packs a day will never develop lung cancer, while many non-smoking vegetarians will develop that disease. To complicate things still further, most smokers are also consumers of leafy green vegetables, so both external factors are exerting an influence on them. The best we can do is to talk about *populations.*

The external factors affecting language are far murkier than those affecting health. It would therefore be a serious mistake to entertain the idea of linking statements in particular grammars with functional motivations, as is entailed by AF. Rather, we need to set the more modest goal associated with HF, namely, that of accounting for typological generalizations. But that is hardly an insignificant goal. If accomplished, it will have achieved one of the central tasks facing theoretical linguistics today—coming to an understanding of the relationship between grammatical form and those external forces that help to shape that form.

5.6 More on Optimality Theory, functional explanation, and typology

The following sections continue the critique of atomistic functionalism, begun above, but focus on features that are specific to OT—that is, not shared by other AF-oriented approaches that attempt to link directly grammatical constructs and their functional motivations. Given the fact that OT in general and, even more so, functionally based OT (henceforth 'FOT') in particular have appealed to their seeming ability to account for typological generalizations as one major ingredient of their desirability, it seems appropriate to devote a considerable amount of space to a critique of such claims. I will argue that the typological program of OT in general is severely flawed, a deficiency not remedied by pairing each constraint with a functional motivation.

Section 5.6.1 introduces OT syntax and explains why some linguists have found it appealing. Section 5.6.2 then goes on to say that the typological program of standard OT has a crucial flaw. Sections 5.6.3 and 5.6.4 introduce and criticize FOT respectively and §5.6.5 is a brief summary.

5.6.1 Optimality-theoretic syntax

The following two subsections introduce OT approaches to syntax and discuss their appeal respectively.

5.6.1.1 Syntax, phonology, and Optimality Theory

Many syntacticians gaze upon the world of phonological theorizing with wonder and envy. Phonologists appear to have their act together in ways that have long been unknown to syntacticians. For one thing, new approach after new approach in phonology seems to rally most of the field behind it. Lexical phonology, metrical phonology, and autosegmental phonology all had the effect of sparking a research program that was endorsed—if not always practiced—by a great majority of the world's phonologists. And now for a decade, Optimality Theory (OT) has followed suit. While there are holdouts, of course, and an increasing number of individuals with reservations about the enterprise, it seems accurate to use the expression 'swept the field' to describe the impact of OT in phonology.

Secondly, and even more impressively, these different approaches are not at root incompatible—they simply focus on different aspects of phonological patterning. So, there is no intellectual inconsistency, say, in writing a metrical paper one year, an autosegmental the next, and having as one's current research program the task of recasting some of the generalizations in these works in OT terms.

The world of syntactic theorizing could not be more different. Every new approach has tended to reject fundamental aspects of its predecessor. In syntax, rival approaches are just that—for the most part at root incompatible. The move from Government-Binding to the Minimalist Program or from GPSG to HPSG entailed abandoning central hypotheses of the earlier models. Only an intellectual schizophrenic or anarchist would write an LFG paper one year and a categorial grammar paper the next, without having had severe qualms about the adequacy of the former and having been intrigued by the possibilities of the latter. And it goes without saying that there exists a plethora of 'functionalist' and 'cognitive' approaches to syntax that do not share even the questions that formal approaches ask, much less the answers. As a consequence, syntax is in a highly fragmented state.

Given the relative degree of harmony among phonologists, it might seem surprising that models of syntax have not borrowed more conceptual apparatus from phonology. Until recently, autolexical syntax (Sadock 1991) and the 'case in tiers' theory of Yip, Maling, and Jackendoff (1987) were perhaps the sole modern approaches to syntax whose architecture had phonological roots. If phonologists know something that we (syntacticians) don't know, then why not adapt this knowledge to our own work? The answer to this question is not a mystery—for the most part syntax is simply too different from phonology for any attempt to calque the former on the latter to meet with a great deal of success. Also, given the predominant view that the phonological component takes as its input the output of the syntactic component, phonologists *have to* pay attention to syntax, while syntacticians can—and often do—feel free to ignore the latest developments in phonology.

OT, however, promises to reverse this trend. A significant number of syntacticians have looked to this model—one designed originally to handle phonology—for the purpose of capturing typological generalizations in morphosyntax. The reason that OT has the potential for winning over syntacticians is that it is, at root, not a theory of phonology per se. Rather, it is a theory governing the interaction of constraints. Where the constraints come from is another question—a question that is independent of whether or not one has chosen the OT approach to constraint interaction.

Despite its success in phonology, however, OT has not swept the field of syntactic theory. Predictably, perhaps, it has simply increased the fragmentation of an already-fragmented area of investigation. Part of the explanation for that fact derives from the very nature of OT. It provides no new theory of UG in itself, but merely organizes the principles provided by existing theories of UG. So in other words, assessing the adequacy of an OT syntactic analysis involves not just assessing the results of constraint interaction in that analysis, but also the constraints themselves and, therefore, the theory that provides the constraints. In the past, one could work, say, in the MP, in LFG, or in functionalist syntax. Now, one can work in the MP, with or without an OT orientation, in LFG, with or without an OT orientation, and in functionalist syntax, with or without an OT orientation. The possibilities open to syntacticians are therefore double what they were before the advent of OT.

This section presents a critical, mainly negative, appraisal of OT syntax. It is intended to make no claim, positive or negative, about OT approaches to phonology. Some of the criticism will clearly transfer to phonological work within OT, and some will not. But it is left to others to argue for that transfer. A basic knowledge of the mechanics of OT will be assumed here; the following section will give a short overview of how OT might work for syntax and discuss briefly what there is about this approach that some syntacticians have found appealing.

5.6.1.2 The appeal of OT syntax

As in OT phonology, constraints in OT syntax are universal and violable. What is language-specific is the ranking of the constraints. The first question to ask, then, is what might compose a candidate set, whose members 'compete.' The answer is simple enough in phonology. The input is the underlying form of the word and the output an annotated phonetic representation. The competition set is an infinite set of forms, though because of faithfulness constraints only those bearing some plausible phonological connection to the input have any chance of surfacing as the output. As far as syntax is concerned, it is not totally obvious what competes with what. Following the most cited paper in OT syntax, Grimshaw (1997), the input is generally taken to be an extended projection—that is, a lexical head and associated arguments and functional elements. So for a verbal extended projection, the input is a lexical head and its associated argument structure, along with the associated tense and aspect elements. The input is passed to GEN, which generates all extended projections conforming to X-bar principles. The nature of GEN, of course, depends on the framework being assumed. Grimshaw, for example, assumes some version of principles-and-parameters syntax in her work, while Bresnan (1997, 2000a,b) presents an LFG-based approach to OT.[10] So at least in the simplest cases a competition set is made up of phrases with the same heads and dependents, but which differ in their arrangement (Legendre, Smolensky, and Wilson (1998) argue that competing structures may have, but need not have the same LF). In fact, the literature reveals a world of variety with respect to what can constitute a competition set. We find in competition whole sentences, sentence fragments that are not even constituents, different forms of personal pronouns, and so on. Expository convenience accounts for some of this variety, but certainly not for all of it.

Let us examine a simple (and simplified) tableau which demonstrates how OT might account for a fundamental typological difference among languages—the presence or absence of overt *Wh*-Movement in their grammars. Two crucial constraints are posited, STAY and OP-SPEC:

[10] Bresnan (2000a: 21) writes that 'GEN must be universal. That is, the input and the candidate set are the same for all languages. Systematic differences between languages arise from different rankings...' This remark is puzzling, since in all OT work, including Bresnan's own, candidate sets contain language-particular functional morphemes (such as auxiliary *do*), as well as language-particular expletive elements.

(36) STAY: Trace is forbidden

(37) OPERATOR IN SPECIFIER (OP-SPEC): Syntactic operators must be in specifier position

Tableau 5.1 represents the ranking of STAY and OP-SPEC in a language with overt *Wh*-Movement, Tableau 5.2 their ranking in a language without.

If OP-SPEC ≫ STAY, the candidate with overt *Wh*-Movement is the winner; if STAY ≫ OP-SPEC, it is the candidate without overt movement.

It is easy to see why an OT approach to syntax has won a number of adherents. The idea of violable universal constraints as opposed to parameters rigidly set for a particular language is very seductive. Such an approach allows for flexibility, in that constraints need not be an all-or-nothing affair, and demands precision, in that the exercise of ranking constraints demands more formalization than is typically found in P&P approaches to syntax.[11] Also the possibility of violable universal constraints as opposed to rigid parameters allows for interesting empirical predictions. By hypothesis, all constraints are operative in all languages—the only difference is in their ranking. What this means is that even high-ranked constraints can be violated in a language if a higher one exists and that the effects of low-ranked constraints can become evident, given the right requirements imposed by higher-ranked constraints. Let us examine briefly each possibility.

The first example is of a high-ranked constraint being violated. Costa (1998: 22–4) posits the following two constraints:

Tableau 5.1. *A language with overt* Wh-*Movement*

	OP-SPEC	STAY
☞Who$_i$ did you see t$_i$		*
You saw who	*!	

Tableau 5.2. *A language without overt* Wh-*Movement*

	STAY	OP-SPEC
Who$_i$ did you see t$_i$	*!	
☞You saw who		*

[11] Though it must be said that the *content* of the constraints is often not well formalized, or even formalized at all.

(38) CASE: Move NP to a case-licensing position (e.g. subjects to [Spec, IP]; objects to [Spec, AgrOP]).
(39) WEIGHT: Postpose heavy NPs.

Now CASE is obviously a high-ranked constraint: its GB ancestor, the Case Filter, was presented as an inviolable universal property of grammars. But notice that it *can* (seemingly) be violated. A sufficiently 'heavy' NP can (or must) move to a position to which Case is not assigned. In other words, WEIGHT appears to outrank CASE in English:

(40) a. Mary regards John fondly.
b. ?Mary regards fondly John.
c. ?Mary regards all the students in her evening class in Optimality Theory fondly.
d. Mary regards fondly all the students in her evening class in Optimality Theory.

Tableau 5.3 illustrates.

The second example, that of a low-ranked constraint surfacing, is provided in Grimshaw (1997). STAY is a very low-ranked constraint in English, a language which is quite promiscuous in its movement possibilities. Yet Subject-Auxiliary Inversion does not apply in simple matrix declaratives. Why? Because higher-ranked constraints conspire to prevent movement. The relevant constraints are the following:

(41) OPERATOR IN SPECIFIER (OP-SPEC): Syntactic operators must be in specifier position.
(42) OBLIGATORY HEADS (OB-HD): A projection has a head.
(43) ECONOMY OF MOVEMENT (STAY): Trace is not allowed.

Observe in Tableau 5.4 how this ranking conspires to block inversion. The second entry violates the constraint against empty-headed projections and the third, in which movement takes place, violates STAY. So in English *John will read books* is the grammatical declarative.

5.6.2 *Standard OT sheds no light on typology*

It has become commonplace in OT syntax literature for a paper in that framework to conclude with remarks along the following lines:

TABLEAU 5.3. *Weight effects dominating the Case requirement in English (Costa 1998)*

	WEIGHT	CASE
[[SV [$_{VP}$ Adv t] [Heavy NP]]		*
[SV [$_{AgrOP}$ Heavy NP [$_{VP}$ Adv t t]]]	*!	

Not only has our analysis provided an elegant treatment of [whatever syntactic phenomenon], but it makes non-trivial predictions as well. As has been demonstrated, no possible ordering of the constraints proposed could yield [whatever ungrammatical sentences]. Hence free constraint ranking admits a much smaller class of languages than might be expected. An OT account is thus capable of explaining important facts about the typological distribution of grammatical elements.

Claims of this sort are—in every case that I have examined—without foundation. What they presuppose is that the only relevant constraints are those proposed in the particular research paper to handle the phenomena under immediate analysis. That is, the paper demonstrates that any combination of *those particular constraints* will not yield the targeted impossible forms. But it must be remembered that constraints are universal. If a constraint is necessary for the grammar of one language, then, by hypothesis, it exists in the grammars of all languages. All it takes is one of these 'additional' constraints to subvert the claim that one's OT account has explained the non-existence in principle of some particular set of sentences. And since all rankings of constraints are permitted by the theory, there is no OT-internal possibility of accounting for why a ranking utilized by only one or two languages in the world should be rare.

Section 5.6.2.1 presents an OT analysis of subject universals, in which a typological claim is put forward. Section 5.6.2.2 illustrates how such a claim—and others of the same form—can be subverted.

5.6.2.1 Grimshaw and Samek-Lodovici on subject universals

Let us turn to the analysis of subjects in Italian and English in Grimshaw and Samek-Lodovici (1998). Italian has many more possibilities subject-wise than English, given that subjects can be null even in tensed clauses and may occur postposed. Here are the relevant constraints that Grimshaw and Samek-Lodovici propose, presented in ranked order for Italian:

(44) DROPTOPIC: Leave arguments coreferent with the topic structurally unrealized [failed by overt constituents which are coreferential with the topic].

TABLEAU 5.4. *The surfacing of a low-ranked constraint (Grimshaw 1997)*

Candidates	OP-SPEC	OB-HEAD	STAY
☞ $[_{IP}$ DP will $[_{VP}$ read books]]			
$[_{CP}$ e $[_{IP}$ DP will $[_{VP}$ read books]]]		*!	
$[_{CP}$ will$_i$ $[_{IP}$ DP e$_i$ $[_{VP}$ read books]]]			*!

(45) PARSE: Parse input constituents [failed if an element of the input does not appear in the output].
(46) ALIGN FOCUS: Align the left edge of focus constituents with the right edge of a maximal projection [failed by non-aligned foci].
(47) FULL-INTERPRETATION: Parse lexical conceptual structure [failed by expletives and auxiliary *do*].
(48) SUBJECT: The highest A-specifier in an extended projection must be filled [failed by clauses without a subject in the canonical position].

An interesting result of this particular ranking of these particular constraints is that when the subject is focused, it has to be postverbal. As Tableau 5.5 illustrates, a focused subject can be neither null nor overtly occurring in canonical subject position.

In English, PARSE is the highest-ranked constraint, with SUBJECT also ranked very high, so a focused overt subject may indeed occur in canonical subject position.

Grimshaw and Samek-Lodovici, however, go on to make a universal typological claim about subjects, namely that:

> this system of constraints makes the non-trivial prediction that a contrastively focused subject can never be null, i.e., undergo pro-drop. This follows from the fact that a subject will be realized unless it is topic-connected and hence under the influence of DROPTOPIC. Its realization will be mandated by PARSE and SUBJECT... This universal prediction... (Grimshaw and Samek-Lodovici 1998: 214)

In other words, languages may have null topics as subjects, but never null contrastively focused subjects.

TABLEAU 5.5. *Italian focused subjects (Grimshaw and Samek-Lodovici 1998: 211)*

Input: <gridare (x), x=focus, x=Gianni>

Candidates	DROP TOPIC	PARSE	ALIGN FOCUS	FULL-INT	SUBJECT
☞ha gridato Gianni 'has screamed John'					*
Gianni ha gridato			*!		
ha gridato, Gianni			*!		*
ha gridato		*!			*
[*null structure*]		*!*			
expl. ha gridato Gianni				*!	

5.6.2.2 Generating null focused subjects

Grimshaw and Samek-Lodovici are correct in their claim that no reranking of the constraints that they propose in their paper will yield null focus in subject position. But why should these be the only relevant constraints? If we add the following constraint to UG, everything changes:

(49) DROPFOCUS: Leave arguments coreferent with the focus structurally unrealized [failed by overt constituents which are coreferential with the focus].

If DROPFOCUS is ranked more highly than the other constraints we have looked at (as in Tableau 5.6), we get just the supposedly prohibited form.

In other words, there is a constraint ordering that *does* allow null focused subjects. One's immediate reaction, however, might be to object that DROPFOCUS is an absurd constraint. Indeed, one might object that a focused element can *never* be null. But such an objection would be without foundation. Given the right discourse conditions, focus, like topic, can be pragmatically retrievable. Consider the following exchange in English:

(50) Q: Who broke the plate?
A: You know who!

In most accounts of the notion 'focus,' a grammatical element is considered to be in focus if it provides the answer to a *wh*-question. In (50), however, there is no grammatical constituent that plays such a role. Focus is determined wholly pragmatically. Now imagine a null subject language with the following exchange:

(51) Q: Who broke the plate?
A: e broke the plate. (INTERPRETATION: 'You/I/we both/some third person know(s) who broke the plate')

TABLEAU 5.6. *How null focused subjects might be derived*

Input: <V (x), x=focus, x=DP>

Candidates	DROP FOCUS	DROP TOPIC	PARSE	ALIGN FOCUS	FULL-INT	SUBJECT
AUX V DP	*!					*
DP AUX V	*!			*!		
AUX V, DP	*!			*!		*
AUX V			*			*
[*null structure*]			*!*			
expl. AUX V DP	*!				*!	

In such a situation, a reasonable syntactic-pragmatic analysis would be to posit a null focus in subject position licensed by a constraint like DROPFOCUS. In fact, we find examples like (51) in Portuguese (Madalena Cruz-Ferreira, personal communication):

(52) Q: Quem é que partiu o prato?
A: Partiu o prato?

As long as the reply has question intonation, it can be understood as having a null focus in subject position.

Serbo-Croatian allows for a similar, though more restricted, possibility (Zvjezdana Vrzic, personal communication):

(53) Q (asked by somebody who most likely did it, but is trying to cover it up):
Tko je razbio čašu?
Who broke the glass?
A (With an ironic intonation):
Razbio, razbio
Broke, broke (interpretation: 'You know who did it—it was you')

In conclusion, some languages do permit null focused subjects. In such languages, DROPFOCUS would have to be a high-ranked constraint. But if it has a high ranking in Portuguese and Serbo-Croatian, why should the ranking be so low in most other languages? OT provides no answer to that question and hence no explanation for the typological rarity of the phenomenon in question.[12]

As a more general point, there are countless grammatical phenomena that are confined to a very small number of languages. For example, of all languages, only Chamicuro is known to have tensed definite articles (Parker 1999; Raritätenkabinett #43);[13] only English to have relative pronouns as the only target for agreement in animacy (Raritätenkabinett #84); and only Washo in which third-person independent pronouns are the only NPs inflectionally to distinguish subject and object (Raritätenkabinett #92). The unusual ranking of constraints responsible for these phenomena could easily be the norm—as far as OT is concerned.

5.6.3 *Functionally based Optimality Theory*

This section outlines the research program that attempts to link each syntactic constraint of OT with an external functional motivation, as a means not only for

[12] An anonymous reader has questioned the constraint DROPFOCUS for Portuguese and Serbo-Croatian, remarking that *not any* focus can be omitted in that language, but only those manifesting some highly specific discourse properties. I have no problem with that, since my general point holds whatever (high-ranked) constraint licenses the relevant sentence types in those languages.

[13] The Raritätenkabinett is an online collection assembled by Frans Plank of extremely rare typological features. The URL is <http://ling.uni-konstanz.de:591/universals/introrara.html>.

capturing typological generalizations (as in standard OT), but for explaining them as well. Section 5.6.3.1 explains the appeal of such a program. Section 5.6.3.2 introduces some of the grammatical hierarchies that play a role in both formalist and functionalist work, and the following two sections outline an OT treatment of these hierarchies.

5.6.3.1 On the ontological status of OT constraints

The essence of OT is that constraints are universal. Indeed, such is the very first property of constraints that are mentioned in René Kager's introduction to that approach (Kager 1999: 11). OT loses much of its appeal if purely language-particular constraints are allowed.[14] Now how might a universal come to be instantiated in the grammar of a particular language?[15] There are really not that many possibilities. One is that the universal might be an instance of innate, purely linguistic knowledge. Such has been posited, for example, for the principle of Subjacency in the Government-Binding theory (Hoekstra and Kooij 1988). Another possible explanation is that it could be an instance of innate knowledge that is derivative of more general cognitive principles. Haspelmath (1992) considers it plausible that the principles appealed to in grammaticalization research have this property. A third possibility is that the aspect of language in question is learned, but in some sense of the term so 'useful' that all languages will manifest it. An example might be the universal fact that every language has words that refer to the sun and the moon, which presumably arises by virtue of the functional utility of being able to identify the two most prominent celestial bodies.

Interestingly, the standard assumption in OT is that all constraints are innate: 'We propose that a learner starts with an initial ranking of the constraints' (Tesar and Smolensky 1998: 237). But if all (or a large percentage) of OT constraints are innate, then we are committed to a degree of innate knowledge that far exceeds anything Chomsky ever dreamed of. Not surprisingly, this fact has led to discomfort among some OT practitioners and has engendered a program, described

[14] Along these lines, in their comments on a language-particular *r*-insertion rule proposed in McCarthy (1993), Halle and Idsardi (1997: 26) make the reasonable observation that 'Conceptually, reliance on arbitrary stipulation that is outside the system of Optimality is equivalent to giving up on the enterprise. Data that cannot be dealt with by OT without recourse to rules are fatal counter-examples to the OT research program.' McMahon (2000: 10) argues that many of the allegedly universal constraints of OT phonology are 'effectively language-specific, and that OT cannot in fact function without the addition of parochial rules, or mechanisms which in some way mimic the operations found in traditional derivational models.'

[15] Many universals of language of course are not part of linguistic knowledge, but rather are an emergent (i.e. epiphenomenal) result of some other principle or principles, which themselves might be innate or learned. For example, it is a universal that no language has prefixes that does not also have suffixes. Children do not 'know' this fact; rather, it appears to be an epiphenomenal by-product of the fact that processing considerations favor suffixes over prefixes (Hall 1992). For more discussion, see Ch. 1.

above in §5.2, for grounding constraints, directly or indirectly, in their functional utility.

5.6.3.2 Functionally motivated hierarchies

Since grammatical hierarchies play such a central role both in typological-functionalist theorizing and in the FOT attempt to bridge the results of that theorizing with formal linguistics, I begin by outlining a few of the more important ones. Historically, the first such hierarchy proposed was the Thematic Hierarchy, one version of which is presented in (54):

(54) Thematic Hierarchy (Bresnan and Kanerva 1989: 23): Agent > Beneficiary > Recipient/Experiencer > Instrumental > Theme/Patient > Location

Fillmore (1968) argued that one can predict subject choice in English and other languages by reference to the position on such a hierarchy of the thematic role (or, as he called it, the 'case' role) borne by the NP. Hierarchies of thematic roles have been appealed to in the explanation of such diverse phenomena as antecedence for reflexivization (Jackendoff 1972), argument structure in morphology (Carrier-Duncan 1985), and the choice of controller in embedded infinitivals (Culicover and Jackendoff 2001).

Grammatical relations (or functions) have also been argued to be hierarchically organized. As noted earlier, Keenan and Comrie (1977) suggested that we can explain interesting cross-linguistic facts about relativization possibilities by appealing to the following hierarchy:

(55) Relational Hierarchy (Comrie and Keenan 1979: 650): Subject > Direct Object > Indirect Object > Oblique > Genitive > Object of Comparative

Another hierarchy of long-standing is the Animacy Hierarchy (which is often treated separately from its proper subhierarchy, the Person Hierarchy). Silverstein (1976) was possibly the first to notice that a wide variety of grammatical processes in a number of languages, in particular those involving word order, grammatical relation choice, and case marking, seem to be sensitive to the relative degree of animacy of the noun phrases involved. Here are more recent versions of both hierarchies:

(56) Animacy Hierarchy (Dixon 1979: 85): First-Person Pronoun > Second-Person Pronoun > Third-Person Pronoun > Proper Noun > Human Common Noun > Animate Common Noun > Inanimate Common Noun

(57) Person Hierarchy (Croft 1990: 149): Local (First, Second) > Third

A related hierarchy pertains to the degree of 'identifiability' of the participants in a discourse and is formulated as the Definiteness Hierarchy:

(58) Definiteness Hierarchy (Comrie 1989: 134–6): Personal Pronoun > Proper Noun > Definite NP > Indefinite Specific NP > Non-specific NP

Finally, a number of studies have pointed to the relative 'discourse prominence' of the phrases in an utterance as a factor in grammatical patterning, where the more 'discourse prominent' element is, in some sense, more at the center of attention of the participants of the discourse. Hence, the following hierarchy:

(59) Prominence Hierarchy (Tomlin 1985): Discourse Prominent > Not Discourse Prominent

The above hierarchies have entered into typological-functionalist theorizing in two separate ways. First, all of the hierarchies, to one degree or another, appear to have functional (or at least external) motivation, in that they are based on facts about language users. Intuitively, one might say, all seem to arrange themselves in a decreasing degree of cognitive salience or importance. Human NPs are more central to the human experience than inanimates; agents are more central than instruments; subjects are more central than objects of prepositions; and so on. Second, and more importantly, functionalists formulate typological generalizations by means of direct reference to these hierarchies. In the view of Croft (1995), all universal aspects of language are functionally motivated and representable by implicational hierarchies such as those described above. Grammars of individual languages, in this view, are (to simplify only a little) collections of statements about where particular phenomena fall on particular hierarchies.

As noted above, hierarchies of thematicity, animacy, and so on are given an OT realization in two papers by Judith Aissen (Aissen 1999, 2003). The first, which deals with subject choice, is discussed in the following subsection; the second, which treats differential object marking from an explicitly FOT perspective, is discussed in §5.6.3.4.

5.6.3.3 Aissen on subject choice

Aissen (1999:674) characterizes the person/animacy and thematic hierarchies (and, by implication, the others as well) as 'important result(s) in universal grammar.' Languages differ typologically with respect to the degree that subject and object choice is a function of hierarchically organized scales of personhood, thematic role, and prominence. The goal of her paper is to capture these different realizations in an optimality-theoretic framework. Aissen works with a proper subset of the relevant hierarchies, as follows:

(60) Relational: Subject > Object > Oblique
(61) Person: Local (1st, 2nd) > 3rd
(62) Thematic: Agent > Patient
(63) Prominence: Discourse Prominent (X) > Not Discourse Prominent (x)

Following the technique proposed in Prince and Smolensky (1993), she aligns these hierarchies harmonically, interleaving them so that the ranking within each is preserved. Hence the intuition is captured that local subjects are more natural than third-person subjects, agent subjects are more natural than patient subjects, and discourse prominent subjects are more natural than non-prominent subjects. The actual constraints take the form of the prohibition against some grammatical relation being linked to some element on one of the other hierarchies. Hence, they are stated as follows:

(64) a. *Su/Pat
b. *Su/x
c. *Obl/Local

In other words, we have universal violable constraints prohibiting subjects from being patients (64a), prohibiting subjects from being non-discourse prominent (64b), and prohibiting oblique forms from being first or second person (64c).

Since the ranking within each hierarchy is preserved under alignment, a ranking such as that depicted in (65a) will be allowed, but not one such as in (65b):

(65) a. *Su/Pat ≫ *Su/Ag
b. *Su/Ag ≫ *Su/Pat

Agents outrank Patients in the Thematic Hierarchy, so a constraint prohibiting subject Agents cannot outrank a constraint prohibiting subject Patients.[16]

Let us now turn to how Aissen captures typological differences among languages with respect to subject choice, beginning with English. The highest-ranked relevant constraint is the one forbidding non-prominent subjects. Notice that in Tableau 5.7, that constraint dominates the one forbidding patient subjects (i.e. *Su/x ≫ *Su/Pat). Passives can be generated, then, if the Patient is prominent and the Agent is non-prominent.

Fox (Tableau 5.8) has no passives at all, a result that Aissen obtains by a high ranking of the prohibition against patient subjects (i.e. *Su/Pat ≫ *Su/x).

Other languages restrict actives and passives to particular persons. Lushootseed, for example, as is illustrated in Table 5.3, does not allow first- or second-person passive agents.

Aissen derives this result by means of a high ranking of *Obl/Local (Tableau 5.9).

Lummi is like Lushootseed, except that, as is illustrated in Table 5.4, *actives* are disallowed when the subject is third person and the object is first or second (Jelinek and Demers 1983).

Aissen derives this generalization by means of a high ranking of *Oj/Local in Tableau 5.10.

[16] It is important to stress that from the fact that *Su/Ag never outranks *Su/Pat, it does not follow that no language allows agent objects. Such languages indeed exist. As Aissen notes (2003: 686): 'Languages in which agents are realized as objects... will only emerge if there are higher-ranked constraints which force the appearance of object agents.'

TABLEAU 5.7. *English (prominent patient) (Aissen 1999: 689)*

V(Agt/3/x,Pat/1/x)	*Su/x	*Su/Pat	*GR/Pers
ACTIVE Agt/Su/3/x-Pat/Oj/1/X	*!		**
☞PASSIVE Pat/Su/1/X-Agt/Obl/3/x		*	**

TABLEAU 5.8. *Fox (Aissen 1999: 687)*

V (Agt/3, Pat/1)	*Su/Pat	*GR/Pers
☞ACTIVE Agt/Su/3-Pat/Oj/1		**
PASSIVE Pat/Su/1-Agt/Obl/3	*!	

TABLE 5.3. *Distribution of voice by person in Lushootseed (Aissen 1999: 690–1)*

Agt ⇓ Pat ⇒	1	2	3
1	-	active/*passive	active/*passive
2	active/*passive	-	active/*passive
3	active/passive	active/passive	active/passive

TABLEAU 5.9. *Lushootseed (Aissen 1999: 691)*

V(Agt/1/x, Pat/3/X)	*Obl/Local	*Su/x	*Su/Pat	*GR/Pers
☞ACTIVE Agt/Su/1/x-Pat/Oj/3/X		*		**
PASSIVE Pat/Su/3/X-Agt/Obl/1/x	*!		*	*

TABLE 5.4. *Distribution of voice by person in Lummi (Aissen 1999: 692)*

Agt ⇓ Pat ⇒	1	2	3
1	-	active/*passive	active/*passive
2	active/*passive	-	active/*passive
3	*active/passive	*active/passive	active/passive

Tableau 5.10. *Lummi (1st person patient) (Aissen 1999: 692)*

V (Agt/3/X, Pat/1/x)	*Obl/Local	*Oj/Local	*Su/x	*Su/Pat	*GR/Pers
ACTIVE Agt/Su/3/X-Pat/Oj/1/x		*!			*
☞PASSIVE Pat/Su/1/x-Agt/Obl/3/X			*	*	**

5.6.3.4 Aissen on differential object marking

Aissen (2003) provides an OT account of differential object marking (DOM), discussed in Chapter 4, §4.9.2. Again, in many languages, whether direct objects are case-marked is a function of the degree of animacy or definiteness of that object. The higher in the hierarchy of animacy and/or definiteness the object is, the more likely it is to be case-marked. Aissen employs the following hierarchies in his paper:

(66) Animacy: Human > Animate > Inanimate
(67) Definiteness: Personal Pronoun > Proper Noun > Definite NP > Indefinite Specific NP > Non-specific NP

As Aissen notes, the typological correlation of overt marking with animacy and/or definiteness appears to have a functional explanation: 'It is those direct objects which are most in need of being distinguished from subjects that get overtly case-marked' (2003: 437).

Employing the technique of harmonic alignment discussed in the previous section, Aissen arrives at the following constraint rankings:

(68) *Oj/Hum » *Oj/Anim » *Oj/Inam
(69) *Oj/Pro » *Oj/PN » *Oj/Def » *Oj/Spec » *Oj/NSpec

In other words, no language will prohibit inanimate objects that does not prohibit human objects; no language will prohibit non-specific objects that does not prohibit pronominal objects; and so on.

Now, then, the goal is to ensure that if in a particular language a direct object with a particular value for animacy or definiteness is case-marked, then objects with animacy or definiteness values higher on their respective hierarchies will also be case-marked. Aissen's first steps to achieving this result are to propose constraint (70) and locally conjoining it with the constraints of (68–69) (see Table 5.5):

(70) *$Ø_C$ 'Star Zero': Penalizes the absence of a value for the feature CASE.

TABLE 5.5. *Local conjunction of *$\emptyset_C$ with object-oriented subhierarchies (Aissen 2003: 448)*

Local conjunction of *$\emptyset_C$ with the subhierarchy on object animacy (68)	Local conjunction of *$\emptyset_C$ with the subhierarchy on object definiteness (69)
*Oj/Hum & *$\emptyset_C$ »	*Oj/Pro & *$\emptyset_C$ »
*Oj/Anim & *$\emptyset_C$ »	*Oj/PN & *$\emptyset_C$ »
*Oj/Inam & *$\emptyset_C$	*Oj/Def & *$\emptyset_C$ »
	*Oj/Spec & *$\emptyset_C$ »
	*Oj/NSpec & *$\emptyset_C$

If nothing more were said, the constraints of Table 5.5 would force case on all objects. Therefore, the next step is to propose a constraint that is, in essence, the inverse of (70), namely one that penalizes the presence of morphological case:

(71) *STRUC$_C$: Penalizes a value for the morphological category CASE.

Aissen is now in a position to propose language-particular tableaux capturing the object case-marking generalizations for each language. Consider Hebrew and Turkish. In Hebrew, all and only definite objects (i.e. personal pronouns, proper names, and other definites) are case-marked. In Turkish, these objects are case-marked, and specifics are as well. This result is achieved by the relative ranking of the locally conjoined constraints of Table 5.5 and constraint (71). The competition sets consist of a case-marked object and a non-case-marked object of the same degree of definiteness. Tableaux 5.11 and 5.12 illustrate. In other words, since in Hebrew the prohibition against case marking dominates the constraint prohibiting non-case-marked specifics, it follows that that language will disallow case-marked specifics. In Turkish, on the other hand, the prohibition against case marking is dominated by the constraint prohibiting non-case-marked specifics. Therefore, case-marked specific objects are allowed in that language. In short,

TABLEAU 5.11. *Hebrew specific indefinite patients (Aissen 2003: 455)*

Patient: specific indefinite	*Oj/Def & *$\emptyset_C$	*STRUC$_C$	*Oj/Spec & *$\emptyset_C$	*Oj/NSpec & *$\emptyset_C$
Oj: specific indefinite CASE: ACC		*!		
Oj: specific indefinite CASE:			*	*

TABLEAU 5.12. *Turkish specific indefinite patients (Aissen 2003: 455)*

Patient: specific indefinite	*Oj/Def & *$ø_C$	*Oj/Spec & *$ø_C$	*$STRUC_C$	*Oj/NSpec & *$ø_C$
Oj: specific indefinite CASE: ACC			*	
Oj: specific indefinite CASE:		*!		*

given the Definiteness Hierarchy, the function of constraint (71) (*$STRUC_C$) is to mark the point in the hierarchy where case marking is disallowed.[17]

5.6.4 *The failure of functionally based Optimality Theory*

Any linguist committed both to the explanation of typological generalizations and to a rapprochement between formal and functional linguistics will find in the FOT synthesis an immediate intuitive appeal. If this synthesis were able to resolve the most bitter and long-standing division in the field of linguistics, that would be a marvelous result. However, upon close examination, FOT fails to bridge the gap between the two opposing tendencies. The remainder of this section will document the problems that such an approach faces. Section 5.6.4.1 raises some conceptual and empirical difficulties inherent in the idea that each constraint is, by hypothesis, both functionally motivated and innate and §5.6.4.2 points out that the lack of any direct relationship between mean cross-linguistic constraint ranking and the functional motivation of a constraint undercuts the right of FOT to call itself a 'functionalist' theory. Section 5.6.4.3 argues that the Thematic Hierarchy is of doubtful existence as a property of UG and that, given FOT assumptions, the Relational Hierarchy cannot underlie putatively universal constraints. It goes on to argue that even where hierarchies *are* motivated, the machinery inherent to Optimality Theory leads to a cumbersome and uninsightful treatment of the phenomena to be explained.

5.6.4.1 Functional motivation versus innateness

If one takes the mainstream OT position that the full set of constraints is innate, then one has 'solved' the learnability problem for constraints. There *is* no problem—though, of course, explaining the acquisition of language-particular

[17] Differential case marking with respect to animacy is handled in analogous fashion. Aissen goes on to discuss the handling of 'two-dimensional' differential object marking, in which marking is sensitive to *both* definiteness and animateness. Given the considerable space that would be required to present her treatment and the fact that any critique of her approach to one-dimensional marking carries over *ipso facto* to that of two-dimensional, the latter will not be discussed here.

rankings still presents more than a minor challenge. But what about FOT? It is by no means clear how the requirement that each grammatical constraint have an accompanying 'user constraint' can be made to be compatible with constraints being universal. The central theme of the functionalist literature is that functional motivation is an *alternative* to innateness. Functionalists argue that by showing how grammars are rooted in language-external functional and cognitive human attributes, the idea of an innate UG can be dispensed with:

Indeed, because the functionalist working hypothesis about innate linguistic abilities is that they are part of a more general cognitive-learning schema, the avenue of 'explaining' some phenomenon by declaring the rule describing it to be innate is not available... (Foley and Van Valin 1984: 13).

...as an empirical claim innateness remains empty.... (Comrie 1989: 25)

It would be nothing less than bizarre to claim that all constraints are *both* innate and functionally motivated. As Haspelmath (1999b: 184) has trenchantly observed, '[functional] justifications are irrelevant in a theory that assumes innate constraints.' But if some constraints are functionally motivated but *not* innate, then how could the full set of constraints possibly be universal? For example, consider a language L in which one never finds operators (i.e. *wh*- and other quantifier-like elements) in specifier position. Presumably in the grammar of L, OP-SPEC would have to be a very low-ranked constraint. If OP-SPEC is simply innate, then the child learning L would, in the acquisition process, keep 'demoting' it to a lower and lower ranking. But if constraints are functionally motivated, there would be no reason for the child acquiring L to acquire OP-SPEC at all! Hence, given FOT, constraints cannot be universal.

Despite all that, practitioners of FOT continue to moot the idea that the set of OT constraints is innate:

There is no logical inconsistency in a constraint being both functionally motivated and innate... many aspects of the more abstract grammatical constraint systems may be grounded in and motivated by theories of higher-level human cognitive and social processes and structures, which are also, in part, innate. While we do not wish to speculate here on the phylogenetic origins of language, recent coevolution scenarios (Kirby 1998; Briscoe 2000) show how functionally motivated constraints operative in many languages could become innate because language learners who assumed these constraints would have acquired language faster. (Bresnan and Aissen 2002: 89)

Consider the implications. Since constraints are stated in terms of phrase-structure configurations, syntactic categories and features, and so on, it follows that the entire stock of mechanisms of generative grammar would have to be innate. I doubt that many functionalists would find such a view palatable.[18]

[18] Bresnan and Aissen, in citing Kirby and Briscoe, point to the Baldwin Effect as a possible factor in nativizing functionally useful constraints (for a description of this effect, see Ch. 1, *n*. 5). Kirby (p. c.) and, I believe, all other language evolution researchers have come to reject a Baldwinian account of constraints (for relevant critical discussion, see Yamauchi 2001).

5.6.4.2 Functional motivation and constraint ranking

An advocate of FOT (or AF in general) might suggest that there is, in fact, a way of supplying empirical content to the idea that rules or constraints need to be grounded functionally. Perhaps one might expect some direct correlation between the functionality of a particular grammatical construct and its frequency of occurrence in the grammars of the world (in traditional functional linguistics) or its typical cross-linguistic ranking (in functionally based OT). That is, the better motivated the constraint functionally, the higher in general we would expect its ranking to be. For example, consider whatever grammatical mechanism determines basic word order in the clause. Clearly, more grammars have whatever it takes to generate SVO order than to generate OSV order. Translated into OT terms, it follows that in more grammars the constraint that licenses subject-before-object order dominates the constraint that licenses object-before-subject order than vice versa. One might attempt to explain such a state of affairs by appealing to work such as Tomlin (1986), which argues that the former order is better motivated functionally than the latter.

Such a suggestion presents two serious problems, however. First, given the present limited state of our knowledge of what external factors are the best motivators of syntactic structure, we have no non-circular way of ranking functions. For example, we might be tempted to say that faithfulness constraints tend to be more highly ranked than markedness constraints because they play a more important function. But our only evidence for their serving a more important function is that they are more highly ranked. There exists no theory of functionality from which it follows that faithfulness is more important than markedness.

Even in phonology, where functionality is better understood than in syntax, there is no clear relationship between the importance of the function that a constraint serves and its typical ranking. For example, Hayes (1998) devises an algorithm for showing how some OT constraints are more phonetically grounded than others, but does not go on to demonstrate how this translates into cross-linguistic constraint rankings. As far as I know, nobody has produced a successful demonstration along those lines.

But in fact, those who take a functionalist view of OT explicitly *reject* the view of a relationship between the functional motivation of a constraint and any particular typological generalization:

> [T]here is no expected correlation between functional motivation and mean cross-linguistic ranking. The ranking of constraints is a conventional property of grammars... [T]he 'mean cross-linguistic ranking' of OT constraints is a constant, the same for all constraints: 'mean cross-linguistic ranking' = $(n + 1) / 2$. (Bresnan and Aissen 2002: 86)

Given such a view, it is worth asking in what sense the approach advocated by Bresnan and Aissen even merits the attribution 'functionalist.' It is a staple of functionalist theorizing that the better motivated an external principle is in functional terms, the more common (typologically) will be grammars that reflect that principle. Bresnan and Aissen, therefore, can provide no explanation for why SVO order should predominate over OSV order. The best that they can do is to point out that for some (unknown arbitrary) reason, more languages present the set of constraint rankings that lead to the former order than to the latter. The same point could be made for genitive–noun order in English, discussed above in §5.4.2. All one needs to do to challenge FOT is to find some constraint—*any* constraint—that would disfavor animate pre-head genitives or inanimate post-head genitives. An OT approach has no way of explaining why such a constraint would be, in general, ranked lower than one whose effects are the reverse. Do such constraints exist? Certainly they do. For example, as is well known, possessors tend to be definite (Haspelmath 1999a) and there is functional pressure for definites to occur in specifier (i.e. subject) position. Hence, we would need to posit one constraint that favors (72a) (something like 'INANIMATES LATE') and another constraint that favors (72b) (something like 'DEFINITES EARLY'):

(72) a. the leg of the table
     b. the table's leg

For Bresnan and Aissen, it is a wholly arbitrary fact that speakers are more likely to say (72a) than (72b). A different ranking of the two relevant constraints would have yielded the opposite preference.

5.6.4.3 Grammatical hierarchies and FOT

The grammatical hierarchies discussed by Aissen and incorporated into her version of OT are interesting in that they are plausibly both innate attributes of UG and functionally motivated. Consider the statement that humans are higher ranked than non-humans, agents are higher ranked than patients, and so on. It is not implausible that we are born with some sort of knowledge of 'cognitive importance', i.e. that animates are more central to human cognition than inanimates, that agents are more central than patients, and so on. It would seem that FOT might be on safe ground, then, in positing these (externally motivated) hierarchies to be part of UG. If the hierarchies are innate attributes of human cognition, then the dilemma discussed above with respect to parochial constraints such as OP-SPEC does not arise.

This subsection, however, first argues that the Thematic Hierarchy is not part of UG. Second, it makes the point that the Relational Hierarchy can be provided by UG only in a non-functionally based theory that permits knowledge of morphosyntax without exposure to evidence leading to that knowledge. Third, it questions whether an insightful treatment of differential object marking is possible given the assumptions of FOT or, indeed, given optimality-theoretic assumptions in general.

The Thematic Hierarchy There is very good reason to doubt the existence of a Thematic Hierarchy provided by UG. How else can one explain the fact that after more than three decades of investigation, nobody has proposed a universal hierarchy of theta-roles that comes close to working? Here is just a sampling of the versions of the Thematic Hierarchy that have been proposed over the years:[19]

(73) Versions of the Thematic Hierarchy:

a. Fillmore (1968: 33):
Agent > Instrumental > Objective

b. Jackendoff (1972):
Agent > Location/Source/Goal > Theme

c. Ostler (1980):
(relational predicates) Theme > Goal > Source > Path
(actional predicates) Source > Path > Theme > Goal

d. Givón (1984: 139):
Agent > Dative/Beneficiary > Patient > Locative > Instrument/Associative > Manner

e. Kiparsky (1985: 20):
Agent > Source > Goal > Instrument > Theme > Locative

f. Carrier-Duncan (1985: 7):
Agent > Theme > Goal/Source/Location

g. Larson (1988: 382–3):
Agent > Theme > Goal > Location (and other obliques)

h. Wilkins (1988: 211):
Agent > Patient > Location/Source/Goal > Theme

i. Randall (1988: 138) (for effects of lexical rules on argument structure):
Theme > Agent > Instrument/Source/Path/Goal/Location/...

j. Bresnan and Kanerva (1989: 23); Bresnan and Moshi (1990: 169); Alsina (1996: 688):
Agent > Beneficiary > Recipient/Experiencer > Instrumental > Theme/Patient > Location

k. Baker (1989: 544):
Agent > Instrument > Patient/Theme > Goal/Location

l. Grimshaw (1990: 8):
Agent > Experiencer > Goal/Source/Location > Theme

m. Jackendoff (1990: 261):
Agent > Patient/Beneficiary > Theme > Source/Goal/Reference Object > Identificational Goal/Reference Object

[19] Bresnan and Aissen (2002) attempt to defuse the problem posed by too many thematic hierarchies by claiming that '[t]he exception-ridden, variable, and "soft" nature of [hierarchies like the Thematic Hierarchy] is predicted from the OT theory of constraint interaction' (p. 90). I find that remark extremely puzzling. It is crucial to the analyses in Aissen (1999, 2003) that the Thematic Hierarchy (and other hierarchies) are *preserved* from grammar to grammar. Language-particular differences fall out from how these (fixed) hierarchies interact with other grammatical constraints.

n. Langacker (1990):
Agent > Instrument > Patient/Mover/Experiencer ('Energy Flow Hierarchy' for subject choice)
Agent > Experiencer > Other ('Initiative Hierarchy')

o. Speas (1990: 16):
Agent > Experiencer > Theme > Goal/Source/Location > Manner/Time

p. Dowty (1991); Rugemalira (1994):
Proto-Agent > Proto-Patient

q. Godard (1992); Kolliakou (1999); Sag and Godard (1994):
Possessor > Agent/Experiencer > Theme

r. Kiefer (1995):
Actor > Agent > Beneficiary > Theme/Patient > Instrument

s. Van Valin and Lapolla (1997: 127), elaborating Foley and Van Valin's (1984: 59) continuum in terms of logical structure argument positions:
Agent > Effector/Mover/User, etc. > Location/Perceiver/Cognizer/Experiencer, etc. > Theme/Stimulus/Implement, etc. > Patient/Entity

The theory of proto-thematic roles argued for in Dowty (1991) is often taken as the solution to the problem of too many thematic hierarchies, and, in fact, Aissen (1999) adopts it. Dowty argued that the proliferation of theta-roles seen in the literature can be dispensed with in favor of two cluster-concepts called 'Proto-Agent' and 'Proto-Patient.' The particular role borne by a particular argument is determined by the number of entailments that the verb gives it. Dowty outlined these entailments as follows:

(74) Contributing properties for the Agent Proto-Role (Dowty 1991):
a. volitional involvement in the event or state
b. sentience (and/or perception)
c. causing an event or change of state in another participant
d. movement (relative to the position of another participant)
e. exists independently of the event named by the verb

(75) Contributing properties for the Patient Proto-Role:
a. undergoes change of state
b. incremental theme
c. causally affected by another participant
d. stationary relative to movement of another participant
e. does not exist independently of the event, or not at all

Dowty suggested that the argument whose predicate entails the greatest number of Proto-Agent properties will be lexicalized as the subject of the predicate; the argument having the greatest number of Proto-Patient entailments will be lexicalized as the direct object.

Unfortunately for the proto-theta-role approach, it is not difficult to find transitive verbs whose subjects and objects do not measure up to Dowty's thematic criteria for them. Consider such stative predicates as *receive, inherit, undergo,* and *sustain.* To illustrate the problem, let us measure sentence (76) against Dowty's Proto-Agent entailments (77):

(76) John received a letter from Mary

(77) a. VOLITION: *Mary*
b. SENTIENCE/PERCEPTION: does not apply
c. CAUSATION: *Mary*
d. MOVEMENT: *the letter*
e. INDEPENDENT EXISTENCE: *John, Mary*

John is a 'Proto-Agent' only by one-half of a test, while *Mary* passes two-and-a-half. Hence; one would predict that *Mary,* not *John,* should be subject.

One might, on the other hand, choose to interpret Dowty's criteria as governing the *necessary* properties of the roles associated with each predicate, rather than focusing on individual sentences (such as (76)) in which that predicate occurs. By this interpretation, the verb *receive* fares no better, as Table 5.6 illustrates.

If the assignments in Table 5.6 are correct, then for the verb *receive,* the theme should be the subject and the recipient should be the direct object, i.e. we should have sentences like **A package received John from Mary.* As far as subject properties are concerned, the theme necessarily moves and has an independent existence, while the only necessary property of the recipient is its independent

TABLE 5.6. *Proto-Agent and Proto-Patient properties of the verb* receive

Proto-Agent properties	[recipient]	[theme]	[source]
Volition	no	no	no
Sentience	no	no	no
Cause	no	no	no
Movement	no	yes	no
Independent existence	yes	yes	yes
Total	1	2	1
Proto-Patient properties	**[recipient]**	**[theme]**	**[source]**
Change of state	no	no	no
Incremental theme	no	no	no
Causally affected	yes?	yes	no
Relatively stationary	yes	no	no
No independ. existence	no	no	no
Total	2	1	0

existence. (Note that sentences like *The wall received a coat of paint* illustrate that the recipient need not be sentient.) As far as object properties are concerned, recipients are, I believe, always causally affected by another participant and stationary relative to the movement of another participant.[20]

It is worth pointing out that passive sentences (and most likely A-movements in general) pose a lethal problem for the attempt to link any approach that incorporates the UTAH (Baker 1988) and the hypothesis of proto-thematic-roles.[21] Consider the active–passive pair (78a–b). For the past two decades, or longer, it has been assumed that (78b) has a derivation schematically represented as (79) (the intermediate trace in [Spec, VP] may or may not be required given current 'minimalist' assumptions):

(78) a. Mary ate the chicken.
b. The chicken was eaten by Mary.

(79)

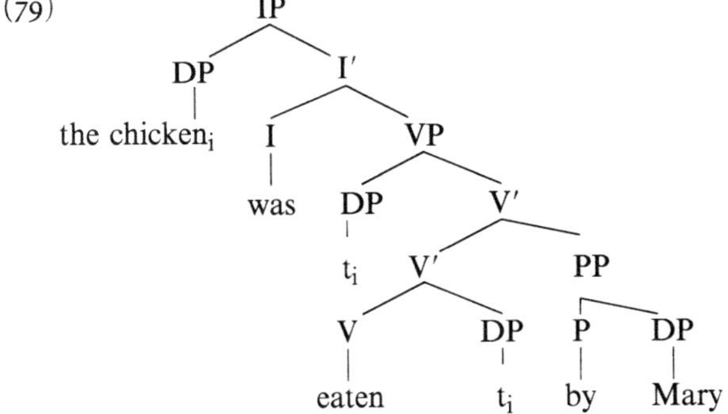

Such a derivation, however, violates the UTAH. *Mary* has identical Θ-roles in (78a) and (78b) and, therefore, by the UTAH, would have to be in identical D-structure positions in those two sentences. But agent phrases of passives have not been analyzed as originating in deep subject ([Spec, IP]) position since before Emonds (1970)—and the Theta-Criterion, of course, explains *why* they cannot originate there. So we have a fundamental conflict between the UTAH and the Theta-Criterion. Worse, however, is the fact that (79) leads to the assignment of the wrong Θ-roles, given a Dowtyan analysis. The argument with the most Proto-Agent properties is not a deep subject; indeed the deep subject, being empty, has no thematic properties at all. That presents no problems for a semanticist like

[20] Bresnan and Aissen (2002: 90) object to the above argument, writing that Dowty restricts himself 'to subject selection in two-place verbs.' They are mistaken on that point (see, for example, Dowty 1991: 576).

[21] According to the UTAH (Uniformity of Theta Assignment Hypothesis), identical thematic relationships between items are represented by identical structural relationships between those items at the level of D-structure. Virtually all principles-and-parameters approaches adopt the UTAH, I believe. See Baker (1997, 2001b) for an attempt to effect a linkage between the UTAH and Dowtyan proto-roles. For criticism of this attempt, see Newmeyer (2001b).

Dowty, who rejects null elements in syntactic derivations, but is highly problematic for the standard principles-and-parameters approaches. Even worse, the agent phrase can be omitted:

(80) The chicken was eaten.

As Dowty makes clear in his paper, in sentences with only one DP argument, that argument is assigned the subject position by default. But in (78b), *the chicken* needs to be an underlying direct object.

Even if something like proto-thematic roles could be motivated for subject and object choice, more fine-grained roles would still be necessary for other facets of the grammar. This fact undercuts any theoretical parsimony argument for reducing the number of roles to two. For example, a tradition in word-formation studies going back at least as far as Carrier-Duncan (1985) states morphological generalizations in terms of a variety of theta-role labels. Or consider the analyses of control phenomena in Sag and Pollard (1991) and Culicover and Jackendoff (2001). In the latter analysis, the controller is identified differently for different verb classes, verbs in each class picking a particular theta-role as controller. For example, the controller might be an Agent (81a), an Addressee (81b), a Patient (81c), a Recipient (81d), a Source (81e), or a Holder (81f) (the controller is identified in boldface):

(81) a. **Mary** attempted to take a vacation.
b. Bill told **Mary** to come visit him.
c. I persuaded **John** to see the doctor.
d. We taught **the dog** to roll over.
e. **Sam** promised Mary to write more often.
f. Tom required **Alice** to hand in the assignment.

I see no way to handle the control facts by appealing only to the roles Proto-Agent and Proto-Patient.[22]

In short, while grammatical processes might well have to refer to individual thematic roles, there is little evidence for a Thematic Hierarchy forming an integral part of UG.[23]

The Relational Hierarchy Let us now turn to the Relational Hierarchy. It is repeated below as (82):

(82) Relational Hierarchy: Subject > Direct Object > Indirect Object > Oblique > Genitive > Object of Comparative

[22] See Primus (1999) for arguments that even for the linking of grammatical relations and thematic roles, more proto-roles are needed than Proto-Agent and Proto-Patient. Primus motivates the need for the role 'Proto-Recipient.'

[23] The same conclusion is reached in Jelinek (1993); Meinunger (1999); Davis and Koenig (2000); and Jelinek and Demers (1983).

Are grammatical relations innate constructs? Frameworks that accord them the status of grammatical primitives, such as Relational Grammar and Lexical-Functional Grammar (LFG), have tended to answer this question in the affirmative. For example, Steven Pinker, writing from an LFG perspective, has remarked:

> The child is assumed to know, prior to acquiring a language, the overall structure of the grammar, the formal nature of the different sorts of rules it contains, and the primitives from which those rules may be composed. (Pinker 1984: 31)

Pinker goes on to suggest that the child uses semantic bootstrapping to identify agentive arguments of active action predicates as subjects and then expects 'without further learning' (p. 44) that entities labeled SUBJ will be the leftmost NP daughter of S, can be controlled by an argument of a matrix predicate, and so on.

Such a view seems consistent with standard versions of OT. If constraints involving reference to grammatical relations are innate, then it follows that grammatical relations are innate. But, for the reasons discussed in §5.6.4.1, if the 'F' of FOT has any meaning, then FOT has no choice but to abandon the idea of innate constraints. For a functionalist, a constraint can be universal only if it is manifested morphosyntactically in every language unless there is some function-based explanation for their absence.[24] Van Valin and Lapolla (1997) and Kibrik (1997), however, provide evidence that grammatical relations are not universally instantiated.[25] That is, they demonstrate that not all languages present evidence to the language learner that would lead him or her to posit distinct grammatical relations such as 'subject,' 'direct object,' and so on. Such relations can be motivated for a particular grammar only when semantic oppositions are neutralized morphosyntactically. English is typical in this respect. Consider the following active–passive pair:

(83) a. John kills the ducklings.
     b. The ducklings are killed by John.

It is the agreement pattern that is of interest to us. The verb agrees in (83a) with the agent and in (83b) with the patient. In other words, agreement is not purely semantically determined; rather it needs to make reference to some

[24] In Chomskyan versions of UG theory, universals need not be exemplified morphologically or syntactically in every language. They are simply available to the learner and will be activated for grammatical purposes if there is evidence for them in the primary data. Functionalist approaches, however, reject the idea of uninstantiated (i.e. innate) morphosyntactic knowledge (again, see §5.6.4.1).

[25] In mainstream transformational approaches, grammatical relations have generally been defined derivatively in terms of configurational structure, so the question of their innateness/universality has been discussed only in the context of the innateness/universality of particular structural configurations. A subject, for example, was originally defined simply as an NP immediately dominated by S. The situation is more complicated now, given the VP-internal subject hypothesis. In principles-and-parameters accounts, there are several 'subject positions,' each correlated with different subject properties, and not all which need be filled in every language (see McCloskey 1997 for discussion).

morphosyntactic category, in this case the 'subject.' Languages differ, of course, as to which processes exhibit neutralization of semantic oppositions for morphosyntactic purposes and in that way provide evidence for grammatical relations. In those languages in which agreement is subject to purely semantic conditions, there is no argument derivable from this process for the existence of distinct grammatical relations in that language.

Now, as it turns out, there exist languages in which there is *never* restricted neutralization of semantic roles. Based on the work of Mark Durie (1985, 1987), Van Valin and Lapolla identify Acehnese as one such language and Primus (1999) makes the same point with respect to Guarani and Tlingit. No learner of these languages would be led to posit a distinction between subjects and objects. Therefore, grammatical relations are not universal, nor can any hierarchy involving them be universal. FOT is forced either to give up the universality of constraints or, more seriously, to explain how speakers can have in their grammars functionally motivated constraints for which they have no evidence.[26]

The FOT treatment of differential object marking The principal objection that can be raised against the treatment of DOM in Aissen (2003) is not based on its empirical inadequacy, but rather on its conceptual complexity. The FOT framework requires far more theoretical machinery than is necessary to capture the relevant generalizations. The remainder of this section will support this assertion.

The generalization that Aissen's analysis is designed to capture is simply stated, as in (84):

(84) The higher in prominence a direct object, the more likely it is to be overtly case-marked.

I now present an analysis that captures this generalization in a simpler manner than Aissen's (see §5.6.3.4). First, assume that the Animacy Hierarchy and the Definiteness Hierarchy (repeated below) are provided by UG,[27] with each position on each hierarchy indexed along the lines indicated:

(85) Animacy Hierarchy: First-Person Pronoun$_a$ > Second-Person Pronoun$_b$ > Third-Person Pronoun$_c$ > Proper Noun$_d$ > Human Common Noun$_e$ > Animate Common Noun$_f$ > Inanimate Common Noun$_g$

(86) Definiteness Hierarchy: Personal Pronoun$_a$ > Proper Noun$_b$ > Definite NP$_c$ > Indefinite Specific NP$_d$ > Non-specific NP$_e$

[26] Individual languages might still hierarchize grammatical relations, of course. For example, Pollard and Sag (1992) make a strong case that anaphor binding in English is sensitive to such a hierarchy.

[27] These are by no means uncontroversial assumptions. Hierarchies of animacy have been implicated in phenomena as diverse as noun classification, numeral classifiers, number marking, and voice systems, as well as in object marking. It remains to be seen whether there is a smooth mapping from one hierarchy to another, as would be required if UG itself provides the Animacy Hierarchy. (I am indebted to William Croft for discussion of this issue.)

Now assume the following universal principle governing object case marking:[28]

(87) Grammars in which object case is overtly marked choose a point on the Animacy and/or Definiteness Hierarchies and mark case at that point and at every point of higher prominence.

Hence, the grammars of Hebrew and Turkish will include the following statements:

(88) a. Hebrew: Object case-mark point c on the Definiteness Hierarchy.
b. Turkish: Object case-mark point d on the Definiteness Hierarchy.

Universal principle (84) and language-particular statements such as (88) capture the essence of object case marking cross-linguistically and replace the bulk of the theoretical machinery that Aissen proposes.

In large part, the complexities of Aissen's analysis are due to the general nature of OT. In that framework there is no way for a correct form to emerge without competition between rival forms. Therefore one needs to set up a proliferation of candidate sets, simply to ensure that a 'winner' results. So for each language with object case marking it is necessary to posit a separate tableau in which, for each point on the relevant hierarchy, a case-marked form and a non-case-marked form compete with each other (see Tableaux 5.11 and 5.12). The fundamental problem with such an approach can be appreciated by means of an analogy. Suppose that Smith and Jones are weight-lifters who train with weights of 100, 200, 300, 400, and 500 pounds. Smith is able to lift a 200 pound weight (and, of course, all lighter ones) and Jones is able to lift a 300 pound weight (and, of course, all lighter ones). How might we provide an efficient characterization of their abilities? First, we would state a 'principle' like (89):

(89) If an individual can lift a weight of *x* pounds, then he or she can lift a lighter weight.

Second, we would characterize the limits of Smith's and Jones's abilities as follows:

(90) a. Smith can lift 200 pounds.
b. Jones can lift 300 pounds.

To handle the same generalizations the 'OT way,' however, we would have to posit a set of tableaux for Smith and Jones, one for each weight category, and ranked constraints in which weight categories are locally conjoined with a constraint that

[28] Things are slightly more complicated, since, as Aissen notes, some languages optionally case-mark objects and such NPs are intermediate in the hierarchies between those obligatorily case-marked and those not case-marked. For example, in the Spanish of El Cid, human-referring pronouns and proper nouns are obligatorily case-marked and human referring definites and indefinite specifics as well as inanimate proper nouns are optionally marked. Hence the grammar of this stage of Spanish selects two points on each hierarchy.

penalizes the lack of the ability to lift weights. Surely my alternative analysis is both conceptually simpler and equal in its empirical coverage.

It is never clear from a reading of the OT literature how literally (in terms of claims about I-language) one is to take the tableaux that form the centerpiece of every OT analysis. If tableaux like 5.11 and 5.12 are simply metaphorical in nature, then one would have to object that such metaphors do little to promote understanding. But a non-metaphorical interpretation seems remote. Could it really be the case that for each language, for each degree of definiteness, case-marked and non-case-marked objects are in a separate competition in speakers' heads with each other? If OT is incapable of formulating the following generalization in so many words—that in language L objects with property *x* are case-marked and objects with property *y* are not case-marked—then one would have to conclude that that framework is less than appealing as an approach to UG.

One might object that while empirically the analyses are equivalent, at a metatheoretical level they differ. The constraints of Aissen's analysis have explicit functional motivation, as is required by FOT. For example, Aissen attributes constraint (70), which penalizes the absence of case marking, to a hearer-based need for clarity. The constraints of Table 5.5, which locally conjoin (70) with the animacy and definiteness object-oriented subhierarchies, are regarded as being rooted in 'iconicity,' since they favor morphological marks for marked configurations. Constraint (71), on the other hand, is said to have an economy-based motivation, since it reduces the amount of structure that needs to be processed. Since such constraints (arguably) are motivated by their functions, one might claim that the extra complexity of the FOT analysis is justified.

That would be true, however, only if it were correct to pair the constraints of a synchronic grammar with their functional motivations. But as I have argued at length in this chapter it is *not* correct, so the more complex FOT approach is not motivated at a metatheoretical level either. Thus this discussion of DOM brings us back to the question of linking functional motivations to synchronic grammatical constructs. As a closing note, it is worth pointing out that Martin Haspelmath (personal communication) has demonstrated that the functional grounding of constraints like DOM can be deeply embedded in arbitrary lexical facts. Consider some facts about German morphology discussed in Haspelmath (2002). In German, a small subclass of nouns manifest a nominative–accusative distinction in their inflectional morphology, as well as in the article that they take:

(91) a. der Bote (NOM) / den Boten (ACC) 'messenger'
b. der Schütze (NOM) / den Schützen (ACC) 'archer'
c. der Philologe (NOM) / den Philologen (ACC) 'philologist'
d. der Hase (NOM) / den Hasen (ACC) 'hare'

Since the great majority of these nouns are animate, it looks on the surface like we have an instance of DOM within inflectional morphology. But the problem with expressing the generalization in such terms is that the majority of animate nouns do *not* belong to this inflection class. The question posed by Haspelmath is how it could be possible to devise a synchronic constraint system that generated the right inflectional forms and at the same time incorporated Aissen's functionally motivated DOM constraints.

At the same time, the *diachronic* evidence for DOM as a factor is quite striking. As Otto Behaghel observed nearly a century ago, in Old High German, the *n*-declension had both animate and inanimate members:

(92) *knoto/knoton* 'knot,' *hufo/hufon* 'heap,' *garto/garton* 'garden,' etc.

But it was only the inanimate members that lost this distinction, so modern German has *Knoten, Haufen, Garten*, with no case distinction. This differential treatment of animates and inanimates in language change can be explained quite easily in the kind of holistic functionalist approach that I advocate, but not in the atomistic approach adopted by Aissen.

5.6.5 *Summary*

This section has examined 'functionally based Optimality Theory' (FOT), the version of Optimality Theory that requires that each constraint be paired with an external functional motivation. It has argued that, at least as far as syntactic constraints are concerned, FOT suffers from severe deficiencies. Such a pairing incorrectly locates the form–function interplay in the mental grammar itself, rather than seeing the response of form to function as emerging from language use and acquisition. Furthermore, FOT seems incompatible with the standard OT assumption that constraints are universal. Finally, two of the functionally motivated hierarchies that are central to FOT theorizing, the thematic and relational hierarchies, are highly problematic, while incorporating the hierarchies of animacy and definiteness into an FOT analysis leads to otherwise unnecessary complexity.

5.7 Conclusion

The hypothesis that typological generalizations are, on the whole, functionally motivated, leads to an important question: how direct is the linkage between functional pressures and the typological distribution of formal elements that represents a response to those pressures? There are two radically different answers to this question. According to atomistic functionalism, the link between grammatical constructs and functional motivations is very close, whereas holistic functionalism maintains that the relationship between the two is extremely indirect. I conclude that holistic functionalism is better motivated than atomistic.

Afterword

Formal and functional linguists alike have placed on their research agendas the task of accounting for typological variation in language. Each has assumed a somewhat 'imperialistic' stance in their attempts to carry out this task. Formalists have resorted on the whole to theory-internal mechanisms, in particular parameters provided by Universal Grammar. Functionalists, on the other hand, have generally seen typological variation as being wholly predictable from facts about language use. In this work, I have attempted to demonstrate that both are partly right and partly wrong. Functionalists are certainly correct that the cross-linguistic distribution of morphosyntactic elements is to a large extent predictable from linguistic performance, a fact that renders unnecessary recourse to the formally defined parameter settings of much generative work. On the other hand, there is merit to the formalist view that neither grammar-internal nor cross-linguistic properties of language can be properly understood without taking as an underlying assumption the idea that at the heart of each language lies a structural system, whose rules and principles have no direct synchronic linkage to the functional forces that helped to shape them.

References

ABNEY, STEVEN P. (1987), 'The English Noun Phrase in Its Sentential Aspect', Ph.D. dissertation, MIT.

—— (1996), 'Statistical Methods and Linguistics', in J. L. Klavans and P. Resnik (eds.), *The Balancing Act: Combining Symbolic and Statistical Approaches to Language* (Cambridge, MA: MIT Press), 1–26.

ACKERMAN, FARRELL and WEBELHUTH, GERT (1998), *A Theory of Predicates* (Stanford: CSLI Publications).

AISSEN, JUDITH (1999), 'Markedness and Subject Choice in Optimality Theory', *Natural Language and Linguistic Theory* 17: 673–711.

—— (2003), 'Differential Object Marking: Iconicity vs. Economy', *Natural Language and Linguistic Theory* 21: 435–83.

ALDAI, GONTZAL (2003), 'The Prenominal [-Case] Relativization of Basque: Conventionalization, Processing, and Frame Semantics', Unpublished manuscript, USC and UCLA.

ALLEN, CYNTHIA L. (1995), *Case Marking and Reanalysis: Grammatical Relations from Old to Early Modern English* (Oxford: Clarendon Press).

ALLEN, SHANLEY E. M. and SCHROEDER, HEIKE (2003), 'Preferred Argument Structure in Early Inuktitut Speech Data', in J. W. Du Bois, L. E. Kumpf, and W. J. Ashby (eds.), *Preferred Argument Structure: Grammar as Architecture for Function* (Amsterdam: John Benjamins), 301–38.

ALSINA, ALEX (1996), 'Passive Types and the Theory of Object Asymmetries', *Natural Language and Linguistic Theory* 14: 673–723.

ANDERSEN, HENNING (ed.) (2001), *Actualization: Linguistic Change in Progress*, Amsterdam Studies in the Theory and History of Linguistic Science, Series IV: Current Issues in Linguistic Theory, vol. 219 (Amsterdam: John Benjamins).

ANDERSEN, PAUL K. (1983), *Word Order Typology and Comparative Constructions* (Amsterdam: John Benjamins).

ANDERSON, STEPHEN R. (1977), 'On the Mechanisms by Which Languages Become Ergative', in C. Li (ed.), *Mechanisms of Syntactic Change* (Austin: University of Texas Press), 317–63.

—— and KEENAN, EDWARD L. (1985), 'Deixis', in T. Shopen (ed.), *Language Typology and Syntactic Description. Volume 3: Grammatical Categories and the Lexicon* (Cambridge: Cambridge University Press), 259–308.

—— and LIGHTFOOT, DAVID (2002), *The Language Organ: Linguistics as Cognitive Physiology* (Cambridge: Cambridge University Press).

ANSHEN, FRANK (1975), 'Varied Objections to Various Variable Rules', in R. W. Fasold and R. W. Shuy (eds.), *Analyzing Variation in Language: Papers from the Second Colloquium on New Ways of Analyzing Variation* (Washington, DC: Georgetown University Press), 1–10.

ARISTAR, ANTHONY R. (1991), 'On Diachronic Sources and Synchronic Patterns: An Investigation into the Origin of Linguistic Universals', *Language* 67: 1–33.

Arnold, Jennifer E., Wasow, Thomas, Losongco, Anthony, and Ginstrom, Ryan (2000), 'Heaviness vs. Newness: The Effects of Structural Complexity and Discourse Status on Constituent Ordering', *Language* 76: 28–55.

Ashby, William J. and Paola Bentivoglio (1993), 'Preferred Argument Structure in Spoken French and Spanish', *Language Variation and Change* 5: 61–76.

—— —— (2003), 'Preferred Argument Structure across Time and Space: A Comparative Diachronic Analysis of French and Spanish', in J. W. Du Bois, L. E. Kumpf, and W. J. Ashby (eds.), *Preferred Argument Structure: Grammar as Architecture for Function* (Amsterdam: John Benjamins), 60–80.

Aske, Jon (1998), *Basque Word Order and Disorder: Principles, Variation, and Prospects* (Amsterdam: John Benjamins).

Babyonyshev, Maria, Ganger, Jennifer, Pesetsky, David M., and Wexler, Ken (2001), 'The Maturation of Grammatical Principles: Evidence from Russian Unaccusatives', *Linguistic Inquiry* 32: 1–43.

Bach, Emmon (1962), 'The Order of Elements in a Transformational Grammar of German', *Language* 38: 263–9.

—— (1965), 'On Some Recurrent Types of Transformations', in C. W. Kreidler (ed.), *Approaches to Linguistic Analysis, Language and Society, Teaching Language Skills*, Monograph Series on Languages and Linguistics No. 18; 16th Round Table Meeting (Washington, DC: Georgetown University Press), 3–18.

—— (1970), 'Is Amharic an SOV Language?', *Journal of Ethiopian Studies* 8: 9–20.

—— (1971), 'Questions', *Linguistic Inquiry* 2: 153–66.

—— and Horn, George M. (1976), 'Remarks on "Conditions on Transformations"', *Linguistic Inquiry* 7: 265–99.

Baker, C. L. (1970), 'Notes on the Description of English Questions: The Role of an Abstract Question Morpheme', *Foundations of Language* 6: 197–219.

Baker, Mark C. (1988), *Incorporation: A Theory of Grammatical Function Changing* (Chicago: University of Chicago Press).

—— (1989), 'Object Sharing and Projection in Serial Verb Constructions', *Linguistic Inquiry* 20: 513–53.

—— (1996), *The Polysynthesis Parameter* (New York: Oxford University Press).

—— (1997), 'Thematic Roles and Syntactic Structure', in L. Haegeman (ed.), *Elements of Grammar: Handbook of Generative Syntax* (Dordrecht: Kluwer), 73–137.

—— (2001a), *The Atoms of Language: The Mind's Hidden Rules of Grammar* (New York: Basic Books).

—— (2001b), 'Phrase Structure as a Representation of "Primitive" Grammatical Relations', in W. Davies and S. Dubinsky (eds.), *Objects and Other Subjects: Grammatical Functions, Functional Categories, and Configurationality* (Dordrecht: Kluwer), 21–51.

—— (2002), 'Building and Merging, Not Checking: The Nonexistence of (Aux)-S-V-O Languages', *Linguistic Inquiry* 33: 321–8.

—— (2003), *Lexical Categories: Verbs, Nouns, and Adjectives*, Cambridge Studies in Linguistics, vol. 102 (Cambridge: Cambridge University Press).

Bates, Elizabeth (1997), 'On Language Savants and the Structure of the Mind: A Review of Neil Smith and Ianthi-Maria Tsimpli *The Mind of a Savant*', *International Journal of Bilingualism* 1: 163–79.

Bayer, Josef and Kornfilt, Jaklin (1994), 'Against Scrambling as an Instance of Move-Alpha', in N. Corver and H. van Riemsdijk (eds.), *Studies on Scrambling* (Berlin: Mouton de Gruyter), 17–60.

Beaken, Mike (1996), *The Making of Language* (Edinburgh: Edinburgh University Press).

Beghelli, Filippo and Stowell, Timothy A. (1997), 'Distributivity and Negation: The Syntax of *Each* and *Every*', in A. Szabolcsi (ed.), *Ways of Scope Taking* (Dordrecht: Kluwer), 71–107.

Belletti, Adriana (2001), 'Agreement Projections', in M. R. Baltin and C. Collins (eds.), *The Handbook of Contemporary Syntactic Theory* (Oxford: Blackwell), 483–510.

Bennis, Hans and Hoekstra, Teun (1984), 'Gaps and Parasitic Gaps', *Linguistic Review* 4: 29–87.

—— and Koster, Jan (1984), 'GLOW Colloquium 1984, Call for Papers: Parametric Typology', *GLOW Newsletter* 12: 6–7.

Berdan, Robert (1973), *The Use of Linguistically Determined Groups in Socio-Linguistic Research*, Professional Paper 26, Los Alamitos, CA: Southwest Regional Laboratory for Educational Research and Development.

Berkenfield, Catie (2002), 'The Role of Frequency in the Realization of English *That*', in J. L. Bybee and P. Hopper (eds.), *Frequency and the Emergence of Linguistic Structure* (Amsterdam: John Benjamins), 281–307.

Bernstein, Judy B. (2001), 'The DP Hypothesis: Identifying Clausal Properties in the Nominal Domain', in M. Baltin and C. Collins (eds.), *The Handbook of Contemporary Syntactic Theory* (Oxford: Blackwell), 536–61.

Berwick, Robert C. (1985), *The Acquisition of Syntactic Knowledge* (Cambridge, MA: MIT Press).

—— (1998), 'Language Evolution and the Minimalist Program: The Origins of Syntax', in J. R. Hurford, M. Studdert-Kennedy, and C. Knight (eds.), *Approaches to the Evolution of Language: Social and Cognitive Bases* (Cambridge: Cambridge University Press), 320–40.

Biber, Douglas (1988), *Variation across Speech and Writing* (Cambridge: Cambridge University Press).

—— (1995), *Dimensions of Register Variation: A Cross-Linguistic Comparison* (Cambridge: Cambridge University Press).

—— Johansson, Stig, Leech, Geoffrey, Finegan, Edward, and Conrad, Susan (1999), *Longman Grammar of Spoken and Written English* (London: Longman).

Bichakjian, Bernard H. (2002), *Language in a Darwinian Perspective* (Frankfurt am Main: Peter Lang).

Bickel, Balthasar (2001), 'What Is Typology?—a Short Note', unpublished paper, University of Leipzig.

—— (2003), 'Referential Density in Discourse and Syntactic Typology', *Language* 79: 708–36.

—— and Nichols, Johanna (2001), 'Syntactic Ergativity in Light Verb Complements', *Berkeley Linguistics Society* 27.

Bickerton, Derek (1973), 'Quantitative Versus Dynamic Paradigms: The Case of Montreal *Que*', in C.-J. N. Bailey and R. W. Shuy (eds.), *New Ways of Analyzing Variation in English* (Washington, DC: Georgetown University Press), 22–43.

—— (1990), *Language and Species* (Chicago: University of Chicago Press).

Bierwisch, Manfred (1963), *Grammatik des deutschen Verbs*, Studia Grammatica, Vol. 2 (Berlin: Studia Grammatica).

—— (1966), 'Regeln für die Intonation deutscher Sätze', *Studia Grammatica* 7: 99–201.

Blansitt, Edward L. (1988), 'Datives and Allatives', in M. Hammond, E. Moravcsik, and J. Wirth (eds.), *Studies in Syntactic Typology* (Amsterdam: John Benjamins), 173–91.

BOBALJIK, JONATHAN D. (1995), 'Morphosyntax: The Syntax of Verbal Inflection', Ph.D. dissertation, MIT.

—— and THRÁINSSON, HÖSKULDUR (1998), 'Two Heads Aren't Always Better Than One', *Syntax* 1: 37–71.

BOD, RENS (1998), *Beyond Grammar: An Experience-Based Theory of Language*, CSLI Lecture Notes, vol. 88 (Stanford: Center for the Study of Language and Information).

—— HAY, JENNIFER, and JANNEDY, STEFANIE (eds.) (2003), *Probabilistic Linguistics* (Cambridge, MA: MIT Press).

BOECKX, CEDRIC (2001), 'Head-Ing toward PF', *Linguistic Inquiry* 32: 345–55.

BOERSMA, PAUL and HAYES, BRUCE (2001), 'Empirical Tests of the Gradual Learning Algorithm', *Linguistic Inquiry* 32: 45–86.

BONDRE, PRIYA (1993), 'Parameter Setting and the Binding Theory: No Subset Problem', in G. Fanselow (ed.), *The Parametrization of Universal Grammar* (Amsterdam: John Benjamins), 17–35.

BORER, HAGIT (1984), *Parametric Syntax: Case Studies in Semitic and Romance Languages*, Studies in Generative Grammar, vol. 13 (Dordrecht: Foris).

—— and KENNETH WEXLER (1987), 'The Maturation of Syntax', in T. Roeper and E. Williams (eds.), *Parameter Setting* (Dordrecht: Reidel), 123–72.

BOUCHARD, DENIS (2003), 'The Origins of Language Variation', *Linguistic Variation Yearbook* 3: 1–41.

BOWERMAN, MELISSA (1985), 'What Shapes Children's Grammars?' in D. I. Slobin (ed.), *The Crosslinguistic Study of Language Acquisition* (Hillsdale, NJ: Erlbaum), 1257–319.

BOYLE, JOHN A. (1966), *Grammar of Modern Persian* (Wiesbaden: Otto Harrassowitz).

BRESNAN, JOAN W. (1970), 'On Complementizers: Toward a Syntactic Theory of Complement Types', *Foundations of Language* 6: 297–321.

—— (1997), 'The Emergence of the Unmarked Pronoun: Chichewa Pronominals in Optimality Theory', in A. C. Bailey, K. E. Moore, and J. L. Moxley (eds.), *Berkeley Linguistics Society 23: Special Session on Syntax and Semantics of Africa* (Berkeley: Berkeley Linguistics Society), 26–46.

—— (2000a), 'Explaining Morphosyntactic Competition', in M. Baltin and C. Collins (eds.), *The Handbook of Contemporary Syntactic Theory* (Oxford: Blackwell), 11–44.

—— (2000b), 'Optimal Syntax', in J. Dekkers, F. van der Leeuw, and J. van de Weijer (eds.), *Optimality Theory: Syntax, Phonology, and Acquisition* (Oxford: Oxford University Press), 334–85.

—— and AISSEN, JUDITH (2002), 'Optimality and Functionality: Objections and Refutations', *Natural Language and Linguistic Theory* 21: 81–95.

—— DINGARE, SHIPRA, and MANNING, CHRISTOPHER D. (2001), 'Soft Constraints Mirror Hard Constraints: Voice and Person in English and Lummi', in M. Butt and T. H. King (eds.), *Proceedings of the LFG-01 Conference* (Stanford: CSLI Publications), 13–32.

—— and KANERVA, JONNI (1989), 'Locative Inversion in Chichewa: A Case Study of Factorization in Grammar', *Linguistic Inquiry* 20: 1–50.

—— and MOSHI, LIOBI (1990), 'Object Asymmetries in Comparative Bantu Syntax', *Linguistic Inquiry* 21: 147–85.

BRISCOE, TED (2000), 'Grammatical Acquisition: Inductive Bias and Coevolution of Language and the Language Acquisition Device', *Language* 76: 245–96.

BRODY, JILL (1984), 'Some Problems with the Concept of Basic Word Order', *Linguistics* 22: 711–36.

BUCKLEY, EUGENE (2000), 'What Should Phonology Explain?', unpublished paper, University of Pennsylvania.

BYBEE, JOAN L. (1985), *Morphology: A Study of the Relation between Meaning and Form.* Typological Studies in Language, vol. 9 (Amsterdam: John Benjamins).

—— and DAHL, ÖSTEN (1989), 'The Creation of Tense and Aspect Systems in the Languages of the World', *Studies in Language* 13: 51–103.

—— and PAUL J. HOPPER (2001b), 'Introduction to Frequency and the Emergence of Linguistic Structure', in J. L. Bybee and P. Hopper (eds.), *Frequency and the Emergence of Linguistic Structure* (Amsterdam: John Benjamins), 1–24.

—— —— (eds.) (2001), *Frequency and the Emergence of Linguistic Structure*, Typological Studies in Language, vol. 45 (Amsterdam: John Benjamins).

——., PERKINS, REVERE D., and PAGLIUCA, WILLIAM (1994), *The Evolution of Grammar: Tense, Aspect, and Modality in the Languages of the World* (Chicago: University of Chicago Press).

CAMPBELL, LYLE (1996), 'Typological and Areal Issues in Reconstruction', in J. Fisiak (ed.), *Linguistic Reconstruction and Typology* (Berlin: Mouton de Gruyter), 49–72.

CARRIER-DUNCAN, JILL (1985), 'Linking of Thematic Roles in Derivational Word Formation', *Linguistic Inquiry* 16: 1–34.

CARSTAIRS, ANDREW (1984), 'Inflectional Complexity in Relation to Phonology', *Te Reo* 27: 29–46.

CARSTAIRS-MCCARTHY, ANDREW (1999), *The Origins of Complex Language: An Inquiry into the Evolutionary Beginnings of Sentences, Syllables, and Truth* (Oxford: Oxford University Press).

CASALI, RODERIC F. (1997), 'Vowel Elision in Hiatus Contexts: Which Vowel Goes?', *Language* 73: 493–533.

CEDERGREN, HENRIETTA J. and SANKOFF, DAVID (1974), 'Variable Rules: Performance as a Statistical Reflection of Competence', *Language* 50: 333–55.

CHAO, WYNN (1981), 'Pro-Drop Languages and Nonobligatory Control', *University of Massachusetts Occasional Papers* 6: 46–74.

CHEN, MATTHEW and WANG, WILLIAM S.-Y. (1975), 'Sound Change: Actuation and Implementation', *Language* 51: 225–81.

CHENEY, DOROTHY and SEYFARTH, ROBERT (1990), *How Monkeys See the World* (Chicago: University of Chicago Press).

CHENG, LISA L.-S. (1991/1997), *On the Typology of Wh-Questions* (New York: Garland).

CHOMSKY, NOAM (1957), *Syntactic Structures*, Janua Linguarum Series Minor, vol. 4 (The Hague: Mouton).

—— (1962), 'Explanatory Models in Linguistics', in E. Nagel, P. Suppes, and A. Tarski (eds.), *Logic, Methodology, and Philosophy of Science* (Stanford: Stanford University Press), 528–50.

—— (1965), *Aspects of the Theory of Syntax* (Cambridge, MA: MIT Press).

—— (1970), 'Remarks on Nominalization', in R. Jacobs and P. Rosenbaum (eds.), *Readings in English Transformational Grammar* (Waltham, MA: Ginn), 184–221.

—— (1973), 'Conditions on Transformations', in S. Anderson and P. Kiparsky (eds.), *A Festschrift for Morris Halle* (New York: Holt, Rinehart, and Winston), 232–86.

Chomsky, Noam (1975), *Reflections on Language* (New York: Pantheon).

——(1977a), 'Introduction', *Essays on Form and Interpretation* (New York: North-Holland), 1–21.

——(1977b), 'On *Wh*-Movement', in P. Culicover, T. Wasow, and A. Akmajian (eds.), *Formal Syntax* (New York: Academic Press), 71–132.

——(1981), *Lectures on Government and Binding*, Studies in Generative Grammar, vol. 9 (Dordrecht: Foris).

——(1982a), *The Generative Enterprise: A Discussion with Riny Huybregts and Henk Van Riemsdijk* (Dordrecht: Foris).

——(1982b), *Some Concepts and Consequences of the Theory of Government and Binding* (Cambridge, MA: MIT Press).

——(1986a), *Barriers* (Cambridge, MA: MIT Press).

——(1986b), *Knowledge of Language: Its Nature, Origin, and Use* (New York: Praeger).

——(1988), *Language and Problems of Knowledge: The Managua Lectures*, Current Studies in Linguistics, vol. 16 (Cambridge, MA: MIT Press).

——(1991a), 'Linguistics and Cognitive Science: Problems and Mysteries', in A. Kasher (ed.), *The Chomskyan Turn: Generative Linguistics, Philosophy, Mathematics, and Psychology* (Oxford: Blackwell), 26–55.

——(1991b), 'Some Notes on Economy of Derivation and Representation', in R. Freidin (ed.), *Principles and Parameters in Comparative Grammar* (Cambridge, MA: MIT Press), 417–54. [Repr. in Noam Chomsky (1995), *The Minimalist Program* (Cambridge, MA: MIT Press), 129–66.]

——(1995), *The Minimalist Program* (Cambridge, MA: MIT Press).

——(1998), 'Noam Chomsky's Minimalist Program and the Philosophy of Mind. An Interview [with] Camilo J. Cela-Conde and Gisèle Marty', *Syntax* 1: 19–36.

——(2000), 'Minimalist Inquiries: The Framework', in R. Martin, D. Michaels, and J. Uriagereka (eds.), *Step by Step: Essays on Minimalist Syntax in Honor of Howard Lasnik* (Cambridge, MA: MIT Press), 89–155.

——(2001), 'Derivation by Phase', in M. Kenstowicz (ed.), *Ken Hale: A Life in Language* (Cambridge, MA: MIT Press), 1–52.

——(2002), *On Nature and Language* (Cambridge: Cambridge University Press).

——and Halle, Morris (1968), *Sound Pattern of English* (New York: Harper and Row).

——and Lasnik, Howard (1977), 'Filters and Control', *Linguistic Inquiry* 8: 425–504.

Chung, Sandra (1984), 'Identifiability and Null Objects in Chamorro', *Berkeley Linguistics Society* 10: 116–30.

——(1990), 'VPs and Verb Movement in Chamorro', *Natural Language and Linguistic Theory* 8: 559–620.

Cinque, Guglielmo (1981), 'On Keenan and Comrie's Primary Relativization Constraint', *Linguistic Inquiry* 12: 293–308.

——(1982), 'On the Theory of Relative Clauses and Markedness', *Linguistic Review* 1: 297–343.

——(1994), 'On the Evidence for Partial N Movement in the Romance DP', in G. Cinque, J. Koster, J.-Y. Pollock, L. Rizzi, and R. Zanuttini (eds.), *Paths Towards Universal Grammar* (Washington, DC: Georgetown University Press), 85–110.

——(1996), 'The "Antisymmetric" Program: Theoretical and Typological Implications', *Journal of Linguistics* 32: 447–65.

——(1999), *Adverbs and Functional Heads: A Cross-Linguistic Perspective* (Oxford: Oxford University Press).

Clahsen, Harald, Eisenbeiss, Sonia, and Penke, Martina (1996), 'Underspecification and Lexical Learning in Early Child Grammars', in H. Clahsen and R. Hawkins (eds.), *Generative Approaches to First and Second Language Acquisition* (Amsterdam: Benjamins), 129–60.

——and Penke, Martina (1992), 'The Acquisition of Agreement Morphology and Its Syntactic Consequences: New Evidence on German Child Language from the Simone-Corpus', in J. Meisel (ed.), *The Acquisition of Verb Placement: Functional Categories and V2 Phenomena in Language Acquisition* (Dordrecht: Kluwer), 181–224.

Clancy, Patricia M. (2003), 'The Lexicon in Interaction: Developmental Origins of Preferred Argument Structure in Korean', in J. W. Du Bois, L. E. Kumpf, and W. J. Ashby (eds.), *Preferred Argument Structure: Grammar as Architecture for Function* (Amsterdam: John Benjamins), 81–108.

Clark, Brady (2005), 'On Stochastic Grammar', *Language* 81: 207–17.

Clark, Robin (1994), 'Finitude, Boundedness, and Complexity', in B. Lust, G. Hermon, and J. Kornfilt (eds.), *Syntactic Theory and First Language Acquisition: Cross-Linguistic Perspectives* (Hillsdale, NJ: Erlbaum), 473–89.

——and Roberts, Ian (1993), 'A Computational Theory of Language Learnability and Language Change', *Linguistic Inquiry* 24: 299–345.

Claudi, Ulrike (1994), 'Word Order Change as Category Change: The Mande Case', in W. Pagliuca (ed.), *Perspectives on Grammaticalization* (Amsterdam: John Benjamins), 191–232.

Cole, Peter and Hermon, Gabriella (1998), 'Long Distance Reflexives in Singapore Malay: An Apparent Typological Anomaly', *Linguistic Typology* 2: 57–77.

——and Sung, Li-May (1994), 'Head Movement and Long Distance Reflexives', *Linguistic Inquiry* 25: 355–406.

——and Wang, Chengchi (1996), 'Antecedents and Blockers of Long Distance Reflexives', *Linguistic Inquiry* 27: 357–90.

Collins, Chris (1997), 'Argument Sharing in Serial Verb Constructions', *Linguistic Inquiry* 28: 461–97.

Comrie, Bernard (1981), *Language Universals and Linguistic Typology* (Chicago: University of Chicago Press).

——(1984), 'Language Universals and Linguistic Argumentation: A Reply to Coopmans', *Journal of Linguistics* 20: 155–64.

——(1988), 'Linguistic Typology', in F. Newmeyer (ed.), *Linguistics: The Cambridge Survey*, Volume 1 (Cambridge: Cambridge University Press), 447–61.

——(1989), *Language Universals and Linguistic Typology*, 2nd edn. (Chicago: University of Chicago Press).

——(1998), 'Reference-Tracking: Description and Explanation', *Sprachtypologie und Universalienforschung* 51: 335–46.

——and Keenan, Edward L. (1979), 'Noun Phrase Accessibility Revisited', *Language* 55: 649–64.

Coopmans, Peter (1983), 'Review of *Language Universals and Linguistic Typology* by B. Comrie', *Journal of Linguistics* 19: 455–74.

——(1984), 'Surface Word-Order Typology and Universal Grammar', *Language* 60: 55–69.

Corbett, Greville G. (1991), *Gender* (Cambridge: Cambridge University Press).

—— (2000), *Number* (Cambridge: Cambridge University Press).

Costa, João (1998), 'Parameters vs. Soft Constraints in the Analysis of Discourse-Configurationality', in M. C. Gruber, D. Higgins, K. S. Olson, and T. Wysocki (eds.), *CLS 34, Part 2: Papers from the Panels* (Chicago: Chicago Linguistic Society), 18–30.

Cowart, Wayne (1997), *Experimental Syntax: Applying Objective Methods to Sentence Judgments* (Newbury Park, CA: SAGE Publications).

Craig, Colette G. (1987), 'The Rama Language: A Text with Grammatical Notes', *Journal of Chibchan Studies* 5.

Crain, Stephen and Mckee, Cecile (1986), 'Acquisition of Structural Restrictions on Anaphora', *North Eastern Linguistic Society* 16, 94–110.

—— and Pietroski, Paul (2002), 'Why Language Acquisition Is a Snap', *Linguistic Review* 19: 163–83.

Creider, Chet (1979), 'On the Explanation of Transformations', in T. Givón (ed.), *Syntax and Semantics, Volume 12: Discourse and Syntax* (New York: Academic Press), 3–22.

Croft, William (1988), 'Agreement vs. Case Marking and Direct Objects', in M. Barlow and C. A. Ferguson (eds.), *Agreement in Natural Language: Approaches, Theories, Descriptions* (Stanford: Center for the Study of Language and Information), 159–79.

—— (1990), *Typology and Universals* (Cambridge: Cambridge University Press).

—— (1995), 'Autonomy and Functionalist Linguistics', *Language* 71: 490–532.

—— (2000), *Explaining Language Change: An Evolutionary Approach* (London: Longman).

—— (2003), *Typology and Universals*, 2nd edn. (Cambridge: Cambridge University Press).

Crowley, Terry (1982), *The Paamese Language of Vanuatu* (Canberra: Pacific Linguistics).

—— (1994), *An Introduction to Historical Linguistics*, 2nd edn. (Auckland: Cambridge University Press).

—— (2002), *Serial Verbs in Oceanic: A Descriptive Typology* (Oxford: Oxford University Press).

Culicover, Peter W. (1999), *Syntactic Nuts: Hard Cases, Syntactic Theory, and Language Acquisition* (Oxford: Oxford University Press).

—— and Jackendoff, Ray (2001), 'Control Is Not Movement', *Linguistic Inquiry* 32: 493–512.

Cysouw, Michael (2003), *The Paradigmatic Structure of Person Marking* (Oxford: Oxford University Press).

Dahl, Östen (2000a), 'Egophoricity in Discourse and Syntax', *Functions of Language* 7: 33–77.

—— (2000b), 'Grammaticalization and the Life-Cycles of Constructions', unpublished paper, University of Stockholm.

Damonte, Federico (2004), 'The Thematic Field: The Syntax of Valency-Enriching Morphology', Ph.D. dissertation, University of Padua.

Davies, William D. and Dubinsky, Stanley (eds.) (2001), *Objects and Other Subjects: Grammatical Functions, Functional Categories, and Configurationality* (Dordrecht: Kluwer).

Davis, Anthony R. and Koenig, Jean-Pierre (2000), 'Linking as Constraints on Word Classes in a Hierarchical Lexicon', *Language* 76: 56–91.

Deane, Paul D. (1987), 'English Possessives, Topicality, and the Silverstein Hierarchy', *Berkeley Linguistics Society* 13: 65–77.

——(1992), *Grammar in Mind and Brain: Explorations in Cognitive Syntax*, Cognitive Linguistics Research, vol. 2 (The Hague: Mouton de Gruyter).

Déchaine, Rose-Marie A. (1993), 'Predicates across Categories: Towards a Category-Neutral Syntax', Ph.D. dissertation, University of Massachusetts.

DeLancey, Scott (1985), 'The Analysis-Synthesis-Lexis Cycle in Tibeto-Burman: A Case Study in Motivated Change', in J. Haiman (ed.), *Iconicity in Syntax* (Amsterdam: John Benjamins), 367–90.

den Besten, Hans (1983), 'On the Interaction of Root Transformations and Lexical Deletion Rules', in W. Abraham (ed.), *On the Formal Syntax of the Westgermania* (Amsterdam: Benjamins).

Denham, Kristin (2000), 'Optional Wh-Movement in Babine-Witsuwit'en', *Natural Language and Linguistic Theory* 18: 199–251.

Déprez, Viviane and Pierce, Amy (1993), 'Negation and Functional Projections in Early Grammar', *Linguistic Inquiry* 24: 25–67.

Derbyshire, Desmond C. (1985), *Hixkaryana and Linguistic Typology* (Arlington, TX: Summer Institute of Linguistics).

de Waal, Frans B. M. (1996), *Good Natured: The Origins of Right and Wrong in Humans and Other Animals* (Cambridge, MA: Harvard University Press).

Dick, Frederic and Elman, Jeffrey L. (2001), 'The Frequency of Major Sentence Types over Discourse Levels: A Corpus Analysis', *Newsletter of the Center for Research in Language, University of California, San Diego* 13: 3–19.

Dik, Simon C. (1986), 'On the Notion "Functional Explanation"', *Belgian Journal of Linguistics* 1: 11–52.

——(1989), *The Theory of Functional Grammar; Part 1: The Structure of the Clause*, Functional Grammar Series, vol. 9 (Dordrecht: Foris).

Dimmendaal, Gerrit J. (1983), *The Turkana Language* (Dordrecht: Foris).

Dixon, R. M. W. (1977), 'Where Have All the Adjectives Gone?' *Studies in Language* 1: 1–80.

——(1979), 'Ergativity', *Language* 55: 59–138.

——(1994), *Ergativity*, Cambridge Studies in Linguistics, vol. 69 (Cambridge: Cambridge University Press).

Donohue, Mark and Brown, Lea (1999), 'Ergativity: Some Additions from Indonesia', *Australian Journal of Linguistics* 19: 57–76.

Dowty, David R. (1991), 'Thematic Proto-Roles and Argument Selection', *Language* 67: 547–619.

Dryer, Matthew S. (1988a), 'Object–Verb Order and Adjective–Noun Order: Dispelling a Myth', *Lingua* 74: 185–217.

——(1988b), 'Universals of Negative Position', in M. Hammond, E. Moravcsik, and J. Wirth (eds.), *Studies in Syntactic Typology* (Amsterdam: John Benjamins), 93–124.

——(1989a), 'Discourse-Governed Word Order and Word Order Typology', *Belgian Journal of Linguistics* 4: 69–90.

——(1989b), 'Large Linguistic Areas and Language Sampling', *Studies in Language* 13: 257–92.

——(1991), 'SVO Languages and the OV:VO Typology', *Journal of Linguistics* 27: 443–82.

——(1992), 'The Greenbergian Word Order Correlations', *Language* 68: 81–138.

——(1997a), 'On the Six-Way Word Order Typology', *Studies in Language* 21: 69–103.

DRYER, MATTHEW S. (1997b), 'Why Statistical Universals Are Better Than Absolute Universals', in K. Singer, R. Eggert, and G. Anderson (eds.), *CLS 33: Papers from the Panels* (Chicago: Chicago Linguistic Society), 123–45.

DU BOIS, JOHN (1985), 'Competing Motivations', in J. Haiman (ed.), *Iconicity in Syntax* (Amsterdam: John Benjamins), 343–65.

——(1987), 'The Discourse Basis of Ergativity', *Language* 63: 805–55.

DURIE, MARK (1985), *A Grammar of Acehnese* (Dordrecht: Foris).

——(1987), 'Grammatical Relations in Acehnese', *Studies in Language* 11: 365–99.

EISENBEISS, SONIA (1994), 'Kasus und Wortstellungsvariation im deutschen Mittelfeld', in B. Haftka (ed.), *Was determiniert Wortstellungsvariation?* (Opladen: Westdeutscher Verlag), 277–98.

——(2002), 'Merkmalsgesteuerter Spracherwerb: Eine Untersuchung zum Erwerb der Struktur und Flexion von Nominalphrasen', Ph.D. dissertation, Heinrich-Heine Universität Düsseldorf.

ELMAN, JEFFREY L., BATES, ELIZABETH A., JOHNSON, MARK H., KARMILOFF-SMITH, ANNETTE, PARISI, DOMENICO, and PLUNKETT, KIM (1996), *Rethinking Innateness: A Connectionist Perspective on Development* (Cambridge, MA: MIT Press).

EMONDS, JOSEPH E. (1970), 'Root and Structure-Preserving Transformations', Ph.D. dissertation, MIT.

——(1976), *A Transformational Approach to English Syntax* (New York: Academic Press).

——(1978), 'The Complex V—V' in French', *Linguistic Inquiry* 9: 151–75.

——(1980), 'Word Order in Generative Grammar', *Journal of Linguistic Research* 1: 33–54.

ENGLAND, NORA C. (1988), 'Mam Voice', in M. Shibatani (ed.), *Passive and Voice* (Amsterdam: John Benjamins), 525–45.

EVERETT, DANIEL L. (2004), 'Cultural Constraints on Grammar and Cognition in Pirahã', unpublished paper, University of Manchester.

EWERT, MANFRED and HANSEN, FRED (1993), 'On the Linear Order of the Modifier-Head-Position in NPs', in G. Fanselow (ed.), *The Parametrization of Universal Grammar* (Amsterdam: John Benjamins), 161–81.

FALTZ, LEONARD M. (1977/1985), *Reflexivization: A Study in Universal Syntax*, Outstanding Dissertations in Linguistics (New York: Garland).

FANSELOW, GISBERT (1992), 'Zur biologischen Autonomie der Grammatik', in P. Suchsland (ed.), *Biologische und Soziale Grundlagen der Sprache* (Tübingen: Niemeyer), 335–56.

FERGUSON, CHARLES A. (1978), 'Historical Background of Universals Research', in J. H. Greenberg (ed.), *Universals of Human Language. Vol. 1: Method and Theory* (Stanford: Stanford University Press), 7–32.

FILLMORE, CHARLES J. (1968), 'The Case for Case', in E. Bach and R. Harms (eds.), *Universals in Linguistic Theory* (New York: Holt, Rinehart, and Winston), 1–90.

FISCHER, OLGA C. M. (1992), 'Syntax', in N. Blake (ed.), *The Cambridge History of the English Language, II: 1066–1476* (Cambridge: Cambridge University Press), 207–408.

FODOR, JANET D. (1983), 'Phrase Structure Parsing and the Island Constraints', *Linguistics and Philosophy* 6: 163–223.

——(1984), 'Constraints on Gaps: Is the Parser a Significant Influence?' in B. Butterworth, B. Comrie, and Ö. Dahl (eds.), *Explanations for Language Universals* (Berlin: Mouton), 9–34.

——(2001a), 'Parameters and the Periphery: Reflections on Syntactic Nuts', *Journal of Linguistics* 37: 367–92.

——(2001b), 'Setting Syntactic Parameters', in M. Baltin and C. Collins (eds.), *The Handbook of Contemporary Syntactic Theory* (Oxford: Blackwell), 730–67.

——and Crowther, Carrie (2002), 'Understanding Stimulus Poverty Arguments', *Linguistic Review* 19: 105–45.

Foley, William A. and Van Valin, Robert D. (1984), *Functional Syntax and Universal Grammar*, Cambridge Studies in Linguistics, vol. 38 (Cambridge: Cambridge University Press).

Fox, Barbara A. (1994), 'Contextualization, Indexicality, and the Distributed Nature of Grammar', *Language Sciences* 16: 1–38.

Francis, Hartwell S., Gregory, Michelle L., and Michaelis, Laura A. (1999), 'Are Lexical Subjects Deviant?', *Chicago Linguistic Society* 35/1: 85–98.

Freidin, Robert and Quicoli, A. Carlos (1989), 'Zero-Stimulation for Parameter Setting', *Behavioral and Brain Sciences* 12: 338–9.

Frisch, Stefan (1999), 'Review of *Linguistic Structure and Change: An Explanation from Language Processing* by T. Berg', *Journal of Linguistics* 35: 597–601.

Fry, J. (2001), 'Ellipsis and Wa-Marking in Japanese Conversation', Ph.D. dissertation, Stanford University.

Fukui, Naoki (1986), 'A Theory of Categorial Projection and Its Applications', Ph.D. dissertation, MIT.

——(1988), 'Deriving the Differences between English and Japanese: A Case Study in Parametric Syntax', *English Linguistics* 5: 249–70.

——(1993), 'Parameters and Optionality', *Linguistic Inquiry* 24: 399–420.

——(1995), *Theory of Projection in Syntax*, Studies in Japanese Linguistics, vol. 4 (Stanford: CSLI Publications).

——and Speas, Margaret (1986), 'Specifiers and Projections', *MIT Working Papers in Linguistics* 8: 128–72.

——and Takano, Yuji (1998), 'Symmetry in Syntax: Merge and Demerge', *Journal of East Asian Linguistics* 7: 27–86.

Genetti, Carol and Crain, Laura D. (2003), 'Beyond Preferred Argument Structure: Sentences, Pronouns, and Given Referents in Nepali', in J. W. Du Bois, L. E. Kumpf, and W. J. Ashby (eds.), *Preferred Argument Structure: Grammar as Architecture for Function* (Amsterdam: John Benjamins), 197–223.

Gibson, Edward and Wexler, Kenneth (1994), 'Triggers', *Linguistic Inquiry* 25: 407–54.

Giddens, Anthony (1984), *The Constitution of Society: Outline of the Theory of Structuration* (Cambridge: Polity Press).

Gil, David (1997), 'The Structure of Riau Indonesian', *Nordic Journal of Linguistics* 17: 179–200.

——(2000), 'Syntactic Categories, Crosslinguistic Variation, and Universal Grammar', in P. M. Vogel and B. Comrie (eds.), *Approaches to the Typology of Word Classes* (Berlin: Mouton de Gruyter), 173–216.

——(2001), 'Creoles, Complexity, and Riau Indonesian', *Linguistic Typology* 5: 325–71.

Gilligan, Gary M. (1987), 'A Cross-Linguistic Approach to the Pro-Drop Parameter', Ph.D. dissertation, University of Southern California.

Ginzburg, Jonathan and Sag, Ivan (2000), *Interrogative Investigations: The Form, Meaning, and Use of English Interrogatives* (Stanford: Center for the Study of Language and Information).

Giorgi, Alessandra and Pianesi, Fabio (1997), *Tense and Aspect: From Semantics to Morphosyntax* (Oxford: Oxford University Press).

Givón, Talmy (1971), 'Historical Syntax and Synchronic Morphology: An Archaeologist's Field Trip', *Chicago Linguistic Society* 7: 394–415.

——(1976), 'Topic, Pronoun, and Grammatical Agreement', in C. Li (ed.), *Subject and Topic* (New York: Academic Press), 149–88.

——(1979), *On Understanding Grammar* (New York: Academic Press).

——(1983a), 'Topic Continuity in Discourse: An Introduction', in T. Givón (ed.), *Topic Continuity in Discourse: A Quantitative Cross-Language Study* (Amsterdam: John Benjamins), 1–42.

——(ed.) (1983b), *Topic Continuity in Discourse: A Quantitative Cross-Language Study.* Typological Studies in Language, vol. 3. (Amsterdam: John Benjamins).

——(1984), *Syntax: A Functional-Typological Introduction, Vol. 1* (Amsterdam: John Benjamins).

——(1985), 'Iconicity, Isomorphism, and Non-Arbitrary Coding in Syntax', in J. Haiman (ed.), *Iconicity in Syntax* (Amsterdam: John Benjamins), 187–220.

——(1991), 'Isomorphism in the Grammatical Code: Cognitive and Biological Considerations', *Studies in Language* 15: 85–114.

Godard, Danièle (1992), 'Extraction out of NP in French', *Natural Language and Linguistic Theory* 10: 233–77.

Godfrey, J., Holliman, J., and Mc Daniel, J. (1992), 'Switchboard: Telephone Speech Corpus for Research and Development', *Proceedings of ICASSP-92*, 517–20.

Greenberg, Joseph H. (1963), 'Some Universals of Language with Special Reference to the Order of Meaningful Elements', in J. Greenberg (ed.), *Universals of Language* (Cambridge, MA: MIT Press), 73–113.

——(1966), *Language Universals, with Special Reference to Feature Hierarchies* (The Hague: Mouton).

——(1978), 'Introduction', in J. H. Greenberg, C. A. Ferguson, and E. A. Moravcsik (eds.), *Universals of Human Language, vol. 1: Method and Theory* (Stanford: Stanford University Press), 1–5.

——Osgood, Charles E., and Jenkins, James J. (1963), 'Memorandum Concerning Language Universals', in J. H. Greenberg (ed.), *Universals of Language* (Cambridge, MA: MIT Press), xv–xxvii.

Grice, H. P. (1975), 'Logic and Conversation', in P. Cole and J. Morgan (eds.), *Syntax and Semantics, Vol. 3: Speech Acts* (New York: Academic Press), 41–58.

Grimshaw, Jane (1977), 'English Wh-Constructions and the Theory of Grammar', Ph.D. dissertation, University of Massachusetts.

——(1986), 'Subjacency and the S/S' Parameter', *Linguistic Inquiry* 17: 364–9.

——(1990), *Argument Structure* (Cambridge, MA: MIT Press).

——(1997), 'Projection, Heads, and Optimality', *Linguistic Inquiry* 28: 373–422.

——and Samek-Lodovici, Vieri (1998), 'Optimal Subjects and Subject Universals', in P. Barbosa, D. Fox, P. Hagstrom, M. McGinnis, and D. Pesetsky (eds.), *Is the Best Good Enough?: Optimality and Competition in Syntax* (Cambridge, MA: MIT Press), 193–219.

GROAT, ERICH and O'NEIL, JOHN (1996), 'Spell-out at the LF Interface', in W. Abraham, S. D. Epstein, H. Thráinsson, and C. J.-W. Zwart (eds.), *Minimal Ideas: Syntactic Studies in the Minimalist Framework* (Amsterdam: John Benjamins), 113–39.

GROHMANN, KLEANTHES K. and NEVINS, ANDREW A. (2004), 'Echo Reduplication: When Too-Local Movement Requires PF-Distinctness', *University of Maryland Working Papers in Linguistics* 14: 84–108.

GUILFOYLE, EITHNE (1990), 'Functional Categories and Phrase Structure Parameters', Ph.D. dissertation, McGill University.

GUNDEL, JEANETTE K. (1988), 'Universals of Topic-Comment Structure', in M. Hammond, E. Moravcsik, and J. Wirth (eds.), *Studies in Syntactic Typology* (Amsterdam: John Benjamins), 209–39.

——HEDBERG, NANCY, and ZACHARSKI, RON (1990), 'Givenness, Implicature, and the Form of Referring Expressions in Discourse', *Berkeley Linguistics Society* 16: 442–53.

HAEGEMAN, LILIANE (1987), 'Register Variation in English: Some Theoretical Observations', *Journal of English Linguistics* 20: 230–48.

——(1990), 'Understood Subjects in English Diaries: On the Relevance of Theoretical Syntax for the Study of Register Variation', *Multilingua* 9: 157–99.

HAIDER, HUBERT (1993), 'Principled Variability: Parameterization without Parameter Fixing', in G. Fanselow (ed.), *The Parametrization of Universal Grammar* (Amsterdam: John Benjamins), 1–16.

——(1994), '(Un-)heimliche Subjekte—Anmerkungen zur Pro-Drop Causa, im Anschluß an die Lektüre von Osvaldo Jaeggli and Kenneth J. Safir, eds., *The Null Subject Parameter*', *Linguistische Berichte* 153: 372–85.

——(2000a), 'Branching and Discharge', in P. Coopmans, M. Everaert, and J. Grimshaw (eds.), *Lexical Specification and Insertion* (Amsterdam: John Benjamins), 135–64.

——(2000b), 'OV Is More Basic Than VO', in P. Svenonius (ed.), *The Derivation of VO and OV* (Amsterdam: John Benjamins), 45–67.

HAIMAN, JOHN (1983), 'Iconic and Economic Motivation', *Language* 59: 781–819.

——(1985), *Natural Syntax: Iconicity and Erosion* (Cambridge: Cambridge University Press).

HALE, KENNETH (1973), 'A Note on Subject-Object Inversion in Navajo', in B. B. Kachru, R. B. Lees, Y. Malkiel, A. Pietrangeli, and S. Saporta (eds.), *Issues in Linguistics: Papers in Honor of Henry and Renée Kahane* (Urbana: University of Illinois Press), 300–9.

——(1976), 'Linguistic Autonomy and the Linguistics of Carl Voegelin', *Anthropological Linguistics* 18: 120–28.

——(1982), 'Preliminary Remarks on Configurationality', *North Eastern Linguistic Society* 12: 86–96.

——(1983), 'Warlpiri and the Grammar of Nonconfigurational Languages', *Natural Language and Linguistic Theory* 1: 5–47.

——(1992), 'Basic Word Order in Two "Free Word Order" Languages', in D. Payne (ed.), *Pragmatics of Word Order Flexibility* (Amsterdam: John Benjamins), 63–82.

——and KEYSER, SAMUEL JAY (1993), 'On Argument Structure and the Lexical Expression of Syntactic Relations', in K. Hale and S. J. Keyser (eds.), *The View from Building 20: Essays in Honor of Sylvain Bromberger* (Cambridge, MA: MIT Press), 53–110.

HALE, MARK and REISS, CHARLES (2000), '"Substance Abuse" and "Dysfunctionalism": Current Trends in Phonology', *Linguistic Inquiry* 31: 157–69.

Hall, Christopher J. (1992), *Morphology and Mind: A Unified Approach to Explanation in Linguistics* (London: Routledge).

Halle, Morris and Idsardi, William J. (1997), '*R*, Hypercorrection, and the Elsewhere Condition', in I. Roca (ed.), *Derivations and Constraints in Phonology* (Oxford: Clarendon Press), 331–48.

Hankamer, Jorge (1971/1979), *Deletion in Coordinate Structures* (New York: Garland).

—— (1973), 'Why There Are Two *Than's* in English', in C. Corum, C. C. Smith-Stark, and A. Weiser (eds.), *You Take the High Node and I'll Take the Low Node* (Chicago: Chicago Linguistic Society), 179–91.

Harris, Alice C. (2000), 'Word Order Harmonies and Word Order Change in Georgian', in R. Sornicola, E. Poppe, and A. Sisha-Halevy (eds.), *Stability, Variation, and Change of Word Order Patterns over Time* (Amsterdam: Benjamins), 133–63.

—— and Campbell, Lyle (1995), *Historical Syntax in Cross-Linguistic Perspective*, Cambridge Studies in Linguistics, vol. 74 (Cambridge: Cambridge University Press).

Harris, Roy (1980), *The Language-Makers* (Ithaca: Cornell University Press).

—— (1981), *The Language Myth* (London: Duckworth).

Harris, Tony and Wexler, Ken (1996), 'The Optional-Infinitive Stage in Child English: Evidence from Negation', in H. Clahsen (ed.), *Generative Perspectives on Language Acquisition: Empirical Findings, Theoretical Considerations, and Crosslinguistic Comparisons* (Amsterdam: John Benjamins), 1–42.

Haspelmath, Martin (1992), 'Grammaticalization Theory and Heads in Morphology', in M. Aronoff (ed.), *Morphology Now* (Albany: SUNY Press), 69–82, 194–8.

—— (1993), 'The Diachronic Externalization of Inflection', *Linguistics* 31: 279–309.

—— (1999a), ' Explaining Article-Possessor Complementarity: Economic Motivation in Noun Phrase Syntax', *Language* 75: 227–43.

—— (1999b), 'Optimality and Diachronic Adaptation', *Zeitschrift für Sprachwissenschaft* 18: 180–205.

—— (1999c), 'Why Is Grammaticalization Irreversible?', *Linguistics* 37: 1043–68.

—— (2002), *Understanding Morphology* (London: Arnold).

—— (2004), 'Does Linguistic Explanation Presuppose Linguistic Description?', *Studies in Language* 28: 554–79.

Hauser, Marc D. (1996), *The Evolution of Communication* (Cambridge, MA: MIT Press).

—— Chomsky, Noam, and Fitch, W. Tecumseh (2002), 'The Faculty of Language: What Is It, Who Has It, and How Did It Evolve?', *Science* 298: 1569–79.

Hawkins, John A. (1979), 'Implicational Universals as Predictors of Word Order Change', *Language* 55: 618–48.

—— (1980), 'On Implicational and Distributional Universals of Word Order', *Journal of Linguistics* 16: 193–235.

—— (1982), 'Notes on Cross-Categorial Harmony, X', and Predictions of Markedness', *Journal of Linguistics* 18: 1–35.

—— (1983), *Word Order Universals* (New York: Academic Press).

—— (1988), 'Explaining Language Universals', in J. A. Hawkins (ed.), *Explaining Language Universals* (Oxford: Basil Blackwell), 3–28.

—— (1990), 'A Parsing Theory of Word Order Universals', *Linguistic Inquiry* 21: 223–62.

—— (1994), *A Performance Theory of Order and Constituency*, Cambridge Studies in Linguistics, vol. 73 (Cambridge: Cambridge University Press).

—— (1999), 'Processing Complexity and Filler-Gap Dependencies across Grammars', *Language* 75: 244–85.

—— (2004a), *Efficiency and Complexity in Grammars* (Oxford: Oxford University Press).

—— (2004b), 'Relative Clause Typology: Patterns, Puzzles, and Processing Efficiency', unpublished paper, USC and MPI-Leipzig.

—— and Gilligan, Gary (1988), 'Prefixing and Suffixing Universals in Relation to Basic Word Order', *Lingua* 74: 219–60.

Hawkins, Roger (1981), 'Towards an Account of the Possessive Construction: NP's N and N of NP', *Journal of Linguistics* 17: 247–69.

Hayes, Bruce P. (1998), 'Phonetically Driven Phonology: The Role of Optimality Theory and Inductive Grounding', in M. Darnell, E. Moravcsik, F. J. Newmeyer, M. Noonan, and K. Wheatley (eds.), *Functionalism and Formalism in Linguistics* (Amsterdam: John Benjamins), 243–85.

Heine, Bernd and Claudi, Ulrike (1986), *On the Rise of Grammatical Categories: Some Examples from Maa* (Berlin: Dieter Reimer).

—— and Kuteva, Tania (2002), 'On the Evolution of Grammatical Forms', in A. Wray (ed.), *The Transition to Language* (Oxford: Oxford University Press), 376–97.

—— and Reh, Mechthild (1984), *Grammaticalization and Reanalysis in African Languages* (Hamburg: Helmut Buske Verlag).

Hengeveld, Kees (1992), *Non-Verbal Predication: Theory, Typology, Diachrony* (Berlin: Mouton de Gruyter).

Hinton, Geoffrey E. and Nowlan, S. J. (1987), 'How Learning Can Guide Evolution', *Complex Systems* 1: 495–502.

Hirsh-Pasek, Kathy and Golinkoff, Roberta (1996), *The Origins of Grammar: Evidence from Early Language Comprehension* (Cambridge, MA: MIT Press).

Hockett, Charles F. (1960), 'The Origin of Speech', *Scientific American* 203: 88–96.

Hodge, Carleton (1970), 'The Linguistic Cycle', *Language Sciences* 13: 1–7.

Hoekstra, Teun and Kooij, Jan G. (1988), 'The Innateness Hypothesis', in J. A. Hawkins (ed.), *Explaining Language Universals* (Oxford: Blackwell), 31–55.

Holmberg, Anders (1986), 'Word Order and Syntactic Features in Scandinavian Languages', Ph.D. dissertation, University of Stockholm.

Hopper, Paul J. (1987), 'Emergent Grammar', *Berkeley Linguistics Society* 13: 139–57.

—— (1988), 'Emergent Grammar and the Apriori Grammar Postulate', in D. Tannen (ed.), *Linguistics in Context: Connecting Observation and Understanding* (Norwood, NJ: Ablex), 117–34.

—— (1998), 'Emergent Grammar', in M. Tomasello (ed.), *The New Psychology of Language: Cognitive and Functional Approaches to Language Structure* (Mahwah, NJ: Lawrence Erlbaum), 155–75.

—— and Thompson, Sandra A. (1980), 'Transitivity in Grammar and Discourse', *Language* 56: 251–99.

Horn, Laurence R. (1972), 'On the Semantic Properties of Logical Operators in English', Ph.D. dissertation, UCLA.

—— (1984), 'Toward a New Taxonomy of Pragmatic Inference: Q- and R-Based Implicature', in D. Schiffrin (ed.), *Meaning, Form, and Use in Context: Linguistic Applications* (Washington, DC: Georgetown University Press), 11–42.

—— (1989), *A Natural History of Negation* (Chicago: University of Chicago Press).

HORN, LAURENCE R. (1993), 'Economy and Redundancy in a Dualistic Model of Natural Language', in S. Shore and M. Vilkuna (eds.), *Sky 1993: Yearbook of the Linguistic Association of Finland* (Helsinki: Linguistic Association of Finland), 33–72.

HORNSTEIN, NORBERT (1999), 'Movement and Control', *Linguistic Inquiry* 30: 69–96.

—— and WEINBERG, AMY (1981), 'Case Theory and Preposition Stranding', *Linguistic Inquiry* 12: 55–92.

HUANG, C.-T. JAMES (1982), 'Logical Relations in Chinese and the Theory of Grammar', Ph.D. dissertation, MIT.

—— (1984), 'On the Distribution and Reference of Empty Pronouns', *Linguistic Inquiry* 15: 531–74.

—— (1994), 'More on Chinese Word Order and Parametric Theory', in B. Lust, M. Suñer, and J. Whitman (eds.), *Syntactic Theory and First Language Acquisition: Cross-Linguistic Perspectives* (Hillsdale, NJ: Erlbaum), 15–35.

HUDSON, GROVER (1972), 'Why Amharic Is Not a VSO Language', *Studies in African Linguistics* 3: 127–65.

HYAMS, NINA M. (1986), *Language Acquisition and the Theory of Parameters* (Dordrecht: Reidel).

INADA, T. (1981), 'Problems of Reanalysis and Preposition Stranding', *Studies in English Linguistics* 9: 120–31.

ISHIKAWA, MASATAKA (1999), 'Morphological Strength and Syntactic Change', *Linguistic Inquiry* 30: 301–10.

JACKENDOFF, RAY (1970), 'Gapping and Related Rules', *Linguistic Inquiry* 2: 21–35.

—— (1972), *Semantic Interpretation in Generative Grammar* (Cambridge: Cambridge University Press).

—— (1977), *X-Bar Syntax: A Study of Phrase Structure* (Cambridge, MA: MIT Press).

—— (1983), *Semantics and Cognition* (Cambridge, MA: MIT Press).

—— (1990), *Semantic Structures* (Cambridge, MA: MIT Press).

JACOBSEN Jr., WILLIAM H. (1980), 'Inclusive/Exclusive: A Diffused Pronominal Category in Native Western North America', in A. E. Ojeda (ed.), *Papers from the Parasession on Pronouns and Anaphora* (Chicago: Chicago Linguistic Society), 204–27.

JAEGGLI, OSVALDO and HYAMS, NINA (1987), 'Morphological Uniformity and the Setting of the Null Subject Parameter', *North Eastern Linguistic Society* 18: 238–53.

—— and SAFIR, KENNETH J. (1989), 'The Null Subject Parameter and Parametric Theory', in O. Jaeggli and K. J. Safir (eds.), *The Null Subject Parameter* (Dordrecht: Reidel), 1–44.

JÄGER, GERHARD (2004), 'Learning Constraint Sub-Hierarchies: The Bidirectional Gradual Learning Algorithm', in R. Blutner and H. Zeevat (eds.), *Pragmatics in Optimality Theory* (Palgrave: Macmillan).

—— (2005), 'Evolutionary Game Theory and Typology', unpublished paper, University of Bern <http://www.ling.uni-potsdam.de/~jaeger/games_dcm.pdf>.

JAKOBSON, ROMAN (1936/1971), 'Beitrag zur allgemeinen Kasuslehre', in R. Jakobson (ed.), *Selected Writings*, Volume 2 (The Hague: Mouton), 23–71.

JELINEK, ELOISE (1993), 'Ergative "Splits" and Argument Type', *MIT Working Papers in Linguistics* 18: 15–42.

—— and DEMERS, RICHARD (1983), 'The Agent Hierarchy and Voice in Some Coast Salish Languages', *International Journal of American Linguistics* 49: 167–85.

JELINEK, FRED (1997), *Statistical Methods in Speech Recognition* (Cambridge, MA: MIT Press).

JOHANSSON, STIG and HOFLAND, KNUT (1989), *Frequency Analysis of English Vocabulary and Grammar Based on the Lob Corpus. Volume 1: Tag Frequencies and Word Frequencies* (Oxford: Clarendon Press).

JONES, CHARLES (1987), 'P for Proper Governor', *West Coast Conference on Formal Linguistics* 6: 115–30.

—— (1988), *Grammatical Gender in English: 950 to 1250* (London: Croom Helm).

JOOS, MARTIN (ed.) (1957), *Readings in Linguistics: The Development of Descriptive Linguistics in America since 1925* (New York: American Council of Learned Societies).

JOSEPH, BRIAN D. (2001), 'Is There Such a Thing as Grammaticalization?', *Language Sciences* 23: 163–86.

JOSEPH, JOHN E. (1992), '"Core" and "Periphery" in Historical Perspective', *Historiographia Linguistica* 19: 317–32.

JUN, JONGHO (1995), 'Place Assimilation as the Result of Conflicting Perceptual and Articulatory Constraints', *West Coast Conference on Formal Linguistics* 14: 221–37.

JURAFSKY, DAN and MARTIN, JAMES H. (2000), *Speech and Language Processing: An Introduction to Natural Language Processing, Computational Linguistics, and Speech Recognition* (Upper Saddle River, NJ: Prentice Hall).

KAGER, RENÉ (1999), *Optimality Theory* (Cambridge: Cambridge University Press).

KALMÁR, IVAN (1985), 'Are There Really No Primitive Languages?' in D. R. Olson, N. Torrance, and A. Hildyard (eds.), *Literacy, Language, and Learning : The Nature and Consequences of Reading and Writing* (Cambridge: Cambridge University Press).

KARIMI, SIMIN (1989), 'Aspects of Persian Syntax, Specificity, and the Theory of Grammar', Ph.D. dissertation, University of Washington.

KAUN, ABIGAIL R. (1994), 'An Optimality-Theoretic Account of Rounding Harmony Typology', *West Coast Conference on Formal Linguistics* 13: 78–92.

KAY, PAUL and MC DANIEL, CHAD (1979), 'On the Logic of Variable Rules', *Language in Society* 8: 151–87.

KAYNE, RICHARD S. (1980), 'Extensions of Binding and Case Marking', *Linguistic Inquiry* 11: 75–96.

—— (1984), *Connectedness and Binary Branching*, Studies in Generative Grammar, vol. 16 (Dordrecht: Foris).

—— (1994), *The Antisymmetry of Syntax* (Cambridge, MA: MIT Press).

—— (2000a), 'On the Left Edge in UG: A Reply to McCloskey', *Syntax* 3: 44–51.

—— (2000b), *Parameters and Universals* (Oxford: Oxford University Press).

KEAN, MARY-LOUISE (1975), 'The Theory of Markedness in Generative Grammar', Ph.D. dissertation, MIT.

KEENAN, EDWARD L. (1985), 'Passive in the World's Languages', in T. Shopen (ed.), *Language Typology and Syntactic Description, Volume 1: Clause Structure* (Cambridge: Cambridge University Press), 243–81.

—— and COMRIE, BERNARD (1977), 'Noun Phrase Accessibility and Universal Grammar', *Linguistic Inquiry* 8: 63–99.

—— —— (1979), 'Data on the Noun Phrase Accessibility Hierarchy', *Language* 55: 333–52.

—— and HAWKINS, SARAH (1987), 'The Psychological Validity of the Accessibility Hierarchy', in E. L. Keenan (ed.), *Universal Grammar: 15 Essays* (London: Croom Helm), 63–99.

Keller, Rudi (1994), *Language Change: The Invisible Hand in Language* (London: Routledge). (Translation from German of book originally published in 1990.)

Kibrik, Aleksandr E. (1997), 'Beyond Subject and Object: Toward a Comprehensive Relational Typology', *Linguistic Typology* 1: 279–346.

Kiefer, Ferenc (1995), 'Thematic Roles and Compounds', in A. Crochetière, J.-C. Boulanger, and C. Ouellon (eds.), *Proceedings of the XVth International Congress of Linguists* (Québec: Presses de l'Université Laval), 167–70.

Kim, Soowon (1990), 'Chain Scope and Quantificational Structure', Ph.D. dissertation, Brandeis University.

Kiparsky, Paul (1985), 'Morphology and Grammatical Relations', unpublished paper, Stanford University.

——(2004), 'Universals Constrain Change: Change Results in Typological Generalizations', unpublished paper, Stanford University.

Kirby, Simon (1997), 'Competing Motivations and Emergence: Explaining Implicational Hierarchies', *Linguistic Typology* 1: 5–31.

——(1998), *Function, Selection and Innateness: The Emergence of Language Universals* (Oxford: Oxford University Press).

——and Hurford, James (1997), 'Learning, Culture, and Evolution in the Origin of Linguistic Constraints', in P. Husbands and H. Inman (eds.), *Proceedings of the Fourth European Conference on Artificial Life* (Cambridge, MA: MIT Press), 493–502.

Kirchner, Robert (2000), 'Geminate Inalterability and Lenition', *Language* 76: 509–45.

Kiss, Katalin É. (1987), *Configurationality in Hungarian*, Studies in Natural Language and Linguistic Theory (Dordrecht: Reidel).

——(1994), 'Scrambling as the Base-Generation of Random Complement Order', in N. Corver and H. van Riemsdijk (eds.), *Studies on Scrambling* (Berlin: Mouton de Gruyter), 221–56.

Kluender, Robert (1992), 'Deriving Island Constraints from Principles of Predication', in H. Goodluck and M. Rochemont (eds.), *Island Constraints: Theory, Acquisition, and Processing* (Dordrecht: Kluwer), 223–58.

Kolliakou, Dimitra (1999), '*De*-Phrase Extractability and Individual/Property Denotation', *Natural Language and Linguistic Theory* 17: 713–81.

König, Ekkehard and Siemund, Peter (2000), 'Intensifiers and Reflexives: A Typological Perspective', in Z. Frajzyngier and T. S. Curl (eds.), *Reflexives: Forms and Functions* (Amsterdam: John Benjamins), 41–74.

Koopman, Hilda (1984), *The Syntax of Verbs: From Verb Movement Rules in the Kru Languages to Universal Grammar*, Studies in Generative Grammar, vol. 15 (Dordrecht: Foris).

Koptjevskaja-Tamm, Maria (1993), *Nominalizations* (London: Routledge).

Kortmann, Bernd (1996), *Adverbial Subordination* (Berlin: Mouton de Gruyter).

——and König, Ekkehard (1992), 'Categorial Reanalysis: The Case of Deverbal Prepositions', *Linguistics* 30: 671–97.

Koster, Jan (1975), 'Dutch as an SOV Language', *Linguistic Analysis* 1: 111–36.

——(1986), *Domains and Dynasties: The Radical Autonomy of Syntax*, Studies in Generative Grammar, vol. 30 (Dordrecht: Foris).

——(1994), 'Predicate Incorporation and the Word Order of Dutch', in G. Cinque, J. Koster, J.-Y. Pollock, L. Rizzi, and R. Zanuttini (eds.), *Paths toward Universal*

Grammar: Studies in Honor of Richard S. Kayne (Washington, DC: Georgetown University Press), 255–76.

Kozinsky, Isaak (1981), 'Nekotorye Grammaticeskie Universalii V Podsistemax Vyrazenija Subjektno-Objektnyx Otnnosenij' [Some Grammatical Universals in Subsystems of Expression of Subject-Object Relations], Ph.D. dissertation, Moskovskij Gosudarstvennyj Universitet.

Krifka, Manfred (2001), 'Quantifying into Question Acts', *Natural Language Semantics* 9: 1–40.

Kroch, Anthony (1994), 'Morphosyntactic Variation', in K. Beals, et al. (eds.), *Papers from the 30th Regional Meeting of the Chicago Linguistic Society, Part 2: The Parasession on Variation in Linguistic Theory* (Chicago: Chicago Linguistic Society), 180–201.

Kumagai, Yoshiharu (2000), 'Ergativity in English Spontaneous Discourse', *Mulberry: Bulletin of the Department of English, Faculty of Letters, Aichi Prefectural University* 39: 45–60.

Kuno, Susumu (1978), 'Generative Discourse Analysis in America', in W. Dressler (ed.), *Current Trends in Textlinguistics* (New York: Walter de Gruyter), 275–94.

Labov, William (1969), 'Contraction, Deletion, and Inherent Variability of the English Copula', *Language* 45: 716–62.

—— (1972), *Sociolinguistic Patterns* (Philadelphia: University of Pennsylvania Press).

—— (1994), *Principles of Linguistic Change. Volume 1: Internal Factors*, Language in Society, Vol. 20 (Oxford: Blackwell).

Lakoff, George (1965/1970), *Irregularity in Syntax* (New York: Holt, Rinehart, and Winston).

—— (1970/1972), 'Linguistics and Natural Logic', in D. Davidson and G. Harmon (eds.), *The Semantics of Natural Language* (Dordrecht: Reidel), 545–665.

—— (1973), 'Fuzzy Grammar and the Performance/Competence Terminology Game', *Chicago Linguistic Society* 9: 271–91.

—— (1974), 'Interview', in H. Parret (ed.), *Discussing Language: Dialogues with Wallace L. Chafe, Noam Chomsky, Algirdas J. Greimas (and Others)* (The Hague: Mouton), 151–78.

—— (1987), *Women, Fire, and Dangerous Things: What Categories Reveal About the Mind* (Chicago: University of Chicago Press).

—— and Johnson, Mark (1999), *Philosophy in the Flesh: The Embodied Mind and Its Challenge to Western Thought* (New York: Basic Books).

—— and Ross, John R. (1967/1976), 'Is Deep Structure Necessary?', in J. D. McCawley (ed.), *Syntax and Semantics, Volume 7: Notes from the Linguistic Underground* (New York: Academic Press), 159–64.

Lambrecht, Knud (1987), 'On the Status of SVO Sentences in French Discourse', in R. Tomlin (ed.), *Coherence and Grounding in Discourse* (Amsterdam: John Benjamins), 217–62.

Langacker, Ronald W. (1974), 'Movement Rules in Functional Perspective', *Language* 50: 630–64.

—— (1987), *Foundations of Cognitive Grammar: Volume 1, Theoretical Prerequisites* (Stanford: Stanford University Press).

—— (1990), *Concept, Image and Signal: The Cognitive Basis of Grammar* (Berlin: Mouton de Gruyter).

Langacker, Ronald W. (2000), 'A Dynamic Usage-Based Model', in M. Barlow and S. Kemmer (eds.), *Usage-Based Models of Language* (Stanford: CSLI Publications), 1–63.

Larson, Richard K. (1988), 'On the Double Object Construction', *Linguistic Inquiry* 19: 335–92.

—— (1991), 'Some Issues in Verb Serialization', in C. Lefebvre (ed.), *Serial Verbs: Grammatical, Comparative, and Cognitive Approaches* (Amsterdam: John Benjamins), 185–210.

Lasnik, Howard and Uriagereka, Juan (2002), 'On the Poverty of the Challenge', *Linguistic Review* 19: 147–50.

Laury, Ritva and Ono, Tsuyoshi (2005), 'Data Is Data and Model Is Model: You Don't Discard the Data That Doesn't Fit Your Model!' *Language* 81: 218–25.

Lavandera, Beatriz R. (1978), 'Where Does the Sociolinguistic Variable Stop?', *Language in Society* 7: 171–82.

Lazard, Gilbert (1984), 'Actance Variation and Categories of the Object', in F. Plank (ed.), *Objects: Towards a Theory of Grammatical Relations* (London: Academic Press), 269–92.

Lebeaux, David (1987), 'Comments on Hyams', in T. Roeper and E. Williams (eds.), *Parameter Setting* (Dordrecht: Reidel), 23–39.

Lee, Young-Suk (1992), 'Case and Word Order Variations in Nominal Clauses', *Language Research* 6: 359–80.

Lefebvre, Claire and Muysken, Pieter (1988), *Mixed Categories: Nominalizations in Quechua*, Studies in Natural Language and Linguistic Theory (Dordrecht: Kluwer).

Legate, Julie A and Yang, Charles D. (2002), 'Empirical Re-Assessment of Stimulus Poverty Arguments', *Linguistic Review* 19: 151–62.

Legendre, Géraldine, Smolensky, Paul, and Wilson, Colin (1998), 'When Is Less More? Faithfulness and Minimal Links in *Wh*-Chains', in P. Barbosa, D. Fox, P. Hagstrom, M. McGinnis, and D. Pesetsky (eds.), *Is the Best Good Enough? Optimality and Competition in Syntax* (Cambridge, MA: MIT Press), 249–90.

Lehmann, Winfred P. (1973), 'A Structural Principle of Language and Its Implications', *Language* 49: 47–66.

Levelt, Willem J. M. (1989), *Speaking: From Intention to Articulation* (Cambridge, MA: MIT Press).

Levine, Lewis and Crockett, Harry (1967), 'Speech Variation in a Piedmont Community', in S. Lieberson (ed.), *Explorations in Sociolinguistics* (The Hague: Mouton), 125–51.

Levine, Robert D. (1984), 'Against Reanalysis Rules', *Linguistic Analysis* 14: 3–30.

Levinson, Stephen C. (2000), *Presumptive Meanings: The Theory of Generalized Conversational Implicature* (Cambridge, MA: MIT Press).

Li, Charles N. (ed.) (1976), *Subject and Topic* (New York).

—— (1977), *Mechanisms of Syntactic Change* (Austin: University of Texas Press).

—— (2002a), 'Missing Links, Issues, and Hypotheses in the Evolutionary Origin of Language', in T. Givón and B. F. Malle (eds.), *Symposium on the Evolution of Language* (Amsterdam: John Benjamins), 83–106.

—— (2002b), 'Some Issues Concerning the Origin of Language', in J. Bybee and M. Noonan (eds.), *Complex Sentences in Grammar and Discourse* (Amsterdam: John Benjamins), 203–21.

Lightfoot, David W. (1979), *Principles of Diachronic Syntax*, Cambridge Studies in Linguistics, vol. 23 (Cambridge: Cambridge University Press).

——(1981), 'The History of NP Movement', in C. L. Baker and J. J. McCarthy (eds.), *The Logical Problem of Language Acquisition* (Cambridge, MA: MIT Press), 86–119.

——(1991), *How to Set Parameters: Arguments from Language Change* (Cambridge, MA: MIT Press).

——(1999), *The Development of Language: Acquisition, Change, and Evolution*, Blackwell/ Maryland Lectures in Language and Cognition, Vol. 1 (Oxford: Blackwell).

——(2002), 'Myths and the Prehistory of Grammar', *Journal of Linguistics* 38: 113–26.

Linell, Per (1982), *The Written Language Bias in Linguistics* (Linköping: University of Linköping).

Löfström, Jonas (1988), *Repliker Utan Gränser. Till Studiet Av Syntaktisk Struktur i Samtal* (Göteborgs Universitet: Institionen För Nordiska Språk).

Longobardi, Giuseppe (2001), 'Formal Syntax, Diachronic Minimalism, and Etymology: The History of French *Chez*', *Linguistic Inquiry* 32: 275–302.

——(2003), 'Methods in Parametric Linguistics and Cognitive History', *Linguistic Variation Yearbook* 3: 101–38.

Lord, Carol (1993), *Historical Change in Serial Verb Constructions* (Amsterdam: John Benjamins).

MacWhinney, Brian (2000), 'Connectionism and Language Learning', in M. Barlow and S. Kemmer (eds.), *Usage-Based Models of Language* (Stanford: CSLI Publications), 121–49.

Maling, Joan (1972), 'On "Gapping and the Order of Constituents"', *Linguistic Inquiry* 3: 101–8.

——(1983), 'Transitive Adjectives: A Case of Categorial Reanalysis', in F. Heny and B. Richards (eds.), *Linguistic Categories: Auxiliaries and Related Puzzles, vol. 1: Categories* (Dordrecht: Reidel), 253–89.

——(1984), 'Non-Clause-Bounded Reflexives in Modern Icelandic', *Linguistics and Philosophy* 7: 211–41.

——and Zaenen, Annie (1978), 'The Nonuniversality of a Surface Filter', *Linguistic Inquiry* 9: 475–97.

Manning, Christopher D. (2002a), 'Probabilistic Syntax', in R. Bod, J. Hay, and S. Jannedy (eds.), *Probabilistic Linguistics* (Cambridge, MA: MIT Press), 289–341.

——(2002b), 'Review of *Beyond Grammar: An Experience Based Theory of Language*, by Rens Bod', *Journal of Linguistics* 38: 441–2.

——and Schütze, Hinrich (1999), *Foundations of Statistical Natural Language Processing* (Cambridge, MA: MIT Press).

Manzini, M. Rita and Wexler, Kenneth (1987), 'Parameters, Binding, and Learning Theory', *Linguistic Inquiry* 18: 413–44.

Marantz, Alec P. (1993), 'Implications of Asymmetries in Double Object Constructions', in S. A. Mchombo (ed.), *Theoretical Aspects of Bantu Grammar* (Stanford: Stanford University Press), 113–50.

——(1995), 'The Minimalist Program', in G. Webelhuth (ed.), *Government Binding Theory and the Minimalist Program: Principles and Parameters in Syntactic Theory* (Oxford: Blackwell), 349–81.

Martin, William A., Church, Kenneth W., and Patel, Ramesh S. (1987), 'Preliminary Analysis of the Breadth-First Parsing Algorithm: Theoretical and Experimental Results', in L. Bolc (ed.), *Natural Language Parsing Systems* (Berlin: Springer Verlag), 267–328.

MAZUKA, REIKO (1996), 'Can a Grammatical Parameter Be Set before the First Word? Prosodic Contributions to Early Setting of a Grammatical Parameter', in J. L. Morgan and K. Demuth (eds.), *Signal to Syntax: Bootstrapping from Speech to Grammar in Early Acquisition* (Mahwah, NJ: Erlbaum), 313–30.

MCCARTHY, JOHN (1993), 'A Case of Surface Constraint Violation', *Canadian Journal of Linguistics* 38: 169–95.

MCCAWLEY, JAMES D. (1968), 'Lexical Insertion in a Transformational Grammar without Deep Structure', *Chicago Linguistic Society* 4: 71–80.

MCCLOSKEY, JAMES (1977), 'An Acceptable Ambiguity in Modern Irish', *Linguistic Inquiry* 8: 604–9.

——(1991), 'Clause Structure, Ellipsis, and Proper Government in Irish', *Lingua* 85: 259–302.

——(1996), 'On the Scope of Verb Movement in Irish', *Natural Language and Linguistic Theory* 14: 47–104.

——(1997), 'Subjecthood and Subject Positions', in L. Haegeman (ed.), *A Handbook of Theoretical Syntax* (Dordrecht: Kluwer), 197–236.

——(1999), 'On the Right Edge in Irish', *Syntax* 2: 189–209.

——(2002), 'Resumption, Successive Cyclicity, and the Locality of Operations', in S. D. Epstein and D. Seeley (eds.), *Derivation and Explanation* (Oxford: Blackwell), 184–226.

——(2004), 'Questions and Questioning in a Local English', *Proceedings of GURT 2004*, Georgetown University, 26 March.

——and HALE, KENNETH (1984), 'On the Syntax of Person-Number Inflection in Modern Irish', *Natural Language and Linguistic Theory* 4: 245–81.

MCDANIEL, DANA and COWART, WAYNE (1999), 'Experimental Evidence for a Minimalist Account of English Resumptive Pronouns', *Cognition* 70: B15–B24.

MCGREGOR, WILLIAM B. (1999), '"Optional" Ergative Marking in Gooniyandi Revisited: Implications to the Theory of Marking', *Leuvense Bijdragen* 87: 491–534.

MCMAHON, APRIL M. S. (2000), *Change, Chance, and Optimality* (Oxford: Oxford University Press).

MEINUNGER, ANDRÉ (1999), 'Topicality and Agreement', in M. Darnell, E. Moravcsik, F. J. Newmeyer, M. Noonan, and K. Wheatley (eds.), *Functionalism and Formalism in Linguistics* (Amsterdam: John Benjamins), 203–20.

MEISEL, JÜRGEN (1990), 'INFL-Ection, Subjects, and Subject-Verb Agreement', in J. Meisel (ed.), *Two First Languages: Early Grammatical Development in Bilingual Children* (Dordrecht: Foris), 237–98.

——and MÜLLER, N. (1992), 'Finiteness and Verb Placement in Early Child Grammars', in J. Meisel (ed.), *The Acquisition of Verb Placement: Functional Categories and V2 Phenomena in Language Acquisition* (Dordrecht: Kluwer), 109–38.

MERCHANT, JASON (2004), 'Fragments and Ellipsis', *Linguistics and Philosophy* 27: 661–739.

MILLER, JIM and WEINERT, REGINA (1998), *Spontaneous Spoken Language: Syntax and Discourse* (Oxford: Clarendon Press).

MILROY, LESLEY (1987), *Language and Social Networks*, 2nd edn. (Oxford: Basil Blackwell).

MILSARK, GARY (1985), 'Case Theory and the Grammar of Finnish', *North Eastern Linguistic Society* 15: 319–31.

MITHUN, MARIANNE (1984), 'How to Avoid Subordination', *Berkeley Linguistics Society* 10: 493–523.

—— (1987), 'Is Basic Word Order Universal?' in R. Tomlin (ed.), *Coherence and Grounding in Discourse* (Amsterdam: John Benjamins), 281–328.

Miyagawa, Shigeru (ed.) (1989), *Syntax and Semantics, Vol. 22: Structure and Case Marking in Japanese* (San Diego: Academic Press).

—— (2001), 'The EPP, Scrambling, and *Wh*-in-Situ', in M. Kenstowicz (ed.), *Ken Hale: A Life in Language* (Cambridge, MA: MIT Press), 293–338.

Moon, Seung Chul (1995), 'An Optimality Approach to Long Distance Anaphors', Ph.D. dissertation, University of Washington.

Moore, Samuel and Knott, Thomas A. (1965), *The Elements of Old English* (Ann Arbor, MI: George Wahr).

Moravcsik, Edith A. (1969), 'Determination', *Stanford University Working Papers on Language Universals* 1: 63–98.

—— (1974), 'Object-Verb Agreement', *Stanford University Working Papers on Language Universals* 15: 25–140.

—— (1978), 'Agreement', in J. H. Greenberg, C. A. Ferguson, and E. A. Moravcsik (eds.), *Universals of Human Language, Vol. 4: Syntax* (Stanford: Stanford University Press), 331–74.

—— (1988), 'Agreement and Markedness', in M. Barlow and C. A. Ferguson (eds.), *Agreement in Natural Language: Approaches, Theories, Descriptions* (Stanford: Center for the Study of Language and Information), 89–106.

—— (1993), 'Government', in J. Jacobs, A. von Stechow, W. Sternefeld, and T. Venneman (eds.), *Syntax: An International Handbook of Contemporary Research* (Berlin: Walter de Gruyter), 705–21.

—— (1995), 'Summing up Suffixaufnahme', in F. Plank (ed.), *Double Case: Agreement by Suffixaufnahme* (Oxford: Oxford University Press), 451–84.

Morelli, Frida (1998), 'Markedness Relations and Implicational Universals in the Typology of Onset Obstruent Clusters', *North Eastern Linguistics Society* 28/2: 107–20.

Morgan, Jerry L. (1973), 'Sentence Fragments and the Notion "Sentence"', in B. B. Kachru, R. B. Lees, Y. Malkiel, A. Pietrangeli, and S. Saporta (eds.), *Issues in Linguistics: Papers in Honor of Henry and Renée Kahane* (Urbana: University of Illinois Press), 719–51.

—— (1989), 'Sentence Fragments Revisited', in B. Music, R. Graczyk, and C. Wiltshire (eds.), *CLS 25: Parasession on Language in Context* (Chicago: Chicago Linguistic Society), 228–41.

Mühlhäusler, Peter and Harré, Rom (1990), *Pronouns and People: The Linguistic Construction of Social Identity* (Oxford: Blackwell).

Müller, Gereon (1999), 'On Common-Sense Justifications of Optimality-Theoretic Constraints', *Zeitschrift für Sprachwissenschaft* 18: 230–4.

Müller-Gotama, Franz (1994), *Grammatical Relations: A Cross-Linguistic Perspective on Their Syntax and Semantics* (Berlin: Mouton de Gruyter).

Musso, Mariacristina, Moro, Andrea, and five others (2003), 'Broca's Area and the Language Instinct', *Nature Neuroscience* 6: 774–81.

Muysken, Pieter and Riemsdijk, Henk van (1986), 'Projecting Features and Featuring Projections', in P. Muysken and H. van Riemsdijk (eds.), *Features and Projections* (Dordrecht: Foris), 1–30.

Nanni, Deborah L. (1978), 'The "Easy" Class of Adjectives in English', Ph.D. dissertation, University of Massachusetts.

Neeleman, Ad (1994), 'Scrambling as a D-Structure Phenomenon', in N. Corver and H. van Riemsdijk (eds.), *Studies on Scrambling* (Berlin: Mouton de Gruyter), 387–430.

Nevalainen, Terttu (1997), 'Recycling Inversion: The Case of Initial Adverbs and Negators in Early Modern English', *Studia Anglica Posnaniensia* 31: 203–14.

Newmeyer, Frederick J. (1983), *Grammatical Theory: Its Limits and Its Possibilities* (Chicago: University of Chicago Press).

—— (1986), *Linguistic Theory in America*, 2nd edn. (New York: Academic Press).

—— (1991), 'Functional Explanation in Linguistics and the Origins of Language', *Language and Communication* 11: 3–28.

—— (1998a), 'The Irrelevance of Typology for Linguistic Theory', *Syntaxis* 1: 161–97.

—— (1998b), *Language Form and Language Function* (Cambridge, MA: MIT Press).

—— (1998c), 'Preposition Stranding: Parametric Variation and Pragmatics', *Languages and Linguistics* 1: 1–24.

—— (2000a), 'On Reconstructing "Proto-World" Word Order', in C. Knight, J. Hurford, and M. Studdert-Kennedy (eds.), *The Emergence of Language* (Cambridge: Cambridge University Press), 372–88.

—— (2000b), 'Why Typology Doesn't Matter to Linguistic Theory', in G. Goodall, M. Schulte-Nafeh, and V. Samiian (eds.), *Proceedings of the Twenty-Eighth Meeting of the Western Conference on Linguistics* (Fresno: Department of Linguistics, California State University at Fresno), 334–52.

—— (2001a), 'Where Is Functional Explanation?' in M. Andronis, C. Ball, H. Elston, and S. Neuvel (eds.), *Proceedings from the Parasessions of the Thirty-Seventh Meeting of the Chicago Linguistic Society*, vol. 37/2 (Chicago: Chicago Linguistic Society), 99–122.

—— (2001b), 'Grammatical Functions, Thematic Roles, and Phrase Structure: Their Underlying Disunity', in W. Davies and S. Dubinsky (eds.), *Objects and Other Subjects: Grammatical Functions, Functional Categories, and Configurationality* (Dordrecht: Kluwer), 53–75.

—— (2001c), 'How Language Use Can Affect Language Structure', in K. Inoue and N. Hasegawa (eds.), *Linguistics and Interdisciplinary Research: Proceedings of the COE International Symposium* (Chiba: Kanda University of International Studies), 189–209.

—— (2002a), 'Commentary on John Hawkins, "Symmetries and Asymmetries: Their Grammar, Typology, and Parsing"', *Theoretical Linguistics* 28: 171–6.

—— (2002b), 'A Rejoinder to Bresnan and Aissen', *Natural Language and Linguistic Theory* 20: 97–9.

—— (2002c), 'Optimality and Functionality: A Critique of Functionally-Based Optimality-Theoretic Syntax', *Natural Language and Linguistic Theory* 20: 43–80.

—— (2003a), 'Grammar Is Grammar and Usage Is Usage', *Language* 79: 682–707.

—— (2003b), 'Reviews of *On Nature and Language* by Noam Chomsky; *The Language Organ: Linguistics as Cognitive Physiology* by Stephen R. Anderson and David W. Lightfoot; *Language in a Darwinian Perspective* by Bernard H. Bichakjian', *Language* 79: 583–99.

—— (2004a), 'Cognitive and Functional Factors in the Evolution of Grammar', *European Review* 12: 245–64.

—— (2004b), 'Typological Evidence and Universal Grammar', *Studies in Language* 28: 527–48.

—— (2004c), '"Basic Word Order" in Formal and Functional Linguistics and the Typological Status of "Canonical" Sentence Types', in D. Willems, B. Defrancq, T. Colleman, and D. Noël (eds.), *Contrastive Analysis in Language: Identifying Linguistic Units of Comparison* (Basingstoke: Palgrave), 69–88.

—— (2004d), 'Against a Parameter-Setting Approach to Language Variation', *Linguistic Variation Yearbook* 4: 181–234.

—— (Forthcoming), 'Negation and Modularity', in B. Birner and G. Ward (eds.), *Drawing the Boundaries of Meaning: Neo-Gricean Studies in Pragmatics and Semantics in Honor of Laurence R. Horn* (Amsterdam: Benjamins).

Nichols, Johanna (1992), *Linguistic Diversity in Space and Time* (Chicago: University of Chicago Press).

Nishigauchi, Taisuke and Roeper, Thomas (1987), 'Deductive Parameters and the Growth of Empty Categories', in T. Roeper and E. Williams (eds.), *Parameter Setting* (Dordrecht: Reidel), 91–121.

Niyogi, Partha and Berwick, Robert C. (1997), 'A Dynamical Systems Model of Language Change', *Linguistics and Philosophy* 20: 697–719.

Ostler, Nicholas (1980), *A Theory of Case Linking and Agreement* (Bloomington: Indiana University Linguistics Club). [Truncated Version of (1979) 'Case Linking: A Theory of Case and Verb Diathesis, Applied to Classical Sanskrit', unpublished Ph.D. dissertation, MIT.

Ouhalla, Jamal (1991a), *Functional Categories and Parametric Variation* (London: Routledge).

—— (1991b), 'Functional Categories and the Head Parameter', Paper presented at the 14th GLOW Colloquium, Leiden.

Parker, Steve (1999), 'On the Behavior of Definite Articles in Chamicuro', *Language* 75: 552–62.

Payne, Doris L. (1990), *The Pragmatics of Word Order: Typological Dimensions of Verb-Initial Languages* (Berlin: Mouton de Gruyter)

—— (1992), 'Nonidentifiable Information and Pragmatic Order Rules in 'O'odham', in D. L. Payne (ed.), *Pragmatics of Word Order Flexibility* (Amsterdam: John Benjamins), 137–66.

Perlmutter, David M. (1971), *Deep and Surface Structure Constraints in Syntax* (New York: Holt, Rinehart, and Winston).

Pesetsky, David M. (1982), 'Complementizer-Trace Phenomena and the Nominative Island Constraint', *Linguistic Review* 1: 297–343.

—— (1995), *Zero Syntax: Experiencers and Cascades* (Cambridge, MA: MIT Press).

—— (1998), 'Some Optimality Principles of Sentence Pronunciation', in P. Barbosa, D. Fox, P. Hagstrom, M. McGinnis, and D. Pesetsky (eds.), *Is the Best Good Enough?: Optimality and Competition in Syntax* (Cambridge, MA: MIT Press), 337–84.

—— and Esther Torrego (2001), 'T-to-C Movement: Causes and Consequences', in M. Kenstowicz (ed.), *Ken Hale: A Life in Language* (Cambridge, MA: MIT Press), 355–426.

Phillips, Betty S. (1984), 'Word Frequency and the Actuation of Sound Change', *Language* 60: 320–42.

Pica, Pierre (1987), 'On the Nature of the Reflexivization Cycle', *North Eastern Linguistic Society* 17: 483–99.

PICA, PIERRE (2001), 'Introduction', *Linguistic Variation Yearbook* 1: v–xii.

PIERCE, AMY (1992), *Language Acquisition and Syntactic Theory: A Comparative Analysis of French and English Child Grammars* (Dordrecht: Kluwer).

PINKER, STEVEN (1984), *Language Learnability and Language Development* (Cambridge, MA: Harvard University Press).

—— (1989), *Learnability and Cognition: The Acquisition of Argument Structure* (Cambridge, MA: MIT Press).

—— and BLOOM, PAUL (1990), 'Natural Language and Natural Selection', *Behavioral and Brain Sciences* 13: 707–84.

—— and JACKENDOFF, RAY (2005), 'The Faculty of Language: What's Special About It?', *Cognition* 95: 201–36.

PINTZUK, SUSAN, TSOULAS, GEORGE, and WARNER, ANTHONY (2000), 'Syntactic Change: Theory and Method', in S. Pintzuk, G. Tsoulas, and A. Warner (eds.), *Diachronic Syntax: Models and Mechanisms* (Oxford: Oxford University Press), 1–22.

PLANK, FRANS (1989), 'On Humboldt on the Dual', in R. L. Corrigan, F. Eckman, and M. Noonan (eds.), *Linguistic Categorization* (Amsterdam: John Benjamins), 299–333.

—— (1994), 'What Agrees with What in What, Generally Speaking?', *EUROTYP Working Papers* 7: 39–58.

POEPPEL, DAVID and WEXLER, KENNETH (1993), 'The Full Competence Hypothesis of Clause Structure in Early German', *Language* 69: 1–33.

POLETTO, CECILIA (2000), *The Higher Functional Field: Evidence from Northern Italian Dialects* (Oxford: Oxford University Press).

POLINSKY, MARIA (1997), 'Dominance in Precedence: SO/OS Languages', in K. Singer, R. Eggert, and G. Anderson (eds.), *CLS 33: Papers from the Panels* (Chicago: Chicago Linguistic Society), 253–69.

POLLARD, CARL and SAG, IVAN A. (1992), 'Anaphors in English and the Scope of Binding Theory', *Linguistic Inquiry* 23: 173–234.

—— —— (1994), *Head-Driven Phrase Structure Grammar* (Chicago: University of Chicago Press).

POLLOCK, JEAN-YVES (1989), 'Verb Movement, Universal Grammar, and the Structure of IP', *Linguistic Inquiry* 20: 365–424.

POPE, EMILY (1971), 'Answers to Yes-No Questions', *Linguistic Inquiry* 2: 69–82.

PRIMUS, BEATRICE (1999), *Cases and Thematic Roles: Ergative, Accusative, and Active* (Tübingen: Max Niemeyer).

PRINCE, ALAN and SMOLENSKY, PAUL (1993), *Optimality Theory: Constraint Interaction in Generative Grammar*, RUCCS Technical Report, vol. 2 (Piscataway, NJ: Rutgers University Center for Cognitive Science).

PRINCE, ELLEN F. (1981), 'Toward a Taxonomy of Given-New Information', in P. Cole (ed.), *Radical Pragmatics* (New York: Academic Press), 223–56.

—— (1985), 'Fancy Syntax and "Shared Knowledge"', *Journal of Pragmatics* 9: 65–82.

PULLUM, GEOFFREY K. (1981a), 'Evidence against the Aux Node in Luiseño and English', *Linguistic Inquiry* 12: 435–63.

—— (1981b), 'Languages with Object before Subject: A Comment and a Catalogue', *Linguistics* 19: 147–55.

—— (1990), 'Constraints on Intransitive Quasi-Serial Verb Constructions in Modern Colloquial English', *Ohio State University Working Papers in Linguistics* 39: 218–39.

—— and SCHOLZ, BARBARA C. (2002), 'Empirical Assessment of Stimulus Poverty Arguments', *Linguistic Review* 19: 9–50.

RADFORD, ANDREW (1988), *Transformational Grammar: A First Course* (Cambridge: Cambridge University Press).

—— (1990), *Syntactic Theory and the Acquisition of English Syntax: The Nature of Early Child Grammars of English* (Oxford: Blackwell).

—— (1994), 'Clausal Projections in Early Child Grammars', *Essex Research Reports in Linguistics* 3: 32–72.

RANDALL, JANET H. (1988), 'Inheritance', in W. K. Wilkins (ed.), *Syntax and Semantics, Vol. 21: Thematic Relations* (New York: Academic Press), 129–46.

RENAULT, RICHARD (1987), 'Genre Grammatical et Typologie Linguistique', *Bulletin de la Société de Linguistique de Paris* 82: 69–117.

REULAND, ERIC J. (1986), 'A Feature System for the Set of Categorial Heads', in P. Muysken and H. van Riemsdijk (eds.), *Features and Projections* (Dordrecht: Foris), 41–88.

RICHARDS, NORVIN (2001), *Movement in Language: Interactions and Architectures* (Oxford: Oxford University Press).

RIEMSDIJK, HENK VAN (1978), *A Case Study in Syntactic Markedness: The Binding Nature of Prepositional Phrases*, Studies in Generative Grammar, vol. 4 (Dordrecht: Foris).

RIZZI, LUIGI (1982), *Issues in Italian Syntax*, Studies in Generative Grammar, vol. 11 (Dordrecht: Foris).

—— (1986), 'Null Objects in Italian and the Theory of *Pro*', *Linguistic Inquiry* 17: 501–57.

—— (1989), 'On the Format for Parameters', *Behavioral and Brain Sciences* 12: 355–6.

—— (1997), 'The Fine Structure of the Left Periphery', in L. Haegeman (ed.), *Elements of Grammar: Handbook of Generative Syntax* (Dordrecht: Kluwer), 281–337.

—— (2004), 'On the Study of the Language Faculty: Results, Developments, and Perspectives', *Linguistic Review* 21: 323–44.

ROBERTS, IAN (1993a), 'A Formal Account of Grammaticalization in the History of Romance Futures', *Folia Linguistica Historica* 13: 219–58.

—— (1993b), *Verbs and Diachronic Syntax: A Comparative History of English and French*, Studies in Natural Language and Linguistic Theory, vol. 28 (Dordrecht: Kluwer).

—— (1998), 'Review of *Historical Syntax in Cross-Linguistic Perspective* by A. C. Harris and L. Campbell', *Romance Philology* 51: 363–70.

—— (1999), 'Verb Movement and Markedness', in M. DeGraff (ed.), *Language Creation and Language Change: Creolization, Diachrony, and Development* (Cambridge, MA: MIT Press), 287–327.

—— and ROUSSOU, ANNA (1999), 'A Formal Approach to "Grammaticalization"', *Linguistics* 37: 1011–41.

—— —— (2002), 'The History of the Future', in D. W. Lightfoot (ed.), *Syntactic Effects of Morphological Change* (Oxford: Oxford University Press), 24–56.

ROEPER, THOMAS and DE VILLIERS, JILL (1994), 'Lexical Links in the *Wh*-Chain', in B. Lust, G. Hermon, and J. Kornfilt (eds.), *Syntactic Theory and First Language Acquisition: Cross-Linguistic Perspectives* (Hillsdale, NJ: Erlbaum), 357–90.

ROEPER, THOMAS and SIEGEL, MUFFY (1978), 'A Lexical Transformation for Verbal Compounds', *Linguistic Inquiry* 9: 199–260.

ROHRBACHER, BERNHARD (1994), 'The Germanic VO Languages and the Full Paradigm: A Theory of V to I Raising', Ph.D. dissertation, University of Massachusetts.

Rosenbach, Anette (2002), *Genitive Variation in English: Conceptual Factors in Synchronic and Diachronic Studies* (Berlin: Mouton de Gruyter).

—— (2003), 'Aspects of Iconicity and Economy in the Choice between the *S*-Genitive and the *of*-Genitive in English', in B. Mondorf and G. Rohdenburg (eds.), *Determinants of Grammatical Variation in English* (Berlin: Mouton de Gruyter), 379–411.

—— (2005), 'Comparing Animacy Versus Weight as Determinants of Grammatical Variation in English', *Language* 81.

—— and Vezzosi, Letizia (2000), 'Genitive Constructions in Early Modern English: New Evidence from a Corpus Analysis', in R. Sornicola, E. Poppe, and A. Shisha-Halevy (eds.), *Stability, Variation, and Change of Word Order over Time* (Amsterdam: John Benjamins), 285–307.

Ross, John R. (1967), 'Constraints on Variables in Syntax', Ph.D. dissertation, MIT. [Published in 1985 as *Infinite Syntax!* (Norwood, NJ: Ablex).]

—— (1970), 'Gapping and the Order of Constituents', in M. Bierwisch and K. Heidolph (eds.), *Progress in Linguistics* (The Hague: Mouton), 249–59.

—— (1973a), 'A Fake NP Squish', in C.-J. N. Bailey and R. Shuy (eds.), *New Ways of Analyzing Variation in English* (Washington, DC: Georgetown), 96–140.

—— (1973b), 'Nouniness', in O. Fujimura (ed.), *Three Dimensions of Linguistic Theory* (Tokyo: TEC Company, Ltd.), 137–258.

—— (1973c), 'The Penthouse Principle and the Order of Constituents', in C. Corum, C. C. Smith-Stark, and A. Weiser (eds.), *You Take the High Node and I'll Take the Low Node* (Chicago: Chicago Linguistic Society), 397–422.

Rugemalira, Josephat M. (1994), 'The Case against the Thematic Hierarchy', *Linguistic Analysis* 24: 62–81.

Rumelhart, David E. and McClelland, John L. (1986), 'On Learning the Past Tenses of English Verbs', in J. L. McClelland and D. E. Rumelhart (eds.), *Parallel Distributed Processing: Explorations in the Microstructure of Cognition* (Cambridge, MA: MIT Press), 216–71.

Sabel, Joachim (2002), 'A Minimalist Analysis of Syntactic Islands', *Linguistic Review* 19: 271–315.

Sadock, Jerrold M. (1991), *Autolexical Syntax: A Theory of Parallel Grammatical Components* (Chicago: University of Chicago Press).

Safir, Kenneth J. (1985), *Syntactic Chains* (Cambridge: Cambridge University Press).

—— (1987), 'Comments on Wexler and Manzini', in T. Roeper and E. Williams (eds.), *Parameter Setting* (Dordrecht: Reidel), 77–89.

Sag, Ivan A. and Godard, Danièle (1994), 'Extraction of *De*-Phrases from the NP', *North Eastern Linguistic Society* 24: 519–41.

—— and Pollard, Carl (1991), 'An Integrated Theory of Complement Control', *Language* 67: 63–113.

Sampson, Geoffrey (1978), 'Linguistic Universals as Evidence for Empiricism', *Journal of Linguistics* 14: 183–206.

Scancarelli, Janine S. (1985), 'Referential Strategies in Chamorro Narratives: Preferred Clause Structure and Ergativity', *Studies in Language* 9: 335–62.

Schiffrin, Deborah (1987), *Discourse Markers*, Studies in Interactional Sociolinguistics, vol. 5 (Cambridge: Cambridge University Press).

Schiller, Eric (1990), 'The Typology of Serial Verb Constructions', *Chicago Linguistic Society* 26: 393–406.

SCHUCHARDT, HUGO (1885/1972), 'On Sound Laws: Against the Neogrammarians', in T. Vennemann and T. Wilbur (eds.), *Schuchardt, the Neogrammarians, and the Transformational Theory of Phonological Change* (Frankfurt: Athenäum), 39–72.

SCHUETZE-COBURN, STEPHAN (1987), 'Topic Management and the Lexicon: A Discourse Profile of Three-Argument Verbs in German', Ph.D. dissertation, UCLA.

SCHÜTZE, CARSON (1996), *The Empirical Basis of Linguistics: Grammaticality Judgments and Linguistic Methodology* (Chicago: University of Chicago Press).

SEDLAK, PHILIP A. S. (1975), 'Direct/Indirect Object Word Order: A Cross-Linguistic Analysis', *Stanford University Working Papers on Language Universals* 18: 117–64.

SEIDENBERG, MARK S. (1997), 'Language Acquisition and Use: Learning and Applying Probabilistic Constraints', *Science* 275: 1599–603.

SEILER, WALTER (1985), *Imonda, a Papuan Language*, Pacific Linguistics, Series B, vol. 93 (Canberra: Australian National University).

SHIBATANI, MASAYOSHI and BYNON, THEODORA (1995), 'Approaches to Language Typology: A Conspectus', in M. Shibatani and T. Bynon (eds.), *Approaches to Language Typology* (Oxford: Clarendon Press), 1–25.

SHOPEN, TIMOTHY (1971), 'Caught in the Act', *Chicago Linguistic Society* 7: 254–63.

SIEWIERSKA, ANNA (1988), *Word Order Rules* (London: Croom Helm).

—— (1991), *Functional Grammar* (London: Routledge).

—— and BAKKER, DIK (1996), 'The Distribution of Subject and Object Agreement and Word Order Type', *Studies in Language* 20: 115–61.

SILVERSTEIN, MICHAEL (1976), 'Hierarchy of Features and Ergativity', in R. M. W. Dixon (ed.), *Grammatical Categories in Australian Languages* (Canberra: Australian Institute of Aboriginal Studies), 112–71.

—— (1981), 'Case Marking and the Nature of Language', *Australian Journal of Linguistics* 1: 227–46.

SMITH, NEIL (1981), 'Consistency, Markedness and Language Change: On the Notion "Consistent Language"', *Journal of Linguistics* 17: 39–54.

—— and CORMACK, ANNABEL (2002), 'Parametric Poverty', *Glot International* 6: 285–7.

—— and TSIMPLI, IANTHI-MARIA (1995), *The Mind of a Savant: Language Learning and Modularity* (Oxford: Blackwell).

—— —— (1997), 'Reply to Bates', *International Journal of Bilingualism* 1: 180–6.

SMITH, WENDY (1996), 'Spoken Narrative and Preferred Clause Structure: Evidence from Modern Hebrew Discourse', *Studies in Language* 20: 163–89.

SMOLENSKY, PAUL (1999), 'Grammar-Based Connectionist Approaches to Language', *Cognitive Science* 23: 589–613.

SNYDER, WILLIAM (2001), 'On the Nature of Syntactic Variation: Evidence from Complex Predicates and Complex Word-Formation', *Language* 77: 324–42.

SPEAS, MARGARET J. (1990), *Phrase Structure in Natural Language*, Studies in Natural Language and Linguistic Theory, vol. 21 (Dordrecht: Kluwer).

—— (1994), 'Null Arguments in a Theory of Economy of Projection', *University of Massachusetts Occasional Papers* 17: 179–208.

—— (1997), 'Optimality Theory and Syntax: Null Pronouns and Control', in D. Archangeli and D. T. Langendoen (eds.), *Optimality Theory: An Overview* (Oxford: Blackwell), 171–99.

—— (2000), 'Constraints on Null Pronouns', in G. Legendre, J. Grimshaw, and S. Vikner (eds.), *Optimality-Theoretic Syntax* (Cambridge, MA: MIT Press), 393–425.

Stassen, Leon (1992), 'A Hierarchy of Main Predicate Encoding', in M. Kefer and J. van der Auwera (eds.), *Meaning and Grammar. Cross-Linguistic Perspectives* (Berlin: Mouton de Gruyter), 179–201.

—— (2000), '*And*-Languages and *with*-Languages', *Linguistic Typology* 4: 1–54.

Steedman, Mark (1999), 'Connectionist Sentence Processing in Perspective', *Cognitive Science* 23: 615–34.

Steele, Susan (1978), 'Word Order Variation: A Typological Study', in J. H. Greenberg, C. A. Ferguson, and E. A. Moravcsik (eds.), *Universals of Human Language* (Stanford: Stanford University Press), 585–623.

—— (1981), *An Encyclopedia of Aux* (Cambridge, MA: MIT Press).

Stowell, Timothy A. (1981), 'Origins of Phrase Structure', Ph.D. dissertation, MIT.

Stromswold, Karin (1988), 'The Acquisitional Implications of Kayne's Theory of Prepositions', unpublished paper, MIT.

—— (1989), 'Using Naturalistic Data: Methodological and Theoretical Issues (or How to Lie with Naturalistic Data)'. Paper presented at the 14th Annual Boston University Child Language Conference, October 13–15.

—— (1990), 'Learnability and the Acquisition of Auxiliaries', Ph.D. dissertation, MIT.

Stuurman, Frits (1985), *Phrase Structure Theory in Generative Grammar* (Dordrecht: Foris).

Suchsland, Peter (1993), 'The Structure of German Verb Projections—a Problem of Syntactic Parameterization?' in G. Fanselow (ed.), *The Parametrization of Universal Grammar* (Amsterdam: John Benjamins), 123–43.

Svorou, Soteria (1994), *The Grammar of Space* (Amsterdam: John Benjamins).

Szabolcsi, Anna and Dikken, Marcel den (1999), 'Islands', *Glot International* 4/6: 3–8.

Tai, James H.-Y. (1973), 'Chinese as a SOV Language', *Chicago Linguistic Society* 9: 659–71.

Takano, Yuji (1996), 'Movement and Parametric Variation in Syntax', Ph.D. dissertation, University of California, Irvine.

Talmy, Leonard (1983), 'How Language Structures Space', in H. L. Pick and L. P. Acredolo (eds.), *Spatial Orientation: Theory, Research, and Application* (New York: Plenum Press), 225–82.

—— (1985/2000), 'Lexicalization Patterns: Semantic Structure in Lexical Forms', in L. Talmy (ed.), *Toward a Cognitive Semantics* (Cambridge, MA: MIT Press), 21–212.

—— (1988), 'Force Dynamics in Language and Cognition', *Cognitive Science* 12: 49–100.

Tanaka, Hidekazu (2001), 'Right-Dislocation as Scrambling', *Journal of Linguistics* 37: 551–79.

Taraldsen, Knut T. (1980), 'On the Nominative Island Constraint, Vacuous Application and the *That*-Trace Filter', Bloomington: Indiana University Linguistics Club Publication.

Tesar, Bruce and Smolensky, Paul (1998), 'Learnability in Optimality Theory', *Linguistic Inquiry* 29: 229–68.

Thomason, Sarah G. and Everett, Daniel L. (2001), 'Pronoun Borrowing', *Berkeley Linguistics Society* 27.

Thompson, Sandra A. (1988), 'A Discourse Approach to the Cross-Linguistic Category "Adjective"', in J. Hawkins (ed.), *Explaining Language Universals* (Oxford: Basil Blackwell), 167–85.

—— and Hopper, Paul J. (2001), 'Transitivity, Clause Structure, and Argument Structure: Evidence from Conversation', in J. L. Bybee and P. Hopper (eds.), *Frequency and the Emergence of Linguistic Structure* (Amsterdam: John Benjamins), 27–60.

Thráinsson., Höskuldur (1996), 'On the (Non)-Universality of Functional Categories', in W. Abraham, S. D. Epstein, H. Thráinsson, and C. J.-W. Zwart (eds.), *Minimal Ideas: Syntactic Studies in the Minimalist Framework* (Amsterdam: John Benjamins), 253–81.

——(2001), 'Object Shift and Scrambling', in M. R. Baltin and C. Collins (eds.), *The Handbook of Contemporary Syntactic Theory* (Oxford: Blackwell), 148–202.

Tomasello, Michael (ed.) (1998), *The New Psychology of Language: Cognitive and Functional Approaches to Language Structure* (Mahwah, NJ: Lawrence Erlbaum).

Tomasello, Michael (2000), 'Primate Cognition (Special Issue)', *Cognitive Science* 24/3: 351–61.

Tomlin, Russell S. (1985), 'Interaction of Subject, Theme, and Agent', in J. Wirth (ed.), *Beyond the Sentence: Discourse and Sentential Form* (Ann Arbor, MI: Karoma), 61–80.

——(1986), *Basic Word Order: Functional Principles* (London: Croom Helm).

Traugott, Elizabeth C. and Dasher, Richard B. (2002), *Regularity in Semantic Change* (Cambridge: Cambridge University Press).

Travis, Lisa (1984), 'Parameters and Effects of Word Order Variation', Ph.D. dissertation, M.I.T.

——(1989), 'Parameters of Phrase Structure', in M. R. Baltin and A. S. Kroch (eds.), *Alternative Conceptions of Phrase Structure* (Chicago: University of Chicago Press), 263–79.

Ultan, Russell (1978), 'Toward a Typology of Substantival Possession', in J. H. Greenberg, C. A. Ferguson, and E. A. Moravcsik (eds.), *Universals of Human Language, Vol. 4: Syntax* (Stanford: Stanford University Press), 11–50.

Uriagereka, Juan (1999), 'Multiple Spell-Out', in S. D. Epstein and N. Hornstein (eds.), *Working Minimalism* (Cambridge, MA: MIT Press), 251–82.

Vainikka, Anne (1989), 'Deriving Syntactic Representations in Finnish', Ph.D. dissertation, University of Massachusetts.

——and Levy, Yonata (1999), 'Empty Subjects in Finnish and Hebrew', *Natural Language and Linguistic Theory* 17: 613–71.

Valian, Virginia V. (1990), 'Logical and Psychological Constraints on the Acquisition of Syntax', in L. Frazier and J. de Villiers (eds.), *Language Processing and Language Acquisition* (Dordrecht: Kluwer), 119–45.

——(1991), 'Syntactic Subjects in the Early Speech of Italian and American Children', *Cognition* 40: 21–81.

Van Valin, Robert D. and LaPolla, Randy J. (1997), *Syntax: Structure, Meaning, and Function* (Cambridge: Cambridge University Press).

Vardul', Ivan F. (1969), *Jazykovye Universalii I Lingvisticeskaya Tipologia [Language Universals and Linguistic Typology]* (Moscow: Nauka).

Vennemann, Theo (1973), 'Explanation in Syntax', in J. Kimball (ed.), *Syntax and Semantics*, Vol. 2 (New York: Seminar Press), 1–50.

Verrips, M. and Weissenborn, Jürgen (1992), 'The Acquisition of Functional Categories Reconsidered'. Paper presented to the Workshop on Crossing Boundaries, Tübingen.

Wang, William S.-Y. (1969), 'Competing Changes as a Cause of Residue', *Language* 45: 9–25.

—— (ed.) (1977), *The Lexicon in Phonological Change* (The Hague: Mouton).

Wasow, Thomas (2002), *Postverbal Behavior* (Stanford: CSLI Publications).

WEBELHUTH, GERT (1992), *Principles and Parameters of Syntactic Saturation* (Oxford: Oxford University Press).

WEBER, DAVID J. (1989), *A Grammar of Huallaga (Huánaco) Quechua* (Berkeley: University of California Press).

WEDGWOOD, DANIEL (1995), 'Grammaticalization by Reanalysis in an Adaptive Model of Language Change: A Case Study of the English Genitive Constructions', Ph.D. dissertation, University of Edinburgh.

WEINREICH, URIEL, LABOV, WILLIAM, and HERZOG, MARVIN I. (1968), 'Empirical Foundations for a Theory of Language Change', in W. Lehmann and Y. Malkiel (eds.), *Directions for Historical Linguistics* (Austin: University of Texas Press), 95–188.

WIERZBICKA, ANNA (1981), 'Case Marking and Human Nature', *Journal of Linguistics* 1: 43–80.

WILKINS, WENDY K. (1988), 'Thematic Structure and Reflexivization', in W. K. Wilkins (ed.), *Syntax and Semantics, Vol. 21: Thematic Relations* (New York: Academic Press), 191–214.

—— and WAKEFIELD, JENNIE (1995), 'Brain Evolution and Neurolinguistic Preconditions', *Behavioral and Brain Sciences* 18: 161–226.

WILLIAMS, EDWIN (1981), 'Language Acquisition, Markedness, and Phrase Structure', in S. L. Tavakolian (ed.), *Language Acquisition and Linguistic Theory* (Cambridge, MA: MIT Press), 8–34.

WU, ANDI (1994), 'The Spell-out Parameters: A Minimalist Approach to Syntax', Ph.D. dissertation, UCLA.

WUNDERLICH, DIETER (1996), 'Lexical Categories', *Theoretical Linguistics* 22: 1–48.

—— (2004), 'Why Assume UG?', *Studies in Language* 28: 615–41.

WURZEL, WOLFGANG U. (1994), *Grammatisch initiierter Wandel* (Bochum: Brockmeyer).

YAMAUCHI, HAJIME (2001), 'The Difficulty of the Baldwinian Account of Linguistic Innateness', in J. Kelemen and P. Sosík (eds.), *Advances in Artificial Life: 6th European Conference, ECAL 2001* (Prague: Springer), 391–400.

YANG, CHARLES D. (2004), 'Universal Grammar, Statistics, or Both?', *Trends in Cognitive Sciences* 8: 451–6.

YIP, MOIRA, MALING, JOAN, and JACKENDOFF, RAY (1987), 'Case in Tiers', *Language* 63: 217–50.

ZANUTTINI, RAFFAELLA (2001), 'Sentential Negation', in M. Baltin and C. Collins (eds.), *The Handbook of Contemporary Syntactic Theory* (Oxford: Blackwell), 511–35.

ZEPTER, ALEX (2000), 'Mixed Word Order: Left or Right, That Is the Question', unpublished manuscript, Rutgers University.

ZIPF, GEORGE (1935), *The Psychobiology of Language* (New York: Houghton Mifflin).

—— (1949), *Human Behavior and the Principle of Least Effort* (Cambridge, MA: Addison-Wesley).

ZUBIZARRETA, MARIA LUISA (1982), 'Theoretical Implications of Subject Extraction in Portuguese', *Linguistic Review* 2: 79–96.

ZWART, C. JAN-WOUTER (1993), 'Dutch Syntax: A Minimalist Approach', Ph.D. dissertation, University of Groningen.

—— (1997), *Morphosyntax of Verb Movement: A Minimalist Approach to the Syntax of Dutch* (Dordrecht: Kluwer).

—— (2001), 'Syntactic and Phonological Verb Movement', *Syntax* 4: 34–62.

ZWICKY, ARNOLD M. (1999), 'The Grammar and the User's Manual'. Paper presented at Linguistic Society of America Summer Institute Forum Lecture, Urbana.

Index

Notes, tables, and tableaux are indexed as **n**, **t**, and **tb**. If more than one table or tableau appears on a page, they are numbered consecutively as **a**, **b**, **c** etc.